The Disciplinary Revolution

The Disciplinary Revolution
Calvinism and the Rise of the State in Early Modern Europe

Philip S. Gorski

THE UNIVERSITY OF CHICAGO PRESS
Chicago and London

The University of Chicago Press, Chicago 60637
The University of Chicago Press, Ltd., London
© 2003 by The University of Chicago
All rights reserved. Published 2003
Printed in the United States of America
12 11 10   3 4 5

ISBN: 0-226-30483-3 (cloth)
ISBN: 0-226-30484-1 (paper)

Chapter 2 of this book appeared earlier as "Calvinism and Revolution: The Walzer Thesis Reconsidered," in *Meaning and Modernity,* edited by Richard Madsen, William M. Sullivan, and Ann Swidler (Berkeley: University of California Press, 2001). Copyright © 2001, The Regents of the University of California; reprinted by permission of the University of California Press.

Library of Congress Cataloging-in-Publication Data

Gorski, Philip S.
 The disciplinary revolution : Calvinism and the rise of the state in early modern Europe / Philip S. Gorski.
  p. cm.
 Includes bibliographical references and index.
 ISBN 0-226-30483-3 (alk. paper)—ISBN 0-226-30484-1 (pbk. : alk. paper)
 1. Sociology, Christian (Reformed Church)—History. 2. Church and state—Reformed Church—History. 3. Church and state—Europe—History. 4. Calvinism—Europe—History. 5. Europe—Politics and government. 6. Europe—Church history. I. Title.

BX9423.S63 G67 2003
306'.094—dc21
                     2002155086

♾ The paper used in this publication meets the minimum requirements of the American National Standard for Information Sciences—Permanence of Paper for Printed Library Materials, ANSI Z39.48-1992.

To my wife, Hella, and our three sons, Jacob, Eric, and Mark

CONTENTS

Preface and Acknowledgments ix
Introduction xv

1 / Body and Soul: Calvinism, Discipline,
and State Power in Early Modern Europe
1

2 / Disciplinary Revolution from Below
in the Low Countries
39

3 / Disciplinary Revolution from Above
in Brandenburg-Prussia
79

4 / Social Disciplining in Comparative Perspective
114

Conclusion 157
Notes 173
Bibliography 209
Index 237

PREFACE AND ACKNOWLEDGMENTS

This book began as an undergraduate term paper for the class "Dutch Art and Civilization during the Golden Age" taught by Simon Schama, then of Harvard. The paper dealt with Foucault's theory of disciplinary power, Weber's study of the Protestant ethic, and the light they shed on Dutch capitalism. Little did I suspect that it would one day evolve into a book. Seventeenth-century Holland was certainly not my first—or even second or third—interest at that time. My focus was postwar European politics, and I had only taken the course because it fulfilled a distribution requirement and because Schama was said to be an excellent lecturer. (He was.) After graduation, I headed off to Germany to do research on the Green Party, the subject of my first book.

When I returned to the United States two years later to begin graduate school in the Berkeley sociology department, the Dutch Republic could not have been further from my mind. But it resurfaced again during the seminar "Comparative-Historical Methods" that I took with Kim Voss during my first year. The syllabus included several books on early modern Europe, including Perry Anderson's *Lineages of the Absolutist State* and Immanuel Wallerstein's *Modern World System*. I was perplexed by the fact that Anderson ignored the Dutch Republic, which I understood to be one of the great powers of the seventeenth century, and I was irked by the absence of Calvinism from Wallerstein's discussion of Dutch capitalism, given the significance which Weber and others had attributed to it. Wasn't there some connection between the Reformation and early modern state-formation, I wondered?

I might not have pursued this question any further if I had not found myself in a seminar, "Sociology of Religion," taught by Ann Swidler and another, "Changing Visions of Community," taught by Reinhard Bendix. It was Swidler who first pushed me to think about the connection between religious organization and social power. And it was Bendix who introduced me to the work of Gerhard Oestreich and Otto Hintze, especially their writings on the importance of discipline and Calvinism in Brandenburg-Prussia. I then began to see some of the historical and theoretical connections that form the subject of this book—among Geneva, the Netherlands, and Prussia; Calvinism, discipline, and state power; and Weber, Foucault, and Elias. The result was a very long term paper. I had not yet given up on studying postwar European politics, however, and without some strong pushing from my advisors—especially Voss, Swidler, and Robert Bellah—I probably would have filed that term paper away forever and written a very different dissertation. Instead, I spent the next several years learning Dutch, reading up on early modern history, and reworking the term paper for publication. This was followed by several more years of research in various libraries and archives in Germany and the Netherlands and many more years of writing, research, and revision. For such a short book, it has taken a very long time to write.

The result of all these labors is a work of comparative-historical sociology, which juxtaposes historical cases to illustrate and refine theoretical arguments about macrosocietal change. In most works of comparative-historical sociology, the cases are countries. In this book, however, the theoretically relevant cases are actually "confessions": Calvinism, Lutheranism, and Catholicism. My argument, in brief, is that the Reformation unleashed a profound and far-reaching process of disciplining—a disciplinary revolution—that greatly enhanced the power of early modern states and that the effects of this revolution were deepest and most dramatic in the Calvinist parts of Europe. The argument is one part Foucault and one part Weber.

I hope that this book will be of interest not only to historical sociologists but also to people working in the areas of social theory, political science, early modern history, and religious studies. Because the interests of these audiences are quite different, it may be useful to provide a brief road map to guide each to those parts of the book that they will find most relevant. Social theorists will probably be most interested in the final section of the introduction, where I present a conceptual and historical critique of Foucault's, Weber's, Elias's, and Oestreich's discussions of social discipline and state power and their relation to religion. Political scientists, on the other hand, may find the critique of realist theories of state power (conclusion) and rational-choice theories of bureaucratization (chapter 4) more pertinent. I expect that Dutch historians will be surprised by my claim that the Dutch republic was a strong state (chapter 2), and I hope that they will be persuaded by the evidence that I present to support it. Prussian historians, meanwhile, will probably be surprised by my argument that Prussian absolutism was born, first and foremost, out of confessional conflict and by my claim that Calvinism was in fact much more important to the development of the Prussian ethos than was Lutheran Pietism (chapter 3). And other early modernists will probably be most interested in chapter 4, where I argue that social-disciplining was a great deal more intensive in the Calvinist parts of Europe than in Lutheran and Catholic regions. I think the most important part of my argument for students of religion is my focus on the religious roots of various social and political technologies, such as confinement and bureaucracy.

As much as I hope that each of these audiences will find something they like in the book, I am quite sure that each will also find things to dislike. Social theorists will probably find my analysis too cautious. They will see many places where I could have pushed it further—in the discussions of subjectification and normalization, for example. Many historians, however, will probably find the analysis too bold. They will discover many exceptions to my arguments and many nuances that I have missed. As for students of religion, they may find that I have said too much about religious organizations and too little about religious ideas.

These differences in disciplinary standards, and the contradictions among them, create certain dilemmas and trade-offs—between theoretical bravado and interpretive nuance, between geographical scope and historical depth, and between institutional and textual analysis—to name only a few of the most salient. In navigating between these conflicting demands, I have generally steered towards the left-hand terms—towards bravado, scope, and institutions—though not, I hope, to the point of drifting entirely off course. The result is a relatively compact book, which covers a great deal of time and territory, and focuses on structure more than ethos, a book therefore that is short on details and not especially hermeneutical, a book, in other words, that leaves out a lot—including a good deal of research done at one time or another.

I have incurred many debts in writing this book—financial, intellectual, and personal, and I would like to acknowledge them gratefully. My research has been supported, at one point or another, by the Foreign Language Area Studies Program, the Columbia Council on European Studies, the Social Science Research Council, the American Council of Learned Societies, the

Berliner Senat, the University of California–Berkeley, and the Graduate School at University of Wisconsin–Madison. And it has been aided by the staffs of various archives and libraries, including the *Evangelisches Zentralarchiv* (Berlin), the *Geheimes Staatsarchiv–Preußischer Kulturbesitz* (Berlin), the *Staatsbibliothek-Preußischer Kulturbesitz,* the *Archiv der Franckeschen Stiftungen* (Halle-S), the *Brandenburgisches Landeshauptarchiv* (Potsdam), the *Universiteitsbibliotheek, Leiden,* the *Rijksarchief van Friesland,* the *Gemeentearchief van Leeuwarden,* and the *Gemeentearchief van Amsterdam.*

The intellectual debts are even more numerous though sometimes harder to identify. I would like to thank the anonymous reviewers of this and other related manuscripts that I have submitted over the years, as well as the audiences to which I have presented this work at UCLA (twice), the University of Chicago (twice), Berkeley, Cornell, Madison, Michigan, Northwestern, NYU, Stanford, and Yale. Their feedback has been enormously helpful. I have also benefited more than I can say, and probably more than I know, from the faculty and graduate students of the sociology departments at UC-Berkeley and UW-Madison that I have been privileged enough to call home while working on the book. I would like to thank Jerry Karabel, Kim Voss, and especially Ann Swidler and Bob Bellah at Berkeley for guiding and teaching me. I would also like to thank three other sets of people from Berkeley: John L. Martin, Ricardo Samuel, Rich Wood, Laura Schmitt, and the other members of the religion reading group, who taught me how to think about religion; and Marc Garcelon, Lyn Spilman, Chuck Stephens, Jim Stockinger, John Torpey, and the other members of the Lowenthal seminar for making me think about other things, sometimes. And I would like to thank Clem Brooks, Claude Fischer, Mike Hout, Jeff Manza, and the other members of the sociology softball team for making me do something besides think. Here, at UW-Madison, I would like to thank my comrades on the eighth floor—Steven Bunker, Chas Camic, Mustafa Emirbayer, Chad Goldberg, Chuck Halaby, Jerry Marwell, Gay Seidman, and Erik Olin Wright—who helped me, wittingly and unwittingly, to finish this book, get tenure, and, perhaps most importantly, to stay (semi-) sane through it all. Finally, I would like to offer special thanks to three generous and open-minded historians who made me feel at home in their discipline, and provided invaluable guidance and support at various stages of this project: Tom Brady, Jr. (Berkeley), Heinz Schilling (Humboldt University, Berlin), and Robert M. Kingdon (Madison).

The biggest debt, though, I owe to my wife, Hella Heydorn, who provided, not only unwavering love and support over the years, but also a sense of balance and perspective about life, which served as a powerful antidote to my own single-mindedness and obsession with work, and to our three boys, Jacob, Eric, and Mark, who have taught me, again and again, that there is much more to life than the life of the mind. It is to all of them that I dedicate this book.

INTRODUCTION

The subject of this book is the early modern state—what it was and how it came to be. A great deal has been written on this topic over the last twenty years; indeed, the study of state-formation has become one of the core concerns, not only of historical sociology, but also of comparative politics and social history. Virtually all of the work in this area has sought to explain state-building in terms of two processes: the military revolution of the sixteenth century or the bourgeois revolutions of the seventeenth and eighteenth centuries.[1] This book focuses on the impact of a third revolution: the disciplinary revolution unleashed by the Protestant Reformation. In particular, it focuses on the role that Calvinism played in this revolution. By refining and diffusing a panoply of disciplinary techniques and strategies, it is argued, Calvin and his followers helped create an infrastructure of religious governance and social control that served as a model for the rest of Europe—and the world.

This argument can perhaps be best elucidated by means of an analogy—an analogy between the disciplinary and industrial revolutions. Most historians and social scientists would agree that modern capitalism would be unthinkable, or at least very different, without the industrial revolution because it laid the material and technological foundations upon which modern capitalism was built. Further, most would agree that the industrial revolution would have been unthinkable without the steam engine because it so dramatically increased the productive powers of industry by unleashing the energies of coal—a well-known but little-used resource—and harnessing them for the purposes of manufacture and transport. It was steam, then, that first unfettered the unparalleled productive powers of modern industrial economies, the capacity to produce more goods with less labor.

My argument is that the relationship between the disciplinary revolution and the modern state was quite similar. Like the industrial revolution, the disciplinary revolution transformed the material and technological bases of production; it created new mechanisms for the production of social and political order. And, like the industrial revolution, the disciplinary revolution was driven by a key technology: the technology of observation—self-observation, mutual observation, hierarchical observation. For it was observation—surveillance—that made it possible to unleash the energies of the human soul—another well-known but little-used resource—and harness them for the purposes of political power and domination. What steam did for the modern economy, I claim, discipline did for the modern polity: by creating more obedient and industrious subjects with less coercion and violence, discipline dramatically increased, not only the regulatory power of the state, but its extractive and coercive capacities as well.

Having briefly outlined my argument, let me now restate it in more analytical terms. What I wish to explain is the emergence of a new infrastructure of governance in early modern Europe and its gradual absorption and appropriation by the early modern state. And what I believe explains this sudden intensification of governance is the disciplinary revolution unleashed by the Protestant Reformation. By "infrastructure of governance," I mean a network of practices and institutions whose goal, to borrow Foucault's words, is "the conduct of conduct": the control of behavior and the shaping of subjectivity. By "disciplinary revolution," I mean a revolutionary struggle, whether from below or above, which has, as one of its chief ends, the creation of a more disciplined polity. The state, from this perspective, may be defined as a "pastoral" organization that claims clear priority (if not complete monopoly) over the legitimate means of socialization within a given territory.

Seeing the state in this way compels one to fundamentally rethink the dynamics of the state-formation process. It forces one to shift from a top-down perspective, in which state-building princes are the main actors and the centralization of power the central story line, to a bottom-up perspective, in which local reformers play the central role and the diffusion of disciplinary practices forms the central motif. And indeed the early modern infrastructure of governance was not the brainchild of centralizing princes. At least in the early stages, the key carriers of the disciplinary revolution were Protestant clerics and reformist magistrates. It was only later that this revolution penetrated and reshaped royal bureaucracies and armies.

Seeing the state in this way also helps address a number of perplexing anomalies in early modern political history. For example, it helps explain why two of the least centralized and least monarchical states in the early modern world—the Netherlands and England—were also among the most orderly and powerful. And it also helps explain why one of the most fragmented and backward monarchies of Europe—Brandenburg-Prussia—eventually became one of the most unified and advanced of the great powers. Unlike most of their competitors, all of these states experienced Calvinist disciplinary revolutions.

Of course, social disciplining was not specific to the Calvinist world. Similar processes can be observed in the Catholic and Lutheran contexts as well. This raises an important question: Were there cross-confessional differences in the disciplining process? Most early modern historians, I think, would probably answer in the negative. They would be apt to emphasize the parallels between Protestant and Catholic reforms—and not without reason. For there *were* similarities between, say, the Genevan consistory and the Spanish Inquisition; as we will see below, both used mutual surveillance to impose religious discipline. But *similar* is not *identical,* and in the comparative chapter of this book I will argue that there were some subtle but important differences between the confessions. In particular, I will argue that the social-disciplining process went further and faster in the Calvinist polities; that Lutheran and Catholic reforms were often inspired by Calvinist precedents; and that this helps to explain the rapid ascent of Calvinist states, such as Holland, England, and Prussia. Finally, I will argue that these differences had religious roots, that Calvinism differed from its competitors in terms of both its ethos (self-discipline) and its ecclesiology (the visible community of saints).

The book is thus organized as follows. In chapter 1, I situate the project in relation to previous work on state-formation, the recent historiography of the Reformation era, and the theories of Max Weber and Michel Foucault, among others. In chapter 2, I examine the Dutch case. I argue that the Dutch state was stronger than existing theories of the state would predict—or allow—and that this strength was partly a function of religiously grounded discipline. In chapter 3, I turn to the case of Brandenburg-Prussia, detailing the ways in which Calvinist disciplinary practices were adapted to the army, bureaucracy, and public schools. Then, in chapter 4, I set these developments within a comparative context, arguing that the social-disciplining process was both more rapid and more intense in the Calvinist countries, and that this was due, in large part, to their ethos and ecclesiology. In the conclusion, finally, I discuss some of the broader historiographical and theoretical implications of this analysis.

Frontispiece of the 1651 edition of Thomas Hobbes, *Leviathan*, depicting the two dimensions of state power—temporal and spiritual—and their various levels

1
Body and Soul: Calvinism, Discipline, and State Power in Early Modern Europe

> Man is not fitted for society by nature, but by discipline.
> *Thomas Hobbes,* De Cive

The differences between the theoretical perspective advanced here and the one adopted in most work on state formation can be easily grasped in terms of a common metaphor, the metaphor of the body politic, and, more specifically, by means of one of its better-known representations, the frontispiece to the first edition of Hobbes's *Leviathan* (see opposite page). At the top, the Leviathan of the state rises up out of the foreground with outstretched arms, in the right hand a sword symbolizing temporal power, in the left a bishop's crosier symbolizing ecclesiastical authority, a crowned head depicting the king, and a composite body, made up of his subjects. At the bottom are two panels, the one on the left representing the various levels of worldly power—the soldiers, arms, artillery, the crown, and a castle—the one on the right representing the various levels of spiritual authority—a church court, the devices of logic and argument, the lightning bolts of divine intervention, the cardinal's crest, and a church.

There are a number of different ways in which one might interpret this drawing. One possibility is to read it from the top down.[1] Such a reading is suggested by the sheer size of the Leviathan and the prominence given to it in the overall composition. The picture would thus appear to be a metaphor for the descending character of royal authority.[2] The outstretched arms are those of the worldly judge, who stands above the institutions of civil government and the church, ready to execute God's laws and enforce them with his sword. This is probably the way in which the picture is most often read today.

It is also possible to read the picture from the bottom up.³ This reading is suggested by the upward-thrusting weapons of war and rhetoric, by the increasingly lighter and more ethereal content of the panels as one moves up, by the upward-looking gaze of the subjects, and by the upward-pointing sword and crosier. The picture now appears as a metaphor for the constitution of civil government out of the institutions of civil society. The outstretched arms could then be seen as those of Christ, welcoming the subject into his firm and secure embrace, with the sword being the worldly arm of his authority. Support for this reading can also be found in Hobbes's text.

There is also the question whether one should read the picture from left to right or from right to left—that is, how one should understand the relative importance of religious and temporal authority in *Leviathan* and the proper relationship of these forms of authority within the state. The fact that the Leviathan holds the sword in his strong hand—the right hand—and the crosier in his weak hand would seem to suggest that the secular arm is the more important. But there are also reasons for seeing the ecclesiastical arm as dominant. For example, the fact that the word *matter* is placed next to the symbols of worldly authority, while the word *form* is set beside the symbols of spiritual authority, suggests that the relationship between the sword and the crosier is one of matter to form, or force to law, and that spiritual authority is thus ultimately superior to worldly authority.⁴

Which of these readings is the right one? I will not attempt an answer here, and I am not sure there is one. Like most texts, the frontispiece appears to contain multiple and contradictory meanings defy the rules of logic while drawing our attention to a central problematic. The point I wish to make here is simply that the frontispiece has generally been read in only one way—from top to bottom and from right to left—and that social-scientific studies of the state exhibit a similar one-sidedness. This book is an attempt to reread the history of state from the opposite direction—from the bottom up and from left to right.

The purpose of this chapter is to lay the groundwork for this rereading. It is divided into three, interconnecting parts. In the first, I review the social-scientific literature on early modern state formation and discuss some of its shortcomings. In particular, I argue that existing theories have failed to explain the rise of the Dutch and Prussian states in a convincing and parsimonious way and that this is at least partly because they ignore the impact of the Reformation. In the second section, I examine the "confessionalization paradigm," which has come to dominate work on the early modern era in recent years. Scholars of confessionalization cannot be accused of ignoring the impact of the Reformation on the development of the state; indeed, they have focused considerable attention on the relationship between religion, social discipline, and state formation (though not systematically enough for a sociologist's taste). But they have tended to see this relationship as a constant. By contrast, I will argue that it was variable and, in particular, that the impact of social discipline on state power was greatest in the Calvinist context. In the third section, finally, I discuss the work of Weber, Foucault, and other social theorists who have dealt with the relationship between religion, discipline, and state power. In brief, I argue that Weber grasped the relationship between religion and discipline, and Foucault theorized the nexus between discipline and the state, but neither put together all three links of the chain. In this sense, my project can be seen as a synthesis—and maybe even a completion—of theirs.

Sociological Theories of State Formation: Review and Critique

In his epic novel, *Joseph und seine Brüder,* Thomas Mann cautions that "treating religion and politics as fundamentally different things is to overlook the unity of the world."[5] Mann was speaking of ancient Egypt, but his caveat applies equally to early modern Europe. For at perhaps no other time in European history were religion and politics more tightly intertwined than in the two centuries following the Reformation. Curiously, however, most historical sociologists have ignored Mann's dictum. They have sought to explain early modern political development solely as the consequence of two processes: capitalist development and military competition.[6] As a result, they have completely ignored the impact of a third factor: the religious revolution known as the Protestant Reformation.

Marxist Models: Class Relations or Exchange Relations?

Over the last two decades, sociological analysis of the state has been dominated by two principal perspectives: a neo-Marxist position, which focuses on material factors, and a bellicist viewpoint, which emphasizes geopolitical ones. Within the neo-Marxist literature on the early modern state, the two most influential works are probably Perry Anderson's *Lineages of the Absolutist State* and Immanuel Wallerstein's *The Modern World System*.

In *Lineages,* Anderson argues that the early modern period was an "age of absolutism." The origins of absolutism, he contends, lie in the "crisis of feudalism" that overtook Western Europe in the fourteenth century, as oversettlement and overpopulation began to weaken the grip of the nobility over the land. At the same time, the revival of commerce gave rise to a new class of urban merchants, which challenged the nobility's monopoly on political power.⁷ The twin threats of peasant unrest in the countryside and merchant dominance in the cities drove the western European nobility into the arms of the Crown. In Spain, France, England, and Austria, a series of "new monarchs" enhanced their power by entering into an alliance with the nobility against the peasants and merchants. This alliance, Anderson argues, provided the social foundation of absolutism. The absolutist state was, in his phrase, "a redeployed and recharged apparatus of feudal domination."⁸ In eastern Europe, socioeconomic conditions were quite different. Unsettled areas remained plentiful, the population sparse, the towns weak. There, it was not an indigenous crisis that toppled the feudal order, but an exogenous threat—the military threat posed by west European absolutism. To meet this threat, Eastern rulers were compelled to construct standing armies and centralized extractive apparatuses to finance them. But because the peasantry and merchant classes were weaker and less able to resist the centralizing onslaught, absolutism took a particularly harsh and despotic form in eastern Europe. Whereas in western Europe, absolutism merely compensated the nobility for its declining social power, in eastern Europe, it actually strengthened the social position of the nobility through the imposition of a "second serfdom." Thus, despite the mediating role he ascribes to international military competition, Anderson explains early modern state-formation in primarily socioeconomic terms. In the last instance, he insists, state structure is determined by the mode of production and the patterns of class relations that result from it.

For Immanuel Wallerstein, exchange relations, not class relations, are primary. A state's structure, he argues, corresponds to its location within the global ecology of production, the "capitalist world system" that first emerges in the early modern period. This system of exchange relations is divided into three major zones: core, periphery, and semiperiphery. In the economically advanced core, which controls the "terms of trade," there arise "strong states," possessing "a strong state machinery coupled with a national culture" and serving the interests of the dominant, merchant classes.⁹ In the economically backward periphery, which serves as a source of raw materials and corvée labor for the core, states are weak, that is, lacking in organization and autonomy, and even the dominant classes are subordinated to their imperial overlords. Between the core and the periphery lies the semiperiphery, a liminal area inhabited by rising and falling states, controlled by social classes in decline or state-building elites on the make. To sum up, Wallerstein explains state development in terms of the following causal chain: varying roles in the world economy "led to different class structures which led to different polities."¹⁰

Bellicist Explanations: The "Fiscal-Military Model"

In contrast to the Marxists, the bellicists view international military competition as the driving force behind state-formation. Bellicists take Marxists to task on two counts. First, they object that Marxist stage theories, in which economic development and state development move together in lockstep, ignore the fact that "many different kinds of states were viable at different stages of European history," a charge to which Anderson seems particularly susceptible.[11] Second, they argue that a monadic emphasis on socioeconomic development within states overlooks the significance of military competition between states, a particularly glaring omission in Wallerstein's work.[12] Recent formulations of the bellicist approach have thus tried to account for the full range of variation in early modern state structure and strength and to incorporate both socioeconomic and geopolitical variables in their models by focusing on the interaction between economic development and military mobilization, an approach that one scholar has aptly dubbed the "fiscal-military model."[13] In this section, I review two versions of this model, Charles Tilly's (1990) *Coercion, Capital and European States* and Brian Downing's (1992) *The Military Revolution and Political Change*, as well as one work that seeks to go beyond them, Thomas Ertman's (1997) *Birth of the Leviathan*.

Tilly explicitly sets out to synthesize bellicist and Marxist models of state development. He begins by reaffirming the bellicist tenet that "war drives state-formation and transformation," but he argues that levels of economic development crucially affect strategies of military mobilization.[14] Variations in state structure, he contends, are thus best explained by the *interaction* between military competition and economic development. Where resources are scarce—that is, in economically backward areas, they must be extracted directly from the population through centralized, extractive and administrative apparatuses. Where resources are plentiful—that is, in economically advanced areas—rulers can obtain resources by making "compacts with capitalists."[15] Some states—the strongest ones—succeed in combining the advantages of economic development (plentiful resources) with those of administrative centralization (effective extraction). Tilly therefore sees three main paths to state-formation: coercion-intensive, capital-intensive, and capitalized-coercion, which correspond historically to three different types of states, tribute-taking empires, territorially fragmented states, and national-states. In the end, he argues, only the latter was able to withstand the heat of military competition. Thus, Tilly aims to set forth a general explanation for the rise of the modern nation-state.

Brian Downing pursues a somewhat different (if no less ambitious) explanatory end. Following in Barrington Moore's footsteps, he seeks to locate the "origins of dictatorship and democracy." He traces the roots of "modern liberal democracy" to "medieval constitutionalism," the tradition of "local government . . . , parliamentary bodies, and the rule of law" common to most of Europe.[16] In some countries, he argues, constitutionalism survived, providing the foundation for democratization. In others, it perished, clearing the path to autocracy. The key turning point, in Downing's view, was the military revolution of the sixteenth century, which led to the creation of standing, mercenary armies. Raising and supporting these armies placed enormous fiscal pressures on early modern rulers. Where they sought to mobilize the necessary resources domestically, as in France and Brandenburg-Prussia, the representative institutions of the *Ständestaat* were destroyed and replaced with a centralized bureaucracy under royal control. The result was "military-bureaucratic absolutism." Where rulers were sheltered from the military revolution by geography, as in England, or found other means for mobilizing resources (for example, capital markets in the Netherlands or military conquest in Sweden), constitutional arrangements were left intact, providing the institutional base for democratization in the nineteenth century. States such as Poland, which simply ignored the imperatives of international military competition, were conquered and destroyed. Downing therefore concludes that the origins of dictatorship and democracy were not so much social as political. They lay not in the effects of commercial agriculture on class structure but in varying national responses to the military revolution.

The fiscal-military model thus distinguishes two basic outcomes: coercion-intensive versus capital-intensive (Tilly) or military-bureaucratic versus constitutionalist (Downing) or, more simply, absolutist and nonabsolutist. The problem with this typology is that it fails to encompass the full range of variation in state and regime structure. In Tilly's analysis, for instance, a wide variety of nonabsolutist political formations—city-states (Venice), urban leagues (the Hansa), and confederal states (the Dutch Republic)—are all lumped together under the rubric capital intensive. Similarly, Downing groups together all those states in which the basic elements of medieval constitutionalism—representative assemblies, local government, and rule of law—withstood the assaults of centralizing monarchs. This category includes states that differed substantially in both structure and strength—for example, Poland's neofeudal "Republic of Nobles," Sweden's conquest-driven military empire, and the republican regime of the Northern Netherlands. Hence, while Tilly and Downing do a good job of explaining absolutist versus nonabsolutist outcomes, they do not discriminate among, much less explain, the various types of nonabsolutist (capital-intensive, constitutionalist) states. The fiscal military model, in sum, leaves a great deal of unexplained (or, rather, unidentified) variance.

This cannot be said of Thomas Ertman's study of "states and regimes in medieval and early modern Europe."[17] Indeed, Ertman takes Tilly and Downing to task for being "too willing to link one kind of political regime with only one kind of state apparatus—absolutism with 'bureaucracy' and constitutionalism/parliamentarism with the absence thereof."[18] In fact, he argues that the other permutations were equally possible—marriages of absolutism and patrimonialism or constitutionalism and bureaucracy—and that we must therefore distinguish between state structure (absolutist versus constitutionalist) and regime structure (bureaucratic versus patrimonial). Building on these typologies, Ertman then distinguishes between four different outcomes of the state-building process: bureaucratic absolutism, patrimonial absolutism, bureaucratic constitutionalism, and patrimonial constitutionalism.[19]

But what explains these vastly different outcomes? Ertman identifies three "independent variables": the type of local government, the timing of the military revolution, and the independent effects of parliamentary institutions. The type of local government is important because it affects the type of representative institutions that emerge, which in turn affects the ability of political elites to resist absolutizing monarchs. The story begins in the era of the Dark Age empires. In those areas of Europe subjected to Imperial domination (that is, Latin Europe and Germany), Ertman argues, institutions of local government were dismantled and could not serve as a foundation for representative institutions. Here, parliaments came to be organized along tricurial lines, that is, as three separate estates (clergy, nobility and towns) that sat and voted apart. And because they sat and voted apart, these parliaments were more vulnerable to an absolutizing policy of divide and conquer. In those areas of Europe that escaped Imperial domination (that is, the British Isles, Scandinavia, Poland, and Hungary), the institutional dynamic was very different. Here, indigenous structures of local government were preserved intact. As a result, representative assemblies were generally organized along bicameral lines, that is, as two separate houses: an upper house consisting, as a rule, of the upper nobility and leading members of the clergy and a lower house consisting of the lower nobility and, in some cases, representatives of the towns, with members of the lower house generally being elected to represent a particular county or city. Ertman argues that bicameral legislatures tended to promote cross-class alliances and maintain links between central and local government and that they were therefore better able to resist the blandishments of absolutist monarchs. For all these reasons, he concludes, it was easier to establish absolutist regimes in the core areas of the old empire than in the pristine landscape of the European periphery.

The second independent variable that Ertman adduces is the onset of sustained geopolitical competition. Like Tilly, Downing, and other proponents of the bellicist model, Ertman views war as the key stimulus in the formation of a centralized administrative infrastructure. Unlike them, however, he argues that the effects of war were not the same in all times and places. In particular, he distinguishes between those states that faced sustained geopolitical competition before 1450 (France, England, Scotland, Spain and the Italian principalities and city-states) and those that first experienced it after 1450 (Germany, Scandinavia, Poland, and Hungary). What makes this date so important, Ertman claims, is the kinds of administrative personnel and the models of administrative and fiscal organization that were available in these two periods. State builders who established their infrastructures before 1450 were forced to rely on the cooperation of powerful (and unqualified) vassals and could draw only on feudal and ecclesiastical models of office holding, in which offices were a form of property that could be bought, sold, inherited, and transferred. Moreover, since there were no national or international money markets or banking systems to speak of prior to this date, rulers were compelled to rely on private financiers for their short-term credit needs—needs that were likely to be great given the fiscal demands of war and the difficulty of collecting taxes. State builders who established their infrastructures after 1450 faced a much more favorable situation. The rapid growth of the European university system during this era meant that there was a growing stock of trained jurists who could be used to fill high-ranking administrative posts, and new models of office holding, which drew on the principle of ad hoc commissions, made it easier to hire, fire, and promote officials according to their merit. In sum, in those areas where sustained geopolitical competition began before 1450, patrimonial and often venal infrastructures were the result, whereas in those areas where geopolitical competition came later, less patrimonial and more bureaucratic infrastructures were the rule.

A model based on these two variables would predict the following outcomes: (1) patrimonial absolutism in Latin Europe (France and the Iberian and Italian peninsulas); (2) bureaucratic absolutism in the German states; (3) patrimonial constitutionalism in Britain; and (4) bureaucratic constitutionalism in Poland, Hungary, Sweden, and Denmark. While the first and second predictions accord well with the observed outcomes, the third and the fourth do not. In Britain, the actual outcome was bureaucratic constitutionalism, in Poland and Hungary patrimonial constitutionalism, in Sweden and Denmark, bureaucratic absolutism. To account for these anomalies, Ertman introduces a third variable: "the independent effect of parliaments." What all six of the deviant cases had in common, argues Ertman, is that they were located on the European periphery and thus had strong, bicameral systems of representative government, whose presence "deflect[ed] them from the path they otherwise would have followed had the effects of timing been able to work themselves out unimpeded."[20] In England, Parliament was able to purge the state infrastructure of its patrimonial elements during the civil wars of 1641–42 and, after the Restoration (1660), to impose a series of proto-bureaucratic reforms on an unwilling king and his corrupt administration. In Hungary and Poland, on the other hand, the existence of powerful representative institutions allowed the landed nobility to block the efforts of their rulers to create the sort of bureaucratic infrastructures that eventually took shape in other late state-builders such as Germany.

This still leaves the cases of Sweden and Denmark. In these cases, argues Ertman, the unexpected outcomes were due to "contingent events" that served to weaken representative institutions: in the former case, the election of Gustav Vasa (1523) "under circumstances which allowed him to replace the country's old territorially based assembly with a new, four-chamber body (the Riksdag)"; in the latter case, "the progressive destruction of a participatory form of local government beginning in the middle ages through the immigration of German knights granted lands at feudal tenure."[21] This third variable and these two contingencies, concludes Ertman, explain "most of the observed variance" in the process of European state-building.

It should be noted that there is one case Ertman does not discuss: the Netherlands. Why? The reason, I suspect, is that it does not fit Ertman's model terribly well. Like England and France, the Netherlands experienced sustained geopolitical competition before 1450, partly because they were situated *between* England and France and were therefore drawn into the Hundred Years' War, and partly because they were fragmented into a coterie of duchies and principalities that were all vying with one another for territorial supremacy. Based on these facts, Ertman's model would predict the emergence of a patrimonial system of venal office holding. And, indeed, we do observe a certain degree of venality in the Dutch Republic, at least at the local level. But it was never formally institutionalized as in France. Indeed, it was explicitly forbidden by the provincial and national parliaments! In this regard, the Netherlands were more like England. So perhaps this was another example of the independent effects of parliaments. For the republic *did* have very strong parliaments. But this very fact represents a serious problem for Ertman. For unlike England and the other peripheral countries, parts of the Netherlands *were* conquered by Charlemagne. Nonetheless, they *did* retain an extraordinarily strong system of local government. Despite this fact, however, they did *not* develop a bicameral legislature. And despite *this* fact, they successfully resisted the blandishments of an absolutist monarch, Philip II of Spain. Thus, the Netherlands defy almost all of Ertman's predictions.

Marxist and Bellicist Models: Some Historical Anomalies

Of course, it would be unfair—and even methodologically suspect—to reject the Marxist and bellicist models because they leave out certain causally relevant factors and/or fail to explain some cases fully.[22] The same charge could be leveled against most works of social science, including the present one. Simply because a model is incomplete does not mean that it is false. In my view, the only fair test of a model's empirical adequacy is whether it fully and parsimoniously explains those outcomes that it regards—for whatever reasons—as most important.[23] In this section, I will subject the Marxist and bellicist models of early modern state-formation to just such a test. I will try to show that even the most fully developed and clearly specified versions of these models—namely, Wallerstein's, Downing's, and Ertman's—are inadequate on their own terms, that they fail to account fully or convincingly for just those cases that they claim to explain best.

For Wallerstein, the key cases are the strong core states of the early modern world—the Netherlands and England. These cases presented the greatest challenge to earlier Marxist models, such as Anderson's, and it is to Wallerstein's credit that he squarely addresses this empirical anomaly in his work. He insists, quite correctly, that these states were strong in the sense that they were able to maintain order internally and project power externally. At the same time, though, he claims that they were relatively liberal, that is, that they lacked the kind of centralized administrative apparatus typical of absolutist monarchies.[24] Clearly, there is something of a riddle here, but Wallerstein simply tries to finesse it by contradicting his earlier statement and asserting, somewhat confusingly, that the core states all possessed a "strong state machinery" and a "unified national culture." While such a claim could perhaps be defended for the English case (though not without compromising its liberal designation somewhat), it clearly does not fit the Dutch Republic, which was, after all, the hub of the world economy for much of the sixteenth and seventeenth Centuries. Wallerstein's world systems theory thus fails to explain one of the two cases that it must account most important—the Netherlands.

The key case for Brian Downing—and perhaps the paradigmatic one for the fiscal-military model in general—is not the Dutch Republic, but Brandenburg-Prussia.[25] For nowhere else in early modern Europe, we are told, were constitutional checks on royal power so completely dismantled and the organs of monarchical power so thoroughly bureaucratized. Following earlier bellicist accounts of Prussian state-building,[26] Downing emphasizes the reign of Frederick William (1640–88), a period in which Prussia was involved in a series of intense and protracted military conflicts. And indeed it was the Great Elector, as he is known to posterity, who established Prussia's first standing army and founded the General War Commissary (*General Kriegskommissariat*), the organizational node around which the Prussian central administration later crystallized.[27]

Yet, as most historians agree, the decisive phase of Prussian state-building actually came later, during the reign of Frederick William I (1713–40), Frederick William's grandson.[28] It was the soldier-king (*Soldatenkönig*) who transformed Prussia's ramshackle mercenary force into one of the largest and most disciplined armies in Europe.[29] And it was he who engineered the expansion of the Prussian civil service into a single fiscal and administrative agency, the General Superior Finance War and Domains Commissary (*General Ober-Finanz- Kriegs- und Domänenrat*). By the end of his reign, Prussia had the largest standing army in Europe, relative to its population and, arguably, the most centralized and efficient administrative system. Ironically, however, this unprecedented mobilization for war occurred during a period of relative peace. The *timing* of Prussian state-building, then, presents something of a conundrum for the bellicist model.[30]

The next case that Downing examines—and probably the second in overall importance for him—is France.[31] The dynamics of the French case, he argues, were much the same as those of the Prussian as were its results; in both cases, the fiscal demands of war (that is, the Thirty Years' War) led to the mobilization of domestic resources (that is, taxes) and the establishment of military-bureaucratic absolutism.

Two objections may be raised to this interpretation. The first, once again, concerns timing. Although there is no consensus on the subject, there are at least some historians who contend that the beginnings of French absolutism are to be found, not in the Thirty Years' War, but in the Wars of Religion (1562–98), and there can be little doubt that Henry IV and Sully did as much to dismantle representative institutions and build up the central administration as did Louis XIII and Mazarin.[32] Similarly, a recent study of the royal army during the late sixteenth century suggests that the Wars of Religion stimulated far-reaching changes in military training, tactics, logistics and administration and that these changes were responsible, in part, for the outcome of the conflict. But this hardly undermines Downing's central argument regarding war and state-building. The second and more serious objection concerns Downing's characterization of French absolutism. For while it was certainly very militaristic, it was not terribly bureaucratic. Indeed, except at the very highest levels, the royal administration did not exhibit any of the features of an ideal-typical bureaucracy enumerated by Weber; the average French *officier* owned his own means of administration, was permitted to buy and sell his post, did not receive a fixed salary, worked out of his home, and so on. And the situation was not much better among the *commissaires* appointed directly by the king; there, too, the tendency was towards venality and spoils. The French "bureaucracy," in short, was not a bureaucracy at all, but an extreme—one could even say pathological—form of patrimonialism. Thus, Downing's model is unable to account for a crucial difference (degree of bureaucratization) between his two central cases (Prussia and France).

At first glance, Ertman's model would not seem to be subject to (serious) objections of this sort. He has a ready account for the strength of the British state (if not for that of the Dutch Republic), and he clearly recognizes the differences between French and Prussian absolutism. Moreover, he adduces a set of three independent variables that are logically sufficient to explain most (if not all) cases of early modern state-formation.

But Ertman's model is not as logically consistent and as theoretically parsimonious as one might like. The question, in other words, is whether there is a more coherent and more convincing explanation for at least some aspects of some of the outcomes that Ertman discusses.

Let us quickly review his model. As the reader may recall, it contained three variables: one (local government) that accounts for regime type (absolutist versus constitutionalist), a second (geopolitical competition) that accounts for state structure (patrimonial versus bureaucratic), and a third (the effects of parliaments) that accounts for some of the deviant outcomes (for example, in Britain, Hungary, and Poland). It also contains an error term (historical contingency) that covers two other deviant outcomes (Sweden and Denmark) and, presumably, a third as well (the Netherlands). It would not be difficult to raise questions and objections about the first and second variables.[33] But the Achilles heel of the model—the spot where its weaknesses shine through—is the third variable. These weaknesses are conceptual insofar as the third variable is not really distinct from the first; ultimately, both have to do with the effects of parliaments. And they are logical insofar as the effects of parliaments are not just independent, but opposite! In England, parliaments promoted bureaucratization; in Poland and Hungary, they retarded it. Why? Ertman offers no answer to this question. Thus, Ertman's model is not as airtight as it first appears. In fact, there is a good deal of empirical leakage, for it fails to account, not only for the Netherlands, but for Britain, Hungary, and Poland as well.

Couldn't there be a simpler and more consistent explanation, another variable that accounts for these deviant outcomes? The answer, I believe, is yes. For what Ertman fails to point out is that the struggle against absolutism in all of these cases was closely linked to the quest for religious reform—in the Dutch revolt against Spain, in the demands of the Polish gentry for the execution of the laws, in the rebellion of the Hungarian nobility against the Catholic Habsburgs, and in the Puritan revolution against Charles I. Indeed, in all four of these cases, Calvinism and constitutionalism went hand in hand. The same was also true in France, of course, where Calvinists and constitutionalists squared off against Catholics and monarchists for nearly three decades during the Wars of Religion; there, however, the Calvinists were politically neutralized (by Henry IV) and then gradually suppressed (by Louis XIII and Louis XIV). This explanation of regime outcomes is considerably more parsimonious than the one advanced by Ertman: where Calvinist insurgents could draw on strong traditions of representative government, constitutionalism was preserved; where such a movement and/or such traditions were lacking, absolutism ultimately prevailed.[34] The key, in other words, was not the structure of representative institutions per se but the (relative) success or failure of antimonarchical insurgency.

Confessional politics, as it turns out, were also key for Sweden, one of the aberrant cases that Ertman explains in terms of historical contingency. The contingency in question, it may be recalled, was Gustav Vasa's election to the throne in 1523. Gustav was one of several prominent nobles involved in the uprising against Danish rule led by Sten Sture in 1517 and one of the few who survived the Stockholm Bloodbath of 1520, and he was chosen as regent in 1521.[35] From the beginning, his relations with the Catholic Church were fraught with tension. The Apostolic See had sided with the Danes in 1517, as had the Swedish archbishop, Gustav Trolle, and one of Gustav's first acts as regent was to dismiss and banish Trolle. Gustav had been forced to borrow heavily to finance his war against the Danes, especially from the city of Lübeck, and he now began eyeing the properties of the Swedish Church. Before launching a frontal attack on the hierocracy, however, he first sought to weaken it from within by appointing reform-minded clergy such as Olavus Petri to important posts within the church.[36] In 1527, he finally made his gambit: he called a meeting of the *Riksdag* at

Söderköping, bemoaned the deplorable state of royal finance, and threatened to abdicate unless a remedy were found—the remedy he preferred being a thoroughgoing secularization of church properties. Lutheranism had made significant inroads among both the nobility and the commoners by this time, and the assembly placed its stamp of approval on the king's proposal. With this independent revenue base, Gustav was able to pay off his debtors in Lübeck, build up the country's defenses, and establish a small standing army, all without seeking additional contributions from the *Riksdag*. He was able, in other words, to set Sweden on the path towards absolutist monarchy.

Confessional politics also played a role in Sweden's return to a more constitutional style of monarchy during the reign of Gustavus Adolphus (1611–32).[37] Like many German princes, Gustavus's father, Charles IX (reigned: 1604–11) was disheartened by the narrow scholasticism that had taken hold within the Lutheran Church and was alarmed by the resurgence of Catholicism and the Empire following the Council of Trent and the Peace of Augsburg. Consequently, he found himself increasingly drawn towards Calvinism, with its fighting spirit and system of lay governance. And while he never went so far as to undertake a "Second" or Calvinist Reformation of the sort introduced introduced by the electors of Brandenburg and the Palatinate and other German rulers, he did appoint a Reformed court preacher (Johannes À Lasco's former assistant, Martin Micron), to purify the Swedish liturgy of "popish remnants" and insert crypto-Calvinist passages into the Swedish confession—much to the chagrin, of course, of the Swedish clergy. He also practiced a style of rule more imperious and aloof than that of his predecessors, and, before long, an antimonarchical front of orthodox clergymen and constitutionalist nobles began to take shape. It was these two parties who Gustavus Adolphus sought to accommodate after taking the throne in 1611. In that year, he signed a compact with church leaders in which he agreed to confirm the unaltered Augsburg Confession (rather than the less orthodox Melancthonian variation), impose Lutheranism on all Swedish subjects (though not on foreign residents), and recognize the right of the Swedish Church to elect its own bishops. And the following year, he signed a royal charter that restored the political power of the nobility by granting it a monopoly over the highest offices of state, and of the estates more generally; all new legislation now required the prior consultation and approval of the *Riksdag*. In this way, he avoided a religiously fueled, antiabsolutist backlash. A focus on confessional politics thus helps us to understand why the Swedish monarchy became so much stronger during the sixteenth century and why representative institutions made a comeback during the seventeenth.

As we will see later, such a focus is also crucial to understanding the Prussian outcome, which was so different than the Swedish. There, the ruling House of Hohenzollern *did* attempt to impose a Second Reformation, did *not* succeed in reconciling the nobility, and chose, in the end, to break with constitutional governance altogether. This result is all the more striking given that the most populous province of the Hohenzollern kingdom, East Prussia, possessed a strong, bicameral legislature. In this instance, at least, confessional dynamics seem to have outweighed institutional ones.

The upshot of the foregoing critique should now be clear: once confessional dynamics are taken into account, many of the anomalies and aberrations that befuddled and defied Ertman's model can be readily comprehended and easily explained. In fact, it is curious that previous work on early modern state formation has paid so little attention to religion. After all, to write a political history of the sixteenth and seventeenth centuries and leave out confessional politics is a bit like writing a political history of the nineteenth and twentieth centuries without class politics; the result is bound to be one-sided to the point of distortion.

Historians, happily, have not been guilty of this error, and it is to recent work on the Reformation that I now turn, for it is there that we will find a theoretical framework more conducive to our explanatory ends: the confessionalization paradigm developed by Ernst Zeeden and Heinz Schilling.

Rethinking the Reformation: Religion and Politics in the Confessional Age

Over the last several decades, early modern historiography has undergone a veritable sea change, as the old framework for studying the Reformation advanced by Ranke almost 150 years ago has given way to a new framework focusing on confessionalization.[38] The traditional accounts of the Reformation with which many readers may be most familiar began with Luther's Ninety-five Theses (1517) and concluded with the Peace of Augsburg (1555) and focused mainly on the diffusion of doctrine. Recent accounts have adopted a very different periodization, dividing the Reformation into three, overlapping segments, each with its own distinctive sociopolitical dynamic: (1) a diffuse evangelical movement (ca. 1517–25), which advocated religious reform based on the Gospels, often with strong social and communal overtones; (2) a reformation from above (*obrigkeitliche Reformation*) (ca. 1520–45), in which the civil authorities effected various liturgical and ecclesiastical reforms; and (3) a confessional age (ca. 1540–1648), in which the construction of national or territorial churches and wars of belief reinforced and drove one another forward.

The Confessionalization Paradigm: Periodization and Dynamics
Let us examine each of these phases in slightly more detail.

Historians generally trace the origins of the *evangelical movement* back to the humanistic agitation for religious reform that began in the late fifteenth century and found its most influential expression in the works of Erasmus. With their insistence on a preaching ministry and the authority of the Gospel, Luther and other reformist clerics stood firmly in this tradition. But by playing on the anticlericalism of the populace and the Erastianism of the elite, they lent the humanistic message a heightened social and political appeal. As a consequence, the evangelical movement soon slipped beyond their grasp and became a vehicle for the political ambitions of disgruntled nobles and the social grievances of the common man, culminating in the Rebellion of the Imperial Knights led by Ulrich von Hutten (1522/23) and the German Peasants War (1525), or Revolution, as some historians now prefer to call it. The failure of these uprisings, it is generally agreed, marks the end point of the evangelical movement.

It did not, however, defuse conflict over the religious question. On the contrary, popular agitation for reform continued, even as Imperial attacks on it hardened. The initiative now passed to the territorial princes and urban rulers. Faced with intense pressure from above and below, political leaders had little choice but to take a stand on the religious question. In the end, most opted for *reform from above,* thus initiating the second phase of the confessionalization process. Making use of the *ius reformandi,* the right of the lower magistrates to reform the church, they effected liturgical, ecclesiastical, and doctrinal changes that accorded with the reformers' emphasis on the Gospel as the sole authority in religious matters. In doing so, it should be noted, they vastly expanded their power over the church—which was surely one reason, though by no means the only one, why so many rulers chose to side with the reformers. Charles V, meanwhile, was determined to reestablish the religious unity of the Empire, and in a series of successful military campaigns, culminating in the defeat of the Schmalkaldian League (1547), he delivered the Protestant princes and towns a string of humiliating defeats. But he failed to translate this military victory into a political one. In the peace negotiations at Augsburg, he was forced to accept the principle of *cuius regio, eius religio,* which gave territorial rulers an almost unlimited right to impose their own confession on their subjects, thus initiating the third phase of the confessionalization process—the creation of territorial churches.

Outside Germany, however, the religious struggle was only beginning. The Swiss and south German reformers—Zwingli, Bucer, Calvin—had never seen eye-to-eye with their counterparts in Saxony and Hessia, and with the establishment of the Genevan mission in 1559 their version of Protestantism was rapidly exported to the north. Meanwhile, the decrees of the Counsel of Trent four years later (1563) signaled a resurgence of the Catholic Church, which was now determined to reconquer the ground which it had lost to Protestantism. The stage was thus set for a three-cornered struggle between Catholics, Lutherans, and Calvinists over religious beliefs and political boundaries. From Edinburgh to Prague, Europe was swept by a series of revolutionary confrontations fought out under the banners of Calvinism and Catholicism—the Covenanter's revolt in Scotland, the French Wars of Religion, the Dutch Revolt against Spain, the gentry movement in Poland, the Hungarian rebellion against the Habsburgs, the revolt of the Bohemian estates. And it was this latter confrontation that touched off a military conflagration that consumed all of Europe—the Thirty Years' War (1618–48). Only the resultant economic and military exhaustion brought the Confessional Age to a close.

The confessionalization paradigm, then, is not just a new periodization of the Reformation; it is a new interpretation of the early modern period as such. It is an attempt to connect the dynamics of the Reformation with the dynamics of social and political development. While the old framework tended to hive off the Reformation and portray it in strictly religious terms by tracing its outbreak to the corruption of the Catholic Church and its diffusion to the mass appeal of Luther's teachings, recent scholarship has attempted to set the Reformation within a wider context, emphasizing the importance of social factors in its reception and of political factors in its propagation. In short, scholars of confessionalization have attempted to understand how the Reformation stimulated and interacted with other historical processes, such as the expansion of commercial capitalism and the formation of the early modern state. This latter connection is of particular interest here.

Confessionalization, Social-Disciplining, and State Formation

In the "confessionalization paradigm," church-building and state-building go hand in hand.[39] Without state support, these scholars point out, church leaders could not hope to put down sectarian movements and impose a uniform set of religious beliefs and practices on the populace. The civil authorities, for their part, were generally happy to cooperate. From their perspective, religious uniformity provided the best foundation for political stability. In the phrase of the age, "religion is the bond that holds society together" (*religio vincula societatis*). Their motives were not entirely pure, of course. The creation of territorial churches also enhanced state power. It did so most directly by greatly increasing the authority of the state over the church. In Lutheran territories, the church came under the de facto control of the ruler, in his capacity as emergency bishop. In Calvinist territories, the church had greater autonomy, but representatives of the magistrate generally sat in the consistories, the boards of church elders that governed each congregation. And even in Catholic territories, where the authority of Rome was maintained, rulers expanded their control over clerical appointments, and even established royal agencies to oversee the church administration. Nor should we forget that the seizure of church property filled the royal coffers of Protestant states.

Church-building also enhanced state power indirectly by establishing new mechanisms of moral regulation and social control. Of course, there was nothing new about attempts to impose social discipline on the populace; urban magistrates and territorial rulers had been attempting to alter the behavior of their subjects for decades and even centuries through a plethora of legislation governing everything from the rations allowed the poor to the clothing permitted the rich.[40] But they generally lacked the administrative capacities to enforce these rules. It was here that the church proved crucial. As Heinz Schilling has aptly put it:

Driven by confessional zeal, the Lutheran pastors, the spiritual counselors of the Tridentine clergy, and Calvinist elders and ministers became . . . the most important mediators of a new system of moral-ethical and political-legal norms. Through household visitations, church discipline and ecclesiastical courts (*Episkopalgerichtsbarkeit*), they monitored and disciplined everyday life-conduct, penetrating into the last house in the most isolated little village.[41]

The Reformation also helped to break down long-standing barriers to social reform. Attempts to rationalize and centralize urban poor-relief had long been opposed by the Catholic Church and especially by the various mendicant orders.[42] By desanctifying the poor and dissolving the monasteries, the Reformation cleared the way for a thoroughgoing reorganization of inequitable and inefficient systems of social welfare in both Protestant and Catholic regions. Beginning in the 1520s, cities throughout Europe issued new poor-relief ordinances, which gave urban magistrates greater control over the dispensation of alms and discriminated between the truly deserving poor—the young, the old, the infirm—and the able-bodied poor, providing aid to the former and setting the latter to work.[43]

The Reformation also stimulated educational reform. In Protestant regions, elementary schools, including classes in how to read the Bible, were created for the poor.[44] In Catholic regions, special academies were founded, especially by the Jesuits, to educate members of the upper classes. And throughout Europe university education was expanded in order to improve the quality of the clergy.[45]

Finally, Catholic and Protestant churches alike sought to tighten and enforce rules governing sexuality and marriage. Marriage ordinances were publicly promulgated, and for the first time baptisms and marriages were recorded in church and parish registers.[46]

In all these areas—poor-relief, education, and the regulation of sexuality and marriage—cooperation between the religious and civil authorities was generally tight. In fact, in most early modern polities, it would have been difficult to draw a clear line between church and state. And in a world where princes served as bishops, bishops as princes, magistrates as elders and elders as magistrates, such a distinction would be purely anachronistic. Not only had the Medieval symbiosis between the two swords persisted, it had grown tighter. But instead of having two centers—the papacy and the Empire—it now had many. In the long run, however, this symbiosis proved more beneficial to one party than the other; ultimately, the state monopolized control over the new infrastructures of power—the prisons and workhouses, the schools and universities, the law and the courts.

Calvinism and Social-Disciplining

The confessionalization paradigm thus highlights just those sources and dimensions of state-formation that are of interest here: the bottom-up creation of new strategies and mechanisms of discipline and governance and their gradual instrumentalization and absorption by political elites. Unfortunately, however, it pays little attention to how these dynamics differed across the confessions. Indeed, Schilling and other exponents of the new approach have long argued that the "modernizing dynamics" unleashed by the Lutheran, Calvinist, and Catholic reforms were "functionally equivalent," and have only recently begun to explore the peculiarities and *propria* of the individual confessions.

No doubt, there is some merit to this perspective. Proponents of the old framework often exaggerated the differences between Catholicism and

Protestantism, and processes of social-disciplining such as those just described occurred throughout confessional Europe. In this sense, the de-emphasis of confessional differences has served as an important corrective.

But it is also possible to overcorrect for past mistakes. After all, there *were* real differences in the doctrines, structures, and politics of the three confessions, and these differences tended to grow sharper over time. One such difference, I will argue, lay in the intensity of the social-disciplining process. For while all three confessions advocated discipline—both religious and social—it was the Calvinists who did so with the greatest fervor and consequence.

There were a number of reasons for this. The first had to do with the Calvinist understanding of *disciplina,* the outward form of the Christian community. For while the Calvinists shared the concern of the Lutherans and Catholics with doctrinal and liturgical uniformity within the church, they gave particular emphasis to the conformity of the church—and indeed of the entire political community—with scriptural law.

This emphasis was not incidental. In fact, its roots are to be found in Calvin's theology. Of course, the theological precept most frequently associated with Calvin's name is predestination. It was Weber who first comprehended the powerful "psychologic" that this doctrine generated within the individual believer. He argued that Calvin's doctrine of the calling harnessed the ideal interest of the believer to worldly work and the accumulation of wealth.[47] But Calvin and his followers gave equal stress to another "sign" of salvation—"justification."[48] Calvin understood justification as the process through which "by [God's] Spirit, we are regenerated into a new spiritual nature" and become capable of living in perfect obedience to God's will.[49] Spiritual growth, Calvin believed, was manifested in the attainment of a "voluntary" and "inward" obedience, a natural harmony between morality and desire.[50] Hence, one might say that Calvinism contained not only a work ethic, but an ethic of self-discipline. For the individual believer discipline was not just a theological problem but a practical one as well, and Calvinists invented a variety of techniques for achieving it: regular Bible reading, daily journals, moral log books, and rigid control over time.[51] Thus, Calvinism propagated new ethics and practices of self-discipline.

It should be stressed that discipline was not only central to Calvinist spirituality but to the Calvinist understanding of the church as well. Indeed, when Calvin used the word *discipline,* it was in relationship to the church, not the individual believer. For him, a disciplined church (*église dressée*) was a congregation that enforced obedience to godly law among its members. In his *Ordonnances ecclésiastiques,* which served as the organizational blueprint for Reformed churches throughout Europe, Calvin outlined a set of institutional mechanisms for maintaining discipline within the church.[52] He directed that each congregation establish a consistory, composed of an elected body of elders together with the church pastor(s). The chief function of the consistory was to supervise the morals of the congregation. To this end, the consistory interviewed prospective members before admitting them to the church. It also interviewed individual church members several times a year in order to ascertain whether they were fit to receive communion. Errant members—for example, drunkards, adulterers, wife beaters, and tax cheats—were excluded from communion until they mended their ways. Particularly recalcitrant individuals who defied the consistory faced excommunication. The purpose of this discipline, however, was not so much to punish individual sinners as to expunge sin from the Christian community. Calvin understood church discipline as a form of witness through which God's will and majesty were made manifest in the world. He was thus more concerned with the purity of the church than the morality of its members per se. For this reason, he regarded public peccadillos, which could bring disrepute to the church, more severely than private transgressions, which could not. Indeed, he felt it important that church members avoid even the appearance of sin. Only by remaining blameless and above all reproach could the church fulfill its testimonial function. Consequently, each individual was not only made responsible for his or her own conduct but was charged to keep a watchful eye over other members of the congregation and to remonstrate with those who strayed from the path of righteousness. In sum, the Reformed Church made each individual responsible not only for their own conduct but for the purity of the church as a whole. Each watched each, and all watched all.

If Calvin's understanding of the church was elitist (in the most literal sense)—and here we discover the third root of Calvinist discipline—it was not strictly speaking sectarian. Calvin saw the church as a gathered community, which should include only the elect, but he did not regard it as a purely spiritual community, which should retreat from the world. On the contrary, he viewed the church as the spiritual arm of the Christian community, as part of a *res publica christiana* or Christian polity.[53] Worldly authority was vested in the civil magistrate. The role of a godly magistrate, argued Calvin, was to protect the true religion and impose Christian discipline on the community as a whole. If the ungodly could not be saved, he reasoned, then they could at least be compelled to obey God's laws. Together, church and magistrate were to work towards the establishment of a "Christian polity" (*res publica christiana*) to effect a thoroughgoing Christianization of social life. Inspired by this vision, many Calvinists became zealous advocates of social improvement, taking up and implementing the reform program first outlined by the Renaissance humanists (Erasmus, Vives), with its focus on popular education and poor-relief. The new schools and workhouses, not surprisingly, employed the same mechanisms of moral surveillance and social control as the Calvinist consistories.[54] Indeed, they may be seen as an attempt to extend the discipline of the Reformed Church to the population as a whole. The Calvinists, in short, aimed at nothing less than the establishment of an all-encompassing regime of moral and social discipline—a disciplinary revolution.

Of course, it is possible to find parallels for the various aspects of Calvinist discipline within the other confessions. Still, I believe it can be shown that the scope and intensity of the disciplining process was greatest in the Calvinist context, and I will present comparative evidence for this contention in chapter 4. It is also possible to find precedents for many of the theoretical points advanced here, especially in the work of Michel Foucault and Max Weber.

Rethinking State Theory: Foucault, Weber, and the Genealogy of Early Modern Governance

Michel Foucault once quipped that we have not chopped off the king's head in political theory.[55] Much the same might be said of state theory. For while a great deal of attention has been devoted to the nerve centers of the state—the fiscal and administrative apparatus—very little has been paid to its torso and limbs—the networks of practices and institutions that it uses to embrace and guide the population.[56]

But state theorists have not only ignored the king's body; they have ignored his "soul" as well. For while they have studied the organization of state institutions and the material interests of state actors in great depth, these theorists have displayed surprisingly little interest in the animating spirit, that is, the "ideal interests" of state rulers and the dominant ethos of their "administrative staffs," and the impact that this spirit had on the sorts of reforms and projects that state rulers deemed relevant and on the diligence and efficiency with which they carried them out.

One of the key challenges for state theory, then, is to analyze the king's body and soul, the infrastructure and animus of the modern state. Of course, a number of theorists have already taken up this challenge. In fact, Foucault's own analysis of capillary power may be seen as an attempt to theorize state infrastructure. And Weber's analysis of sociopolitical ethics may be seen as an effort to theorize the spirit of the state. The works of Gerhard Oestreich and Norbert Elias, though less familiar to American social scientists, may also be seen as an answer to this challenge.

In this section, I examine these efforts to theorize the body and soul of the state and attempt to point up some of their limitations. The problem with Foucault's analysis, as I intimated earlier, is that he ignores—or, rather, represses—the connection between religion and discipline. Weber is guilty of the reverse; he overlooks the relationship between discipline and the state. And while Oestreich and Elias are better attuned to the tripartite connections among religion, discipline, and state power, they tend to see it operating from the top down rather than from the bottom up. It is only by combining their various approaches, I argue, that we are able to understand the early modern disciplinary revolution in all its richness and complexity.

Michel Foucault and the King's Body: Prolegomenon to a Theory of Early Modern Governance

Foucault never wrote a book about the state. His remarks on the subject are scattered through various lectures, interviews, and essays from the 1970s. In an interview from 1972, for example, Foucault argued that "the eighteenth century invented . . . a synaptic regime of power, a regime of its exercise *within* the social body, rather than *from above* it."[57] In *Discipline and Punish*, which appeared in 1975, he used a somewhat different metaphor, arguing that the "Classical Age" gave rise to a new "micro-physics of power," whose purest expression was Jeremy Bentham's (in)famous panopticon, which allowed a single person to watch over and control a large multitude of prisoners. And in another interview, conducted in 1977, he compared the relationship between capillary power and state power to that between "base" and "superstructure."[58] In Foucault's view, then, the state rests upon and grows out of diffuse strategies and mechanisms of discipline and control, such as panopticism and the prison, which it appropriates and absorbs only incompletely.[59] It is a central(izing) node or grand strategy that connects and integrates diffuse networks of power and domination more than it creates or controls them.

As Foucault himself recognized, this view of the state has far-reaching methodological implications. If we accept the premise that state power flows upward as well as downward, then descending analyses of state-formation as a top-down process involving the centralization of control over territory and subjects—the traditional approach—must be complemented by an ascending analysis of state-formation as a bottom-up process in which the capillaries and synapses of power within the social body are gradually plugged into and connected with the central circulatory and nervous systems of the state.⁶⁰ Doing an ascending analysis of the state would mean reconstructing the genealogy or development of particular strategies and institutions of power and the means by and the degree to which they were appropriated or absorbed by various state actors and institutions.

For whatever reasons, Foucault never carried out this research program in any systematic way. But he did seek to sketch out a history of the state from below in various works from the late 1970s, such as his 1978 speech on "governmentality." By *governmentality*, Foucault means "the manner in which the conduct of an ensemble of individuals becomes implicated to a greater and greater degree in the exercise of state power."⁶¹ The growth of governmentality, he argues, can be traced back to the fifteenth and sixteenth centuries—to the decline of feudalism and the onset of the Reformation and, more specifically, to "the establishment of the great territorial, administrative and colonial states," on the one hand, and the growing concern with "how one must be spiritually ruled and led on this earth to achieve salvation," on the other.⁶² Based on this statement, and on Foucault's earlier remarks, one would expect a brief overview of the various disciplinary mechanisms invented by Protestant and Catholic religious reformers and of the ways in which territorial rulers utilized them as part of their strategies of domination. But, instead, Foucault launches into a lengthy discussion of Machiavelli's *Prince* and the various treatises written in reaction to it from the late sixteenth century onwards. In these latter tracts, Foucault discerns the gradual emergence of a discourse on the "art of governance," which he contrasts with the discourse on monarchical sovereignty underlying *The Prince*.⁶³ On the concrete social mechanisms through which this power operated, the central concern of so much of his work, Foucault is strangely silent.

Foucault returned to the connection between religious discourse and the development of the state the following year in an address entitled "Politics and Reason."⁶⁴ Foucault begins the talk by making a sharp distinction between the "centralizing power" of the state and the "individualizing power" of the pastor. In order to illustrate the distinction, he draws a series of contrasts between the prince and the shepherd and the sort of government practiced by each: whereas the prince seeks to control a territory and the people who happen to be within it and is concerned primarily with the welfare of the state and the achievement of glory, the shepherd looks after a flock that he himself gathers together, is concerned with the welfare of each individual member of the flock, and governs out of a sense of duty and self-denial. He traces the roots of the shepherd analogy back to the ancient Hebrews and then follows out its elaboration in the pastoral practices of the Western church, emphasizing the growing concern of the latter with the spiritual welfare of the individual believer and with practices of self-examination and self-knowledge.

At this point, one might have expected Foucault to focus on the marriage between princely and pastoral power that occurred during the Reformation. But he did not. Instead, he chose to focus his energies on a new project: his "history of sexuality."[65] This work was divided into four parts. After disposing with the cliché that repression began with the Victorians and attacking the idea that the history of sexuality could be understood as a process of repression (volume 1), Foucault attempted to demonstrate that the Ancients first made sexuality into a moral problem (volume 2) and that this problematization of the sexual gave rise to various techniques of "caring for the self" (volume 3), which, in turn, formed the precursors for Christian asceticism in general and Medieval monasticism in particular (volume 4, unpublished). Had the last volume of the history been completed it would have brought Foucault back, once again, to the historical threshold he had so carefully avoided during the previous decades—the Reformation. Indeed, one could even see his intellectual trajectory as a sort of extended circumlocution, in which he repeatedly approached the chronological boundaries of the Reformation era from various directions without ever transgressing them.

Why? There are probably several reasons. Throughout his career, Foucault insisted that he was more interested in how power and domination was exercised rather than by whom.[66] Accordingly, he always strove to write "history without a subject" and "books without a face."[67] Of course, it would have been difficult to write a book on the state without any (acting) subjects, and even more difficult to write a book on religion and the state, unless, of course, one chose to focus solely on discourses about the state—which is precisely the path Foucault did choose in his writings on this topic. There may have been another reason for Foucault's resistance as well: any serious study of the connection between the Reformation and the early modern state would have exposed the untenability of Foucault's earlier claims that the disciplinary regime of the classical age first took shape in absolutist France beginning in the mid-eighteenth century.[68] For as we will see below, most of the disciplinary strategies that Foucault identifies (mutual surveillance, compartmentalization of space, the use of written codes, and so on) and all of the disciplinary institutions that he discusses (the prison, the workhouse, the school, the barracks) were more or less fully developed by the end of the seventeenth century at the very latest. What is more, we will see that these disciplinary strategies and institutions were often inspired by religious doctrines and propagated by religious elites. We will see, in other words, that the history of discipline *does* have a subject and that it *did* involve subjection.

As regards the identity of that subject and the nature of that subjection, Weber is a better guide than Foucault.

Max Weber: The Protestant Ethic and the Spirit of the State

Weber never wrote a book by this name. What he did write, of course, was a series of essays that explored the link between ascetic Protestantism and modern capitalism and, more generally, between religion and rationality. But the problem of the state, though secondary, was never far from his mind. In the preface to *The Protestant Ethic,* for example, Weber identifies the modern state as one of the characteristic and distinctive products of Western rationalism, and in the closing paragraph of the book he urges his readers to investigate "the significance of ascetic rationalism for the content of *socio-political* ethics, that is, for the organizational forms and functions of social institutions from the conventicle to the state."[69] What Weber almost seems to be suggesting here is that one conduct an ascending analysis of the state focusing on the effects of ascetic Protestantism, and if one reads his work on the sociology of religion a little more closely and somewhat against the grain, one soon discovers the basic elements out of which such an analysis could be constructed. But Weber, himself, does not put the various elements together. In particular, he fails to draw any connection between the Protestant ethic and the spirit of bureaucracy.

In *The Protestant Ethic* (1905), of course, Weber focuses on the spirit of capitalism—that peculiar and paradoxical combination of acquisitiveness and thrift which he sees as the cultural foundation of capitalist accumulation. Weber argues that the spirit of capitalism has an elective affinity (*Wahlverwandtschaft*) with the Protestant ethic, and that the Protestant ethic, is rooted in Calvinist theology, specifically, the Calvinist doctrine of double predestination. There is a problem with this argument, however; there were some denominations that developed an ethic of "innerworldly ascetisicm" but rejected the doctrine of predestination. Weber is aware of this problem, of course, and he repeatedly emphasizes that "similar ethical maxims" can arise out of "dis-similar dogmatic foundations."[70] This is an important point. But it raises a further question: What produced the similarity in "ethical maxims"? Towards the end of *The Protestant Ethic,* Weber suggests an answer: the common denominator uniting the various forms of ascetic Protestantism, he argues, is not a particular doctrine (pre-destination) but a certain ecclesiastical polity (*Kirchenverfassung*).[71]

This argument is developed at greater length in Weber's essay on "The Protestant Sects" (1919–20). What distinguished the ecclesiastical polity of the ascetic churches and sects, he suggests, was that they all possessed a system of congregational discipline (*Gemeindezucht*), which was quite different from the system of ecclesiastical discipline practiced by the Catholic Church and other hierocratic denominations, such as Lutheranism and Anglicanism.[72] In the former, says Weber, discipline was enforced by the laity, was communal in character, and focused on the moral qualities of the individual believer. It was public and it was imposed by one's peers. In the latter, by contrast, discipline was enforced by the clergy, was authoritarian in character, and was triggered by specific offenses. It was private and it was applied by the priestly class. For all these reasons, Weber concludes, communal discipline tended to be more intensive than hierocratic discipline. To understand the development of innerworldly asceticism, then, one must look not simply at theological doctrines, but also at ecclesiastical discipline.

But what does ecclesiastical discipline have to do with state power? How did the Protestant ethic affect the early modern state? Again, Weber never addresses these questions directly, but in various parts of *Economy and Society* he does point to some important connections between the Protestant ethic and the spirit of the state. The first has to do with the relationship between ascetic Protestantism and social reform. The Calvinists, as Weber recognized, were not content with a disciplined church; they wanted a disciplined society, as well. And one of the mechanisms through which they sought to achieve this new society was poor-relief. It was the Calvinists, contends Weber, who first did away with "received forms of charity" and replaced them with a rational system of poor-relief (*sachlicher Armenpflegebetrieb*), and it was they, too, who first used the poor law as an instrument of labor discipline.[73]

The second connection that Weber points to is between ascetic Protestantism and political revolution.[74] This connection is not entirely new. At least within the ethical religions, argues Weber, there have always been religious ascetics who chose to renounce the otherworldly universe of the cloister cell in order to assume the activist role of the prophet, individuals who demanded "an ethically rational ordering and disciplining of the world" that accorded more fully with the "methodical and rational form of self-discipline" they themselves practiced.[75] But the radical Calvinists went further than this. They aspired to the political "domination of the religious virtuosos belonging to the church" and to the "imposition of godly law upon the world."[76] And where such tendencies became fully expressed, as in the Dutch Revolt or the English Revolution, the energy and discipline of the Calvinists helped them to achieve these goals, at least for a time.[77]

The third connection is between the Protestant ethic and the spirit of bureaucracy. Generally speaking, says Weber, "bureaucracy tends to be characterized by a deep contempt for all irrational religiosity."[78] It follows from this that bureaucracy should have an elective affinity to rational religiosity. This was true in China, Weber argues, and it was also true in Prussia, where the bureaucratic ethos owed much to Lutheran Pietism.[79]

In the "Protestant Sects" essay, Weber also points to a fourth connection. There, he argues that American democracy is not a "sand pile of individuals," as is often believed, but "a tangle of highly exclusive voluntary associations," which intensely police the qualities of their members and control their access to various social and material goods (prestige, business contacts, and so on).[80] These practices, he continues, have their roots in traditions of church discipline, and they, he implies, are the real foundation of democratic government and political stability in the United States. Here, Weber's analysis of social discipline and political order sounds very much like Foucault's discussion of capillary power and liberal regimes or neo-Tocquevillian discussions of social capital and democratic governance.[81] In sum, Weber suggests that the Protestant ethic tended to promote poor-law reform, political revolution, bureaucratization, and social order more generally.

But, suggestive as this analysis is, Weber never draws an explicit connection between discipline and the state. In fact, his theory of the state tends to obscure the significance of this connection, insofar as it focuses on the threat of violence and coercion rather than on the capacity for discipline and control. And insofar as Weber advances a theory of state-formation, it is clearly a bellicist one.[82] Thus, the ascending analysis of state-formation suggested by Weber's writings on the sociology of religion is deeply at odds with the descending analysis of the state advanced in his writings on the sociology of domination. In order to trace out the cultural affinities and historical connections between the Protestant ethic and the spirit of absolutism, it will be necessary to adopt a more Foucauldian understanding of the state and its development, one that emphasizes the pastoral or embracing character of state power, rather than its repressive and judicial dimension, and one that underlines the emergence of new governmental projects and technologies below the state as well as their appropriation and centralization by the state. It will be necessary, in other words, to combine Weber's sociology of religion with Foucault's theory of micropolitics.

"The Non-Absolutist in Absolutism": Oestreich and Elias on Social Discipline and State-Formation

Of course, Weber and Foucault are not the only ones who have analyzed the nexus between religion, discipline, and state power. The spate of work on social discipline (*Sozialdisziplinierung*) among early modern historians is inspired by another figure: the constitutional historian, Gerhard Oestreich. Oestreich first introduced the concept of social-disciplining in his essay on the "Structural Problem of European Absolutism."[83] There, Oestreich contrasts the old literature on absolutism, which focuses on the creation and extension of central institutions such as the army and the bureaucracy, with a new literature, which focuses on those areas of social life that remained outside the purview of the absolutist state, what Oestreich provocatively calls "the non-absolutist in absolutism."[84] He then goes on to argue that development of the absolutist state had three distinct dimensions—centralization, institutionalization, and social-disciplining—and he emphasizes that the last of these three processes was by the far the most important. Given the period in question—the sixteenth and seventeenth centuries—and Oestreich's apparent concern with the social, one would expect some discussion of the relationship between religion and discipline, and, in fact, Oestreich does mention Calvin's Genevan church ordinances as an example of social disciplining.[85] But it soon becomes clear that what Oestreich really means by social-disciplining is the myriad of "police legislation" passed by territorial rulers from the Renaissance onwards[86]—laws governing everything from the opening hours of local taverns to the numbers of guests permitted at weddings.[87] The main inspiration for this program of monarchically imposed discipline, says Oestreich, was "late humanism" and Neostoicism.[88] Insofar as religion played a role in this process, he argues, it was primarily negative; by unleashing widespread conflict and bloodshed, says Oestreich, the confessional struggles of the Reformation era sparked "the call for a strong state" and set in motion a "deconfessionalization" and "de-doctrinization" (*Enttheologisierung*) of politics that reinforced the power of the state.[89] "Under the judicial and police state [*Polizei- und Ordnungsstaat*] of the sixteenth century," concludes Oestreich, "the general population and especially the common people were trained to lead disciplined lives"[90]—a peculiar conclusion indeed for someone who emphasized the relative weakness of the absolutist state! Not surprisingly, Oestreich seems to back off somewhat from this position in the closing paragraph of the essay, where he claims that social-disciplining "was not solely a political (*staatlicher*), religious (*kirchlicher*), military or economic process," and in some of his later essays, particularly those on Brandenburg-Prussia, he attributed greater importance to religion and especially to Calvinism. But even in these writings he continued to conceive of social-disciplining mainly as a top-down process emanating from the state.

Much the same can be said of a second body of work that deals with the nexus between social discipline and state power, namely, Norbert Elias's work on the civilizing process. Unlike Oestreich, who never gives a formal definition of *social disciplining*, Elias is quite clear about what he means by *civilizing*: the imposition of external norms and controls on behavior and affect and their gradual internalization within the individual psyche. Oestreich and Elias also differ as to the key embodiment of the new norms: Oestreich sees laws as central, while Elias emphasizes manners. Like Oestreich, however, Elias argues that the spread of civility is intimately bound up with the establishment of absolutism.[91] Of course, Elias does not contend that absolutist rulers were the first to articulate and codify norms of civility; in fact, he traces their antecedents to the Middle Ages. But he does insist that absolutist courts were the first to practice them to any real degree. For in his view it was only with the establishment of the royal courts of the Renaissance, and especially of the French court at Versailles, that a social "figuration" was put into place that could impose civility on its members and, through them, on the wider population. The court, in other words, was the key mechanism or conduit through which civility was imposed and diffused. The complex codes of behavior and etiquette that governed daily life at court forced members of the nobility to restrain their affects and emotions and channeled their ambitions and envy into highly controlled forms of ritual competition; the manners of the nobility were then imitated by upwardly mobile and status-conscious members of the *haute bourgeoisie* and professional classes and, somewhat later, by the middling sort as well.[92] For Elias, then, the royal courts in general and Versailles in particular form the motor of the civilizing process, the epicenter from which the entire movement derives its energy and direction.[93] Elias also suggests that there are feedback effects between state-building and disciplining, insofar as the gradual spread of aristocratic manners helps to forge a pacified population that can be more easily governed and controlled by a highly centralized state apparatus—an important insight that will be discussed at length in the pages that follow.[94] But except for a passing remark about the role of the church as an important transmission belt for the new models of behavior,[95] he makes no mention of religion and appears to have attributed even less weight to it than did Oestreich. For him, the Middle Ages are followed by the Renaissance and the Renaissance by the modern age; there is no place for the Reformation in his periodization[96]—or his theory.

Oestreich's theory of social disciplining and Elias's theory of the civilizing process are thus quite similar in their aims—and their limitations. On the one hand, both seek to extend the scope of traditional theories of the state, albeit in somewhat different ways. While Oestreich focuses on the efforts of early modern rulers to impose new and more rational standards of social conduct on their subjects, Elias draws attention to the effects that the court configuration had on the aristocracy and, through them, the middle classes. And both emphasize the ways in which these cultural transformations—the spread of discipline and civility—facilitated the establishment and exercise of absolute rule. Clearly, this represents an advance over earlier accounts, which focused solely on the development of the central administration and the military. At the same time, however, neither Oestreich nor Elias really challenges the received notion of state-formation as a process of political and administrative centralization. Oestreich sees absolutism as arising out of a power struggle between territorial rulers and representative estates, while Elias sees it as the result of a natural tendency towards the formation of monopolies (*Monopolbildung*) within all social formations. Both, in other words, continue to portray state-formation as a top-down process driven by outside-in pressures. It is this framework or *épistème*, I suspect, that leads Oestreich and Elias to downplay the significance of the Reformation and to focus on absolutist states. In what follows, I will attempt to develop a conceptual framework that I believe is better able to capture the dynamics of the early modern disciplinary project in all of its richness and complexity.

Summary and Synthesis: Confessionalization, Social Disciplining, and State Power

Discipline and Disciplinary Revolutions: Some Definitions and Distinctions

For the Puritan poet John Milton, discipline was the "axle" of history around which the "flourishing and decaying of all civil societies, all the moments and turnings of human occasions are moved to and fro."[97] Because discipline is also the axle around which the central argument of this book revolves, it is important to define it more clearly before setting that argument in motion.

The building blocks for a comprehensive theory of social discipline can be found in the works of Foucault, Oestreich, Elias, and Weber. As we have just seen, each of them understands discipline somewhat differently. In Foucault's conceptualization, discipline works from outside and emanates from below. It is a set of techniques and strategies (for example, surveillance and normalization) that are embodied in particular domains or institutions (for example, the prison and the asylum) and imposed on particular groups of subjects (for example, criminals and madmen). The kind of social-discipline that Oestreich describes also works from outside, but it emanates mainly from above. It consists of certain ideals and principles codified in various rules and regulations and enforced by the state. The civilizing process analyzed by Elias also emanates from above, but it works from the inside, at least in its most developed form; the principles of civility begin as written codes but are gradually instilled and internalized within the individual subject through a process of social emulation and status competition. Weber's theory of discipline is the sketchiest. The formal definition offered in *Economy and Society* refers primarily to military discipline, that is, to the likelihood that an order will be obeyed. In his writings on the sociology of religion, however, he points to a form of discipline rooted in the ascetic ethos and reinforced by the religious community (the monastery, the sect, the church, and so on), that is, a type of discipline that works from within and emanates from below.

In my view, a general theory of social discipline should be attentive to all of the directions in which discipline can operate—from below and from above, from the inside and from the outside. Accordingly, I would suggest that we distinguish between two different levels and modes of discipline—the individual and social levels and the normative and coercive modes. Combining these two distinctions, we can then distinguish among four different types of discipline: (1) self-discipline (individual and normative); (2) corrective discipline (individual and coercive); (3) communal discipline (social and normative); and (4) judicial or institutional discipline (social and coercive). Of course, like all ideal types, these four kinds of discipline are rarely found in anything like a pure form. They are most often found together, sometimes in tandem, sometimes in opposition. Thus, the self-discipline of the monk is reinforced by the communal discipline of the monastery, the social discipline of the prison is undercut by the communal discipline of the inmates (for example, sanctions against ratting out fellow inmates), and so on.

This typology allows us to distinguish among different sorts of disciplining processes, and to advance some general hypotheses as to their likely effects. In what follows, for example, I will often distinguish between religious discipline, which is primarily (though not exclusively) normative in character, and social discipline, which is primarily (though not exclusively) coercive in character. Similarly, I will often distinguish between disciplining from below, by which I mean discipline carried on outside the purview of the state and especially of the *territorial* state, and disciplining from above, by which I mean discipline imposed by the organs and actors of the state and especially those of the central administration. In most instances, of course, these various types of disciplining are found in combination with one another. The purpose of these distinctions is simply to emphasize which type is *preponderant* within a particular configuration. As to the effects of these various types of disciplining, several general principles can be elaborated. First, normative and individual forms of disciplining are, as a rule, more *intensive* than coercive and social forms because rules that are voluntarily accepted are more likely to be obeyed than ones that are forcefully imposed and because it is easier to monitor a single individual than a large collectivity. It follows from this that the most intensive type of discipline will be self-discipline because the rules are internalized and monitored by the subjects themselves. Second, coercive and social forms of disciplining are, in general, more *stable* than normative and individual forms because the rules are more likely to be formally codified and because they are more likely to be enforced without respect to persons. This implies that the most stable form of disciplining is social-disciplining. Third, normative and social forms of disciplining are likely to have the most profound and *long-lasting effects:* they bring about fundamental alterations in social practices (for example, child raising, pedagogy, courtship, and so on) that tend to outlive their moral justification, and they transform certain aspects of social life into normative problem zones (for example, sexuality, hygiene, work) that become a focus of ongoing moral concern long after the formal rules and codes have lost their judicial force. This suggests that the most profound and long-lasting type of disciplining is communal disciplining. Fourth and finally, individual and coercive forms of discipline tend, on the whole, to be the harshest and most physical forms of discipline; it is harder to reach the soul via the body than vice versa, and it is easier to punish an other than a brother. Based on these principles, we would expect corrective discipline to be the *least* effective of the four types. As regards the present analysis, the key point is this: insofar as one is concerned with the development of societies, rather than the fate of individuals, the impact of disciplining from below will almost invariably be greater than the impact of disciplining from above, particularly insofar as it is normatively inspired. But it should be immediately added that the greatest effect of all is attained when the various types of disciplining process are all strongly present—where communal discipline is reinforced by social discipline, self-discipline by corrective discipline, and so on.

Having said something about the character of discipline, I should also explain what I mean by the term *disciplinary revolution.* I use it in two distinct but interrelated senses. On the one hand, I speak of the early modern disciplinary revolution, by which I mean the introduction and diffusion of disciplinary techniques and strategies, both new and old, and their social and political effects. Here, the term *revolution* refers to a process of rapid innovation and change as in the phrases *industrial revolution* or *scientific revolution*. On the other hand, I speak of the *Dutch disciplinary revolution*, the *Prussian disciplinary revolution* or, more generally, the *Calvinist disciplinary revolution*, by which I mean a political revolution, or set of political revolutions, that stimulated an intense and rapid process of disciplining. Here, I use the term *disciplinary revolution* in much the same way that Marxists use the term *bourgeois revolution*.

In what follows, I will also draw a distinction between disciplinary revolutions from below and disciplinary revolutions from above. The former refers to disciplinary revolutions that were engineered and led mainly by representatives of the church, whether lay or clerical. The latter refers to disciplinary revolutions that were orchestrated mainly by agents of the state. I should emphasize that the distinction is not a sharp one. Disciplinary revolutions from below generally involved disciplining from above and vice versa. I use the terms *below* and *above* only to indicate what I take to be the driving force or principal dynamic behind a particular disciplinary revolution.

Let me close with a couple of caveats and disclaimers. In the text, I often speak of *the* disciplinary revolution or the *Calvinist* disciplinary revolution. In doing so, I do not mean to imply that the early modern disciplinary revolution was the only disciplinary revolution (in the broad sense) or that the Calvinist disciplinary revolution was the only disciplinary revolution (in the narrow sense). One could plausibly argue that the monastic reform movement of the Middle Ages constituted a disciplinary revolution (at least within the Catholic Church). One could also argue that the Iranian revolution was a disciplinary revolution. Perhaps one could even argue that the French and Russian Revolutions were disciplinary revolutions. Thus, when I speak of *the* disciplinary revolution, I do so, not out of scholarly conviction, but as a matter of stylistic convenience.

Confessionalization, Social Discipline, and State Power: Linkages and Mechanisms

This book argues that there were strong linkages between confessionalization, social-disciplining, and state power. Before describing these linkages in greater historical detail, it will be useful to analyze them in broad theoretical terms.

While I have spent a great deal of time discussing other scholar's views of the state and state power in this chapter, I have said very little up to this point about how I understand them. I will address these subjects at greater length in the conclusion. For the purposes of the present analysis, however, we can provisionally adopt Charles Tilly's definition of states as "coercion-wielding organizations that are distinct from household and kinship groups and exercise clear priority in some respects over all other organizations within substantial territories."[98] Accordingly, we can define state power as the capacity to defend and expand a sovereign territory and govern the human and natural resources within it. As this definition suggests, state power is complex and multifaceted. In order to facilitate comparative analysis, it will therefore be useful to break it down further—to define various *types* of state power. We can begin by distinguishing two different modes and spheres of state power: administrative versus coercive and the internal versus external. Administrative power operates through rules and regulations; its paradigmatic instrument is the bureaucrat. Coercive power operates through the threat or application of force; its paradigmatic instrument is the soldier. The internal sphere consists of the indigenous or national population(s). The external sphere consists of colonies or other nations.[99] Combining these distinctions yields four distinct types of state power: regulatory, compulsory, colonial, and military. In practice of course, there is a great deal of overlap among them. For example, a state with strong regulatory capacities can make do with weak compulsory capacities. And military power can easily be translated into compulsory power simply by using soldiers against the domestic population. Likewise, colonial power provides human and natural resources that can be used to build up military power. Hence, when evaluating the power of a particular state, it is important that one look at *all* of these types of state power *and* at the synergy between them.

What makes some states stronger than others? Obviously, there is no simple answer to this question. For the purposes of the present analysis, however, it may be useful to distinguish between *indigenous* sources of power, which inhere in the state qua institution, and *exogenous* sources of power, which derive from its social environment. Key indigenous sources would include the size and quality of the administrative organization and personnel; other things being equal we would expect a state apparatus that is bureaucratic and clean to be more effective and efficient than one which is patrimonial and corrupt. Key exogenous sources might be the size and quality of the national population and territory; other things being equal, we would expect a state whose population and territory are large and developed to be more powerful than one whose population and territory are small and undeveloped (or undevelopable). The fact that state power depends at least partly on exogenous factors suggests a further distinction between *comparative* and *relative* power. Comparative power is power in comparison with other states. Relative power is power relative to exogenous resources. This is an important distinction to bear in mind when comparing the contribution of indigenous and exogenous resources to the power of particular states.

Having defined state power and discussed its bases, we can now turn to the central problematic: the relationship between discipline and state power. This relationship, I would suggest, is both direct and indirect. It is direct insofar as disciplining impinges on the state qua institution, which is to say, the state qua organization and personnel. Other things being equal, we would expect that a state that has honest, hard-working administrators and strong, effective mechanisms for monitoring them will be more efficient than one that does not. Insofar as disciplining impinges on the state's immediate environment, which is to say, society, its effects are indirect. Other things being equal, we would expect that a state with obedient, hard-working subjects and strong, effective mechanisms of social control will be stronger than one that does not. In sum, *discipline increases state power insofar as it increases overall levels of administrative efficiency and social order because a more orderly society is cheaper to govern and a more efficient administration is cheaper to run.*

This brings us to the last—or rather first—link in the causal chain: confessionalization. As we have seen, confessionalization involves two not always adequately distinguished processes: the hardening of interconfessional boundaries and the imposition of intraconfessional uniformity. Obviously, the latter process is of greatest interest to us here, for it is there that the link between confessionalization and disciplining lies. This link, like that between disciplining and state power, was both direct and indirect. It was direct insofar as the imposition of intraconfessional uniformity went hand in hand with the imposition of ecclesiastical discipline and the propagation of self-discipline. And it was indirect insofar as it facilitated or accelerated disciplining processes already underway. This latter connection requires some explaining. It is important to recognize that the campaign to impose greater religious and social discipline antedated the Reformation, and that the motives behind this campaign were never solely religious. Thus, there were numerous efforts to discipline the poor during the centuries before the Reformation, efforts motivated in large part by concerns over urban hygiene and finance; the poor carried disease, and they weighed on the city treasuries. These efforts will be examined more thoroughly in chapter 4. For the moment, the key point is that they met with a good deal of resistance from the Catholic clergy. For some theologians, restrictions on begging and charity were a violation of Christian precepts. And for the mendicant orders, such restrictions were a threat to material and spiritual livelihood. In this and other areas, the Reformation brought a dramatic turning of the tides. It removed the barriers to, and created a new impetus for, social reform. It was in this sense that it indirectly facilitated and accelerated the disciplining process. But it is important to bear in mind that the Reformation was neither the beginning of nor the sole force behind the disciplining process. It was as much catalyst as cause.

Following this forced march through an endless thicket of distinctions and typologies, I suspect that some readers will have lost sight of the forest for the trees. So it may be helpful to conclude this chapter with a brief restatement of the main arguments and a quick preview of the upcoming chapters.

Conclusion

At the beginning of this chapter, I used the metaphor of the body politic and the frontispiece of Hobbes's *Leviathan* to illustrate the shortcomings of current work on the state and to suggest how one might rectify them. I argued that most work on the state had focused on the king's head and that more attention should be paid to his body and soul. I am now in a position to restate this argument in somewhat more concrete and analytical terms.

When I say that state theorists focus on the king's head, I mean that they focus on: (a) the internal organization of state administration and (b) the instrumental motivations of state actors. And I mean that they see the one as explaining the other; from this perspective, it is the ruler's quest for increased power—and that alone—that underlies the development of state administration. I also mean that they tend to see state power as a function of state organization, specifically, the degree of administrative rationalization.

There is a great deal to be said for this point of view; rulers *are* interested in increasing their power, and state organization *does* affect state power. But there is also a great deal that it misses, including (a) the noninstrumental motivations of political actors and (b) the social determinants of state power. The problem with current theorizing about the state is that it pays too little attention to the impact that social political ethics (Max Weber) and social infrastructure (Michael Mann) have on state power. Stated in the most general terms, then, my thesis is that *state capacity is a function, not only of administrative rationalization, but of the strength of the social infrastructure and the rationality of sociopolitical ethics.*[100] The more extensive the infrastructure and the more rational the ethic, the stronger the state will be.

Of course, the book does not—and could not—"prove" this claim. What it does try to show is that the Reformation led to a general expansion of state infrastructure and a progressive rationalization of social-political ethics and thus to a secular increase in state capacity. At the same time, it attempts to show that these processes were most pronounced in the Calvinist parts of Europe and that this helps explain the unusual capacity of several Calvinist states, most notably, the Netherlands and Prussia.

• • •

The empirical core of this book is composed of three chapters: one on the Netherlands (ca. 1550–1700), one on Brandenburg-Prussia (ca. 1640–1750), and one on various Lutheran and Catholic polities (for example, Hessia and Saxony versus Venice and France). These cases obviously differ from one another in many different respects (for example, social structure, political organization, confessional allegiance, time period), and there are several different ways in which one could group them, each of which would yield a somewhat different set of comparisons.

One possibility would be to see the first two cases—the Netherlands and Prussia—as single instances of the same thing, namely, Calvinist disciplinary revolutions. Grouping the cases together in this way would focus attention on the effects of social structure and political organization on the reception and implementation of Calvinist discipline. The obvious comparison would then be between the bourgeois and republican case of the Netherlands and the noble and absolutist case of Brandenburg-Prussia.

Another possibility would be to see these two cases as one case—as successive stages of the Calvinist disciplinary revolution. Grouping the cases together in this way would shift attention to the historical links among the cases, to the ways in which the disciplinary revolution diffused from one to the other. As we will see, these links were very real.

Yet another possibility would be to contrast the Calvinist polities with non-Calvinist polities. Grouping the cases together in this way would call attention to the effects of interconfessional differences on the disciplining process. It would allow one to examine the effects organizational and doctrinal differences between the confessions have on the scope and intensity of the disciplining process within each confession.

No doubt, there are other groupings and comparisons that one might also examine. But these three are of greatest relevance to the argument that I wish to make, and it is on them that I will concentrate in the pages that follow.

2
Disciplinary Revolution from Below in the Low Countries

"The Netherland-Provinces have rendered themselves so conspicuous and considerable amongst the other States of Europe," wrote William Aglionby in 1669, that "scarce any Subject occures more frequent in the discourses of ingenious men, than that of the marvellous progress of this little State." And this progress is all the more astonishing, he remarked, when one considers that "they were continually engag'd in a Warre against the greatest king of this Western World" (that is, the king of Spain) during the time of their ascent. Indeed, he concludes, this war (the Dutch Revolt) only served to "render the Constitution of the State . . . more robust and athletick."[1] What accounts for the remarkable strength of "this little State"? And what made its "Constitution" so "robust and athletick"?

According to the bellicists, the answers to these questions should be found in institutional and organizational factors—in the level of state centralization and bureaucratization and their impact on state capacities. But this answer is very much at odds with the evidence. As we will see, the Dutch state was neither particularly centralized, nor particularly bureaucratized, despite the fact that it was embroiled in one war after the other from the time of its inception. Thus, the Dutch Republic hardly fits the image of the strong state advanced by the bellicists. Was it therefore weak? Is our English interlocutor incorrect?

That is not what the evidence suggests. Despite its diminutive territory and small population, the Dutch Republic fielded a large army and navy, oversaw a far-flung colonial empire, and acquitted itself remarkably well in conflicts with its larger and more populous neighbors: Spain, France, and England. And this external power was mirrored in internal order; despite its puny administration and patriarchal regime, the Dutch Republic appears to have been one of the safest, most stable, and best governed nations in Europe.

Thus, we are confronted with something of a puzzle. The standard theory of state-formation (that is, the bellicist model) implies that the Dutch state should have been weak. But in terms of the usual indicators (namely, external power and internal order)—the very indicators the bellicists prefer—it seems to have been quite strong.[2] How was this possible?

One potential answer is wealth. This is the answer advanced by world systems theory and also by some historical institutionalists, and it is not without merit.[3] After all, most economic historians would probably agree that the Northern Netherlands were the most developed country in Europe during the seventeenth century, and it seems that they also remained the most prosperous during the next century, even after losing their hegemonic status in the world economy to Great Britain.[4] And most historical sociologists would agree that material resources are one of the key ingredients of state power. If war is the ultimate test of a state's strength, and money is the sinews of war, then state capacity will be at least partly a function of monetary resources. Still, this answer is far from complete. In particular, it does not explain why the Dutch state was able to maintain such a high degree of social order—or even why it was able to extract such high levels of material resources. A strong economy may be one potential source of strength, but it is by no means the only possible one.

To fully understand what made the Dutch state so strong, I will argue that we need to look at another factor: religion. Specifically, we need to look at the impact that religious discipline had on social order, particularly at the local level. At that level real power was exercised in the republic, and it is in local institutions, I will argue, that the hidden well-springs of its strength are to be found. Once we have examined the networks of moral regulation and social control woven into the fabric of everyday life in the Golden Age, the capacity of the Dutch state to mobilize resources and maintain order will appear a good deal less mysterious.

But before asking if and why the Dutch state was so strong, it will be useful to examine how and when it came into existence. The simple answer to this question is the Eighty Years' War (1568–1648) between Spain and the Low Countries, and especially the first half of the war, which is generally referred to as the Dutch Revolt (1565–89). For it was the revolt against

Spain that led to the division of the Low Countries into two separate polities—a Spanish appanage to the south, roughly contiguous with present-day Belgium, and a constitutional republic to the north, predecessor of the modern Netherlands. The deeper answer, I will argue, was the rise of Dutch Calvinism and the confessional conflict that followed. For the intractable dispute over the religious question, over the future of the Catholic and Reformed Churches, transformed a high-level political dispute between the Spanish Crown and the Dutch estates into a full-blown revolutionary conflict.

The remainder of this chapter is organized as follows. I begin with a brief overview of the Dutch Revolt and the catalytic role that Dutch Calvinism played in it. I then describe the organization and workings of the Dutch state and present qualitative and quantitative evidence of its external and internal strength. I then show how Calvinist-inspired discipline contributed to state strength. In the conclusion, finally, I put the results of this analysis back into a broader historical and theoretical perspective.

The Dutch Revolt: Confessional Conflict and Social Revolution[5]

During the first half of the sixteenth century, the Spanish Habsburgs worked diligently to consolidate their control over the Low Countries, the seventeen provinces comprising what is now Belgium and the Netherlands.[6] Under Emperor Charles V (1506–55), the central administration in Brussels was reorganized and the powers of the national and territorial assemblies—the States General and the provincial estates—were gradually curtailed. His son, Philip II (1555–98), sought to shift the balance of power even further; in desperate need of resources to finance his campaign against the French, he proclaimed new taxes without the consent of the States General. Tensions were heightened further in 1559 when Philip announced plans to reorganize the church and create a number of new bishoprics,[7] thereby sparking the ire of the upper nobility, which tended to view church offices as their private patrimony. In short, the Habsburgs were attempting to impose a system of absolutist rule.

There was nothing particularly unusual about these conflicts. Relations between Renaissance monarchs and representative assemblies were often tense. But in this case, as in several others, the long-standing constitutional conflict intersected with a precipitous Protestant upsurge. Itinerant Calvinist preachers began crossing into the Low Countries from France during the early 1550s,[8] and by the early 1560s the Calvinist movement had a national following and was actively calling for freedom of worship. Philip II responded by renewing the old anti-Protestant edicts and expanding the activity of the Inquisition courts.

In the spring of 1566 a large group of noblemen forced their way into the chambers of the Spanish governess, Margaret of Parma, and presented her with a letter demanding the retraction of the anti-Protestant edicts.[9] She responded with an act of moderation that was widely interpreted by the Calvinists as a proclamation of religious freedom. The following summer open-air religious services or hedge sermons were held outside many Dutch towns, attracting thousands of worshipers. And in August the Netherlands were swept by the iconoclastic fury, a wave of Calvinist led image breaking.[10] Then, in the fall, a group of rebellious nobles under the Duke of Brederode took up arms against the king, but they failed to muster widespread support and were easily defeated by royal troops under the Duke of Alva, who succeeded Margaret as governor.

Retribution was swift and brutal. A special tribunal was established to try heretics and rebels.[11] Thousands were executed and many more were driven into exile, including William of Orange, the future leader of the rebel movement.[12] At the same time, native nobles were dismissed from many top administrative posts in Brussels and replaced with Spaniards; the new bishoprics plan was revived; and a series of unpopular taxes were unilaterally proclaimed.[13]

Meanwhile, the Calvinist refugees began organizing popular resistance to the Spanish inside and outside the Low Countries, and William of Orange desperately worked to enlist foreign support for military intervention. The next round of conflict began in 1572 when the undefended coastal town of Brill was stormed by the Sea Beggars, a ragtag band of 1,100 Calvinist desperadoes.[14] With the help of local sympathizers, they soon "liberated" much of the Northern Netherlands, "opening" churches to Calvinist worship and replacing uncooperative magistrates with rulers more sympathetic to their cause.[15] William of Orange followed up with a hastily organized invasion from the south. But his troops were thin on the ground, and he was soon forced to beat a hasty retreat to the north, where a Calvinist-dominated republican regime had been established by the provincial estates of Holland and Zeeland.[16]

A financial crisis in Castile soon stalled the Spanish campaign, however, and Philip II was forced to sue for peace. But the negotiations quickly broke down over the religious question. Philip II refused to make any concessions to the "heretics," and William of Orange proved equally unwilling to give any ground. Following the breakdown of the peace talks, the Spanish launched another assault on the north. The Imperial armies, under the command of the new governor-general, Don Louis Requesens, made rapid progress. But, once again, the offensive was brought to a standstill by the fiscal woes of the Spanish Crown.

The death of Requesens the following spring created an opportunity for moderates and *politiques* who yearned for religious peace. For, with his passing, power reverted to the Council of State (the central organ of the territorial administration), which was dominated by moderates under the (Catholic) Duke of Aerschot. Under his leadership, the council hammered out an agreement with Holland and Zeeland, that "solved"—or rather devolved—the religious question by turning it over to the provincial estates—the so-called Pacification of Gent. When Requesens's successor, Don Juan of Austria, finally arrived in the Low Countries in 1577, the States General made their recognition of him as governor contingent upon acceptance of the Pacification of Gent. In the so-called Perpetual Edict, he reluctantly assented.

But the peacemakers were soon overtaken by events, as revolt gave way to revolution. This time, it was the urban *popoli* who took the lead, demanding freedom of worship and an end to oligarchy. In some southern towns, most notably Gent and Bruges, Calvinist-dominated republics were proclaimed.[17] The southern provinces were now in open rebellion against Spain.[18]

During these same years, William of Orange steadily consolidated his control over the northern cities, and in 1579 the seven northern provinces signed a treaty of mutual defense, the Union of Utrecht. In 1581, after another round of fruitless peace talks, the northern provinces did in the letter what they had already done in fact: they renounced Philip II as their lord and sovereign. The stage was now set for a war between the seven United Provinces and the king of Spain.

In October 1578, Don Juan died of the plague and was replaced by Alexander Farnese, Duke of Parma, a shrewd diplomat, a brilliant military tactician, and a convinced Catholic, who was determined to put down what he saw as a heretic rebellion. Through a sustained campaign of siege warfare, Parma reconquered most of the southern Netherlands.[19] By 1585, only Holland, Zeeland, and parts of the surrounding provinces remained under rebel control.

In order to alleviate this increasingly desperate situation, the States General began searching for a powerful protector who could muster much needed military leadership and foreign assistance. They first turned to Francis Hercules, duke of Anjou and brother of Henry III, king of France, but dismissed him after an abortive coup. Then they turned to Robert Dudley,

Earl of Leicester, a protegé of Queen Elizabeth of England.[20] He, too, was dismissed following an attempted coup. Thereafter, the Estates General quietly neglected to name a successor. The provinces of the north were now a republic, in fact, if not yet in name.

Throughout these years, the military situation in the United Provinces had grown increasingly desperate. But the sinking of the Spanish Armada in August 1588 brought a temporary respite, allowing the Dutch to recoup politically and militarily. The fiscal and administrative system was put onto more solid footing by Johan van Oldenbarnevelt, the Grand Pensionary of Holland and de facto leader of the States General.[21] Meanwhile, the army was instilled with new discipline and order by William the Silent's son, Maurice of Nassau, with the assistance of Simon Stevin, a gifted mathematician and engineer.[22] While the war against Spain would continue until 1609, by 1600 the independence of the United Provinces was a *fait accompli*.

This war had given birth to a new state: the Dutch Republic. Geographically, the republic consisted of the seven northern provinces of the Low Countries (Holland, Zeeland, Utrecht, Friesland, Drente, and Overijssel), together with small pieces of Flanders and Limburg. Politically, it had a federalist constitution in which ultimate authority was vested in the States General but limited, both in law and in practice, by the powers of the stadtholder, the provincial estates, and the city magistrates.[23] Religiously, it was a multiconfessional society in which the Reformed Church enjoyed special legal and financial privileges and eventually secured the allegiance of most of the population; but other creeds, including Catholicism, were, in the end, grudgingly tolerated.[24] It was, in short, a state in which republicans and Calvinists, the core of the anti-Habsburg coalition, had gotten much but not all of what they wanted.

The revolt had no single or essential cause. In part, it was rooted in resentment—the resentments of the Dutch grandees against the Spanish court, of the lesser nobles against their social superiors, and of the urban *popoli* against the ruling oligarchs. More immediately, it was precipitated by the proto-absolutist policies of Philip II: in his attempts to centralize power in Brussels, impose taxes without the consent of the Estates General, and rationalize the administration of the church. And it was fanned into a revolutionary conflagration by the militancy of the Calvinists and the intransigence of the Catholics—by religious violence and counterviolence. What transformed the revolt into a revolution was not simply the conjunction of these three sources of discontent, however, but the way in which they interacted and eventually fused with each other. Social, political, and religious grievances reinforced one another, gradually became focused on the king, and served to bridge (and obscure) the diverging interests of the various wings of the anti-Spanish alliance—republicans and Calvinists, conservatives and revolutionaries, merchants and artisans. What emerged, in stages, was a groundswell of anti-Spanish sentiment, a religious "party" led by William of Orange, and, ultimately, a republican regime under the States General. Of course, it is not clear that the revolt would have succeeded had the Spanish state been on firmer financial footing. But it is unlikely that it would have escalated into a revolution in the absence of the religious question. Confessional conflict, in sum, was a necessary, if not sufficient, cause of the Dutch Revolt and thus a key factor in the emergence of an independent state in the Northern Netherlands. It is to the structure and strength of that new state that our discussion now turns.

The Dutch State: Structure and Strength

Structure

The Dutch state was not particularly centralized. Indeed, it was so decentralized that its working can be best explained from the bottom up.[25] At the local level, the basic units of governance were the towns and the bailiwicks (*baljuwen*). Although there was a great deal of local variation, the basic pattern of town government was fairly simple. Typically, the laws were made by the city council (*vroedschap*), implemented by the burgomasters, and enforced by the sheriff (*schout*) and the magistrates (*schepen*). The magistrates and city councilmen were selected from among the town's leading families, and the burgomasters and the sheriff from the city council. The town governments were quite oligarchic and become more so as time went on.[26]

At the regional level, the most important institutions were the provincial diets or "states."[27] Here, too, there was a good deal of variation. In some cases, the provincial states were organized along classical tricurial lines, with one chamber for each estate (clergy, nobility, and burghers) and one vote for each chamber. In other cases, the states were organized along primarily territorial lines. The province was divided up into several different quarters, each of which exercised one vote. In most instances, however, the states combined social and territorial forms of representation. In Holland, for example, the states were composed of representatives of the nobility (*Ridderschap*), which exercised one vote, and the voting cities, which possessed eighteen. In Friesland, on the other hand, the province's three quarters exercised one vote each, while the cities collectively exercised one. In other regards, the diets were very similar. They met regularly and at their own behest. And when they were not in session their powers were exercised by small councils of delegates, usually known as the Deputized States (*Gedeputeerden Staten*). Other important provincial institutions included the pensionaries, the stadtholders, and the courts. In principle, the Pensionaries were employees of the states, responsible for providing legal council and supervising parliamentary deliberations. In practice, they often functioned as *de facto* ministers who controlled the proceedings of the states and represented their interests in external negotiations (for example, in the States General, of which, more directly). Prior to the revolt, the stadtholders had been appointed by the monarch, and the courts had served as their advisory councils. After the Revolt, however, the stadtholders were appointed by the states, and the courts served mainly as courts of law. The stadtholders were always members of the House of Orange-Nassau.

Since the Dutch Republic did not have a monarchical head, the most important institution at the national level was also a representative body: the States General.[28] The States General was composed of delegations from seven provinces: Gelderland, Holland, Zeeland, Friesland, Utrecht, Groningen, and Overijssel; neither the province of Drenthe nor the reconquered parts of the southern Netherlands known as the Generality Lands were allowed a vote. The delegations were chosen by the provincial diets, and usually reflected their makeup fairly closely. There was no formal limit on the size of the delegations, but each cast only one vote. The delegations were given detailed instructions by the diets and generally consulted with them before casting their votes. This could slow the decisionmaking process considerably. Like the provincial diets, the States General appointed a group of Deputy States, as well as various other standing committees; these bodies did most of the real administrative and legislative legwork.[29] Other important national offices included the Council of State and the captain-general. Prior to the revolt, the Council of State had functioned as an advisory council for the monarch and had had far-reaching powers. Later, however, its powers were curtailed, both formally and informally, and it became little more than an executive organ of the States General.[30] The office of captain-general was created during the revolt. Its incumbent was directly responsible to the States General and was invariably a member of the House of Orange.

In principle, the Dutch constitution[31] afforded the States General wide-ranging powers, including the authority to collect taxes, muster troops, and negotiate with foreign powers. In practice, however, the States General could only exercise these powers in consultation with the provincial diets. Consider the tax system.[32] The States General did have direct control over several streams of revenue, including receipts from customs and taxes on the Generality Lands. But these revenues comprised less than 20 percent of the national budget. The remaining 80 percent were collected by the provincial and local governments. The procedure was as follows: Each year, the Council of State prepared a budget proposal known as the state of war (*Staat van Oorlog*), which was then debated before, and adjusted by, the States General. A quota system was then used to distribute the tax burden across the provinces, with the richer and more populous paying a higher quota than the poorer and less populous ones.[33] Accordingly, the largest and richest province, Holland, usually contributed somewhere around 60 percent of the total budget, while the smallest and poorest, Drente, only contributed about 1 percent. Theoretically, the provincial diets were free to raise these funds by any means they chose. In point of fact, most chose some combination of excise taxes (that is, taxes on consumables) and land taxes (for example, the real estate tax known as the *verponding*). The city governments often levied wealth and property taxes of various sorts. Overall, the tax burden seems to have been distributed quite fairly between town and country and poor and rich.

Given the fact that the provinces maintained such a firm grip on the purse strings, it should not be surprising to learn that they also exercised a good deal of influence over the military.[34] Indeed, they generally insisted that any troops on "their" payroll be stationed on "their" territory and vice versa. (As a result a large proportion of tax revenues never left the province in which they were collected; they went directly from the provincial treasury to the provincial regiments). Control over the navy was also very decentralized, though not along provincial lines. Here, too, formal command was in the hands of the States General. But the day-to-day administration was entrusted to five regional admiralty boards, which were composed of varying numbers of representatives from the surrounding provinces—which is to say, representatives from the provincial diets and town governments.[35]

Religious affairs were also under the jurisdiction of the provincial states. Each province had its own set of church ordinances and its own synod. In practice, authority over the church was shared with the local governments because they were the ones who enforced (or ignored) the provincial legislation and approved (or even controlled) the appointments of church officials (that is, pastors, elders, and deacons).

Much the same could be said of social policy. The provincial diets could and did issue mandates regarding marriage, sexuality, criminality, vagabondage, poverty, unemployment, education, and other such matters. But their enforcement was very much in the hands of local officials, who had interests and agendas of their own. It was they who registered the marriages, punished the criminals, dispensed the poor-relief, built the schools, and so on.

The republic was not only politically decentralized; it was administratively decentralized as well. During the early eighteenth century, the States General employed something like 200 people. By contrast, the states of Holland employed around 300, and the city of Amsterdam some 3,000![36] As these figures make clear, administrative power was centered at the bottom, rather than the top.

If the Dutch Republic was not very centralized, politically or administratively, neither was it terribly bureaucratic, at least not in the classic, Weberian sense. Generally speaking, Dutch officials were not chosen on the basis of technical qualifications or paid a fixed money salary. They niether worked solely as administrators nor advanced along clear career ladders, and they were not separated from the "means of administration" or subject to formal discipline and controls. Rather, appointments were determined largely by kinship and patronage ties; salaries were often variable and/or *in natura*; officials worked part-time and/or out of their homes; and positions were frequently passed down to sons and nephews. Most of the real administrative work was done, not by paid civil servants, but by local notables, their clients, and various private entrepreneurs.

Strength

According to the bellicist theory, this lack of centralization and bureaucratization should have led to weakness and inefficiency. But it did not. In fact, by the usual criteria—the capacity to project power and maintain order—the Dutch Republic was actually quite strong.

The most basic measure of external power is military might. At the height of its power, during the late seventeenth and early eighteenth centuries, the Dutch Republic maintained around 50,000 troops in peacetime. During times of war, this number swelled to as many as 120,000. At the same time, it maintained somewhere between 70 and 80 ships-of-the-line. In absolute terms, these numbers were not inordinately high. England's navy had over 120 ships-of-the-line, for example, and its army included nearly 90,000 men. France also had well over 100 ships-of-the-line, at least during the early 1700s, and on paper its army numbered over 400,000 men at one time (though in reality, the figure was undoubtedly a great deal lower than this).[37] Relative to population, however, the Dutch numbers were truly extraordinary. For while the Dutch population never exceeded 2 million during this period, England had around 5.5 million inhabitants, and France over 20 million.[38] This means that the Dutch outfitted about one soldier for every seventeen civilians, and 1 ship for every 25,000. By contrast, England had 1 soldier per 61 civilians and 1 ship per 45,000, while France had (at best) 1 soldier for every 50 civilians and only 1 ship for every

166,000. The intensity of Dutch military mobilization was thus very high, indeed—akin, say, to that of contemporary Israel.

• • •

This raises an obvious question: How could such a small population support such a large army? The obvious answer would seem to be: high taxes. And, in fact, foreign travelers often remarked on the size and number of the excise taxes levied by the local and provincial governments in the Netherlands. This impression is corroborated by the numerical evidence. During the late 1690s, for example, the republic spent over £3 per capita on the military. By contrast, England spent just over £1.5 per capita, while France spent less than £.75. Other European countries spent even less.[39]

Of course, the simple fact that the Dutch state outspent its rivals does not necessarily imply that the Dutch were paying *relatively* higher taxes than the English and the French. After all, the Dutch were more prosperous and better paid than the English or French; indeed, it is generally agreed that wages in the republic were the highest in Europe.[40] So it could be that the higher revenues enjoyed by the Dutch state were purely a function of higher individual wages and greater societal wealth rather than of more intensive material extraction. But that does not appear to have been the case. As we can see from table 1, the Dutch did have a higher per capita income than

Table 1 Estimates of Consumption, Taxes, and Saving per Head of the Population, 1688 and 1695

	England		France		Holland	
	1688	1695	1688	1695	1688	1695
	£ s d	£ s d	£ s d	£ s d	£ s d	£ s d
Consumption	7 4 0	7 3 0	5 0 9	4 18 2	5 0 0	4 13 9
Taxes[a]	7 3	1 4 0	15 0	1 5 0	2 3 2	3 1 7
Saving[b]	6 8	−11 0	7 0	−8 10	18 4	7 7
	7 18 0	7 16 0	6 3 0	5 18 0	8 1 4	8 2 9

Source: Phyllis Deane, "The Implications of Early National Income Estimates for the Measurement of Long-Term Economic Growth in the United Kingdom," *Economic Development and Cultural Change* 4 (1955–56): 12, derived from Gregory King, *Natural and Political Observations and Conclusions upon the State and Condition of England, 1696* (London: J. Stockdale, 1804), p. 55.

[a] Including local government taxation, the English average would be in the region of 10s. per annum.

[b] King sets off poor-relief against total savings by the private sector in arriving at these estimates of net saving per head. His estimated total saving in England, that is, before netting out poor-relief, amounts to about 8s. 9d. per head.

the English and the French; but they also paid a considerably higher proportion of their income in taxes. Thus, even when we "control" for income, the intensity of taxation in the Netherlands was still higher than in England or France.

There is also another factor to take into account when comparing levels of government taxation and expenditure: public borrowing. The Dutch Republic was a pioneer in the development of public finance,[41] and it accumulated a rather substantial national debt, particularly in the years after 1672. Thus, it could be that the higher revenues enjoyed by the Dutch state were largely a function of higher debts. If so, this would be a very important point indeed because the bellicists often argue that the financial vigor of the Dutch state was due to its ready access to capital markets and that the availability of plentiful credit made the creation of centralized extractive machinery unnecessary and thereby prevented the rise of an absolutist system of rule in the Netherlands.[42] Let us take a closer look at the evidence. At the close of the War of the Spanish Succession (1701–13), a costly conflict which left many states mired in red ink, the public debt of the Dutch Republic stood at £12.8 per capita. In France, by contrast, it stood at £7.0 per capita and in England at only £6.8.[43] So the per capita public debt of the Netherlands was almost twice as high as those of France and England. Thus, at least part of the difference in government spending was probably due to differences in public indebtedness. Part of it was also due to differences in the costs of debt service. Interest rates in the Netherlands were substantially lower than they were in England and especially in France. During the early eighteenth century, interest rates on public debts in the Netherlands ran as low as 1.25 percent, did not exceed 3.5 percent, even in wartime, and generally averaged around 2.5 percent.[44] In France, by contrast, interest rates during this period generally ranged between 4 and 5 percent, and exceeded 8 percent during wartime.[45] So while the Dutch national debt was much higher than the French, the actual costs of debt service in the two countries would have been roughly the same in per capita terms. This means that the Dutch state would have been able to spend a larger percentage of the money it borrowed on civil and military expenses. Still, when all is said and done, the fact that the Dutch were able to borrow almost twice as much money as the French state (per capita) for about the same price still does not explain how it could out spend the French four to one (per capita). A good part of this difference was clearly due to the fact that tax rates were much higher in the Netherlands than they were in France, in both real and relative terms. Thus, the bellicist claim that the financial strength of the Dutch state was due solely to its access to capital markets is clearly overblown. And the argument that the Dutch state lacked extractive machinery is plainly false. The problem is that the bellicists have looked in the wrong places; the machinery was not located in The Hague but in the provincial capitals and city governments.

• • •

Having considered the capacity of the Dutch state to project power and extract resources, let us now examine another indicator of state strength that generally receives less attention: the ability to maintain domestic order and stability. This is easier said than done. Social order is not easily measured, especially at a distance of three centuries. However, there are some rough indicators—crime rates, for example. By this measure, at least, the Dutch Republic seems to have been a very orderly place. Without exception, contemporary observers agreed that the level of crime in the Northern Netherlands was exceptionally low. In reference to Amsterdam, one English traveler remarked that: " 'Tis rare to hear of any Disorders committed here in the Night-time, notwithstanding the great number and variety of Inhabitants and Strangers."[46] A German traveler said much the same about Leiden, Holland's second largest city and the seat of its best-known university. "In Leiden," he claimed, "you can go out without a gun and leave your door unlocked, even if you will be away for days,"[47] the implication being that this was not the case in German university towns. The situation in other countries was apparently rather different. During his journey through the Spanish Netherlands, for example, the French priest, Charles Lemaitre, became the victim of an early modern protection racket, when he was strongly advised—meaning forced—to hire an armed escort.[48] A British noblewoman reported a similar experience in the French town of Calais.[49] And John Locke, for his part, was startled by the level of violent crime that he observed in the south of France.[50] Nor does the situation in the north appear to have been any better.[51] Of the student gangs in Paris, one British traveler remarked that: "Penelope's suitors never behaved themselves so insolently in the house of Ulysses, as the Academicks here do in the houses and streets of Paris."[52] Reports about the Iberian peninsula strike a similar note. "It is as dangerous at Madrid as at Lisbon," wrote Aglionby, "for a stranger to be abroad in the Streets in the Night-time. On the contrary one may travel Day or Night in Holland, without fear of being robb'd or otherwise molested."[53] And Germany was apparently no better. Indeed, the northern Rhineland, which was quite close to the Netherlands, not only geographically, but culturally and socially, was generally regarded as the most dangerous area in all of western Europe.[54] In the eyes of these travelers and diarists, then, the Dutch Republic appears as an island of order in a sea of violence.

Of course, individual impressions of this sort are not always accurate. They are usually based on limited experiences and may be influenced by misleading stereotypes. Thus, it would be helpful if we could compare them with more objective sorts of evidence, such as crime rates. Fortunately, evidence of this sort does exist. Over the last several decades, social historians and historical criminologists have collected a wealth of information about early modern crime and criminality.[55] Though incomplete, it, too, suggests that crime rates really were lower in the Netherlands than in most other parts of Europe. Specialists generally agree that murder rates provide the most reliable indicators of real or underlying crime rates. This is because murders are less likely to go undetected, unreported, or unpunished than are other crimes and because murder rates tend to be closely correlated with general rates of crime. We have evidence regarding the murder rate for a number of Dutch cities. In Leiden, for example, just under one hundred people were convicted of homicide during the first quarter of the seventeenth century; during the second quarter, the number declined to less than seventy; during the third quarter it dropped to less than twenty; and by the middle of the eighteenth century, it was well below ten.[56] A similar trend can be observed in Amsterdam. There, the number of people tried for murder remained steady at about one per year throughout the early modern era. But the city's population grew rapidly during this time, from around 15,000 in the year 1500 to 200,000 around 1670, at which point it leveled off and rose gradually to around 217,000 in 1795. This translates into a rate of 6.6 murder trials per 100,000 inhabitants in 1500 as compared to 0.5 in 1670—a very dramatic decline indeed.[57] But, dramatic as it is, it is not inconsistent with evidence from other parts of Holland. In the city of Haarlem, the rate of prosecuted homicides stood at around 0.7 in the mid-eighteenth century.[58] And in a group of six small towns and villages studied by Gijswijt-Hofstra, the rate was lower still.[59] Of course, not all murders resulted in indictments, so the actual homicide rate was undoubtedly a good deal higher than these figures suggest.[60] Drawing on a different set of source materials (namely, coroner's inquests) Pieter Spierenburg has estimated that the actual homicide rate in Amsterdam gradually declined from around 3.5 in the late seventeenth century, to around 2.5 in the mid-eighteenth century and then down to 1.5 in 1800.[61] These figures suggest not only that the rate of homicide really was declining but also that rates of detection were increasing.

Interestingly, similar trends can also be observed in another country that was strongly influenced by Calvinism: England. In Essex, for example, the rate of prosecuted murder was around 5.5 per 100,000 during the years 1559–1603 and around 4.8 in the years between 1647 and 1679.[62] These figures are based on court records; thus, they are surely too low. Using coroner's inquests, J. S. Cockburn has calculated that the real rate of homicides in Kent fluctuated between 3.8 and 6.0 (per 100,000 per year) during the late sixteenth century, between 2.5 and 5.3 in the seventeenth, and between 1.6 and 3.6 in the eighteenth.[63] These figures are fairly similar to those we observe in the Netherlands.

Elsewhere in Europe, murder rates were considerably higher. For example, Eva Österberg has calculated that the murder rate in Stockholm was around 20 per 100,000 in the mid-sixteenth century, 36 per 100,000 in the late sixteenth century, and 32 per 100,000 in the 1620s.[64] The rate then began a slow decline but remained at 3 per 100,000 even in the mid-nineteenth century. And these figures are based on court records, meaning that the real rates will have been a good deal higher. Though it is spotty, the evidence that we have suggests that Paris was even more dangerous than Stockholm. In 1643, for instance, the murder rate in Paris stood at nearly 75 per 100,000; and in June 1644 14 murders were committed in a single day.[65] Obviously, these figures need to be interpreted with caution. But they do support the traveler's reports that the Netherlands—and England—were a good deal safer than other parts of Europe, an impression, moreover, that is borne out when one examines the evidence on other forms of crime, such as theft and assault.[66]

What accounts for these differences? One possible explanation—an explanation in line with the bellicist approach—would be the size and structure of the repressive apparatus. Thus, it could be that the low crime rates in England and the Netherlands were due to larger and more highly developed systems of criminal justice. Alas, this does not appear to have been the case. In fact, the French took the lead in the development of a modern (that is, centralized and bureaucratized) police force, and it was they who employed the largest numbers of police officers—some 3,000 in Paris alone.[67] By comparison, the Dutch and English police systems were much smaller and far less professionalized. Amsterdam had a good number of volunteer night watchmen (500 in 1700), but only two dozen professional law enforcement officers.[68] And London, a good deal larger, had 750 watchmen and 35 police officers.[69] Thus, it would seem that the explanation for variations in the crime rate must be sought elsewhere.

Let us now consider a second measure of social order: extramarital sexuality. Today, of course, extramarital sexuality is still regarded as a sin by some and a private matter by most. But in early modern Europe, it was also treated as a crime and matter of public policy. Here, too, the Dutch enjoyed a special reputation (quite different from the one they know today) for moral rectitude, which is documented in numerous travelers' accounts.[70] Is this reputation borne out by the numbers? Once again, it is. Generally speaking, the most reliable indicator of the rate of extramarital sexual activity is the rate of illegitimate births. Since illegitimacy has been extensively studied by historical demographers, we have a good deal of comparative evidence on this subject. Their work suggests that the Netherlands actually deserved their pan-European reputation as "the moral nation." In the rural areas of northern Holland, for example, the illegitimacy rate remained below 1 percent until the late eighteenth century, when it approached 2 percent.[71] In the cities of Rotterdam and Maasluis, the illegitimacy rate rose somewhat more quickly, reaching a level of 3 percent around 1770.[72] Interestingly, illegitimacy rates in England were also quite low, fluctuating between a nadir of around 1 percent in the 1650s (the period of the Puritan Republic) and a high of about 5 percent in the late eighteenth century.[73] In France, by contrast, they appear to have been a good deal higher. In Paris, for example, the illegitimacy ratio rose from around 8 percent in the 1710s to nearly 25 percent in the 1770s.[74] And in Nantes it climbed from 3 percent to 10 percent during these years.[75] Moreover, the actual number of out-of-wedlock births was probably around twice as high as these figures suggest because illegitimate children in France were abandoned at about the same rates at which they were baptized, and illegitimacy was a common motive for abandonment.[76]

In fairness, it must be added that the rate of premarital sexual activity in the Netherlands and England was undoubtedly a good deal higher than the above numbers imply. For while the number of illegitimate births remained quite low in these two countries, the number of pregnant brides was rather high. In one sample of English parishes, it rose from 16 percent in the first half of the seventeenth century to 33 percent one hundred years later. And in the Holland the rise was sharper still.[77] Thus, what these numbers suggest is not so much lower levels of premarital sexual activity in England and the Netherlands as higher numbers of unwed mothers and abandoned children in France. In other words, they suggest that marital and familial norms were more stringently enforced in the Netherlands and England than they were in France. I will return to this point later.

Dutch society thus seems to have been remarkably orderly. What about Dutch politics? Given the high rates of taxation within the republic, one might predict high levels of rebellion as well; taxation and rebellion generally tended to be associated with one another during this period. And, indeed, taxation *was* the chief cause of rebellion in the republic.[78] But the rebellions themselves seem to have been smaller in number and milder in form than those experienced in other countries.[79] That at least is the impression given by Charles Tilly's comparative analysis of *European Revolutions*. During the years between 1550 and 1800, Tilly counts some nine revolutionary situations in the Netherlands. Elsewhere, the figures were higher: eleven on the Iberian Peninsula, sixteen in the Balkans, twenty-three in the British Isles, and thirty-two in France![80] Little wonder, then, that so many foreigners regarded the republic as a bastion of political stability.

• • •

So the puzzle is real. Despite the fact that the Dutch state was not especially centralized, bureaucratized, or monarchical, it was nonetheless able to maintain a large military, extract significant resources, and maintain a high level of social order. How can we explain this paradox? How can we account for a state that looks so weak in theory but acts so strong in practice? To fully answer this question, I will argue, we must shift our focus from the central to the local, and we must broaden it to include a wider range of institutions. What is more, we must look at the ethos that underlay these institutions. To put it metaphorically, we must pay attention to the body and the soul of the Dutch state. I now turn to a closer examination of the various mechanisms of moral regulation and social control which permeated Dutch social life, beginning with the Reformed consistories and their various sister institutions.

Religious Discipline and Social Order: The Calvinist Consistory in Comparative Perspective

In terms of its basic organization, the system of church discipline practiced by the Dutch Reformed Church was quite similar to those established by other Reformed Churches in early modern Europe.[81] At the local level, discipline was in the hands of a consistory or church council (*kerkeraad*), which consisted of the parish clergy together with the church elders. The elders were usually chosen by the consistory in consultation with the town councils. Not surprisingly, they tended to be drawn from the patriciate and were thus closely intertwined, both institutionally and personally, with local government. Some consistories also appointed clandestine overseers (*opzienders*) to keep watch over church members in particular neighborhoods. At the regional level, the parish clergy were grouped together into a larger unit called a classis.[82] The main responsibility of the classis was to maintain discipline among its own members and examine candidates for the ministry. But the classis often intervened in disciplinary cases involving laypersons, especially if the offense was particularly serious or the circumstances unusually complicated. At the provincial level, the classes were grouped into synods.[83] Like the classes, the synods were dominated by the clergy. But they also included lay representatives from the church consistories and, in many cases, nonvoting delegates from the town councils and provincial states. For the most part, the deliberations of the synods focused on general issues of church doctrine and policy. But the synods were also responsible for adjudicating disciplinary cases involving clergymen and interpreting the rules regarding lay discipline.

The principles and procedures governing the Dutch system were also quite standard. As in Geneva, a sharp distinction was drawn between "private sins" and "sins which are public and are associated with public scandal." Sins known only to a few people were to be remedied by means of "fraternal admonishment."[84] Sins more generally known were referred to the consistory. (In practice, of course, private sins could quickly become public ones. In the towns and villages of the Dutch Republic, where quarters were close, walls were thin, windows were large, and streets were narrow, few acts were truly private. A drunken yelp, a bawdy song, a domestic squabble, or a romantic encounter rarely went unnoticed and often reached the ears of the church council.)[85] Once the consistory had learned of a possible offense, the suspected offender was summoned before the elders. If the offense was minor and the offender repentant, the elders usually dismissed the suspect with a private admonition. If the infraction was more serious or signs of remorse were lacking, however, the offender might be publicly admonished, excluded from communion, or even excommunicated from the church.[86]

Though stringent, this system was not as harsh as it may seem. The consistories were usually more interested in reconciling sinners than in punishing them, and they often went to great lengths to bring lost sheep back into the fold. Months and even years might go by between the time when a wayward parishioner was first summoned before the consistory and the time when they were formally excommunicated. And each step in the process was usually preceded by another visit from the elders and another opportunity to repent. In most cases, the consistories sought the approval of the classis before initiating excommunication procedures.[87] Under these circumstances, it was not unusual for the classis to dispatch a delegation of its own, and even once excommunication procedures were underway efforts to reconcile a wayward church member were generally continued.[88] In some instances, the patience and perseverance of the consistories paid off.[89] In others, it did not.[90] In any event, the powers of the consistories were more pastoral than coercive, in both the literal and the Foucauldian senses.

Of course, a system of discipline that relied so heavily on rumor and hearsay was also vulnerable to error and abuse because people could—and probably did—spread rumors as a means of settling political and familial scores. Church leaders were aware of this danger, and they instituted various rules and procedures to safeguard against this. Formal statements were taken; witnesses were called; testimony was solicited. In particularly serious cases, formal investigations were undertaken.[91] If the evidence was judged insufficient, however, the proceedings were dropped, no matter how serious the charges.[92] In such cases, the consistories sometimes even went so far as to order that the accused be formally exonerated before the entire congregation.[93] Moreover, making false or unsubstantiated allegations against a fellow parishioner was itself a grounds for disciplinary action.[94] Thus, in terms of their basic standards and procedures, the Reformed consistories operated very much like the secular courts.

Who was disciplined? And what were they disciplined for? There are no national level studies of these questions. But there are case studies of a number of cities.[95] While one must be careful about generalizing from small samples, the results of these studies are quite consistent. In all of the cities studied, around half of all disciplinary cases involved social offenses such as drunkenness, fighting, calumny, and disturbing the peace. Sexual offenses—extramarital intercourse of one form or another—constituted another 30 percent. By contrast, less than 10 percent involved heterodoxy. The first question—who was punished—is harder to answer. It is clear that discipline touched all segments and strata of society. But is also clear that the powerful and the well-to-do sometimes got off more lightly than their fellows. In this regard, the Netherlands resembled other Reformed polities. In terms of the offenses themselves, however, it was somewhat different. In England and Scotland, for example, the majority of disciplinary cases focused on sexual morality.[96] And in the Calvinist communities of France and the Rhineland the number of cases involving heterodoxy was about twice as high as in the Netherlands.[97] The key point, for the present argument, is that the consistories of the Netherlands—and Great Britain—focused on social and sexual behavior more than religious belief and practice. As we will see in chapter 4, this was less true of the other confessions.

It should be stressed that the activities of the consistories were actually somewhat broader than the foregoing discussion implies. In their campaigns to achieve congregational purity, the elders often went beyond their formal roles as moral policemen. In their efforts to enforce sexual morality, for example, they sometimes found themselves attempting to reunite married couples, reform abusive husbands, or locate missing fathers. Similarly, in their attempts to maintain social order, they might seek to counsel and rehabilitate alcoholics, reconcile estranged friends and relatives, mediate disputes between employers and workers, or put a family's finances back in order. Thus, they served a preventive as well as a punitive function and often behaved more like modern day social workers than early modern policemen.

• • •

How great were the effects of Reformed discipline on Dutch society? Probably not as deep as they were in Geneva—and for at least three reasons. The first, and most important, is that many Netherlanders were not Calvinists.[98] Confessing Calvinists were still a minority during the early 1600s and probably did not achieve majority status until the last third of the century. The second is that there were many churchgoers who were not official church members and hence not subject to consistorial discipline.[99] The third is that the town councils were generally not as supportive of the consistories as they were in Geneva, especially in the cities of Holland.[100]

Still, the effects of religious discipline should not be underestimated either. While the non-Calvinists were not subject to the consistories, they were often subject to disciplines of their own. The various Baptist sects, for example, which had substantial numbers of followers in the northern and western parts of the country, practiced an even stricter form of discipline than the Calvinists. In their quest to build a community "without spot or wrinkle," they subjugated the spiritual welfare of the individual to the moral purity of the congregation to an even greater degree than did the Calvinists.[101] Sinners were often expelled from the congregation immediately and without warning and then completely and irrevocably cut off from any contact with all members of the sect, including their own spouses.[102] While many Dutch Calvinists thought these practices too severe, others thought them a good example, and some, frustrated by the "laxity" of Reformed discipline, even converted to Baptism.[103] There is also evidence that Lutheran congregations in the Netherlands practiced some form of congregational discipline—something that was not true of German Lutherans.[104] For example, the "church ordinance" passed by the Lutheran synod of 1597 outlined a set of disciplinary procedures virtually identical to the three-step system developed by the Dutch Calvinists.[105] And while Dutch Catholics had no formal system of discipline, they were anxious to avoid any public scandals that might spark a wave of persecution. Nor should we overstate the degree of conflict between church and state. Outside of Holland, the magistrates and the consistories usually worked together in harmony. And even inside of Holland they usually saw eye to eye on matters of social discipline. Perhaps, the skeptical reader may respond, but what does religious discipline have to do with state power? Of course, if one defines the state as a centralized agency that is clearly differentiated from other institutions and that seeks a monopoly over the legitimate means of violence, then the answer is obvious: very little. But if one acknowledges that the state is local as well as national, that it was not clearly differentiated from the church in the Netherlands (or anywhere in early modern Europe), and that it sought to regulate as well as to coerce, then the answer will be: a great deal. From this perspective, the Reformed consistories and their sister institutions appear as local appendages of the territorial state that played a crucial role in the regulation of individual conduct—mechanisms of social control that preserved order at the lowest possible cost.

I now turn to another arm of the local state, a rather more expensive one, the system of social provision.

Social Provision and Social Discipline: Charity and Morality in the Netherlands

The Dutch system of social provision was composed of a variety of agencies and institutions. The agencies in question were both secular and confessional. The former went under various names, including masters of the domestic poor and masters of the Holy Ghost and were effectively, if not always directly, controlled by the town councils. The confessional agencies were usually known as diaconates. The Calvinists were the first to organize local diaconates. But they were soon followed by the Baptists and the Lutherans and eventually by the Catholics and Jews as well. In addition to providing outdoor relief (that is, in-kind and cash benefits) to poor householders who could not support themselves, these agencies funded and supervised different forms of indoor relief, such as orphanages, travelers' hostels (*gasthuizen*), hospitals, retirement homes (*hofjes*), workhouses (*werkhuizen*), and houses of correction (*tuchthuizen*), which were collectively referred to as houses of the Lord (*godshuizen*).

The relationships among these various agencies and institutions were diverse and complex and appear to have changed over time. Since the secular and confessional agencies performed the same basic functions—the provision of indoor and outdoor relief—a certain division of labor had to be established. Logically speaking, three basic arrangements were possible: (1) dualistic: the Reformed diaconates could serve Reformed Protestants and the secular agencies could serve everyone else; (2) church-governed: the secular agencies could be subsumed in or subordinated to the religious agencies or (3) state-governed: the reverse of (2). Important examples of each of these arrangements can be found during the early seventeenth century.[106] By the late eighteenth century, however, most Dutch cities appear to have moved towards a fourth model in which the various churches—Calvinist, Catholic, Baptist, Lutheran, and so on—were responsible for providing relief to their own members, and the secular authorities played a purely subsidiary role, providing relief only to people who were not members of any church. This model might be described as confessional or "pillarized." A recent study of poor-relief in Friesland suggests that a pillarized system of social provision had already emerged there by the late seventeenth century.[107] And there are good reasons for believing that other provinces underwent a similar development.[108]

Comparatively speaking, the Dutch system of social provision seems to have been very extensive and quite well-funded. Such at least was the impression of foreign visitors to the Netherlands, who often commented on the number of almshouses that they encountered during their travels and on the cleanliness of these institutions and the quality of the care they provided.[109] Though fragmentary, the evidence generally corroborate these impressions. Consider the case of Amsterdam. It had numerous agencies and institutions for the relief of the poor, both religious and secular. Virtually every confessional grouping had its own almsmen, and many had their own orphanages and rest-homes, as did the city government.[110] Indeed, it is estimated that some 10 percent of the city population was receiving indoor or outdoor relief by the early seventeenth century.[111] Of course, Amsterdam can hardly be regarded as representative. Besides being the wealthiest city in the Netherlands, it also had the largest total population—and the largest immigrant population. So it probably had more aid to give—and more people in need. Still, it was not all that exceptional. In the early 1620s, the city of Delft was providing outdoor relief to about 740 of its 24,000 residents—a little under 3 percent of the population; and this was a time of relative prosperity, when the poor rolls would not have been particularly large.[112] In 1653, in the town of Tiel, the Reformed diacony provided relief to 95 of its roughly

1,650 parishioners—just under 6 percent of the total.[113] Even in a small town such as Graft around 16 percent of the population was receiving aid of some sort.[114] Like Amsterdam, most of the larger cities also provided indoor relief in the form of orphanages, retirement homes, travelers hospices, and workhouses. Indeed, an extensive system of indoor relief was often a point of civic and confessional pride, and the various towns and churches frequently vied with one another to build the largest and most lavish systems of social provision.

Financial support for these agencies and institutions came from a variety of sources. The most important were private endowments, public subsidies, voluntary contributions, and special sin taxes levied on saloons, theaters, and other forms of public entertainment. The relative importance of these different sources of income has not been much studied.[115] But voluntary contributions do seem to have played a rather significant role, particularly in the diaconates, for whom donations were probably the chief source of revenue.

• • •

Having outlined the organizational structure of social provision in the Dutch Republic, let us now examine its underlying principles. They tended to be quite similar throughout the Netherlands. At their root was a sharp distinction between the deserving and the undeserving poor. Whether a person was categorized as deserving or undeserving depended upon their physical, moral, and civic status. Generally speaking, anyone who was physically capable of earning a living was regarded as undeserving, unless they had more dependents than they could realistically support. Individuals who were incapable of earning their own livings could still be classified as undeserving if they were not established members of the religious or civic community, or if they had violated the norms of those communities. Thus, widows, orphans, the elderly, the sick, and the infirm were generally regarded as deserving. By contrast, the able-bodied, the nonnative, and the morally suspect were not.

In their efforts to implement these principles, local reformers employed a number of different strategies. These included: (1) outlawing or restricting mendicancy and begging; (2) introducing and enforcing strict qualifications for outdoor relief; (3) providing moral and practical education for the young; and (4) attempting to resocialize the rebellious and the indolent. By means of these various measures, the Dutch elites sought to encourage economic self-sufficiency, combat moral degeneracy, and maintain social stability, goals that they tended to see as interconnected.

In order to see how these various strategies were put into practice, it may be useful to look at the process of social reform in a particular city: Amsterdam.[116] During the 1580s and 1590s, the town council of Amsterdam passed a series of measures aimed at ridding the city of beggars. First, they ordered that foreign vagrants not be allowed to stay in the city for more than three days. Then, they passed a law requiring indigenous beggars to obtain a special license from the city government. Finally, they hired a squadron of inspectors to patrol the streets in search of possible violators. The inspectors were kept quite busy. Over the next century, they arrested more than 30,000 people for begging. In fact, in any given year beggars typically made up between one-quarter and one-third of all arrests.

This crackdown on begging was combined with a more stringent and more discriminating approach to poor-relief. In Amsterdam, outdoor relief was organized along dualistic lines. The diaconate provided relief to members of the Reformed Church, and the town almsmen provided relief to everyone else. Anyone desiring aid was required to appear before the appropriate agency in the company of at least two witnesses and then submit to a household visitation by a deacon or almsmen. If the applicant was deemed qualified and deserving—that is, if they were church members or city residents who were physically unable to support themselves and their dependents—his or her name was entered in the poor rolls and a food coupon (*portie* or *broodloodje*) was issued, usually valid for one year, which entitled the bearer to a weekly ration of bread, butter, and cheese in accord with the size of their household.[117] Aid recipients could also submit requests for clothing and medical care. These were usually granted.

Of course, fraud was always a problem, and the authorities took various measures to combat it. Aid recipients were required to renew their applications on an annual basis in person and in the company of their children and spouses so as to prevent false claims about dependents.[118] Since cash benefits were particularly susceptible to abuse, most aid was in kind. The deacons and almsmen had their own bakers, tailors, and cobblers; they even employed full-time medical staffs. The format of the food coupons was also varied regularly to prevent forgery.[119]

Naturally, those receiving aid from the Reformed diaconate were also subject to the rigors of ecclesiastical discipline. They were visited four times a year by the deacons, and any moral faults that were discovered were recorded in special visitation books, transcribed into a central commission book, and then reported to the consistory.[120] The deacons were usually reluctant to strike anyone from the rolls, but they did not hesitate to do so if the offense was grave or the offender recalcitrant.[121] Indeed, particularly truculent beneficiaries were sometimes even placed in a workhouse.[122] And if the deacons suspected that aid recipients were concealing money or property, they were prepared to conduct a search, as in the case of one woman who was discovered to have several sacks of gold stashed away under her cushions.[123] Nor could one escape past misdeeds simply by moving to a new town. New residents were required to submit a certificate-of-good-conduct (*attestatie*) from their old parish, certifying that they were confessing members of the Reformed Church and were not currently under censure; they could not receive aid from the diaconate until they had belonged to their new church for at least six months.[124] The almsmen employed similar standards and procedures.

Not surprisingly, some members of the lower classes sought to evade these controls. In order to cure these individuals of their penchant for indolence and vagrancy, the city fathers of Amsterdam created a new institution: the house of discipline [125] (*Tuchthuis*).[126] First founded in 1596, its operating principle was simple and—to modern eyes—familiar. Through a strict regimen of social isolation, forced labor, corporal punishment, and moral instruction, able-bodied beggars (the undeserving poor) were taught the value of work and transformed into productive citizens. The building itself consisted of nine locking cells grouped around a fully enclosed courtyard and resembled nothing so much as a monastery.[127] Everyday except Sunday the inmates were set to work rasping dyewoods with heavy iron saws, for which reason the *Tuchthuis* was popularly known as the Rasp House. Each prisoner was required to produce a fixed quantity of sawdust whose value was roughly equivalent to the cost of his upkeep.[128] Those who failed to meet their production quotas were punished, while those who exceeded them were rewarded with (meager) cash wages, payable upon release.[129] During their free hours, the inmates were permitted to read, write, or exercise.[130] But they were not permitted to curse or swear, fight or quarrel, gamble or trade, read inappropriate books or sing bawdy songs. Those who violated the official code of conduct were subject to a variety of punishments, ranging from decreased rations to solitary confinement.[131] And those who failed to respond to these sanctions were reportedly subjected to an even harsher method of discipline known as the drowning cell.[132] One foreign visitor described it as follows:

In the vestibule or entrance to the house there is running water, and beside it is a room with two pumps, one on the outside and the other on the inside. The patient was brought thither so that by pumping he might produce an appetite for St. Pono [that is, for work]. Water was pumped into the room first as high as his knees, then as high as his waist, and as he was not yet prepared to give his attention to St. Pono, as high as his armpits, and finally up to his neck when he found that he had been cured of his idleness and, fearing that he would drown, began his devotion to St. Pono by furious pumping until he had emptied the room, when he discovered that his weaknesses had left him and he had to confess his cure.[133]

Certainly, there could be no more dramatic—or Dutch—way of teaching the value of work than an existential battle against rising water![134] Originally intended as a reformatory for sturdy beggars, the Amsterdam *Tuchthuis* quickly became a *sammelsorium* for asocial elements of all kinds: rebellious children, adulterous women, hardened criminals, the mentally ill, and even, on one occasion, a Catholic missionary and two unorthodox pastors.[135] Over the years, however, the *Tuchthuis* gave birth to an array of more specialized and functionally differentiated institutions.[136] The first offshoot was the *Spinhuis*, a special *Tuchthuis* for women established in 1597, where female miscreants of various stripes—beggars, thieves, prostitutes, adulteresses, and other women of ill-repute—were put to work spinning yarn. Several years later, in 1603, a secret wing was added on to the *Tuchthuis*, where rebellious children, most of them well-to-do, were placed under round-the-clock supervision, generally at their parents' expense. Then, in 1650, the city magistrate established a special workhouse where able-bodied beggars and vagabonds captured by the city provosts could be put to work and taught a trade.[137] And in 1694 the inmates of the secret wing of the *Tuchthuis* were moved to a special bettering house run by a private contractor. By the year 1700, then, the city of Amsterdam had established a comprehensive network of carceral institutions, and the original *Tuchthuis* had evolved into a prison in the proper sense of the term.

These efforts to reintegrate deviants were supplemented with efforts to socialize children. One of the most important instruments in this campaign of preventive education were the city's various orphanages. In many regards, the new disciplinary regime introduced in the Dutch orphanages during this period resembled that practiced within the Dutch *Tuchthuizen*. Time was strictly regimented. In the deaconate's orphanage in Amsterdam, for example, children attended school six days a week and seven-and-a-half hours a day (7:30–11:00 A.M. and 1:00–5:00 P.M.) during the summers, with three hours of play time on Wednesdays and Saturdays.[138] On Sundays, mornings and afternoons were spent in church, while evenings were reserved for a question-and-answer session regarding the day's sermon.[139] The weekdays, too, were punctuated by religious exercises: prayers and Bible readings before breakfast, psalms singing and more prayers after dinner.[140] The children were also expected to learn the Lord's Prayer, the twelve articles of the (Reformed) faith, the Ten Commandments, the orders of baptism and communion, and the Heidelberg Catechism—all by heart[141]—and contests were held each year among those children who were preparing for their first communion, with New Testaments and psalm books awarded to the winners.[142] Space, too, was strictly regimented. The boys were separated from the girls, the young children from the old, and no unauthorized traffic between the various parts of the building was permitted. The orphans were also not allowed to leave the building without permission, and to prevent them from doing so the regents assigned each child to a specific bed, conducted roll call in the evenings and before church,[143] and installed bars on the windows, locks on the doors, and guards at the exits.[144] And even when they did leave the orphanage, the children's distinctively colored uniforms and numbered armbands made them readily visible and easily identifiable. Naturally, there were always some orphans who bridled at this unbending regime. Minor offenses were dealt with directly by the house father or mother.[145] A child who skipped church, for example, might be given a stern reprimand or sent to bed without dinner.[146] More serious offenses, however, had to be referred to the regents and generally resulted in harsher punishments, such as solitary confinement and a diet of bread and water[147] or having a heavy wooden block chained to one's leg for several months, the standard penalty for children caught drinking or smoking.[148] Chronic offenders might be also expelled from the orphanage and denied the money allowance (*uitsetting*) and workmen's tools that were usually given to the orphans upon their departure. Particularly grave misconduct could even result in five years of compulsory service for the East India Company—a harsh sentence indeed, given that one in three men died during each tour of duty[149]—as in the case of a boy who raped a fellow orphan,[150] or in confinement to the Workhouse, as in the case of a girl found guilty of stealing.[151] And it was not unusual for children who refused to admit their misdeeds to be locked up or publicly beaten until a confession was forthcoming.[152]

Harsh as it was, there is nothing to suggest that this disciplinary regime was stricter than those practiced in other Dutch orphanages. At the Almsmen's Orphanage in Amsterdam, for example, pregnant girls were routinely placed in the workhouse,[153] one boy found guilty of stealing linens was sentenced to a tour of duty in East India,[154] and another discovered drunk in his room was expelled from the orphanage without his allowance and tools.[155] It is difficult to know how successful this pedagogical program was. Certainly, there were some orphans who made out quite well, as evidenced by the rather substantial legacies they later left to the orphanage.[156] But however one evaluates their success, be it negatively or positively, the social impact of the orphanages was clearly substantial. By 1675, Amsterdam had seven orphanages, some of which housed more than a thousand children.[157] Thus, a substantial percentage of the city's children would have been housed in institutions of this sort—a percentage that might otherwise have lived alone or on the streets.

In assessing the significance of these examples, we need to ask ourselves several different questions. The first is: How representative are they? Certainly, in terms of absolute size and numbers, Amsterdam was exceptional. But in terms of its principles and organization Amsterdam's system of social provision was not atypical. Many Dutch cities reorganized their systems of outdoor relief around a distinction between the deserving and the undeserving poor. Many also expanded their systems of indoor relief by building new orphanages, new retirement villages, new travelers' hospices, and new hospitals.[158] And a good many built houses of correction modeled after the Amsterdam *Tuchthuis*.[159] Of course, the small towns and villages of the Dutch countryside made due with less elaborate and less costly systems. But even they had their deacons and almsmen, who regularly visited those receiving aid and diligently recorded their revenues and expenditures. In retrospect, one cannot help but be struck by the scope and complexity of the Republic's "welfare state." In this area, the Dutch state was truly a Leviathan. It embraced a sizeable percentage of the population, including a great many who might otherwise have drifted into "riotous" and "disorderly" lives.

The second question regards the success of these reforms. Here, of course, the answer depends largely upon how one defines *success*. If one defines it in relation to the goals that the reformers set for themselves—eliminating all begging and vagabondage and completely (re)socializing the weak and the depraved—then they were clearly a failure. Contemporary depictions of beggars and vagabonds and archival reports of indiscipline and recalcitrance in the various *godshuizen* provide ample evidence of that.[160] But if one defines it in relation to the situation in comparable cases (for example, in Paris or Rome) the assessment must be more favorable. As we have seen, foreign eyewitnesses were genuinely amazed by the (relative) scarcity of beggars and vagabonds on the streets of Amsterdam and other Dutch cities and by the order and discipline that prevailed in the Amsterdam *Tuchthuis* and similar institutions. And we know that rates of violence and criminality really were lower in the Netherlands than in most other parts of Europe. Thus, there are good reasons to believe that the Dutch reforms did have some effect.[161]

These effects were probably not limited to the actual beneficiaries. For the Dutch system of social provision was not just an institutional means for delivering material benefits to a particular clientele; it was also a symbolic means for representing cultural norms to a broader public. Thus, the structure and the routines of the orphanages were meant to mirror the structure and routines of an ideal family, with a house father and house mother (*binnenvader* and *binnenmoeder*), a daily regimen of worship and work, a gendered division of labor, a strict accounting of income and expenditures, clean clothes and linens, and so on. In the case of the Amsterdam *tuchthuis*, this mirroring function was quite explicit. The doors were opened to the public on a regular basis. As Foucault remarks of Bentham's panopticon, one wonders who was the watcher and who the watched.

Be that as it may, the foregoing discussion does shed light on one of the puzzles posed at the outset of this chapter, the puzzle regarding the sources of domestic order in the Dutch Republic. The answer, it turns out, is deceptively simple: while the central state in the Netherlands *was* quite weak, the *local* state was extremely strong.[162] And it would be possible to expand this discussion considerably. One might focus on the political and religious mechanisms that the churches and town councils used to enforce marital norms, the role of religious schools in socializing the young, or the importance of the civic militias in preventing and suppressing local uprisings.[163] For the sake of brevity, however, I now turn to another topic: the relationship between discipline and external power.

Bureaucrats and Soldiers: Political and Military Discipline in the Republic

Did the Calvinist disciplinary revolution also affect the external power of the Dutch state? Did it enhance the state's efficiency or efficacy in any way? Before addressing these questions, let us briefly define our terms. We may begin by distinguishing by two types of state efficiency: political and administrative. By political efficiency, I understand the relative speed with which a state makes and implements decisions and policies. By administrative efficiency, I mean the relative volume of resources it consumes in the process. An efficient state, by this definition, is one that is comparatively fast and cheap to run.

How does the republic stack up? Was it efficient in this sense? Certainly, it did not enjoy a reputation for speed. The legislative process within the national and provincial states was slow at best, even slower than in modern forms of representative government. The various delegations were all bound by exacting (and often conflicting) mandates issued by their constituents (for example, the town councils or the provincial states). As a result, the delegations often had to seek an expansion or alteration of their mandates before they could reach an agreement with the other delegations, which could mean traveling back to their home districts to meet with their constituencies. Thus, the Dutch state was not usually quick to act. However, it could be very quick to react. Preparations for the invasion of England in 1688 provide a particularly good example of this. Within the space of a month, the Dutch state mobilized an army of 21,000 troops and outfitted a naval detachment four times the size of the Spanish Armada. Diplomatic observers were "stunned" not only by the size of the operation but with the speed at which it was carried out. "It must be admitted," said one, "that this plan could not have been grander or better orchestrated."[164] But these *were* exceptional circumstances. The Dutch were confronted by the prospect of an Anglo-French alliance, a prospect that served to unite the two most powerful political actors in the republic—the regents of Holland and the House of Orange—a rare event.[165] In this case, the strength of the local and provisional governments, and their close ties to social elites, facilitated a rapid mobilization of men and materiel; in more routine situations, however, these same factors tended to slow decision making.

So the Dutch state was not usually fast. Was it cheap? There is some evidence that it was, at least in comparison to the French state. In 1641, for example, nonmilitary expenditures comprised only 4.6 percent of the States General's total budget.[166] In 1642, by contrast, the French government spent almost as much on administrative salaries as it did on military expenses, 34 million *livres* as opposed to 36 million.[167] The provincial governments seem to have been somewhat less efficient than the States General, though still more efficient that the French government. The provincial states of Holland spent around 30 percent of their total budget on nonmilitary expenses during the first half of the seventeenth century.[168] Unfortunately, we do not have comparable figures for local governments. However, since the salaries of local officials were generally higher than those of provincial ones—yet another indicator of where power really resided in the Republic—it seems likely that administrative costs would have consumed an even larger proportion of the budget.[169]

Of course, in assessing administrative efficiency we need to look not only at the official costs (for example, for salaries and expenses) but also at the unofficial ones (for example, for incompetence and malfeasance). In some countries, like France, these costs were probably quite substantial. There, a system of venality prevailed; public offices were auctioned off to the highest bidder and could be passed on as part of an individual's private patrimony, certainly not a system conducive to high levels of competence.[170] Not surprisingly, perhaps, French officials also enjoyed a rather unsavory reputation for corruption. It seems to have been deserved. Typical forms of fraud included issuing receipts for bogus loans, falsifying expense reports, and taking kickbacks from military recruiters, practices that were all the easier to conceal given that the French state did not adopt a system of double-entry bookkeeping until the early nineteenth century.[171]

Dutch officials were not immune to corruption.[172] Nepotism and clientelism were not unusual, and they became more and more common as time went on.[173] Dutch officeholders often sought to pass their charges on to a son or relative and reserved lesser posts for their clients. And while venality was officially forbidden the sale of offices was not entirely unknown. Nor were Dutch politicians untouchable. In The Hague, at least, some Dutch officials could evidently be bought.[174] Still, there was no officially-sanctioned system of venal office holding in the Netherlands, nor is there evidence of the kind of widespread malfeasance that permeated the fiscal system of the French *ancien régime*.[175] The path to political success in the Netherlands did not pass through the central treasury or the royal court, but through a series of local offices.

To see how this system operated, let us place ourselves in the position of a freshly married, young patrician about to begin his career.[176] Let us assume that between his personal patrimony and his wife's dowry he would have had the means to live comfortably, but not grandly, not an untypical situation. In the quest for greater income and status, two avenues would have been open to him: commerce and politics. The former promised the most money, the latter the greatest prestige. Should he have chosen to devote himself to politics and had he had the proper connections to succeed his first appointment would probably have been to a lesser post with a nominal salary—the board of regents at one of the city orphanages, for example. In this capacity, he would have met regularly with his colleagues to discuss the operation and financing of the orphanage, and he would have been appointed to one of the standing committees that were responsible for routine administrative matters, duties that would have consumed a day or more of his time each week. After a few years of office, if he had acquitted himself well, our young regent could have set his sights on a somewhat loftier and more lucrative position, such as a seat on the municipal court (*schepenenbank*). From the municipal court, he could then have sought election to the town council. And if he were particularly talented and well-connected, his post in the town council could have served as a springboard into the office of burgomaster. Having served a term as burgomaster, he might even have captured the post of sheriff (*schout*), the most lucrative of all. Or he could have tried his hand at provincial or national politics by seeking election to the regional parliament or the States General. Such was the *cursus honorum* of the successful politician.

But not all politicians were successful. The *cursus honorum* was filled with stumbling blocks. One was political strife and collusion. In most towns, the regent class was divided into opposing groups or factions, bound together by ties of blood and marriage, who sought to deprive their rivals of power and monopolize it for themselves.[177] Beginning in the late seventeenth century, the dominant faction or factions within many towns began drawing up so-called contracts of correspondence, formal agreements regulating how municipal offices were to be divided up between the factions and/or rotated among their members—and withheld from the members of opposing factions. Needless to say, the excluded factions did everything they could to undermine these agreements and the familial and factional coalitions on which they rested. This included appealing to the broader citizenry and actively fomenting unrest. Sometimes these intrigues were successful; sometimes they were not. At the provincial and national level, the factions sometimes coalesced into parties, loosely organized political alliances founded mainly on political and religious loyalties. Typically, these conflicts pitted a coalition of orthodox Calvinists and die-hard Orangists against the regents of Holland and their republican and latitudinarian supporters. Such struggles were rare. But when they did occur, as in 1650, 1672, 1702, and 1748, they were usually followed by political purges in which the losing party was excluded from local and provincial offices. Thus, the fortunes of an individual politician were closely bound up with those of his faction and/or party. Another potential stumbling block along the road to success was public scandal.[178] A regent who was found guilty of committing adultery, misusing his office, or perjuring himself could be summarily removed from office, stripped of his rights, and declared infamous or without honor.[179] Thus, a single moral misstep could ruin a regent's career. So could an economic one. Bankruptcy was viewed with especial severity in the Netherlands. For men, it resulted in a loss of face (and business), and for Calvinists, an automatic censure by the consistory.[180]

Thus far, the analysis has focused exclusively on the regents. But they were only one cog in the administrative machine, albeit the largest and most important one. Thus, we must also consider the conduct of their agents and especially of the lesser officials who collected the taxes. We do not know as much about them as we know about the regents. But we do know that the tax farmers were mostly "low and vile persons"—artisans, shopkeepers, and peasants—who used their offices to supplement their regular incomes.[181] And we also know that this was just as the regents wanted it.[182] They feared that the fiscal system might fall into the hands of a small group of powerful financiers, as had happened in France. Accordingly, they kept the tax farms small and the terms short. They were rarely worth more than 10,000 guilders and were generally auctioned off on a semiannual basis.[183] This did not prevent an individual from owning more than one farm or from bidding for the same farm again and again. But it did prevent the emergence of powerful financiers capable of holding the government hostage. And it seems to have kept administrative costs quite low as well. The available evidence suggests that profits on the tax farms were quite low, usually on the order of 2–6 percent.[184] This is not a particularly high figure when one considers that the tax farmers were responsible for all their own expenses—and a pittance when one compares it to the profits reaped by French tax farmers.

So while the Dutch state was hardly an ideal-typical bureaucracy, it did exhibit some semi- or proto-bureaucratic features. There was a (formal, if partial) separation of person and office; offices could not be permanently appropriated by particular individuals or publicly bought and sold, at least not legally. There was an unofficial career ladder, at least for the regents, and progress along that ladder was based, to some degree, on demonstrated competence. And there was a de facto discipline of sorts exerted by one's colleagues and competitors; malfeasance and other misbehavior could have tangible political—and financial—costs. This could not be said of France, Spain, or many parts of Italy.

Having assessed the relative efficiency of the Republic's political and administrative system and outlined some of its inner workings, let us now return to the question posed at the beginning of this section: What impact, if any, did the Calvinist disciplinary revolution have on this system? Where political efficiency is concerned, the impact was probably slight and, perhaps, even negative insofar as the revolt contributed to a weakening of executive authority within the republic. Orthodox Calvinists tended to be die-hard Orangists, of course, but their calls for a strengthening of the stadtholdership were ignored by the urban regents, for obvious reasons. In the realm of administrative efficiency, however, the impact may have been somewhat more significant, not because it promoted administrative rationalization, but rather because it hindered the sort of administrative *ir*rationalization that occurred in other parts of the Spanish empire, where venality and corruption struck deep and lasting roots. (This point is discussed in greater detail in chapter 4.) Calvinism may also have had a positive impact on administrative efficiency insofar as it promoted ascetic values, such as diligence and self-denial, and created an institutional and political context that sanctioned their nonobservance. That said, the impact of Calvinism on Dutch political institutions was certainly not as deep as its impact on Dutch social life. The main effects of the Dutch disciplinary revolution were on state infrastructure, rather than state structure, and on non–state governance, rather than local government.

• • •

What about its effects on Dutch military practices? Was there a link between the Netherlands' disciplinary revolution and its military revolution?

The early modern era was a period of intense military competition in western Europe. It was also a period of rapid military innovation, so rapid, in fact, that many historians speak of an early modern military revolution.[185] Most historians also agree that the Dutch Republic was at the very center of this revolution.[186] The catalyst for military reform in the Netherlands was the threat of Spanish reconquest. During the 1580s, the Dutch Republic experienced a humiliating string of military defeats at the hands of Alexander Farnese, the Duke of Parma. By the early 1590s, the southern Netherlands were again under Habsburg control, and Parma's forces were within striking distance of Holland itself. The republic then undertook a sweeping reorganization of its land forces. The masterminds behind this reorganization were the Dutch stadtholder Maurice of Orange, his uncle, Prince Willem Lodewijk, and the Dutch polymath Simon Stevin. The first and perhaps the most important of their innovations involved the use of systematic drilling. Drilling was hardly new, of course; it had already been practiced by the ancient Romans. Since then, however, it had fallen into desuetude. The Dutch system of drilling had two foci. One was the rapid and efficient use of weaponry. Maurice and his collaborators broke down the process of loading and firing a musket into forty-three separate steps, each of which could be individually practiced.[187] Similar drills were developed for pikemen. The other focus was moving quickly and in unison. To facilitate this process, Maurice and his collaborators developed a system of commands in which the directional command preceded the actional command (for example, left ... face, forward ... march, and so on), making it possible for the individual soldier to prepare for the action mentally before executing it physically—a system still in use today. Dutch soldiers were drilled regularly throughout the year in good weather and bad.[188] The result of the new discipline was greater speed and efficiency. According to one source, the Dutch army could assemble 2,000 men in twenty-two to twenty-three minutes, while other armies required over an hour to assemble one thousand.[189] Greater discipline also facilitated various tactical innovations. The most famous was the countermarch, a tactic that enabled Dutch musketeers to maintain a continuous volley of fire. In principal, the procedure was quite simple. The soldiers were arranged into ranks of five. After firing their muskets, the men in the front rank marched to the rear and began the process of reloading. The men of the second rank then discharged their weapons and marched to the rear. By the time the men of the first rank had advanced to the front again, they had reloaded their weapons and were ready to fire. To take advantage of their greater maneuverability and more rapid rate of fire, Maurice and his collaborators abandoned the square-shaped formation known as the *tercio* in favor of a line formation in which the ranks were thinner but more spread out. To make their battlefield units more mobile, they also reduced the size of their companies from 580 to 250 and increased the number of officers per company from eleven to twelve.[190] In this way, they heightened the level of supervision.

The Dutch reforms attracted a great deal of attention, particularly after Maurice bested Farnese at the Battle of Nieuwpoort (1600), one of the few full-scale, open-field infantry battles of the revolt. In the decades that followed, dozens of princes, nobles, and military men made the journey to Holland to observe the Dutch troops in action.[191] (One of them was Prince Frederick William of Hohenzollern, the future ruler of Brandenburg-Prussia). On the international level, then, the Dutch reforms were enormously influential. From a strategic point of view, however, they were not as important as one might imagine. Open-field battles such as Nieuwpoort were exceptional. The war against Spain was mainly a war of siege in which rates of fire and speed of maneuver were of relatively little importance. Still, the reforms may have been important in another way. Insofar as they promoted discipline and obedience, they also hindered mutiny and disorder—major problems in most armies. Between 1572 and 1607, for example, the Spanish contingent stationed in the southern Netherlands experienced over forty-five mutinies. Just in the years between 1602 and 1605, it lost over three million man-days to mutinies.[192] Needless to say, this seriously compromised its ability to wage war. Unfortunately, we do not have comparable data for the Dutch army. But we do know that it enjoyed a reputation for orderliness and discipline. According to the Venetian ambassador, this reputation was so strong that Dutch cities vied with one another for garrisons and that Dutch burgers competed with one another to billet troops.[193] This was hardly the usual situation. In France, for example, towns and villages often resisted the establishment of new garrisons, and the monarchy sometimes punished rebellious municipalities by stationing troops within their walls, knowing that the soldiers would harass and despoil the population. In the Netherlands, by contrast, where the troops were busy drilling or standing watch most of the day, they had little opportunity to misbehave. And if they did they could be sure that they would be punished severely.[194] Lesser offenses such as stealing were punished with fines and jail sentences; more serious crimes such as rape were punished by hanging. And special judicial officials were posted at each garrison to see that these punishments were carried out. Of course, there was at least one other reason why the Dutch soldiers behaved so well: they were paid regularly and generously, at least in comparison to their foreign colleagues.

Influential as they were, however, the Dutch reforms were not quite as revolutionary as some historians originally believed. Subsequent research has shown that the French and Spanish armies were also moving towards smaller units and thinner formations, and there is even some evidence that suggests that the Spanish may have experimented with a maneuver similar to the countermarch.[195] The really distinctive feature of the Dutch reforms was the introduction of systematic drilling. In this realm, Maurice and his collaborators really do seem to have broken new ground—or, rather, revisited old ground. Their reforms were based on an intensive reading of various classical sources and their application to contemporary problems.[196] The drills, the formations, even the commands—all were based on classical precedents.

Why were Maurice and his colleagues the first to draw on these precedents? Since the seminal essays of Gerhard Oestreich on this subject, historians have typically pointed to the influence of Neostoicism, an intellectual movement inspired by the stoic philosophers and their emphasis on constancy and self-control.[197] In particular, these historians point to the role of Justus Lipsius, a Neostoic man of letters who taught at the University of Leiden during the late sixteenth century. In 1584 Lipsius published a treatise *On Constancy,* which included a chapter on military discipline, and, in 1595, he published another book, *On the Roman Army,* which contained glosses and translations of classical writings on military discipline. Because Maurice studied under Lipsius at the University of Leiden in 1583 and 1584 and maintained a high opinion of him throughout his life, it seems reasonable to conclude that his own study of classical precedents was at least partly inspired by his mentor.[198] But the influence of Lipsius and Neostoicism should not be exaggerated. Maurice and Stevin were pious if not altogether orthodox, and Willem Lodewijk was orthodox as well as pious. And it is generally agreed that the intellectual impetus for the reforms came from William Louis rather than from Maurice, and it is also clear that their experiments with reform antedated the publication of Lipsius's compendium by several years. So their concern with discipline may have had Calvinist as well as Stoic roots, and their interest in drill may have been independent of Lipsius's influence. This is not to say that their military reforms were directly inspired by Calvinism; in this regard, Parma was surely a greater inspiration than Calvin! Still, one wonders whether their might not have been a psychological connection—an elective affinity—between their religious ethos and their military reforms because both placed so much stress on discipline, both as a value and as a practice. It is also interesting to note that the Maurician discipline and the Amsterdam *Tuchthuis* were both "invented" around 1590. This seems to have been a time of creative ferment in the republic, when the new technologies of discipline were applied to a widening array of social realms.

Summary and Conclusion

The argument of this chapter consists of three interconnected claims: (1) that the Dutch state was strong, both internally and externally; (2) that this strength had more to do with state infrastructure than with state structure; and (3) that this infrastructure was in no small part the product of the Calvinist disciplinary revolution. The most direct and important contribution of the Calvinist disciplinary revolution was in the area of nonstate governance and domestic order. But it also had significant, if less direct, effects on administrative efficiency and perhaps also on military efficacy.

Having presented my interpretation of the Dutch case, let me now attempt to insert it into a broader historical and theoretical context.

I begin with two disclaimers: (1) I do not mean to argue that discipline was the sole or even primary source of state strength. As I emphasized earlier, the relative strength of a particular state is a function of many factors, including population, administrative centralization and rationalization, and economic development. My aim in this chapter has not been to deny the (widely recognized) importance of the first three factors but rather to underline the (generally underrecognized) importance of another factor, namely, discipline. (2) I also do not mean to suggest that Calvinism is the only or even predominant source of individual and social discipline. As I stressed earlier, the history of discipline does not begin or end with the rise of Calvinism, whether in the Netherlands or elsewhere. Nor can the history of Calvinist discipline be fully disentangled from the history of other movements, such as Dutch Neostoicism. Where the Netherlands are concerned, though, I feel somewhat more confident in asserting that Calvinism *was* the primary, if not sole, source.

But if state strength was a product of so many different factors and discipline had such a long and complicated history, then how much causal weight should we really attribute to discipline or Calvinism? What if the Northern Netherlands had remained Catholic or become Lutheran? Would this have had an appreciable effect on the strength of the Dutch state? Obviously, we cannot change the parameters of Dutch history. However, we can examine other cases similar to the Netherlands, except with respect to religion. The city-states of northern Italy provide a good example. In terms of economic development, political organization, and social structure, the communes of Florence and Venice were quite similar to the provinces of the Northern Netherlands. They were affluent, oligarchic, and bourgeois. In religious terms, of course, they were different; they remained loyal to the Old Church. But their political trajectories were the mirror image of the republic's. Independent in 1500, Florence was under Habsburg suzerainty a century later. A near-great power at the end of the Renaissance, Venice was a marginal player for most of the early modern era. Would a Calvinist Florence have been able to resist the Medicis and the Habsburgs? Would a Reformed Venice have been better able to maintain its position in European affairs? The case of the Northern Netherlands suggests that they might have. Of course, it would be wrong to conclude from these examples that Calvinism and discipline were the *only* things that mattered. The case of Scotland is good evidence of that. Like the Netherlands, Scotland experienced a Calvinist-led disciplinary revolution. Unlike the Netherlands, however, Scotland was relatively poor. And like Florence it, too, succumbed to the domination of a foreign power: England. From these examples, it seems reasonable to conclude that the small states of early modern Europe were unlikely to remain strong and independent unless they had discipline and wealth, and that the chances of them having these two things were intimately connected to having yet another thing: Calvinism. Thus, while Calvinist discipline was surely not a sine qua non of early modern state-building, it probably did increase the odds of political survival, particularly among smaller states. In this regard, it is striking that two of the small states that lived on into the modern era had Calvinist roots: the Netherlands and Switzerland.

The Dutch case also has some important theoretical implications, which bear restating. Most state theorists have generally (if implicitly) focused their attention on central state institutions and have usually drawn a sharp distinction between state and society. By contrast, the present analysis strongly suggests that we must go beyond the realist fixation on central institutions by incorporating the local state into our analyses. Similarly, it suggests that we should pay less attention to where the line between state and society is drawn and more attention to the way public and private institutions cooperate in the project of popular governance. Finally, it suggests that state power is a function, not only of coercive and extractive capacity, but also of regulatory and normalizing capacity as well.

The territorial expansion of Brandenburg-Prussia under Frederick William, 1640–1688

3
Disciplinary Revolution from Above in Brandenburg-Prussia

In Brandenburg-Preußen war die kleinere Zahl bekanntlich immer die größere.
Theodor Fontane, Der Stechlin

Der Staat ist die wahre Sittlichkeit.
G. W. F. Hegel, Philosophie des Rechts

Historical sociologists and social historians have long viewed early modern Prussia as one of the purest manifestations of absolutist monarchy. And not without reason. There was probably no other state in eighteenth-century Europe where the centralization of power and the rationalization of administration were more complete. And yet, as German historians have long recognized, the rise of the eighteenth-century Prussian state was as unlikely as it was meteoric; there were few states in *seventeenth*-century Europe where the monarchy was so weak and the administration so fragmented. Seventeenth-century Prussia consisted of seven different territories scattered across the length of the Continent: the Baltic provinces of East Prussia and East Pomerania (*Hinter-Pommern*), the electorate of Brandenburg in the center, the Rhineland provinces of Cleve and Mark in the west, and the former bishoprics of Magdeburg and Halberstadt to the south. Each province had its own set of governmental institutions and political prerogatives. And in three of these territories the sovereignty of the Hohenzollerns was either contested—by the Palatinate in Cleve and Mark—or shared—with the Poles in Prussia and the Swedes in Pomerania. To this, one must add that Prussia was riven by deep confessional divisions, particularly between the royal court, which was predominantly Calvinist, and the territorial estates, which were overwhelmingly Lutheran (except in the middle-German and Rhineland provinces of Magdeburg and Halberstadt, Ravensburg, Cleve and Mark, where Reformed Protestantism was the dominant creed). Hardly an auspicious starting point for the development of absolutist rule.

Other German principalities, such as Bavaria and Saxony, would appear to have been better positioned to make the leap to great power status. And, yet, it was Prussia that prevailed. Why?

The literature contains at least three different answers, two of which should already be quite familiar to the reader: (1) A materialist answer that focuses on relations among the Crown, the nobility, and the peasantry; (2) a bellicist answer that focuses on the nexus between war making and state-building; (3) an idealist answer that focuses on the religiopolitical ethos of Prussia's rulers, the Hohenzollerns.

While each of these perspectives has its particular merits, none is entirely satisfactory. I will discuss the shortcomings of each theory in more detail below, but it may be useful to indicate my central qualms at the outset. The problem with the materialist and bellicist answers is simple: they do not really explain the Prussian trajectory. In particular, they do not tell us why Prussia developed so differently than other Central European states, which were similar in terms of their socioeconomic and political structures. This cannot be said of the idealist perspective; it *does* provide an explanation of the Prussian trajectory. But it also places too much emphasis on the religiopolitical ethos of the Hohenzollerns while ignoring another factor: confessional conflict.

At this point, the reader will not be surprised to learn that my own interpretation emphasizes the nexus between confessionalism, Calvinism, and social disciplining. I argue that: (1) the unusual *autonomy* of the Prussian state has its roots in confessional conflict between the Crown and the estates during the reign of Frederick William, the Great Elector (1640–88); and that (2) the unusual *strength* of the Prussian state was due, in no small part, to a disciplinary revolution from above orchestrated by Frederick William's grandson, Frederick William I (1713–40). My argument, then, is that Prussia's divergent path and its rise to power cannot be understood without regard to its religious situation.

The Peculiar Character of the Prussian State

Most scholars of early modern state-building would agree that the Prussian state was unusual in certain ways and perhaps even unique. But it is important to be clear at the outset about how it was unusual. For one thing, the size of its army—83,000 men as of 1740—set it apart from its peers. Only four European countries—France, England, Russia, and Austria—had larger land forces at this time. The size of the Prussian army is even more striking when one considers the size of the Prussian population and the character of the Prussian economy. With its 2.2 million inhabitants, Prussia was a good deal smaller than the other land powers and only a little bit bigger than the other Imperial Electorates (*Kurfürstentümer*)—the seven German principalities that elected the German emperor. In fact, in per capita terms Prussia supported a (relatively) larger army than any other country in Europe, large or small. This would be less remarkable if Prussia had possessed a vibrant commercial economy, such as the Netherlands or England. But it did not. In fact, its economy was actually quite backward. Even as late as 1800, commerce and manufacture made up less than 5 percent of Prussia's national income.[1] Nor was the agricultural sector particularly productive; the soil in Brandenburg was so poor that the Electorate was sometimes derided as the sandbox of the Holy Roman Empire.

How was Prussia able to support such a large army when its population was so small and its economy so backward? This is a question we will return to repeatedly in this chapter. We can glean some important clues from a closer examination of Prussia's public finances. First, consider state expenditures. Prussia spent a much higher proportion of its total budget on the military than most of its competitors, about 80–90 percent on average, as compared to 45–55 percent in most other countries.[2] How was this possible? Part of the answer is that administrative costs were fairly low and court expenses lower still. Another part of the answer is that Prussia had no debts, and hence no debt service.

Now consider the revenue side. Given the size of Prussia's military outlays, one might expect that its tax rates would be extremely high. But that does not appear to have been the case. In 1740, the per capita tax rate in Prussia was just under fl. 2.5. In absolute terms, these rates were a good deal lower than those in the Netherlands, England, and even Saxony and fairly similar to those in Austria and France. Of course, compared to these countries—indeed, compared to almost any country—Prussia had a fairly weak economy, so these taxes probably weighed more heavily on the average Prussian than they did on the average Austrian or Frenchman. But how much more? We can get some sense of the relative tax burden by comparing the proportion of national income which was appropriated as taxes in various states. In England, between 1715 and 1785, the figure ranged from a low of around 16 percent to a high of 22 percent. In France, by contrast, it ranged between 9 percent and 17 percent during these years.[3] For Austria in 1789–90, the figure was just under 12 percent.[4] This figure is probably at the high end of the range.[5] For Prussia, the first year for which there are reliable figures on national income is 1800. In that year, the ratio of tax revenues to national income was 6 percent.[6] We must interpret this figure cautiously because there are good reasons for assuming this represents the low end of range.⁷ Still, it seems unlikely that the average figure for Prussia would have been as high as it was for England or France. So while the evidence is incomplete, it does not suggest that the tax burden in Prussia was especially high.

How could Prussia's rulers keep pace with their richer competitors without imposing high taxes on their subjects? One reason is that they enjoyed substantial revenues from the royal domains, the lands belonging directly to the Crown. In 1740, the Prussian domains generated revenues of fl. 5.1 million or 45 percent of the total budget. Even as late as 1800, domain revenues still made up 40 percent of the state's income. The great powers enjoyed far lower revenues from their domains. In Austria, by contrast, domain revenues made up only 10 percent of the total budget in 1754.⁸ In England, they accounted for 10–15 percent of the budget during the eighteenth century, and in France they comprised only 5–10 percent of the budget during these years.⁹ And while a number of other midsized German principalities—Bavaria, Hanover, the Palatinate, and Saxony—enjoyed substantial domain revenues, they were also burdened with much heavier levels of nonmilitary expenditure.¹⁰

As this brief survey of European state finance makes clear, eighteenth-century Prussia really was somewhat unusual; its army was inordinately large, its court unusually small, and its administration quite efficient. What is more, the kings lived largely of their own rather than off the backs of the populace, and their accounts were always balanced. Taken together, these numbers suggest a strategy: minimize civil expenditure to maximize military expenditure, and avoid public debt, foreign subsidies, and high taxes to avoid financial dependency and economic decline. This strategy was a conscious one.

In retrospect, it was also very rational. It is the very strategy that a rational state builder with meager resources and hostile neighbors should have followed. But it was not the strategy pursued by most central European princes. They usually opted for a strategy of courtly display and royal grandeur à la Louis XIV. And while some of these rulers did seek to rationalize their finances and reduce their expenses, few, if any, were as successful as the Hohenzollerns. To understand Prussia's political trajectory, then, we must understand why the Hohenzollerns chose this strategy, and we must understand why they were able to implement it. In other words, we must attempt to understand the peculiar political rationality of the Hohenzollerns and the peculiar political autonomy of the Prussian state. These are the issues that lie at the heart of the Prussian puzzle.

The Rise of Prussia: Some Possible Explanations

Within the literature on state-building, one finds at least four different explanations for the development of Prussian absolutism. The first is *Marxist* in inspiration and was originally advanced by Francis L. Carsten.[11] It focuses on relations between the Crown and the nobility and, in particular, on a series of legislative agreements (*Landtags-Rezesse*) concluded between the Hohenzollern elector, Frederick William (1620–88), and the territorial estates (*Landtage*) of Brandenburg, Prussia, and Cleve-Mark during the 1650s and 1660s. Carsten argues that these agreements served as the foundation for an enduring alliance between Crown and nobility based on a simple quid pro quo: the nobles gave the Crown greater authority over taxation, enabling the Hohenzollerns to build up a large standing army with which to fend off invasion and conquest; in return, the Crown gave the nobles free reign over the peasantry, thereby allowing the *Junkers* to impose the "second serfdom" and reap huge profits in Western cereal markets. Having gained control of the purse strings, says Carsten, Frederick William then proceeded to build up a standing army, expand the territorial estates, and dismantle the territorial administration, thus laying the military, administrative, and political foundations of Prussian absolutism.

Influential as it has been,[12] the materialist interpretation remains quite problematic. For its central claim—the claim that absolutist rule in Prussia originated out of an alliance or pact between crown and nobility—is very much at odds with the evidence.[13] The word *alliance* implies some degree of good will. And of that there was little, not only during the reign of Frederick William, but during those of his successors as well. In fact, it was not until the reign of Frederick the Great (1740–88) that any real rapprochement took place. But perhaps one could still speak of a pact or compromise, a tacit agreement based on shared interests? Here, too, Carsten's case is actually quite weak, for there is little evidence of cooperation between Crown and nobility in this period.[14] Noble landowners would have liked help clamping down on the peasantry. But Frederick William and his successors were not anxious to provide it. On the contrary, they frequently intervened to *protect* the peasantry against the rapacity of noble landowners, though probably more out of self-interest than warm-heartedness: they understood that a strong state could be built only on the backs of a prosperous peasantry.

Unlike the materialists, the *bellicists* begin with the assumption that relations between the Crown and the estates were inherently antagonistic, not only in Prussia, but throughout Europe. In their view, it was geopolitical pressure, rather than economic transformation, that catalyzed the development of absolutism, not only in Prussia, but in Germany as a whole. But therein lies the problem: the bellicist model assumes that the Prussian state was typical, that it can be viewed as representative of Germany as a whole.[15] As we have just seen, this assumption is clearly untenable. So unless one argues that the level of geopolitical pressure on Prussia was much greater than that on all other midsized German principalities—an argument that has little prima facie plausibility—one cannot explain the rise of Prussia from a purely bellicist perspective.

Having said that, it is important to emphasize that the bellicist model is not without its merits. Seventeenth-century Prussia did face substantial geopolitical pressure—from the Swedes and the Poles in the east and the French and the Dutch in the west—and the policies of the Hohenzollerns—fiscal, administrative, and military—were largely a response to these threats. What the bellicist model does *not* explain, and probably *cannot* explain, is why the Hohenzollerns responded so differently than other dynasties in similar positions. It does not explain the peculiar political rationality of the Hohenzollerns.

This cannot be said of the *idealist* approach. Unlike the bellicists, the idealists begin with the assumption that the Prussian path was atypical, and they explain the Prussian *Sonderweg* in religious terms. There are two versions of the idealist argument. The first and older of them was originally set forth by Prussian "national economists" such as Gustav Schmoller and Otto Hintze during the late nineteenth and early twentieth centuries. It emphasizes the impact of Calvinism on the ethos of the Hohenzollerns. Infused with the "political energy" and "fighting spirit" of western European Calvinism, they argue, the Prussian Electors were able to overcome the passivity and egotism of the Lutheran nobility and forge a strong state that would be capable of defending, and later uniting, Germany.[16] The second and more recent version of the idealist position was originally laid out by the German historians Klaus Depperman and Carl Hinrichs during the 1960s and 1970s.[17] It focuses not on Calvinism but on Lutheranism and, in particular, on Pietism, an ascetic reform movement that emerged within the Lutheran churches of Germany during the late seventeenth century. According to this perspective, the Pietist ethos of discipline and duty and its penetration into Prussian state and society, more than anything else, explain the unlikely rise of this backward principality.

Clearly, the interpretive framework developed here owes a great deal to the idealist model. But there are a couple of important differences that bear emphasis. The first is theoretical. Idealist accounts stress the impact of Calvinism on the political will of the Hohenzollerns. By contrast, the present account stresses its impact on their political rationality. And it treats Calvinism not only as a political ethic but also as a political cleavage—as a source of conflict between Crown and estates. The second difference is empirical. Recent works in the idealist mode tend to stress the impact of Pietism and downplay that of Calvinism. My own researches suggest that the emphasis should be reversed; to me, Calvinism seems to have been more important, at least where the Prussian state is concerned.

Having located my interpretation within the literature, I now turn to my case study of Prussia. It consists of two stories divided by a short vignette. The first story concerns the origins of state autonomy in Prussia and focuses on confessional conflict between Crown and estates during the reign of Frederick William (1640–1688), the Great Elector. The vignette deals with the reign of Frederick I (1688–1713), who pursued a policy of royal grandeur and courtly display à la Louis XIV. The second story concerns the sources of state strength in Prussia and focuses on the disciplinary revolution from above that occurred during the reign of Frederick William I (1713–1740).

The Origins of State Autonomy: Social Compact or Confessional Conflict?

One of the hallmarks of absolute monarchy, as the term is generally understood, is a high degree of state autonomy. For our purposes, state autonomy may be defined as the capacity to make and implement laws and reforms without the consent, or against the will, of social elites. By this definition, most scholars would agree, the Prussian state was highly autonomous. Why? The explanation developed here is idealist in inspiration. It focuses on the impact of religion and, more particularly, on the impact of confessional conflict on relations between the (Calvinist) Crown and the (Lutheran) estates. Specifically, it is argued that fiscally based conflicts between the Crown and the estates were exacerbated by confessionally based ones and that the Crown was able to circumvent and undermine the power of the estates by appointing large numbers of Calvinists and "foreigners" to key administrative posts. Let us begin by tracing out this process in one part of the Hohenzollern patrimony: Brandenburg, the seat of the electorate, and the site of its capital: Berlin.

Like a number of other German principalities, Brandenburg experienced not one Reformation, but two. The first Reformation was Lutheran.[18] It began in the 1520s, took root in the cities during the 1530s, and was formally recognized by the Hohenzollerns in 1540. By the 1570s, Brandenburg was firmly in the fold of orthodox Lutheranism. The second Reformation was Calvinist.[19] It began in 1613, when the Hohenzollern elector, Johann Sigismund, announced his conversion to the Reformed faith. It met with sharp opposition, not only from the Lutheran clergy, but also from the territorial estates and even the general population, who greeted it with a barrage of pamphlets and protests.[20] Eventually, Johann Sigismund was compelled to issue a decree, guaranteeing the free exercise of Lutheranism and foreswearing any attempts to convert the populace to his faith. As a result, Calvinism remained a minority faith, a religion of crown and court, which had few followers outside the provincial capitals. The only exceptions to this rule were the lesser provinces of Cleve, Mark, Minden, and Halberstadt where Calvinism was the dominant faith.

Relations between the Crown and the estates were somewhat more amicable during the reign of Johan Sigismund's successor, George William (1619–40). This was due, in part, to the influence of the Reformed Court preacher, Johannes Bergius, a man of moderate and irenicist views who sought to promote mutual toleration—his term—between the two Protestant confessions.[21] It was also due to the influence of George William himself, who supported the policy of armed neutrality (and low expenditures) favored by the territorial estates.

Alas, this latter policy was short-lived, as was the harmonious relationship between the Hohenzollerns and the native nobles. The Hohenzollerns were eventually forced to enter into the Thirty Years' War.[22] To escape the fighting, they retreated to Königsberg, the capital of East Prussia. The government of Brandenburg fell into the hands of the stadtholder, Count Adam von Schwarzenburg, who imposed heavy taxes on the populace and shifted power to the General War Commissary (GWC).[23] The estates complained bitterly about Schwarzenburg's policy of "absolute dominion" and demanded a return to the old system of "condominat" or shared rule.[24]

Initially at least, the ascendance of Frederick William in 1640 seemed to promise just that. Having spent much of his adolescence in the Netherlands—the Hohenzollerns had strong ties to the House of Orange—the young elector favored a policy of cooperation with the estates of the sort practiced by the Dutch stadtholder, Frederick Henry, his former mentor and future father-in-law.[25] Accordingly, one of his first steps upon taking office was to disband the GWC and reestablish the Privy Council (*Geheimer Rat*), which he staffed with members of the native nobility.[26] The elector also returned to the old policy of armed neutrality favored by the estates, signing a cease fire with the Swedes and authorizing a major reduction in troop strength.[27] In the early years of his reign, then, Frederick William tried to rule with the estates rather than against them.

But relations between Crown and estates deteriorated rapidly thereafter. Serious tensions were already evident at the Diet (*Landtag*) of 1643. Frederick William had summoned the estates in hopes of securing a voluntary contribution towards the defense of the kingdom (*Landesdefension*). The Estates retorted—and not without justice—that their resources had been sorely taxed by years of military conflict and foreign occupation, and they made approval of a new contribution dependent upon the willingness of the elector to address a long list of grievances (*gravamina*)—forty-four in all.[28] Frederick responded positively to most of their complaints.[29] But he remained unbending on one point: religion.[30]

Tensions deepened further at the Diet of 1652–53, and for much the same reason. Once again, Frederick William sought funds to pay for his ever-growing army, this time in the form of a general excise tax.[31] And once again the estates balked, arguing that such a tax was insupportable and even "unconstitutional."[32] Instead, they promised to grant a one-time contribution of 530,000 reichsthaler to be paid out over six years—but only after the king addressed a long list of grievances, including ten *gravamina in puncto religionis*.[33] Frederick William granted most of the estates' demands and explicitly promised to "protect the freedom of conscience of all my subjects."[34] But he summarily rejected their religious grievances and angrily dismissed their charges of religious oppression and discrimination. "For as regards the exercise of the Augsburg [or orthodox Lutheran] Confession," he retorted, "it is undeniable and clear as day that it has been left free and unhindered and that not even the least of my subjects has ever been compelled to believe anything else.... Much less can they complain that they have been excluded from public or ecclesiastical office.... On the contrary, it is clear and evident, that most and highest offices and prebends including those in the noblest commissions are occupied and enjoyed by more Lutherans than Reformed Protestants right up to the present moment."[35] But the estates were not satisfied. They demanded that Frederick William address *all* of their grievances, *especially in puncto religionis,* and they threatened to suspend negotiations if he did not. In the end, a compromise was found and in July 1653 the estates approved a contribution of 530,000 Reichsthaler, but only after two years and seven recesses, thus making the *Landtag* of 1652–53 one of the longest ever held—and the last. Never again did Frederick William, or any of his successors, summon a plenary meeting of the estates.

Over the next decade, relations between Frederick William and the territorial estates continued to deteriorate. The reasons remained the same: money, power, and religion. The First Nordic War (1655–60) had given birth to a permanent standing army, numbering some 3,000 troops, and to a new administrative agency, the GWC, which was responsible for provisioning it.[36] The GWC rapidly assumed control over the collection and administration of taxes throughout Brandenburg and eventually eclipsed the noble-dominated Privy Council in power and authority. Needless to say, these policies enraged the estates, who charged that the GWC was "putting a knife to the throat of the territorial constitution."[37] This was not the only source of their anger however. They were also upset by Frederick William's religious policies. For the elector was doing everything he could to expand the presence of Reformed Protestantism. He did this by installing Calvinist court preachers (*Hofprediger*) in all the royal residences and provincial capitals, establishing biconfessional congregations (*Simultankirchen*) in Berlin, and encouraging immigration by Calvinists from other parts of Europe, most notably from Scotland and France; and, on the other hand, he promoted public dialogues (*Religionsgespräche*) between Lutheran and Calvinist ministers, appointed irenical and syncretist ministers to important posts within the Lutheran Church, and punished outspoken or ultraorthodox Lutheran clergymen or excluded them from office. These measures did not violate the agreements that Frederick William and his forebears had signed with the estates. But they were a direct challenge to confessional homogeneity and Lutheran orthodoxy and, thus, to the fundamental constitution of the electorate. The Lutheran clergy and estates responded with heated protests and angry polemics. In 1662, in a final bid for reconciliation, Frederick William summoned the leading Calvinist and Lutheran theologians of Brandenburg to a *Religionsgespräch* in Berlin. But spirits were high, and the talks failed due, for the most part, to the intransigence of the orthodox Lutherans, who argued that Reformed Protestants were not "brothers and fellow believers" deserving of toleration, nor even "Christians *quatenus tales*."[38] Harsh words, indeed.

In retrospect, it is clear that the mid-1660s were a turning point in Frederick William's relationship to the Lutheran estates, not only in Brandenburg, but in other parts of the kingdom as well. From this time onwards, Frederick William sought to undermine and circumvent the territorial estates and the native nobility by shifting administrative power to the GWC and by staffing it with Calvinists and foreigners. Of course, the elector had long given preference to his coreligionists. In fact, two thirds of the Privy councillors appointed between 1640 and 1651 were Reformed Protes-

Table 2 The Calvinization of the Prussian Royal Service under Frederick William

Year	Percentage Calvinists and "Foreigners"
1640	33.3
1645	18.2
1650	14.5
1655	26.7
1660	46.2
1665	43.8
1670	56
1675	60.9
1680	78.9
1690	81.9

Source: Andreas Nachama, *Ersatzbürger und Staatsbildung. Zur Zerstörung des Bürgertums in Brandenburg-Preußen* (Frankfurt am Main: Peter Lang, 1984), p. 111.

tants.[39] Up until the mid-1660s, however, the majority of upper-level posts outside the Privy Council had still been held by Lutherans. From that time on, however, the proportion of Calvinists grew steadily. By 1675, at least three-quarters of all top-level appointments were occupied by Calvinists, and there is no evidence to suggest that the confessional composition of the lower ranks was any different.[40] This Calvinizing trend did not escape the attention of the estates. In a list of grievances submitted in 1678, for example, they complained bitterly that the king had broken his promise "to favor and promote both Lutheran and Reformed subjects without respect to religion" and that, whereas most "posts and prebends" in the royal administrations were previously occupied by Lutherans, "today, the opposite is true: most posts are filled by Reformed Protestants."[41] The situation of the estates was summed up poignantly in a brief chronicle written by a Lutheran nobleman at the end of Frederick William's reign: "In our Electorate, the Lutheran Estates are still allowed to practice their faith, and one could not say that we live in a state of religious oppression. But since the year 1614 [sic] when Elector Johann Sigismund converted to the Calvinist Religion, the so-called Reformed Protestants have expanded and established themselves to such a degree in the Mark Brandenburg, that they control the church consistories, run the ecclesiastical courts, occupy almost all royal posts in the cities and the domain offices [in the countryside]."[42] That is precisely how Frederick William wanted it. In his "Political Testament" of

1667, the Great Elector explicitly instructed his son to "take on and employ such subjects of the Reformed Religion as are to be found in Your Lands, and since none are present in the Mark Brandenburg, to accept them from other Lands, and to prefer them before the Lutherans."[43]

• • •

The example of Brandenburg has led many historians to conclude that Frederick William was determined to dismantle the territorial estates and impose absolutist rule throughout the Hohenzollern lands. But this interpretation is belied by the case of Cleve-Mark. There, relations between the elector and the estates developed very differently.[44] One reason for this—perhaps the crucial reason—was that the estates of Cleve-Mark were predominantly Calvinist. As a result, confessional tensions did not sour relations between the elector and the estates. Indeed, they actually strengthened them, as we will see directly.

At first, relations between Frederick William and the estates of Cleve-Mark were tense, even hostile. The elector was concerned that Cleve-Mark might be overrun by the Duke of Pfalz-Neuburg, who controlled the neighboring principalities of Julich and Berg, and he secretly hoped to preempt the Duke by invading Julich and Berg. So he insisted on stationing troops in Cleve-Mark and pressed the estates to pay for them. The estates were less than cooperative. They insisted that they would not levy any taxes until the elector confirmed their traditional "constitution and privileges,"[45] evacuated the troops, and dismissed all "foreign advisors."[46] The elector threatened to levy the contribution by force. The estates responded by appealing to the Dutch, who promised to intervene on their behalf.[47] In 1649, after several years of negotiations, Frederick William finally acceded to their demands. In exchange, the estates promised a contribution of 700,000 Reichsthaler.[48] But no sooner was the ink on this agreement dry than the estates began attaching further conditions to the contribution.[49] And so it went, back and forth, for the next several years.

The turning point in relations between Frederick William and the estates came in the early 1650s, following the Hohenzollerns' invasion of Julich and Berg. At first, the estates declared themselves neutral and appealed for protection—this time from the emperor.[50] But the Protestant members of the estates began to have second thoughts about an alliance with the (Catholic) emperor. They feared that Imperial intervention would be followed by the suppression of Protestant worship and the installation of a Catholic ruler (namely, the Duke of Neuburg).[51] Rightly sensing the political significance of these religious divisions, Frederick William instructed the stadtholder of

Cleve-Mark to seek out a compromise with the Protestant members of the estates.[52] He succeeded. The estates agreed to a modest contribution. In exchange, Frederick William reconfirmed their privileges.[53] In the meantime, he arrested the leaders of the Catholic faction within the estates.[54]

From this point onwards, relations between Frederick William and the estates of Cleve-Mark improved steadily. Between 1655 and 1660, the estates contributed 1.5 million Reichsthalers and 20,000 troops to Frederick William's military campaign on the Baltic.[55] And in 1661 they ratified a new *Landtagsrezeß*, which enhanced the elector's authority to raise troops and appoint members of the government.[56] In exchange, Frederick William continued to grant the Estates a substantial degree of autonomy and power, including the right to assemble at their own will, collect and administer taxes, and even raise funds for their own use—rights not dissimilar, it should be noted, to those enjoyed by the English Parliament! What is more, the elector observed these privileges not only in the letter but also in spirit. He did not attempt to centralize power in the hands of the provincial war commissary,[57] nor did he attempt to circumvent the authority of the estates by appointing foreign officials.[58] He did not have to: the estates and their members were already loyal—and Calvinist.[59]

A similar pattern can be observed in Magdeburg and Halberstadt, smallish ecclesiastical principalities that fell into the hands of the Hohenzollerns as a result of the Thirty Years' War. Like Cleve and Mark, Magdeburg and Halberstadt had large Calvinist communities.[60] And, like Cleve and Mark, they were allowed to retain many of their traditional privileges and liberties.[61] The reason, one suspects, is the absence of confessional conflict.[62]

This conclusion is corroborated by the cases of East Pomerania and East Prussia.[63] Like Brandenburg, the territorial estates of these provinces were predominantly Lutheran. And, like Brandenburg, they were slowly stripped of their political powers during the 1660s and 1670s. Even the process was the same: confessional conflict and growing animosity followed by a centralization of power and a Calvinization of the provincial administration.

These outcomes, and the events which led up to them, cannot be readily explained from a materialist or bellicist perspective. The relationship between Crown and estates varied considerably from one province to the next as did the degree of administrative centralization. But these variations are not related to class structure, geopolitics, or legislative organization, at least not in any obvious way. What they are related to, I would argue, is confession. The general pattern seems to have been as follows: During the 1640s and early 1650s, Frederick William pursued a policy of cooperation with the territorial estates throughout his kingdom. In the cases of Cleve-Mark,

Halberstadt, and Magdeburg, this policy was eventually successful. The estates provided Frederick William with a steady stream of contributions, and he granted them considerable autonomy and influence. In the cases of Brandenburg, Prussia, and Pomerania, by contrast, the policy of cooperation was a failure. While the elector and the estates were able to reach an agreement on the financial question, often in rather short order, the religious question proved intractable and eventually poisoned relations between them. In each case, the turning point seems have come sometime between 1663 and 1665. From this time onwards, Frederick William refused to summon or negotiate with the estates in these three provinces and began centralizing power in the war commissaries, which he staffed with Calvinists and foreigners.

Seen from this perspective, the puzzle of state autonomy is suddenly less puzzling. The result of Frederick William's policies was the formation of a new elite—a Calvinist elite—which was opposed to the old elites—Lutheran nobles and burghers—in outlook and interest. This elite was concentrated in the royal residences and provincial capitals of the Hohenzollern lands, and its core was made up of court preachers and royal officials. It included a few native subjects who had adopted the religion of their ruler, but it was dominated by foreigners who had come to Prussia in search of work or fled from religious persecution in their home countries. This elite lived its life in the shadow of Crown and court. It worked in the Crown's offices and attended the court's churches, which were usually located in the royal residences and sometimes side by side. And it was resented and persecuted by the old elites and their clerical supporters, who envied its status and excoriated its beliefs. In short, this elite owed everything to the Crown and nothing to the estates. And that, I would argue, is one of the main reasons why the Prussian state was so autonomous:[64] it was composed of men who had no links to Prussian society. Such a state could implement laws and policies without regard to the interests of entrenched elites; it could orchestrate a disciplinary revolution from above. But that revolution would not occur for another generation.

French Intermezzo: The Reign of Frederick I[65] (1688–1713)

"The reign of [Frederick I]," writes Hintze, "was not one of those great creative epochs, in which the basic features of the Prussian state system and its peculiar social and political constitution were established."[66] Rather, it was one of those unusual eras in which Brandenburg-Prussia followed along the well-worn path trodden by its neighbors, in this case, the path towards baroque absolutism first blazed by Louis XIV, with its cult of courtly display, its system of royal patronage—and the administrative and fiscal indiscipline that inevitably accompanied them.⁶⁷

A sensitive but weak-willed man, who was more interested in collecting jewelry than in administering his kingdom, Frederick I introduced few changes in the administration that he inherited from his father. During the first decade of his reign, state finances were kept on an even keel by the "prime minister," Eberhard von Danckelmann and his able assistant, Dodo von Knyphausen.⁶⁸ But they deteriorated rapidly after 1697 when Danckelmann fell from grace and was replaced by Duke August of Sayn-Wittgenstein, an ambitious and unscrupulous courtier. In his efforts to please the king and court—and enrich himself and his friends—Wittgenstein funneled an ever-growing share of the royal revenues into the court treasury. At the same time, he took over the central domains administration (*Hofkammer*) and filled its provincial offices (*Domänenkammer*) with his clients and lackeys. The result, not surprisingly, was profiteering and corruption; domain lands were exploited and alienated en masse, and soon the royal treasury was hovering on the brink of collapse. With his revenues dwindling, Frederick I became increasingly dependent on foreign subsidies to support his army.⁶⁹ The precariousness of the situation was clearly recognized by certain members of the court, including the crown prince, Frederick William I.⁷⁰ But the king remained blind to Wittgenstein's fiscal machinations until 1708. In that year, famine struck East Prussia. When the king ordered Wittgenstein to dispatch half a million Reichsthalers in aid, he balked. Eventually, the truth came out: the state was broke and had been for some time.⁷¹

Of course, there was nothing particularly unusual about this state of affairs. Most baroque monarchies lived on the verge of bankruptcy, buoyed from one fiscal crisis to the next by the ingenuity of their finance ministers and the ruthlessness of their tax collectors. Rather, what is striking about the Prussian bankruptcy of 1709 is that it led to a far-reaching reform of the entire fiscal and administrative system. To understand this unexpected turn of events, however, it is necessary to examine the religiopolitical ethos that animated the crown prince and his followers.

Prussian Puritanism: The Religiopolitical Ethos of Frederick William I

The roots of Prussia's disciplinary revolution from above are to be found in the religious ethos and worldview of Frederick William I. Like his forebears, Frederick William I was brought up in the Reformed religion. He eventually rejected the doctrine of predestination,[72] but he retained the spirit of Calvinist asceticism. In some ways, his ethos was very much like that of the bourgeois ascetics originally described by Weber. For example, the king laid great store by thrift. Already as a young boy, he had kept careful records of his financial transactions. Every expenditure, no matter how small, was recorded in a special ledger. And these habits persisted into adulthood. Frederick William I was also extraordinarily austere. He eschewed all pomp and display. His quarters in the royal castle were decorated in the simplest manner: no carpets, no tapestries, no lavish appointments, just whitewashed walls and the plainest wood furnishings, a decor more typical of a monk's cell than a royal bedchamber.[73] He also lived according to a strict schedule. His routine included frequent prayer, psalms singing, Bible reading and—above all—ceaseless activity.[74] His pleasures were simple and practical; his free hours, such as they were, were spent hunting in his estates in Wusterhausen and Potsdam or discussing politics and finance with the members of the Tobacco Board (*Tobakskollegium*), a small circle of military officers and civil servants which assembled several times a week at the royal castle in Berlin. But there was one respect in which the King's ethos diverged sharply from that of the bourgeois ascetic: for him, divine grace and personal salvation were manifest, not in the accumulation of wealth, but in the accumulation of power. As a child, his tutor, the Huguenot nobleman Philippe Rebeur, had taught him that the fortunes of the Hohenzollern kingdom were bound up with the beliefs of their rulers; since their conversion to Calvinism, he learned, his family had been blessed by God and would continue to be thus blessed as long as they kept His commandments. The argument stuck. As an adult, the king espoused this same view to his own son; if he worked hard, lived an upright life, and enforced God's laws, the kingdom would continue to grow and prosper.[75] But if he "loafed about," engaged in "fornication," and permitted dances, comedies, and other "abominations," he would bring down God's wrath on himself and his subjects.[76] In this regard, he was more like Oliver Cromwell than Benjamin Franklin. There is one other feature of Frederick William I's religiopolitical ethos that is worth mentioning and that is his profound mistrust of his fellow human beings. Of course, many rulers mistrusted their counselors and administrators—and with good reason. More unusual, perhaps, was Frederick William I's conviction that he could control his underlings by means of constant surveillance—the same means he used to control his own "weaknesses." It was this belief in the efficacy of discipline, and the possibility for transforming the world more generally, that was distinctively Calvinist and became distinctively Prussian.

The king's ethos was extreme. But it was not unique. There was a group of royal officials and Calvinist clergymen who shared his outlook on life.[77] The King's religious asceticism and worldly activism were also shared by pietistically inclined members of the Lutheran clergy and their lay supporters. These groups helped Frederick William I carry out his disciplinary revolution from above.

Disciplinary Revolution from Above

In 1700, there were no signs of revolution on the horizon. In the city of Königsberg, preparations were underway for the coronation of Frederick I as King in Prussia. Hundreds of dignitaries were invited from all over Europe. The triumphal procession alone lasted over four hours![78] In Berlin, meanwhile, dozens of artists, engineers, scholars, and architects were busy transforming the city of Berlin into a proper baroque capital; castles, museums, churches, and tree-lined boulevards were under construction, and two Royal Academies were being organized, one for the sciences and a second for the fine arts.[79]

Against this background, Frederick William I's ascension to the throne in 1713 resembled a sort of royal *Bildersturm*.[80] As crown prince, he had observed the rituals and intrigues of the Berlin court with growing consternation and had spent years plotting out a strategy for strengthening the monarchy.[81] And he wasted no time putting it into effect. Immediately after taking leave of his dead father, he strode vigorously past the milling courtiers and called a meeting of his leading advisors. Thereafter, he retired to his estate in Wusterhausen. Over the next several months, he introduced a radical austerity program: the court was shrunk, salaries were slashed, the palace treasures melted down or sold—even feed rations for the courtiers' horses were cut.[82] The royal gardens were cleared of trees and transformed into a drilling ground.[83] In the course of a single year, the budget of the royal court was reduced from 420,000 Reichsthalers to just over 100,000.[84] Many officials were fired, and those who were lucky enough to keep their jobs saw their salaries cut by one-half or even two-thirds. These savings were then used to finance a sizeable hike in military salaries and a 33 percent increase in troop strength (from 30,000 to 40,000). "My father," he told his advisors, "found joy in beautiful buildings, large quantities of jewelry, silver, gold and furniture and external magnificence—please allow me my pleasure as well, which consists mainly in a large number of good troops."[85] The effect of the king's strategy upon the royal capital was immediate and dramatic: courtiers packed their bags, ministers took their hats, merchants closed their shops, craftsmen took to the road. "It is incomprehensible," reported one

Dutch diplomat, "how one can see such a large change in the way of life in so short a time."[86] The changes continued. Over the next thirty years, Berlin evolved from a city of castles and boulevards to one of garrisons and parade grounds.[87]

But the king's avowed goal—"to make [my] sovereignty as stable as a bronze cliff"[88]—could not be achieved through austerity measures alone. Prussia could not compete with the great powers on their own terms. For that, its economic base was too thin, its population too small, its territory too fragmented. The only way to compensate for these shortcomings, realized Frederick William I, was through discipline and hard work and, more specifically, through a loyal and well-trained army, an honest and efficient administration, and an obedient and hardworking population. These, the pillars of Prussia's future greatness, Frederick William I now set out to fashion.

"Like the Best Made Watch": Frederick William I's Military Reforms

By the standards of the day, the Prussian army was a superior fighting force even before Frederick William I took the throne. But it was under the tutelage of Frederick William I that the Prussian army was first transformed into what was widely regarded as the most disciplined and effective fighting force in Europe. The movements of the Prussian infantry, boasted Frederick II of his father's regiments, are like those of "the best made watch"[89]: "in each line there is only one movement, only one sound; so that in firing, only one shot is heard, in marching, only one step; so that every movement is exactly like that of a machine, when its switch is turned on."[90] As a result of this unparalleled coordination and speed, most Prussian regiments were able to maintain a rate of fire considerably greater than that achieved by other armies, probably around three salvos per minute as compared to the usual two.[91] In this way, Frederick William I was able to substitute quality for quantity, that is, to compensate for numerical inferiority with tactical precision. The Prussian army, he confidently asserted, could take on a force that outnumbered it by a ratio of $3:5$[92]—a claim later vindicated by the successes of Frederick the Great on the battlefields of Silesia.

What was the secret of this superior discipline?

In part, of course, it lay in the ruthless and often violent means through which obedience and subordination were imposed upon the enlisted man. Frederick William I believed firmly in the value of corporal punishment. But so, too, did most rulers. The real hallmark of the Prussian army under Frederick William I—what set it apart from other fighting forces and later gave it a decisive edge on the battlefield—was its intensive system of drilling.[93] While the Prussian system was not altogether unique—the use of drill was quite common by this time—it was unusual in at least three respects. First, it was *uniform*. In most armies, there were as many drill codes as there were drill masters.[94] In the Prussian army, by contrast, there was only one: the royal *Reglement* of 1714 and the revised and expanded *Reglement* of 1718 and 1726.[95] Every officer received a copy of the latest *Reglement* or extracts of the relevant passages and was expected to study it carefully and learn it by heart.[96] This was no small task, for the *Reglement* specified every command and every movement, from the placement of the soldier's boots on the assembling line to the position of his fingers on the rifle grip. New recruits sometimes spent several weeks just learning how to hold and present their muskets, and it took most enlisted men one to two years before they had fully mastered the routine—not surprising when one considers that loading, charging, and firing a musket, only one of several drilling routines, was broken down into sixty-seven commands and 167 movements.[97] The second distinctive feature of Prussian drill was its *intensity*. Elsewhere, drills tended to be short and sporadic—perhaps a few hours each week. In Brandenburg-Prussia, by contrast, drills were long and regular. During the drilling season (*Exerzierzeit*), which lasted from March through May, they generally began at 5:00 AM and rarely ended before noon, and during the week of the annual review, usually held in June, soldiers might rise as early as 1:00 AM and be on their feet until the early evening.[98] The third distinctive feature of the Prussian drill is that it was *overseen by officers*. In most armies, drilling was regarded as dirty work and was left to low-born drill sergeants. In the Prussian army, by contrast, drilling was not only a central part of every officer's duty it was absolutely essential to his advancement through the ranks. During the annual review, the king inspected and observed each regiment in person, and those whose troops were orderly and, above all, fast could expect raises and promotions, while those whose troops were disorderly or, God forbid, slow often faced demotion, dismissal, or even imprisonment.[99]

The impact and the aim of military drilling and discipline, moreover, went far beyond the parade ground, for the Prussian army, unlike its competitors, was composed primarily of native subjects. Frederick I had already recruited the majority of his troops from within Brandenburg-Prussia,[100] and Frederick William I declared military service a national duty. "All young men," he declared, "are obligated and required to place their lives and livelihoods (*Gut und Blut*) at [our] disposal according to their natural station in life and [by] the order and commandment of the Almighty God."[101] And, indeed, it is estimated that around two-thirds of all enlisted men were native subjects of the Hohenzollern lands during the reign of Frederick William I. The reason for this policy was dual: on the one hand, reasoned the king, native subjects were generally more loyal and obedient because they were serving their own lord; and, on the other hand, military service was itself a good means of reinforcing loyalty and obedience among one's subjects. This latter consideration was of particular importance where the nobility was concerned, so important, in fact, that Frederick William I explicitly forbade young noblemen from serving in foreign armies[102]—something that noblemen did in other kingdoms quite routinely. Large segments of the (Lutheran) nobility, as he well knew, were still distrustful of their (Calvinist) sovereign, and a military career was one way of winning their allegiance. "Bringing up the entire nobility in your service," he advised the crown prince, "has the advantage that they will know no other lord than God and the King of Prussia."[103] The habits of obedience and subordination learned in the army, he hoped, would be carried over into daily life in the civilian sphere.

The danger of this policy was that it would breed popular unrest and undermine agricultural production. This danger was quite real. There were almost 3,500 cases of desertion during the first year of Frederick William I's reign, and in 1718 so many young men fled the military recruiters that large areas of the countryside fell out of cultivation.[104] At first, the king responded by imposing harsher punishments and stepping up surveillance.[105] These measures do not appear to have been very effective, and the king later shifted his strategy. First, he introduced a "furlough system" (*Beurlaubungssystem*), which allowed soldiers to work their farms or practice their trades during the off-season, when they were not drilling (that is, July–February).[106] Then, he introduced the so-called canton system (*Kantonsverfassung*). It required eligible young men to enroll with the military recruiters before they reached draft age, but allowed them to serve in or near their home district after they were called up.[107] In this way, Frederick William I sought to make military service more bearable for the popular classes (and less draining on the Prussian economy). And not without success: the desertion rate at the end of his reign was only 5 percent of what it had been at the beginning.[108]

"Plusmacherei": Frederick William I's Fiscal and Administrative Reforms

Like its army, Prussia's administration was already quite advanced (that is, centralized and rationalized) when Frederick William I took the throne. The territorial estates had little voice and less power (except in the Calvinist provinces of Cleve-Mark and Halberstadt); power was concentrated in the hands of three royal administrative bodies (the GWC, the Court Treasury [*Hofkammer*], and the Domains Directory); and administrative procedures were becoming increasingly uniform and standardized. By 1700, Prussia already had the germ cell of a royal bureaucracy and the rudiments of a central budget.[109]

Under Frederick I, the process of administrative centralization and rationalization stalled and even reversed. But it picked up steam again during the reign of Frederick William I. In 1713, immediately after his accession to the throne, the king dissolved the Court Treasury and the Domains Directory and created a single body responsible for administering all domain lands, which he christened the General Finance Directory.[110] Then, in 1723, he merged the General Finance Directory with the GWC into a single agency, the General Superior Finance, War and Domains Directory (*General Ober-Finanz, Kriegs- und Domainendirectorium*).[111] It was responsible for all aspects of state administration except religious affairs and foreign policy. Prussia now had one of the most, perhaps *the* most centralized systems of public administration in all of Europe.

Centralization went hand in hand with rationalization. This was particularly evident in the area of administrative organization, which is to say the degree of bureaucratization. In fact, of the ten features of bureaucratic organization discussed by Weber, only two were wholly absent from the Prussian administration: mutually binding labor contracts between the ruler and the administrator and exemption of the administrator's private life from public scrutiny. (And it is revealing that these are features that are in the interest of the administrator, but not the ruler.) The other eight were all present to one degree or another: (1) a clear chain of command that stretched from the king himself through the central and provincial administrative colleges right down to the local tax collectors (hierarchy of offices); (2) increasingly standardized certificates of appointment (*Bestallungsurkunden*) that specified the duties and prerogatives attached to a particular office (job descriptions); (3) university-level programs in the administrative sciences (*Kameralwissenschaften*) at several Prussian universities,[112] and a system of apprenticeship (*Auscultatorensystem*) within the provincial War and Domains boards (technical qualifications); (4) money remuneration, generally via a fixed, annual salary; (5) the emergence of public administration as a full-time job; (6) the beginnings of a career ladder in which a gifted and hardworking official could move up through the ranks;[113] (7) "the separation of the administrator from the means of administration"; and (8) strict and continuous monitoring and supervision (discipline).[114] Of course, the Prussian system still diverged from the Weberian ideal in a variety of ways, besides the two already mentioned above. The central and provincial administrative boards were organized collegially rather than hierarchically; job descriptions were not fully codified or standardized; appointment was not dependent upon passage of an exam; and salaries were determined not by rank but by the king, as was promotion. But the question here is not whether the Prussian state was an ideal-typical bureaucracy but how bureaucratic it was in comparison with other early modern states. And the answer to that question, as we will see in more detail in the next chapter, is that it was easily the most bureaucratic state in Germany and one of the two most bureaucratic states in all of Europe.

The Prussian administration was not only one of the most centralized and rationalized in Europe; it was also one of the most meritocratic. For Frederick William I, the most important qualifications for office were "loyalty, diligence and accuracy" (*Treue, Fleiß und Accuratesse*).[115] The General Directory, he told his leading ministers, "should take on the ablest people wherever they may be found, [people] who understand finance and administration (*Wierdtschaft*) [and] have an open mind."[116] And, indeed, Frederick William I seems to have given little weight to social rank and family background in making appointments to royal office. In fact, most Prussian officials were of non-noble origin. Only 43 percent of those who occupied high-level office—a rank of War and Domains councillor or higher—had names containing the noble predicates *von* or *d,*'[117] and a great many of these had received their titles from Frederick William I or his father. Nor do family connections seem to have played a significant role in hiring and promotion. To be sure, there were a number of *Beamtensippen* or civil servants clans that produced leading officials across several generations. But nepotism in the strict sense was actually quite limited; less than 5 percent of those who achieved a rank of War and Domains councillor or higher appear to have been sons or nephews of other officials.[118] Talent and hard work, by contrast, could result in rapid promotion. George Wilhelm von Aschersleben, for example, began as a copyist for the General Directory in 1723, served as an apprentice (*Auscultator*) to the War and Domains Council in the Kurmark from 1724 to 1726, was promoted to the rank of War Commissar in 1726, and served in this capacity in Prussia until 1736, at which time he was appointed president of the War and Domain Council in Stettin.[119] One of his colleagues in the General Directory, Samuell von Marschall, experienced an even more meteoric rise. Over the course of two decades, he rose from a position in the mail room to a seat in the royal cabinet. More typical, perhaps, was the case of Bernhard Friedrich Becquer, the son of a Huguenot officer who fell in the war against France under Frederick I, was taken on as an apprentice by the War and Domains Council in Magdeburg following the completion of his studies at the University of Halle, and was promoted first to auditor of the treasuries (*Kassenrevisor*), then to War and Domains councillor.[120] Under Frederick William I, then, the Prussian civil service was truly a career open to talent.

Rationalization in state administration was accompanied by rationalization in state finance. This was particularly evident in the new auditing and control procedures introduced by Frederick William I.[121] They began at the provincial level, in the regional War and Domains chambers. Each chamber was responsible for drawing up its own annual budget. This budget was then presented to the chamber president, who reviewed it for accuracy, signed it, and forwarded it to Berlin, where it was reviewed once again by representatives of the General Directory and the Royal Accounting Office (*Ober Rechenkammer*). They were concerned not only with its numerical accuracy but with its legitimacy and its bottom line. Revenues and outlays had to be documented, and changes in them had to be justified, particularly if they involved decreases in revenues or increases in outlays. The latter required a royal signature; the former often resulted in a royal investigation. Once the ministers were satisfied, they signed the budget and forwarded it to the king, who reviewed it for a third time.

But the king was not content to rely solely on these procedural controls. He introduced other safety mechanisms as well. All financial officials were required to submit sizeable deposits (*Kautionen*)—often three or four times their annual salaries—before taking their office. In the event of suspected malfeasance, the deposits were retained and, if necessary, their personal property confiscated. In order to prevent connivance and collusion of any kind, Frederick William also stipulated that royal officials be employed outside their home provinces if possible.[122] In addition to these formal mechanisms, Frederick William I also maintained an informal network of spies and informers.[123] The most famous of these was the general auditor, Christoph von Katsch, who secretly monitored the internal workings of the General Directory—who was working hard and who was not, if there were intrigues among the ministers, and so on.[124] The king also recommended that his ministers in Berlin "maintain special correspondents in their [home] provinces, who inform them about everything that is going on."[125] Where money was involved, however, Frederick William I was not content to rely solely on the probity and loyalty of others. He not only spent long hours poring through papers and reports submitted by the various branches of the government but toured his kingdom regularly, a habit that earned him the epithet King of the Country Roads.[126]

Of course, even so industrious and activist a king as Frederick William I could not hope to uncover every act of negligence or corruption committed by his officials. But when he did discover one, it was punished swiftly and severely. The most (in)famous case of official malfeasance during Frederick William I's reign was undoubtedly that of Albrecht von Schlubhut, a War and Domains councillor in Königsberg, who was charged with embezzling 2,800 Reichsthalers from the royal treasury in Königsberg and extorting another 1,000 from officials under his supervision.[127] Citing the lack of hard evidence against Schlubhut, the royal prosecutor recommended six years of forced labor, a lenient sentence for that time. But the king balked. Since Schlubhut's property was worth less than the money he had allegedly stolen, argued the king, there was only one possible penalty: death. An even more gruesome fate was reserved for one of Schlubhut's colleagues, the Prussian *Landrentmeister* Adam Friedrich Hesse, after a discrepancy of 4,000 Reichsthalers was discovered in the royal accounts.[128] Pointing to various mitigating circumstances—the accounts, it seems, had not been checked since Hesse took over the office from his father over ten years ago—the royal prosecutor again requested a light sentence, which the king again rejected: in order to set an example, he ordered that Hesse be hanged with a string of lead coins. If the king's goal was to instill the fear of God into his officials, he evidently succeeded. When Andreas Titius, a tax collector in Brandenburg, was accused of defrauding the Crown several years later, he first sought to flee the country, and, following his capture and imprisonment, took his own life rather than await the final judgement of the king.[129] While acts of malfeasance particularly roused the king's ire, other forms of corruption were also punished severely. A military official in Potsdam, the *Ober-billetier* Hans Drave, was sentenced to six years of forced labor for trying to secure a second post in Berlin and enlisting one of the "tall grenadiers" to plead his case before the king.[130] Even simple negligence could have serious consequences. A royal engineer overseeing the construction of a new fortress in Wesel, for example, was brought to trial for exceeding his budget.[131] A postmaster who overslept was dismissed from office and evicted from his house.[132] The king's watchful eye even extended to the private sphere. When Frederick William I discovered that one of his ministers, Ludwig Otto Edler von Plotho, was keeping a mistress, he scolded him severely before the Privy Council; while there were no suspicious looking persons entering through the front door, the king is reported to have said, the back door was another matter.[133] Plotho's colleague, Ehrenreich Bogislav von Creutz, received an even more severe reprimand. When the king discovered that Creutz was sleeping with a young courtesan, a certain Fräulein Wagenitz, he accused him of neglecting his duties and immediately suspended him without pay. "I could have you sent to [the military prison in] Spandau," the king stormed, "but I will leave it at this."[134] Creutz later returned to his old post within the General Directory, but he never fully recovered Frederick William I's respect: "if it were not for his passions," the king later commented, "he could have become a very able financier."[135] Even those whose "passions" were less pronounced than Creutz's were sometimes made to feel the king's wrath. The state prosecutor (*General-Fiscal*), Johann Tobias Wagener, for example, was placed in stocks (*krumgeschlossen*) and then dismissed from office for slapping his wife.[136] During the 1720s, Frederick William I even tried to establish a formal system of moral surveillance; the directing ministers in the General Directory and the presidents of the provincial War and Domains boards were ordered to submit a special report to the king in which they reviewed the private and public conduct of all the officials under their supervision.[137]

The Effects: Administrative Efficiency in Longitudinal Perspective

Administrative centralization, meritocratic hiring and promotion, formal and informal surveillance mechanisms, severe and exemplary punishments—these were some of the strategies that Frederick William I used to encourage obedience, hard work, and probity within the royal bureaucracy. Which brings us to a crucial question: Did these measures actually increase the level of administrative efficiency in Brandenburg-Prussia? And if so, By how much?

Before addressing this question, we must be clear about what we mean by administrative efficiency. For the purposes of the present analysis, let us define it as the *ratio of administrative input to administrative output,* and let us further define input in terms of material and/or human resources and output in terms of coercion, extraction, and/or regulation. Under this definition, the administrative efficiency of any given state could be expressed as the ratio between (1) total administrative expenditures and/or personnel and (2) total troop strength, total tax revenues, and/or the overall level of social order.

With these definitions in mind, let us examine the evidence. It is not always as complete or exact as we might like. But it does reveal some important trends. Under Frederick I, total nonmilitary expenditure averaged slightly less than 2 million Reichsthalers per year.[138] Around 20–25 percent of these funds were consumed by the royal court.[139] Unfortunately, it is not clear how much of the remainder was consumed by state administration. What is clear is that total nonmilitary expenditure declined considerably under Frederick William I to an average of 1.17 million Reichsthalers per year.[140] Since this figure includes expenditures for the maintenance of the court (an average of 183,000 Reichsthalers per year), the purchase of new territories and domain lands (approximately 7 million Reichsthalers), the financing of public works (2 million Reichsthalers total), and the reconstruction and resettlement of plague-ravaged East Prussia (6 million Reichsthalers), it is also safe to assume that actual administrative expenditures would have been considerably lower than 1.17 million Reichsthalers.[141] If we subtract these expenditures from the total, we arrive at average administrative costs of 430,000 Reichsthalers per year. This result squares well with the calculations of Friedrich von Reden, which suggest total administrative costs of around 530,000 Reichsthalers for the final year of Frederick William's reign.[142] It also fits well with what we know about the salaries of Prussian administrators during this period, namely, that they were reduced quite drastically in 1713 and that they remained a good deal lower than salaries in other German principalities, particularly at the lower ranks, and were competitive at the upper ranks only insofar as one ignores emoluments of various sorts, which formed a rather considerable part of the total compensation packages for royal officials in Bavaria and Hannover.[143]

What about the second measure of administrative input, namely, administrative personnel? Drawing on various sources, it is possible to construct a rough estimate of the total number of royal officials for the final year of Frederick William I's reign. In that year, the various branches of central administration employed around 165 men.[144] The provincial administration probably employed another 700–900.[145] The number of local officials is somewhat more difficult to estimate because there is no comprehensive treatment.[146] Extrapolating from a regional study of Prussia, we arrive at a minimum figure of 600 officials total. Since there is one important category of subaltern not included in the study, the actual figure is probably higher, perhaps by as many as 200–300. If these calculations are correct, then the Prussian state would have employed somewhere between 1,200 and 1,400 officials in 1740.

How does this compare with earlier periods? It is not possible to answer this question with any great precision, given the present state of our knowledge—and of the archives.[147] But it seems very unlikely that the number of officials would have expanded much during Frederick William I's reign; in fact, it may have actually declined. Of course, the expansion of state activity during these years did generate demands for an expansion of the state apparatus, especially from the officials themselves. But Frederick William I was extremely resistant to these demands; indeed, he sought to shrink the number of officials by means of administrative centralization and reorganization. The ebb and flow of nonmilitary expenditure suggests the following pattern: a dramatic contraction of personnel in the early years of the reign (ca. 1713–16), an equally rapid expansion during the middle years (ca. 1717–27)—the years of "reconstruction" in East Prussia—followed by (re)contraction and equilibrium during the later years (ca. 1728–40).

If the foregoing analysis is correct, then total administrative input (that is, administrative expenditures and personnel) did not increase significantly during Frederick William I's reign and may have even declined. What about administrative output? Unfortunately, the evidence on regulatory output is scant at best and does not allow us to make precise statements or meaningful comparisons.[148] But if we conceive of output in military or fiscal terms, then it most certainly increased: the size of the army more than doubled, rising from 40,000 men to 83,000; total tax revenues increased from 2.5 million to 3.6 million Reichsthalers; and total domain revenues increased from 1.5 million to 3.3 million Reichsthalers.

Putting these various numbers together, it seems safe to conclude that administrative efficiency increased during the reign of Frederick William I, probably by a factor of two or three. In the next chapter, we will attempt to place these results in a comparative perspective. Before doing so, however, we must first finish the story of Prussia's disciplinary revolution.

Social Disciplining from Below: The Pietist Movement and Social Reform

Prussia's disciplinary revolution was primarily a revolution from above, led by the Crown. But it was buttressed by a revolution from below, sparked by the Pietist movement, an ascetic and reformist tendency within the Lutheran Church. Like English Puritanism and the Dutch "Further Reformation," by which it was heavily influenced, the (Lutheran) Pietist movement in Germany was a reaction against the consolidation of orthodoxy and the hairsplitting quarrels to which it had given rise. While the Pietists claimed to accept the basic tenets of Luther's teaching—*sola fide, sola gratia, sola scriptura*—they vehemently rejected the emphasis on pure doctrine that had become the hallmark of mainstream Lutheranism. They argued that the reformation of doctrine had not yet given rise to a reformation of life. Indeed, in their view, concern with right doctrine had actually hindered the Christianization of everyday life insofar as it led individual believers to focus on abstract principles rather than individual conduct. Faith, they argued, should bear fruits. In particular, it should give rise to an active love of one's neighbor (*tätige Nächstenliebe*) and to the rebirth of the individual believer—their transformation from a helpless slave of sin into a powerful instrument of divine will.

• • •

The most influential and outspoken representative of the Pietist standpoint during the late seventeenth century was undoubtedly Philipp Jacob Spener (1635–1705).[149] The son of a pious, Alsatian lawyer, Spener was exposed early on not only to Pietist authors but also to a variety of Puritan works. Later, as a young theology student, he attended the Lutheran University of Strasbourg as well as the Calvinist universities of Basel and Geneva. Shortly after completing his studies, Spener was appointed superintendent of the Lutheran Church in the city of Frankfurt am Main, a multiconfessional trading center with a large and powerful Calvinist refugee community. Spener's energy and abilities as an inter-Protestant conciliator, a preacher and pastor, and a social and religious reformer soon won him an avid following both within and without the city. His reputation grew even further, following the publication of the *Pia Desideria* (1675), a short and concise essay that transformed the vague and inchoate demands of the early Pietists into a modest but coherent program of religious reform, focusing on (1) the propagation of the Word, not only through simple and accessible sermons, but through the establishment of lay devotional circles (so-called conventicles or *ecclesiola in ecclesia*); (2) the restoration of the laity, and especially of the "third estate," to its proper place in ecclesiastical government as the foundation of a true "priesthood of all believers"; (3) the Christianization of everyday life through "active love of one's neighbor"; (4) the pursuit of reconciliation among all Christians by means of fervid but peaceful dialogue among the confessions; (5) a reform of pastoral education, emphasizing the practical side of the ministry—preaching and pastoral counseling; and (6) a return to simplicity in theology. If all these measures were implemented, concluded Spener, the result would be a "general conversion" followed by a "worldly flowering."

Ironically, however, it was not a Lutheran principality but a Calvinist one—Brandenburg-Prussia—that became the site of this Pietist "flowering." Spener's fame had grown steadily following the publication of the

Pia Desideria, and in 1685 he was appointed to the most prestigious and powerful post within the Lutheran churches of Germany: Superior Court Preacher at the Electoral Court of Saxony. But Spener's relations with the Court soured rapidly—he openly criticized the sin and depravity of the courtly lifestyle—and it soon became known that the elector of Saxony was anxious to be rid of him. Frederick I, meanwhile, was seeking to mend fences with the Lutheran Church in Brandenburg-Prussia, and his eye, not surprisingly, fell upon Spener, whom he offered a position as provost of the St. Nicolai Church, the oldest and largest in Berlin. Spener happily agreed, and in 1691 he took up residence in the Prussian capital where his doctrine of Christian activism (*tätiges Christentum*) and his tolerant stance towards Reformed Protestantism soon won him powerful and enthusiastic supporters within the court.[150] In fact, the enthusiasm for Spener was so great during the 1690s and early 1700s that his sermons at the St. Nicolai Church were regularly attended by members of the court, including the king himself.[151] Some prominent Calvinists even asked Spener to perform their funeral orations (*Leichenpredigten*).[152]

As a result of these connections, Spener was able to exert a level of political influence that far exceeded his official powers. This was evident, first of all, in the leading role he played in the poor-law reforms introduced by Frederick I during the 1690s.[153] The large influx of religious refugees during the 1680s had put enormous strains on the existing system, and in 1693 Frederick I established a committee to study the vagrancy problem.[154] Spener was one of its most outspoken members. He argued that most poor-relief was going to the wrong people—to "vagrants" and "sturdy beggars" rather than to the helpless and the infirm—and he recommended the creation of a central hospital, which would be responsible for distributing alms to the deserving and resocializing the undeserving.[155] Spener's recommendations were subsequently adopted, and in 1695 a new and comprehensive set of poor-laws was issued. Henceforth, all poor-relief funds were to be collected in a single treasury, the *Almosenkasse,* and administered by a central agency, the *Armenkommission.* All forms of social provision (and control), moreover, were to be distributed from one place, the royal Frederick's Hospital. The next decade witnessed further reforms of various kinds. To assure a steady stream of revenues, sin taxes were imposed on popular forms of entertainment (puppeteers, comedians, storytellers), a system of "voluntary" house-to-house collections was established within the city, and churches throughout Brandenburg were ordered to send in regular "donations." Gradually, a more functionally differentiated set of social institutions was established. Vagrants and "sturdy beggars" were banished or sent to the workhouse in Spandau, and the Frederick's Hospital evolved into an orphanage. But these were at most minor adjustments and improvements in the system established in 1695—a system that went back to Spener's recommendations of 1693.

Spener and the Pietists also played a central role in efforts to improve ecclesiastical discipline. In contrast to most of its sister churches in Germany, the Lutheran Church of Brandenburg had conserved the Catholic practice of auricular confession. What is more, parishioners in most congregations were required to pay a small fee to the minister—the so-called *Beichtpfennig*—before receiving absolution.[156] While this practice was somewhat controversial even among orthodox clergymen, it aroused particular anger among the Pietists. The *Beichtpfennig*, they charged, allowed affluent sinners to purchase absolution and prevented repentant paupers from taking communion.[157] Frederick I was sympathetic to their arguments, and in 1698 he did away with the *Beichtpfennig* and gave the church consistories the power to exclude the "unworthy" from communion.[158]

Another area in which Spener and the Pietists made their influence felt was in appointments to the clergy. Through his connections with the court and his position within the consistory, Spener was able to secure posts for his followers throughout Brandenburg-Prussia.[159] One of the first beneficiaries of Spener's patronage, and by far the most influential, was August Hermann Francke (1663–1727). A gifted scholar and energetic reformer, Francke had first come to Spener's attention while a student at the University of Leipzig, where he orchestrated a successful if short-lived revolt against orthodox members of the theological faculty, which included sit-down strikes and student-led seminars. Through Spener's efforts, he was appointed to a vacant parish in the town of Glaucha in 1692, and, shortly thereafter, to a professorship in near Eastern languages at the newly established University of Halle. Here, under the protecting hand of the Hohenzollerns, Francke was able to put his Pietist vision of religious and social reform into practice. He began modestly in early 1694 with the catechization of poor children from the steps of his back porch.[160] Then, in the spring of 1695, he established a small school for poor children. By the following year, he already had fifty–sixty students, and soon he decided to take in some of his pupils.[161] In order to care for his steadily growing brood, Francke hired a monitor (*Aufseher*), Georg Heinrich Neubauer (1666–1726), and engaged a dozen local theology students, who taught two hours a day in exchange for free meals at the orphanage.[162] He also decided to build a large addition on to the parsonage because there was no more room left in the little building that had been used to house the orphans.[163] Construction was completed in 1701. By this time, the orphanage was but one of several educational enterprises under Francke's supervision. The most important of these was the *Pädagogium,* a boarding and preparatory school that offered instruction in religion, languages, and the natural and human sciences for the scions of the powerful and well-to-do.[164] There was also a Latin school, which prepared burger children for university studies, several German schools, which gave lower-class children instruction in religion and the three Rs, and a *seminarium praeceptorum,* which prepared university students for teaching careers. Buoyed by a steady stream of donations and a series of royal privileges,[165] Francke continued to build and expand over the next several decades,[166] and at the time of his death in 1727, his schools had more than 2,000 students,[167] an astronomical figure by the standards of the day.

Diverse as their curricula were, however, Francke's institutes had one thing in common: their pedagogy. Francke's method, as he called it, diverged from prevailing practices in a variety of ways, such as its inclusion of practical subjects (*Realien*) like botany and home economics and its attention to the abilities and inclinations of individual students. But the most significant feature of Francke's method—at least from the standpoint of the present analysis—was its use of continual activity and uninterrupted supervision to instill and maintain Christian discipline. All of Francke's schools adhered to a strict, daily schedule. In the *Pädagogium* and the Latin school, the day began at dawn, when the children were roused for their early morning prayers.[168] After breakfast and a reading from the Bible, students filed off to their lessons, which generally lasted until midday. After lunch and an inspirational reading, they returned to classes until the late afternoon, at which time they were assembled for yet another round of religious exhortation, followed by the evening meal. The children even attended school on Sundays—before and after church. Their free time, such as it was, was also filled with activities of one kind or another, for Francke thought little of "childish games" that had no practical aim.[169] Evenings were often spent touring the school grounds or visiting Francke's natural history collection. On the weekends, children might learn various handicrafts, such as drafting and woodworking, or go on excursions—to a local craftsman, say, or to the orphanage, where a wooden model of the city of Jerusalem was on display.[170] Even breaks between classes were occupied with various activities, such as knitting socks and learning Bible stories,[171] and during dinner each night, one of the students read a chapter from the Bible and Luther's interpretation of it.[172] This continual flow of activity was complemented by a regime of uninterrupted supervision. Each student was assigned to a group room and each room was assigned to a particular teacher, who was personally responsible for monitoring the children during the morning and evening hours and reporting any misbehavior to the inspector.[173] The inspectors, in turn, met each week to discuss any problems. Students who violated the school code were punished according to a formal *gradus admonitonum*, which is reminiscent of the three steps of the Calvinist system: three warnings, followed by a verbal admonition, and, finally, by corporal punishment. Particularly flagrant or offensive acts could result in immediate expulsion.[174]

The intellectual development of the students was also carefully monitored. Teachers were required to submit a progress report on their classes each week, and examinations were held according to a rigorous schedule. Even on the spiritual level nothing was left to chance. Students were encouraged to keep a spiritual journal (*Seelenregister*) in which they detailed the course of their own conversion. And there was no escape from this unrelenting regime. Students were not allowed to leave the school compound except in the company of a teacher. School vacations were unknown.[175] Even visits home were discouraged; Francke felt they "upset" and "confused" the students.[176] By means of these measures, Francke argued, it was possible not only to prevent internal weakness (*innerliche Bosheit*) from breaking out, but also "to gradually weaken the inner desires and to unlearn the bad habits acquired through an improper upbringing."[177]

Naturally, Francke's method had its critics. The students themselves often complained about the "lack of freedom," the "hard treatment," "the lack of physical activity," even the "bad food," and some members of the faculty shared their sentiments.[178] A number of outside observers also questioned the efficacy of Francke's method.[179] Other writers compared the Franckean institutes to a *Tuchthuis*.[180] This charge, as it turns out, was not without foundation, for in the spring of 1696, while making plans for the new orphanage building, Francke consulted a book on the work- and poorhouses of Amsterdam,[181] and shortly thereafter, in June 1697, he dispatched his assistant, Georg Neubauer, on a fact-finding mission to Holland.[182]

Nonetheless, Francke's detractors seem to have been outnumbered by his supporters. "Not a day goes by," claimed the local postman, "where there's not more money sent to the orphanage."[183] Some pious well-wishers even sent in fine jewelry and gold embroidery,[184] so many, in fact, that Francke decided to set up a gold and silver refinery at the orphanage![185] The donations must have been quite considerable as well, for they were apparently sufficient to cover the running expenses for the orphanage, which were already over 100 Reichsthalers a week in 1698,[186] and to finance the numerous additions to the orphanage complex undertaken after 1700. Francke also received hundreds of letters from parents and guardians who wished to enroll their children in one of his schools. Indeed, competition for places in the *Pädagogium* was so keen, that Francke was often forced to turn down qualified applicants. Teachers trained in Halle were also in high demand. Graduates of the *seminarium selectorum praeceptorum* commanded a substantial premium on the job market,[187] and many left before completing their studies; they were continually being hired away as tutors and governors.[188]

By the 1720s, Halle had become the center of a "national" and, indeed, international movement of religious, social, and educational reform. Francke's writings rolled off the printing presses of the orphanage at a blistering pace—almost 500,000 copies of his various sermons and devotional tracts were sold just in the years between 1717 and 1723[189]—and Pietist conventicles sprang up in Lutheran churches throughout Brandenburg-Prussia.[190] Francke's students and disciples opened Halle-style schools and orphanages throughout the Hohenzollern lands.[191] In many cities, including Cleve, Berlin, Stettin, Königsberg and, of course, Halle itself, Reformed Protestants followed suit, reorganizing their schools along Franckean lines and starting orphanages of their own, and Francke's *seminarium praeceptorum* also found ready imitators.[192]

And, yet, this outpouring of reformist activity would hardly have been possible were it not for the protecting hand of the Prussian state. For the Pietist movement faced strong opposition right from the start, not only from the orthodox clergy, but, in many cases, from the territorial estates as well. Again and again Frederick I and his ministers were forced to intervene on behalf of Spener, Francke and their followers—in Cleve, in Stettin, in Königsberg, and in Halle itself.[193] Moreover, under Frederick William I, the Prussian state not only protected the Pietist movement but positively promoted it. Francke's students were given special preference in appointments to the ministry, and after 1736 all candidates for the clergy were required to study for at least two years at the University of Halle.[194] Pietist influence was also strong within the large and growing network of military chaplains (*Feldprediger*) who served the Prussian army. Pietists were also placed in leading positions throughout the Lutheran Church as theology professors, high school rectors, and church inspectors. Thus, the Lutheran clergy in Brandenburg-Prussia came to be dominated to an ever-increasing extent by Pietists and Pietist sympathizers.[195]

Frederick William I did not observe these developments passively, however. On the contrary, he actively participated in the process of religious, social and educational reform inspired by the Pietists. In 1717, for example, he sought to impose a system of Genevan, presbyterial discipline on all Protestant churches in Brandenburg-Prussia.[196] Several years later, in 1724, he established a Halle-style military orphanage in Potsdam that housed over 2,000 children. And during the early 1730s, he initiated a comprehensive program of reconstruction in plague-ravaged East Prussia, which included the construction of over 1,000 new schools, all organized (at least on paper) along Franckean lines.[197] He also tightened discipline within the *Joachimsthalsches Gymnasium,* a Reformed high school in Berlin, which was established to prepare future clergymen and civil servants for their university studies.[198] Thus, while the impetus for religious and social reform came primarily from the Pietist movement, it also received substantial and active support from the Prussian state.

It is sometimes claimed that the Pietist movement injected a new ethos into the Prussian state, and, more concretely, that Lutheran Pietists were heavily represented within the royal service.[199] I have not found any evidence to support this view.[200]

Conclusion

The central thesis of this chapter has been that the rise of Prussia cannot be adequately explained unless one takes account of religious factors. More specifically it has been argued (1) that the unusual autonomy of the Prussian state was the product of confessional conflict between the Lutheran estates and the Calvinist Crown and of the Calvinization of the royal administration that followed in its wake; and (2) that the extraordinary strength of the Prussian state was the product of a disciplinary revolution from above orchestrated by Frederick William I and, to a lesser degree, of a disciplinary revolution from below sparked by the Pietist movement.

This interpretation builds on previous accounts insofar as it focuses on conflict between crown and nobility, military competition and fiscal crisis, and Calvinism and Pietism, the mainstays of the materialist, bellicist, and idealist models. But it also diverges from previous work to the degree that it denies the existence of a compact or alliance between Crown and nobility; insists that the Prussian response to the military revolution was atypical; and locates the principal source of this atypicality in Calvinism rather than Pietism. It is not, and does not pretend to be, a "falsification" of previous studies; rather, it is a work of synthesis, which puts confessional cleavages and religious ethics back into political conflict and state development—and vice versa.

It would have been possible to extend this interpretation by including the reign of Frederick the Great (1740–88). One could then have shown how Frederick used his father's fiscal-military apparatus to enlarge the kingdom; how he reached out to the old (Lutheran) nobility and (re)integrated them into the army and the royal administration, albeit on his own terms; and how he secularized the Prussian political ethos by drawing on Stoicism and Enlightenment rationalism. But my argument did not require me to extend the argument in this way, and for brevity's sake I have chosen not to do so.

What my argument *does* require me to do is to place the Prussian case within a larger, comparative framework. And it is to that task that I now turn.

4
Social Disciplining in Comparative Perspective

In the preceding two chapters, I have tried to show two things: (1) that the Dutch and Prussian states were unusual in certain respects, the former mainly in terms of its regulatory power, the latter in terms of its administrative efficiency; and (2) that these peculiarities were at least partly the product of Calvinist-inspired religious, social, and political disciplining.

In the present chapter, I will address several broader issues that arise out of this analysis. The first regards the scope of the disciplining process. Was it specific to Calvinist-dominated polities, such as the Netherlands and Prussia? Or was it part of a more general development during the early modern period, a secular trend towards greater discipline? As will become clear below, I incline to the latter view. I believe that disciplining was a general feature of the confessional era. This is, by now, a relatively uncontroversial claim among early modern historians. The second issue concerns variations in the disciplining process, particularly variations across the confessions. Specifically, I ask how disciplining in Calvinist countries compared with disciplining in Lutheran and Calvinist countries. Was it more intense, less intense, or about equal? My conclusion, to anticipate, is that it was somewhat more intense. Because this claim is somewhat at odds with the prevailing wisdom among early modernists, I begin by reviewing some of the relevant arguments before presenting and defending my own.

The Debate about Discipline: Arguments and Evidence

Much of the debate about discipline has been focused, not on discipline in the broad sense, but on poor-relief. Until the early 1970s, most early modern historians agreed that there had been substantial differences between Protestant and Catholic forms of poor-relief and that the main source of these differences was theology, particularly Luther's (and Calvin's) stance towards the worldly calling (positive) and good works (negative).[1] By emphasizing work and deemphasizing works, the argument went, Protestantism engendered a fundamental shift in attitudes towards the poor and poor-relief: the poor, once apotheosized as incarnations of the Christ, were now demonized as the embodiment of vice—of criminality, debauchery and sloth—while poor-relief, once a form of Christian charity—and a means towards salvation—now became an aspect of social policy.

This interpretation was first challenged during the late nineteenth and early twentieth centuries by Catholic historians such as Franz Ehrle and Georg Ratzinger, who argued that the social reforms of the sixteenth century were originally initiated by "Catholic" cities such as Nuremberg and Ypres and had their roots in the pre-Reformation period.[2] Ehrle's and Ratzinger's writings provoked a pointed counterattack by Protestant historians such as G. Ulhorn and Otto Winckelmann, who argued—convincingly in my view—that the principal reformers in Nuremberg were Protestants or Protestant sympathizers and that the Ypres reforms were modeled directly after those undertaken in Nuremberg.[3] Their views became the dominant views, not only among mainstream historians of poor-relief, but also among prominent sociologists of religion, such as Max Weber and Ernst Troeltsch.[4]

During the late 1960s and early 1970s, however, the dominant view (now associated with the names of Weber and Troeltsch) came under attack once again, this time by secular historians of Catholic countries, such as Brian Pullan, Natalie Zemon Davis, and Jean-Pierre Gutton.[5] In his voluminous case study *Rich and Poor in Renaissance Venice*, for example, Brian Pullan argued that the reform of charitable institutions had begun long before the Reformation and that the resulting system had many typically Protestant features, including a sharp discrimination between the deserving and undeserving poor, a high degree of centralization and laicization, and the use of enclosure or indoor relief.[6] These conclusions were echoed in Gutton's and Davis's studies of another Catholic city: Lyon. There, too, social reform took a startlingly Protestant form and even enjoyed the support of some Catholic clergymen.[7] Writing in a somewhat more programmatic vein during the mid-1970s, Pullan proclaimed that "the Catholic and Protestant community showed an almost equally strong tendency to transform the wandering penniless stranger into the fearful and repulsive figure of the vagrant."[8] The real source of the changes, he concluded, was humanism, not Protestantism. Later studies of German and Spanish cities seemed to confirm these results,[9] and by the 1990s Pullan's view had become the dominant view.[10]

Historians of the poor were not the only ones to highlight the parallels between the Protestant and Catholic developments. A similar (though slightly later) movement can also be observed among Reformation historians (as we saw in chapter 1). Until the mid-1980s, standard accounts portrayed the Reformation as a battle between two opposing theologies, and their public spokesmen (Luther, Calvin, Loyola, and so on). And they assumed, at least implicitly, that differences in religious belief gave rise to two different forms of social organization, one modern (and Protestant), the other archaic (and Catholic). Beginning in the mid-1970s, however, this interpretation came under fire from Catholic historians such as Ernst Walter Zeeden and Wolfgang Reinhard, who argued that post-Tridentine Catholicism could also be seen as a modernizing force.[11] With the help of other historians, especially the Protestant historian Heinz Schilling, Reinhard gradually elaborated these arguments into a full-fledged research program, the so-called confessionalization paradigm, which emphasized similarities in the mechanisms (state/church cooperation) and outcomes (social disciplining) of the Protestant and Catholic Reformations.[12] While critical voices can now be heard, I think it would be fair to say that confessionalization is currently the dominant paradigm among Reformation historians.

Different as they are, all three of these interpretations are similar in at least one respect: they focus mainly on cultural and ideological factors (Protestantism, humanism, confessionalism). As one might expect, there are also other scholars who regard social and material factors as key. In his extensive writings on poverty, for example, Bronislaw Geremek has highlighted the connection between demographic crisis and social reform.[13] The introduction of new poor laws, he argues, often coincided with periods of famine and recession. Faced with wandering hordes of hungry peasants and dormant masses of idle workers, urban rulers were compelled to streamline and rationalize existing systems of poor-relief. Writing in a slightly different, but equally materialist vein, Catharina Lis and Hugo Soly have argued that the new poor laws were first and foremost an instrument of labor discipline, a product of the transition from feudalism to capitalism.[14] Of course, a discussion of the debate on social discipline would not be complete without a mention of the man who coined the term: Gerhard Oestreich. As we saw earlier, Oestreich conceived of social disciplining mainly as a princely project, a strategy for pacifying populations and harnessing them to the state.[15] His approach has obvious affinities with Norbert Elias's notion of the civilizing process, Marc Raeff's analyses of the well-ordered police state, and also with more recent work that portrays early modern social reform as a response of urban elites to the problem of social disorder and dislocation.[16] These approaches have been influential, but they have never attained a paradigmatic status of the sort enjoyed by their more culturally oriented rivals.

Surveying this debate, we can distinguish six basic models of social disciplining: (1) an ur-confessionalist model that emphasizes the role of religion and the distinctiveness of Protestantism; (2) an anticonfessionalist model that downplays the role of religion and emphasizes the impact of humanism; (3) a neoconfessionalist model that emphasizes the role of religion but downplays the distinctiveness of Protestantism; (4) a neo-Malthusian model that focuses on the catalytic role of famine and pestilence; (5) a neo-Marxist model that asserts a decisive role for economic factors; and (6) a neo-Machiavellian model that underlines the interests of political elites (see table 3). It should be emphasized that these models are not necessarily exclusive of one another. The neoconfessionalist model is partly inspired by the neo-Machiavellian model à la Oestreich. And the anticonfessionalist model is often found in tandem with the neo-Malthusian approach, and, more recently, with a neo-Machiavellian approach as well. It should also be noted that the various models differ not only with regard to the *explanans* (independent variable) but also with respect to the *explanandum* (dependent variable). That is, they are not only offering different explanations, but explaining different things. Four of the models (ur-confessionalist, anticonfessionalist, Malthusian, and Marxian) focus on social reform—the disciplining of the poor and the marginal, while the neoconfessionalists focus mainly on ecclesiastical discipline and the neo-Machiavellians on social disciplining in a broader and more inclusive sense.

Table 3 Social Disciplining in Early Modern Europe: The Models Compared

Model	Explanans	Explanandum	Period
Ur-Confessional	Protestantism	Poor-relief	ca. 1517–1555
Anticonfessional	Humanism	Poor-relief	ca. 1450–1550
Neoconfessional	Confessionalization	Religious discipline	ca. 1550–1648
Malthusian	Famine, epidemics	Poor-relief	ca. 1500–1800
Marxian	Labor discipline	Poor-relief	1500–present
Neo-Machiavellian	Political elites	Social discipline	ca. 1500–1800

As should now be clear, my position on these issues is somewhat unorthodox. Insofar as I insist on the importance of religion, I am at odds not only with the materialists but also with the anticonfessionalists. And insofar as I emphasize the distinctiveness of Calvinism, I am at loggerheads with the neoconfessionalists as well. Nor are my views identical to those of the ur-confessionalists either, insofar as I see differences not only between Protestants and Catholics but also between Lutherans and Calvinists.

My reasons for rejecting the existing models are of two sorts. The first concerns their theoretical and temporal scope. Five of the models focus on a single aspect of social disciplining, four of these focus only on poor-relief, and three of these focus only on a relatively short period of time (ca. 1450–ca. 1550). In my view, this is much too narrow a foundation on which to base any general conclusions about the early modern period as a whole. Insofar as possible, one should consider all aspects of the disciplining process (for example, religious, social, and political) across the entire period (ca. 1500–1750). Once we expand the scope of the analysis in this way, the impact of religion and the distinctiveness of Calvinism become quite clear—or so I will argue. My second criticism of the existing models concerns their empirical scope. Much of the work which has been done in this area, particularly on church discipline and poor-relief, has taken the form of case studies, usually of single cities or villages (for example, Venice and Lyon). This approach has much to recommend it, of course. But it is difficult—even dangerous—to generalize on the basis of a single case, no matter how confident we feel about our interpretation of that case. Is the case representative of its genre (for example, Catholic city, Lutheran principality), or is it atypical or an outlier? While it has pitfalls of its own, historical comparison provides a useful tool for addressing questions of this sort. Once we look at a larger number of cases in a comparative perspective, I believe that the impact of confession will become evident, especially in the areas of religious and political discipline, but also in the arenas of social and even military discipline. The organization of this chapter follows directly from the foregoing concerns. It begins with a discussion of religious discipline in the Lutheran, Catholic, and Calvinist contexts, moves on to the topic of social discipline, which is also treated comparatively, and concludes with a consideration of political discipline.

Having stated my argument in the broadest possible terms, let me now qualify it in two important ways. The first qualification has to do with the breadth of my claims. While I believe that religion was an important source of discipline in the early modern period, I certainly do *not* believe that it was the *only* source. In fact, I would even go so far as to say that *all* of the factors adduced in the six models outlined above probably played some role, as did a few that are not named (for example, the Neostoicist movement). My only contention at this point is that the importance of religion—and confession—are not sufficiently appreciated at the present moment. The second qualification has to do with the quality and interpretation of evidence; it is not as high or as easy as one might like. Some aspects of the disciplining process (for example, Calvinist ecclesiastical discipline) have been better researched than others (for example, Lutheran ecclesiastical discipline). Similarly, some effects of the disciplining process (for example, the degree of bureaucratization) are simpler to evaluate than others (the intensity of moral regulation). Thus, the arguments I present here are of a provisional nature; they are based on reinterpretations of existing evidence, rather than on the development of new evidence.

Ecclesiastical Discipline: Lutheran, Catholic, and Calvinist

Unlike Calvin, Luther initially harbored deep reservations about the use of ecclesiastical discipline. He placed his hopes for religious and social transformation in the power of the Word, and he argued that the task of enforcing God's laws should be left to the state rather than the church. There were others in the Protestant camp who felt differently, and Luther himself eventually concluded that church discipline was appropriate in some circumstances.[17] But he insisted that the power of excommunication remain in the hands of the clergy and rejected the view that laymen be given some role in church discipline.[18]

That is where Luther stood in principle. How did Lutheran discipline work in practice? Given the enormous number of Lutheran principalities and the relative paucity of detailed case-studies,[19] it is somewhat difficult to generalize. But two basic models seem to have been particularly common and influential.[20] In the first, which was pioneered by electoral Saxony and emulated by a number of east German territories, such as Prussia, authority over church discipline was centered in regional or territorial consistories.[21] Like their Calvinist counterparts, the Lutheran consistories began as marriage courts, included both lay and clerical members, and gradually assumed power, not only over ecclesiastical discipline, but also over church visitations, book censure, and the day-to-day administration of the church. Unlike the Calvinist consistories, however, the Lutheran bodies were usually centralized bodies under the direct supervision of the sovereign. It seems unlikely that a system of this sort would have been very effective at the local level, and the evidence that we have regarding church discipline in states such as Saxony appears to confirm this; it suggests widespread "ignorance" and "sinfulness."[22] Only in those places where parish clergy and village elites cooperated with one another does this system seem to have been effective.[23]

In the second pattern, typified by Württemberg and found in several other parts of northern and western Germany as well as in Sweden and Finland, authority over church discipline was centered in regional visitation committees.[24] Like the consistories, these committees included both clerical and lay members and accumulated wide-ranging powers over doctrine and liturgy and slowly evolved into a part of the royal administration.[25] Unlike them, however, they do seem to have exercised somewhat more regular and intensive control over the local population, at least in Württemberg and Sweden.[26]

There were also other, less common variants of Lutheran discipline. In Hessia, a Calvinist-style presbyterian system was put into place.[27] Württemberg also established a presbyterian system, though not until the mid-seventeenth century.[28] In Hohenlohe, a small principality near Württemberg, the parish clergy were given the power to impose the ban.[29] The city of Magdeburg had a similar system.[30] And, in a few other cases, such as Strasbourg, proto-Erastian systems of discipline were established in which urban patricians had full or partial authority over use of the ban.[31] These systems also seem to have been very effective.[32]

On balance, then, the existing evidence suggests that the Lutheran system of church discipline was probably more intensive than was previously realized, though probably not as intensive, overall, as the Calvinist system. For while a good many large and influential Lutheran states lacked a locally embedded system of church discipline (for example, Saxony and Denmark), only a few Calvinist polities did. And it is interesting to note: (1) that most of the Lutheran states which had more intensive forms of church discipline, were concentrated in southwest Germany, an area far from Wittenberg and close to Geneva, both geographically and theologically; (2) that all of these states, Sweden included, had large and/or influential Calvinist minorities during the second half of the sixteenth century and that some of them, such as Hessia-Cassel and Magdeburg, were eventually swept up into Germany's "Second Reformation"; and (3) that only one of these states, Hessia, established its system of communal discipline prior to 1542, the year in which Calvin published his ecclesiastical ordinances in Geneva. In other words, there are good reasons for believing that their efforts to impose a more stringent form of religious discipline were at least partially inspired by the Calvinist example.

• • •

The Catholic reformation did not produce anything quite like the Calvinist consistory. But it did produce disciplinary mechanisms of other kinds. The most famous—and infamous—of these was the Spanish Inquisition. The Spanish Inquisition went through several phases of development. It was established during the late fifteenth century to ferret out *conversos*, Jews who had formally converted to Christianity but were reputed to practice their traditional faith in secret. During the early sixteenth century, it shifted its sights towards the "Lutherans," that is, towards Protestants and Protestant sympathizers. All of this is well-known.[33] Less well-known, until recently, is a third shift that occurred around the time of the Tridentine Decrees.[34] During this period, the Inquisitors turned their attentions to the beliefs and behaviors of the Catholic population, itself. Of the nearly 44,000 cases brought before the Inquisition between 1540 and 1700 in the kingdoms of Aragon and Castile, the core areas of the Spanish monarchy, fully one-quarter involved doctrinal or moral errors on the part of professed Catholics, and over one-quarter of these cases (more than 7 percent of the total) involved sexual offenses (that is, bigamy and solicitation).[35]

While some scholars have focused on what the Inquisition did, others have examined how it worked.[36] One of the most important findings that emerges from these studies, regards the role of the *familiares*, local informers who served as the eyes and ears of the inquisitors in exchange for certain legal and fiscal privileges. While no one has as yet attempted a global census, the existing evidence suggests that an average of about 1,000 *familiares* for each of the fourteen tribunals for a total of 14,000.[37] If we assume a total population of 7–8 million, this yields a ratio of 1 *familiare* for each 500–600 people. And since the *familiares* were disproportionately concentrated in the larger cities and along the coastline, the ratios in these areas would have been even higher. Obviously, the old image of the Inquisition as a top-down clerical campaign needs to be modified.

The activities of the Inquisition on the Italian peninsula are not as well known. Only three areas have been thoroughly studied: Venice, Naples, and the Friuli. At first glance, it is the contrasts that are most striking. The Italian tribunals seem to have been somewhat less concerned with sexual and moral offenses and a good deal more concerned with witchcraft and magic. While extramarital sex between laypersons accounted for nearly 6 percent of the cases that came before the Spanish Inquisition, it accounted for less than 1 percent of all cases in Venice and the Friuli.[38] By contrast, trials involving witchcraft and magic made up nearly one-third of the total caseload in each of the three tribunals. But these numbers are actually somewhat misleading.

Sexual offenses actually made up 16 percent of all cases which came before the Neapolitan inquisitors, and the numbers would probably have been similar in Venice had it not been for the existence of a special secular court, known as the Antiblasphemy Commission (*Essecutori contro la bestemmia*), which handled many cases of this kind. Similarly, the number of witchcraft trials would have been much higher in Spain had it not been for the intervention of one particularly scrupulous inquisitor, who dismissed dozens of cases on cause.[39] In all probability, then, the interests and agendas of the Spanish and Italian Inquisitors and their lay supporters were probably very similar; heresy was always their paramount concern, but after 1560 or so morality was a close second.[40]

The Inquisition had little impact outside of the Iberian and Italian peninsulas. But the Catholic Church also had other instruments of discipline. One was the sacrament of confession. The post-Tridentine church encouraged laypeople to confess—and commune—more frequently,[41] and some theologians argued that the confessor should inspire—and demand—remorse and repentance before pronouncing absolution. It is impossible to know how many confessors actually did so, though it is clear that frequent communion and confession were encouraged, not only by the parish clergy, but by missionary and preaching orders such as the Jesuits and the Franciscans.[42] Confraternities were another source of discipline. These lay brotherhoods were hardly new; in some parts of Europe, they had existed since at least the twelfth century.[43] But the post-Tridentine era witnessed a revival and transformation of the confraternal tradition; old confraternities were reformed, and new ones were founded.[44] The penitential confraternities established by many reformist bishops placed special emphasis on lay discipline, as did the Marian sodalities founded by the Society of Jesus.[45] And since all confraternities placed emphasis on communal harmony, they sometimes became involved in mediating conflicts and disputes among their members.

In some instances, the clerical hierarchy was also involved in attempts to discipline the laity. Post-Tridentine bishops were strongly encouraged to tour their parishes on a regular basis.[46] The principal target of these visitations was the parish clergy. But some bishops also met with local parishioners in order to address troubles and scandals within particular communities. And in some places the old diaconal courts continued to play a role in policing popular morality and mediating social conflict.[47]

Taken together, these various mechanisms constituted a formidable machine for the inculcation of religious discipline, more formidable, in all likelihood, than the disciplinary machinery originally produced by the Lutheran Reformation.

But how does Catholic discipline compare with Reformed discipline? Was it more intense or less intense? Obviously, this is a difficult question to answer. But there are reasons for believing that Calvinist discipline was more intensive—reasons of scope, focus, and duration.

Take the geographical scope of the Inquisition. It was effectively limited to the Iberian and Italian Peninsulas. The countries of western and central Europe—which is to say, the majority of the Catholic population—remained virtually untouched. A similar point could be made about the sociological scope of the religious confraternities. Since their memberships consisted almost entirely of middle- and upper-class men, they had little (direct) impact on women or the poor. In the Reformed world, by contrast, church discipline was much more comprehensive, both geographically and socially. Almost every Reformed polity had some form of locally embedded communal discipline to which all church members were subject. Church councils, kirk sessions, consistories, presbyteries, choir- and marriage-courts—the names were different, but the structures and procedures were similar; laymen and clerics sat together to monitor and judge the morals and beliefs of their peers.

The focus of the two systems of discipline also seems to have been different. In both Spain and Italy, the inquisitors focused the bulk of their attentions on heresy, blasphemy, and witchcraft. Moral offenses, such as bigamy and solicitation, generally accounted for less than 15 percent of all cases and never for more than 20 percent.[48] Interestingly enough, the cases that came before the Archdiaconal Court (*Sendgericht*) of Munster display a similar distribution.[49] By contrast, the Calvinist consistories and their Reformed analogues focused very little attention on heresy, blasphemy, and witchcraft. Less than 15 percent of the cases that came before the Amsterdam consistory between 1578 and 1700 involved doctrine or witchcraft.[50] The same is true of Delft and Emden.[51] And in Scotland the numbers were even lower.[52] The bulk of the cases concerned social behavior of one sort or another: fornication, assault, drunkenness, bankruptcy, and so on.[53]

While the evidence on this score is not as complete as we might like, there also appear to have been differences in the duration of the disciplinary campaigns. In Emden and Amsterdam, at least, the number of disciplinary cases heard by the Reformed consistories does not seem to have declined in any lasting way until at least the late seventeenth century. Much the same can be said of the tribunals of the Roman Inquisition, but not of their Spanish counterparts. There, the number of cases dropped precipitously between 1610 and 1620 and had slowed to a trickle by century's end. By the eighteenth century, the Spanish Inquisition had essentially ceased to operate.

Of course, these differences in scope, focus, and duration might not have translated into differences in intensity; in fact, they may not have had much impact on behavior at all. But that is not what the evidence suggests. The Calvinist societies of early modern Europe really do seem to have been more disciplined and orderly than their Catholic counterparts. As we saw in chapter 2, illegitimacy rates varied substantially from one part of early modern Europe to the next. What is striking about the variations is the degree to which they line up with confession; illegitimacy rates seem to have been significantly lower in Calvinist-dominated societies such as the Netherlands, England, and Scotland than in Catholic societies such as Spain, France, and Italy. This suggests that rates of premarital sexuality were lower and/or that rates of postconceptual nuptiality were higher. And it suggests that sexual and marital norms were more strictly observed and/or enforced. The evidence on criminality points to a similar conclusion.

But this conclusion evokes a question: why was Reformed discipline more effective? There are several possible answers. One has to do with its organization. There is a growing body of research that suggests that communally organized systems of church discipline were more effective than hierarchically organized ones; they have more eyes and a steadier gaze.[54] Needless to say, one can find elements of hierarchy within the Reformed system (for example, in the Calvinist system of consistories, classes, and synods) and elements of communalism in the Catholic and Lutheran systems (for example, in Catholic confraternities or Lutheran marriages courts). Still, it seems fair to say that Reformed systems were generally closer to the communal end of the spectrum than were Catholic and Lutheran ones. There is also another possible explanation for the peculiar intensity of Reformed discipline, one which has to do, not with organization, but with theology and, more specifically, with Calvin's soteriology and ecclesiology. For Calvin and his followers, the justification of the individual believer was a gradual process in which the old Adam died, and a new Adam was reborn. This process of conversion or rebirth was marked by growing conformity of the believer's actions to biblical law, that is, by increasing self-discipline.[55] From a Calvinist perspective, however, self-discipline was actually less important than communal discipline. For no amount of private self-discipline could alter God's eternal decree regarding an individual's spiritual fate, but the presence of an unrepentant public sinner at the communion table could sully the city on the hill and provoke God's holy wrath. It is for this reason that Calvin urged his followers to look, not only within their own souls, but also into the hearts—and houses—of their brothers and sisters. Of course, one can find analogous beliefs outside the Calvinist fold, especially in the Pietist and Puritan movements and sects of the seventeenth and eighteenth centuries, but neither Lutheranism and nor post-Tridentine Catholicism drew such tight links between individual and congregational discipline on the one hand and salvation and communal well-being on the other. Needless to say, these two explanations need not be exclusive of one another. One could argue that varying conceptions of conversion and community pushed religious institution builders towards varying systems of church discipline, some of which had greater effects on social behavior than others.

Did they also push social reformers towards varying systems of poor-relief? That is the question to which I now turn.

Social Discipline: Religion, the Reformation, and the Restructuring of Poor-Relief

The answer that most historians would give to this question is that they did not. Today, the dominant view is that there were no significant differences in the principles and practices of Protestant and Catholic poor-relief, and that the reforms themselves were due, not to the Reformation or to religion more generally, but to hunger or humanism or some combination of the two. Are they correct? Let us examine the evidence more closely, beginning, once again, with the Lutheran case.

In many regards, Luther's views on poverty and poor-relief did simply echo those set forth by various Catholic reformers and humanist scholars during the fifteenth and early sixteenth centuries.[56] Like Kaysersberg, Erasmus, and others,[57] Luther believed that no one "should live in idleness off another's labor";[58] that "there should be no begging among Christians";[59] and that the administration of poor-relief should be turned over to the secular authorities.[60] In some regards, however, Luther's views diverged quite sharply from those of the Catholic and humanist reformers.[61] For, unlike them, he believed that the prohibition on begging should be extended to the regular clergy and that the enormous wealth of the mendicant orders and religious brotherhoods should be used to support the poor.[62] Clearly, this is an argument that few Catholic loyalists were willing to accept, and it would be mistaken to see it simply as a more pragmatic or developed version of the Catholic or humanist program. For Luther's views on poor-relief were rooted in his understanding of grace, which is precisely what set his theology apart from that of the Catholic Church. Because the believer is justified by faith rather than works, Luther argued, living in poverty (whether genuine or self-imposed) does not represent a mark of grace and providing succor to the poor does not and cannot increase one's store in heaven. Hence, the church's glorification of the poor and propertylessness and its vast machinery of mendicancy and charity were without scriptural brief or salvational significance and could and should be abolished and eliminated. However much they may have sympathized with Luther's positions, few Catholics would have been willing to go this far. Indeed, the position that lay and religious leaders staked out on these questions was probably one of the factors which influenced their allegiances in the confessional struggles of the sixteenth century.

So there *were* certainly differences in principles, even if they were not as sharp as some ur-confessionalists once claimed. Were there also differences in practice?

Luther first attempted to translate his program into reality in the Order for a Common Purse (*Beutelordnung*) which he drafted for the City of Wittenberg sometime in late 1520 or early 1521.[63] It called, among other things, for the establishment of weekly collections for the poor; the establishment of a "common chest" where donations would be stored; and routine visitations to those receiving alms. While the *Beutelordnung* was never published, many of its provisions were included in the Order for a Common Chest (*Kastenordnung*) written by Luther's right-hand man, Andreas Bodenstein (a.k.a. Karlstadt) and formed part of the Wittenberg church ordinances of 1522.[64] In 1523, a similar ordinance was passed by the city of Leisnig, this time with Luther's full cooperation and approval.[65] Like the previous ordinances, it stipulated the construction of a common chest where relief funds were to be kept. But it differed from them in that it explicitly forbade begging by mendicant clergy, drew a clear line between vagabonds and foreign beggars, on the one hand, and the shame-faced and deserving poor (that is, the young, the old, and the sick), imposed a quarterly poor-rate on local residents, both householders and servants, and secularized incomes and properties belonging to the various religious and charitable institutions in the city. It was the Lesnig ordinances, rather than the Wittenberg Ordinances, that Luther recommended as a model to his followers and that subsequently served as the basis for poor-relief reform throughout electoral Saxony.[66]

Another important center of reform was the city of Nuremberg, which introduced a comprehensive new poor law in 1522.[67] The city fathers had been trying to reshape the existing system for centuries. They had first attempted to regulate begging in the late fourteenth century and had strengthened the existing prohibitions as recently as 1521.[68] The poor law of 1522, however, went beyond the previous legislations in a number of respects: it fully "secularized" control over the administration of poor-relief, placing it in the hands of twelve lay administrators (*Armen-Pfleger*), who were assisted by four servants (*Knechte* or *Bettel-Vögte*), one for each quarter of the city; and it required all those desiring alms to submit to a formal examination before the *Armen-Pfleger* regarding their need and eligibility, which was then checked by the *Bettel-Vögte* and required them, if their request were approved, to wear a special badge issued by the city, thus easing the job of official surveillance.[69] While the ordinance was not written by Luther, it was clearly inspired by him. This is evident both from the preamble, which argues that charity should be based on the imperative of brotherly love (rather than the doctrine of good works), and from some of its special provisions, which were lifted directly from the Wittenberg ordinances of 1522.[70]

The Nuremberg legislation soon inspired reforms in a number of other Lower and west German cities. The Strasbourg ordinances of 1523, for example, were closely modeled on the Nuremberg laws.[71] They placed control over poor-relief in the hands of the town council and other secular officials and required that alms seekers submit to regular interviews, the first of which was carried out in April 1523.[72] The new poor laws enacted by the Flemish city of Ypres in 1525 were also closely modeled on the Nuremberg ordinances.[73] They called for the secularization of church properties and poor-relief administration and the institution of strict eligibility criteria and regular visitations.[74] But the two laws diverged in one important—and highly-instructive—regard: in Ypres, the prohibition on begging was not extended to the regular clergy and, indeed, the mendicant orders were permitted to continue their regular collections, for Ypres, unlike Nuremberg and Strasbourg, was still firmly under Catholic control. The local clergy, however, was not satisfied with this arrangement and sought to undermine the prohibition on begging by distributing alms on its own. The city eventually appealed to the theological faculty of the Sorbonne, which issued a statement supporting the limitations on begging. But without the support of the clergy the magistrate was never able to implement the new poor laws to its complete satisfaction. An interesting contrast is provided by the city of Frankfurt am Main, a Protestant city subject to Imperial authority.[75] Afraid of offending the emperor, the city council never officially passed a new set of poor laws, though it discussed doing so as early as 1523.[76] However, it did establish a common chest, expand its control over church incomes, and clamp down on begging and institute new eligibility criteria. In short, it reformed poor-relief without changing the poor laws. The connection between Protestantism and poor-relief, then, was both direct and indirect;

while Luther's teachings provided a theological brief for secularizing and rationalizing relief—something urban magistrates had been attempting for decades and even centuries—Lutheran reforms swept away the main obstacle to serious change—the mendicant orders, the lay confraternities; and their theological supporters.

Beginning in the late 1520s, the process of reform moved to the territorial level. One of the first German princes to seize the initiative was Philip of Hessia, who ordered the establishment of common chests throughout Hessia in 1527,[77] followed by a directive specifying "how the administrators of the common chests should perform their offices" in 1530.[78] In effect, the two directives required that every city and village reform its system of poor-relief along Lutheran lines. Not surprisingly, some local magistrates failed to carry out the law to its letter. While they were only too happy to take control over church properties, they were wont to spend the new funds on church construction or public works rather than on alms for the poor.[79] But Philip reacted quickly, sending his trusted advisors, Adam Krafft and Heinrich von Lütern on a series of local visitations to ensure compliance with the laws.[80] Over the next decade, control over the day-to-day administration of local poor-relief was gradually shifted towards the Lutheran deacons, who could be more easily supervised and controlled by the church visitors and the territorial bureaucracy, and in 1566 the collection, distribution, and administration of alms was made an official part of the deacons' duties.[81]

In Württemberg, the reform process began somewhat later. The duchy had fallen under the control of the Habsburgs in 1519, and Protestantism was not introduced until 1534 when the dukes were returned to power.[82] The first *Kastenordnung* was promulgated two years later, in March 1536.[83] It was based on the Hessian *Kastenordnungen* of 1530 and 1533 and the Habsburg antivagrant ordinance of 1531.[84] Like other Lutheran *Kastenordnungen,* it prohibited all begging and stipulated that local church property be unified into a single, common chest under the oversight of the local magistrate. Duke Ulrich also turned various church buildings over to the local *Armenmeister,* and the sale of these properties generated considerable revenue for the *Armenkasten*—almost 5,000 guilders in Stuttgart, for example.[85] And in 1551, his son Duke Christoph channeled the income of various prebends, cloisters, and beguineries into a territorial church fund (*Kirchengut*), which was used to pay for church repairs and provide subsidies to the *Armenkasten.*[86] In this way, civic poor-relief was placed on a solid financial footing. Since much of the population initially remained loyal to the old faith, there was naturally some resistance to the new *Kastenordnung.* But by stripping the Catholic clergy of their prebends, forbidding the monasteries from taking in new recruits, and seizing the properties of the lay brotherhoods, Duke Ulrich had frightened away the most determined opponents of reform, and by 1540 most cities were in compliance with the new law.[87] The *Kastenordnung* brought changes, not only in who controlled relief funds, but in who received them and how they were distributed. During a typical year in Stuttgart, for example, somewhere around half of the money was used to clothe and educate orphan children, another third was dispensed to the shame-faced poor (*hausarme Leute*), while only about 5 percent was given to foreigners and travelers.[88] Relief, which generally consisted of bread and a small cash allowance, was distributed, not by the clergy, but by lay deacons or *Almosenpfleger,* usually on Sundays, and could be denied to anyone suspected of drinking, whoring, or other forms of immorality.[89]

Thus, by the mid-sixteenth century, the three lead states of the German Reformation (Saxony, Hessia, and Württemberg) had implemented territorial-level reforms. And by the late sixteenth century, Lutheran princes all over Germany were asserting control over poor-relief as part of their general police powers.[90] This represented an extraordinary degree of laicization and centralization in the field of social provision.

• • •

The systems of poor-relief that took shape in the Reformed societies of western Europe were very similar to those which emerged in Lutheran Germany and Scandinavia. Laicization of control, centralization of organization, discrimination between the deserving and the undeserving—these were common trends that cut across the confessional divide. But there were differences as well, both inter- and intraconfessional. Let us begin with the latter. At one end of the spectrum is the Dutch system. Comparatively speaking, it displayed a relatively low degree of laicization and centralization. There were a few cities where relief funds were placed in a common chest controlled by the magistrate, Leiden being the best-known example. And there were also a few where relief funds for the entire city were placed under the control of the Reformed deacons, who dispensed them to needy residents, regardless of confession; here, Dort provides a good example. But Leiden and Dort were the exceptions. In most cities, poor-relief was provided by a variety of funds and institutions. These included civic relief agencies (for example, Almoners, Masters of the Holy Spirit), Reformed diaconates and their non-Calvinist analogues (Baptist, Catholic, Lutheran, Jewish), and specialized institutions aimed at particular populations (for example, orphanages, workhouses, hospitals, guesthouses, homes for the aged). The people who governed these institutions were invariably laypeople and usually members of the patriciate. But they were not necessarily representatives of the city magistrate. England represents the other end of the spectrum.[91] It displayed a far greater degree of laicization and centralization. There, poor-relief was dispensed and controlled by the state. It was established by an act of parliament, administered by state officials (the local J.P.s and their hired hands), and funded through taxes (the parish poor rates). These were the basic principles, and by the seventeenth century this was also the practice in most places. The cities of Switzerland and southwest Germany—the birthplace of Reformed Protestantism—fall somewhere between these two extremes. They usually had a single institution or fund (for example, the General Hospital of Geneva) that was controlled by lay officers of the church.[92] On average, then, the Reformed systems were probably less centralized and definitely less laicized than their Lutheran analogues. In Reformed polities, control over poor-relief was sometimes decentralized, not only in fact, but in principle as well, the most notable example being the Netherlands. I do not know of any Lutheran polities where this was the case. Similarly, in Reformed polities poor-relief officials were usually lay officials of the church; in Lutheran polities, by contrast, they were usually representatives of the state. No doubt, the reasons for these variations were legion and often very specific. Insofar as they were general in scope and religious in character, however, they had to do with Calvin's conviction that poor-relief was a part of the church's ministry and with the diaconal system which flowed from that conviction.[93]

There is one other feature of the Reformed system that bears notice: its focus on disciplining and reforming the poor. As we saw in chapter 3, the Amsterdam *Tuchthuis* was the first house of correction on the Continent. It was not, however, the first house of correction in Europe. That honor, if it is one, must go to London's Bridewell Hospital, which was transformed into a "workhouse" in 1557.[94] The driving force behind the new "house of occupations" was a group of merchants and tradesmen with strongly Protestant views.[95] Their goal, as it took shape in the early 1550s, was to establish a comprehensive system of civic hospitals that would cater to the varying categories of the poor: those who were poor "by impotence" (the fatherless, aged, blind, and lame); "by casualty" ("wounded soldiers," "decayed householders," and those "visited by disease"); and those who were poor by "thriftelessness" (the "rioter that consumeth all," the "vagabond that will abide in no place" and the "ydel person, as strumpet and other").[96] Bridewell catered to the latter group. During the early years of its existence, thousands of vagrants, beggars and ne'er-do-wells passed through the hospital's gates, where they were forced to grind corn, fashion nails, or spin thread as part of a program of moral and spiritual reform.[97] Later in the century, the ranks of the hospital's inmates swelled to include bigamists, adulteresses, and religious dissenters, and the number of occupations practiced within Bridewell grew to some twenty-four.[98] The example of London soon inspired a host of imitators. Several towns established Bridewells during the 1560s.[99] In 1576, Parliament ordered that houses of correction be established in every English county. And by 1630 there was a Bridewell in every English county for which records remain.[100] As in London, the driving force behind these reforms was usually a godly alliance between reformist magistrates and precisionist clergymen.[101] Of course, England and the Netherlands were not the only countries to build houses of correction. The Lutheran cities of northern Germany followed suit during the early seventeenth century, and by the beginning of the eighteenth century houses of correction could be found throughout Europe. Still, the fact that English and Dutch reformers "discovered" the workhouse independently of one another is very striking indeed. One could interpret it as mere coincidence. Or one could see it as symptomatic—of a stronger will to discipline the unruly, a weaker will to defend the poor, of a harsh view of the indigent and an optimistic attitude towards reform.

• • •

Were these changes in ideology and policy rooted in, and specific to, Protestantism? As we have seen, most historians once believed that they were. [102] They argued that there was a radical break between medieval and modern systems of relief and that the chief catalyst for this break was the Reformation. In recent years, however, a growing number of historians have argued that they were not.[103] The opening salvo in this attack was fired by Natalie Z. Davis in her seminal article on the *Aumône générale* of Lyon.[104] First established by the municipal authorities in 1531 in response to a period of famine, epidemic, and unrest, the *Aumône*'s task was to aid the deserving poor—and police the undeserving. It distributed bread, policed the streets, and aided young orphans. All in all, the *Aumône* looked very much like the agencies established in many Protestant cities. But the *Aumône*'s backers were not all Protestants. They included a number Catholic laymen and even a few Catholic clergymen. The common denominator among these men, argues Davis, was not Protestantism but humanism. And the thing that spurred them to action was not ideology but crisis—the presence of starving and plague-stricken beggars on the city's streets.

The next shot was fired by Brian Pullan in his equally influential study of *Rich and Poor in Renaissance Venice*.[105] At first glance, Venice would appear to confirm the stereotype of Catholic charity, rather than to challenge it. Poor-relief there was distributed through a dizzying array of institutions (for example, hospitals, confraternities, and local parishes), most of which were officially religious in character. But as Pullan shows, it is important to look below the surface. For many of these agencies and institutions were supervised or controlled by the city government either directly or indirectly. This allowed the city rulers to coordinate the actions of the various institutions and to orchestrate targeted relief efforts in times of crisis. Thus, the Venetian system was actually more centralized and laicized than it seemed. It was also more discriminate than one might imagine. Parish priests and religious confraternities often channelled their funds towards those they deemed especially pious or deserving. What is more, all of these processes—laicization, centralization, and discrimination—can be traced back to at least the late fifteenth century. Pullan concludes that the real driving forces behind social reform were economic crisis and civic humanism; religion was not a factor. The work of Davis and Pullan has inspired many imitators, and their conclusions have been echoed in case studies of many other Catholic cities, not only in Italy and France, but also in Spain and Germany.

Based on this evidence, it seems safe to conclude that early modern social reform was not a purely Protestant affair, that its causes were not solely religious in character, and that its onset antedated the Reformation. Can we also conclude that there were no important differences between Catholic and Protestant approaches to the poor? And that religion and the Reformation had no significant effects on the reform process? While a few dissenting voices can now be heard,[106] most early modern historians would probably answer "yes" to both questions. I am not so sure they are justified in doing so.

Like their Protestant counterparts, Catholic systems of poor-relief display a wide range of variation. At one end of the spectrum, we find French cities such as Lyon, Paris, Rouen, Grenoble, and Lille, where we observe very high degrees of centralization, laicization, and discrimination.[107] During the middle decades of the sixteenth century, responsibility for poor-relief in all of these cities, and in many other parts of France as well, was placed in the hands of a municipal agency and funded at least partly through "voluntary" taxes.[108] This rationalization and secularization of social provision was almost always accompanied by aggressive campaigns to expel foreign beggars and put the able-bodied to work, usually on public works projects, such as road construction. Experiments with enclosure inspired by the Amsterdam *Tuchthuis* can be observed in a few cities during the early seventeenth century, but the enclosure movement or *grand renfermement* did not really take off until the establishment of the *Hôpital général* in Paris in 1656.[109] On the other end of the spectrum, we find the kingdom of Castille in Spain.[110] Castile was by no means immune to reform. A number of Castilian cities promulgated new poor laws during the 1540s. Many local hospitals were amalgamated during the 1580s. And various schemes for enclosing the poor were set forth during the 1590s and early 1600s. But the Castilian reforms were not as thoroughgoing or as successful as the French reforms. While the Castilian poor laws did prohibit begging by foreigners, they did not prohibit begging as such. Neither did Pérez de Herrera's proposal for a network of shelters for the poor. On the contrary, it presumed that residents would feed themselves by collecting alms! Nonetheless, it was never realized. Meanwhile, the campaign to centralize local hospitals stalled out in the 1590s and was even reversed in some places. In Castile, then, we observe a very low degree of centralization, laicization, and discrimination. Indeed, of the various systems considered so far, Castile's seems to come closest to the hoary stereotype of "medieval charity" propagated by Protestant apologists.

One must be especially cautious in generalizing about the Italian case. Because of its political fragmentation, the Italian peninsula displays even greater internal variation than France or Spain.[111] But the pattern that Pullan describes for Venice seems to have obtained for many of the larger cities of northern Italy, including Bologna, Florence, and Genoa:[112] hospital amalgamation during the late fifteenth century; governmental oversight of the confraternities by the early sixteenth century; new poor laws and new offices of the poor during the 1540s; and large beggars' hospitals towards century's end. A similar process can also be observed in Turin, though reform began somewhat later there, as well as in Rome, though here the dominant political force was not the city council, of course, but the papal Curia.[113] This was not the only pattern, however. In Habsburg-dominated areas, such as Naples and Lombardy, the reform process did not go as far; the clergy retained greater control over charity, municipal relief remained more fragmented, and mendicants were given freer reign.[114] Considered as a whole, then, Italian efforts seem to have fallen somewhere between the cases of Spain and France.

• • •

Let us now return to the question posed earlier regarding the similarities and differences between Protestant and Catholic systems of poor-relief. Are the anticonfessionalists right? Were there no significant differences between the two? This is not an easy question to answer. As we have seen, there was a great deal of variation *within* the Protestant and Catholic systems. What is more, this variation occurred along a number of different dimensions that are analytically separable and potentially independent of one another. Thus, it is important that we not simply focus on a single case because that case may be atypical and unrepresentative. And it is important that we not focus on a single aspect of reform. Insofar as the evidence permits, we should try to look at the full range of variation within each system (Lutheran, Reformed, and Catholic) along all of the theoretically relevant dimensions (for example, centralization, laicization, discrimination, and incarceration).

Let us begin with the issue of centralization. Clearly, there were some Catholic cities, such as Lyon, that displayed a degree of centralization equal to or perhaps even greater than that observed in certain Protestant cities, such as Amsterdam. But I think it would be fair to say that Lyon represented the high end of the Catholic spectrum, while Amsterdam fell towards the low end of the Protestant spectrum. One can also think about this contrast in terms of extremes. There was probably no large Protestant city with a system of social provision as decentralized as, say, Salamanca's, just as there was probably no Catholic city with a system as centralized as, say, Wittenberg's. What is more, I suspect that these differences grew over time. The post-Tridentine period witnessed a veritable explosion of new institutions—monastic orders, lay confraternities, pious foundations, and so on—many of which were engaged in charitable activities. Further, these charitable activities were often devoted to a highly specific clientele (for example, prisoners, prostitutes, lepers, syphilitics, and so on). Of course, it is possible to find analogous developments within the Protestant world, such as the schools and orphanages founded by German Pietists or the societies for the improvement of morals established by English Puritans. But these developments seem to have occurred on a much smaller scale.

What about laicization? Here, too, we see areas of overlap, especially between Catholic and Reformed cities. In Venice and Amsterdam, for example, a significant share of total relief was distributed by lay officers of religious bodies (members of the *Scuoli grande* and the various diaconates, respectively) who were loosely supervised by the city magistrate. But we also see significant differences, especially between Lutheran and Catholic cities. In the former, relief was collected, administered, and distributed by civic agencies; in the latter, religious institutions that did most of the work. And there are good reasons to believe that these differences also grew over time. The Council of Trent strongly urged the secular and regular clergy to reassert their control over charity, and there are certainly cases in which they did so. Further research will be necessary in order to determine whether these cases were typical or exceptional.

Now consider discrimination and incarceration. Clearly, it would be misleading to characterize Catholic charity as indiscriminate. All of the Catholic societies we have examined drew distinctions between the deserving and undeserving and tried to channel relief accordingly—towards the deserving and away from the others. And most of them experimented with various forms of indoor relief and enclosure. This said, there were some subtle and not so subtle differences between Catholic and Protestant policies. One concerns legislation on begging. In Protestant societies, bans against begging seem to have almost universal; not so in Catholic societies. While begging was almost always regulated, it was not usually prohibited. There were exceptions, not only for the mendicant orders, but often for other categories of people as well. The other difference concerns enclosure. In Protestant societies, indoor relief was usually a synonym for workhouse—for moral reform through continual supervision and hard labor. In Catholic societies, it usually connoted something rather different: a place where the poor could seek shelter, receive medical care, and perhaps learn a trade. Of course, the workhouse movement did not leave Catholic Europe untouched. But it came later and met with more resistance and less success. In Italy, for example, the first workhouses were not opened until the late seventeenth century. And, once they were opened, they often met with considerable opposition. Indeed, in Rome, Genoa, and Turin, the opposition was so great that the newly established workhouses had to be shut down.[115] In Lucca and Siena, similar plans were nipped in the bud.[116] Nor does Italy appear to have been the exception. In the Empire, sixty-nine workhouses were opened during the Seventeenth Century. Of these, sixty-three were Protestant, and only six Catholic, and the latter were all established towards century's end.[117]

If my reading of the evidence is correct, then the anticonfessionalists have overstated their case; there *were* significant differences between Protestant and Catholic (and Lutheran and Calvinist) systems of relief, and it seems very likely that these differences had something to do with religion. The anticonfessionalists have failed to see these differences for at least two reasons. The first is that they focused too much on individual cases (for example, Lyon and Venice) and too little on how representative these cases are. A handful of exceptional cases is not sufficient to demonstrate that there were no significant differences. The second problem is that anticonfessionalist analyses rarely extend beyond the mid-sixteenth century. Because confessional differences were only just taking shape during this period, we would not expect them to be fully manifest in the organization of social provision at this point in time. The distortions that arise from this foreshortened perspective become obvious when we apply the anticonfessionalist logic to the field of religious discipline. Because the Catholic Church had not yet focused its disciplinary machinery of inquisition, confraternities, and visitations on the old believers, we might be tempted to conclude that it had no disciplinary machinery whatsoever. But as we have already seen, this would be a highly erroneous conclusion.

Does this mean that the ur-confessionalists are right? Should we draw a sharp line between medieval charity and modern social policy, and define the Protestant Reformation as the turning point from the one to the other? Obviously, this would also be an oversimplification. For there were parallels between the Protestant and Catholic systems and precedents to the sixteenth-century reforms. This much the anticonfessionalists have clearly shown. And the ur-confessionalist perspective is also problematic in another respect as well: it lumps together Lutherans and Calvinists. As we have seen, there were real differences within the Protestant camp.

The truth, I believe, lies somewhere between the ur- and anticonfessionalist positions. Catholic systems of poor-relief *did* change during the early modern era; but they didn't change as much as Protestant ones did. And while the Reformation was not *the* turning point in the transition from medieval charity to modern social policy, it was certainly *a* turning point. That much seems clear. But why? Why did the Reformation stimulate reform? And why did confession influence the shape the reforms took? The answer, it seems to me, has to do not only with ideas, as the ur-confessionalists thought, but also with actors and institutions. For the Reformations, both Protestant and Catholic, involved changes, not only in how people thought about good works towards the poor, but also in the relationship between clergy and laity and church and state, changes that created space for reform—and channelled the reforms in different directions. In the Lutheran countries, for example, the soteriology of good works was replaced by an emphasis on salvation by faith alone; the clerical hierarchy was integrated into the royal administration; and the boundaries of the church were made coterminous with those of the state. Such, at least, was the typical development in the principalities and kingdoms of Germany and Scandinavia, where Lutheranism was most influential. This constellation tended to channel reformist energies in the direction of secularization, laicization, and centralization; the church turned poor-relief over to the local authorities, who were placed under the supervision of territorial rulers. Calvinism created a slightly different constellation. The doctrine of works was rejected, of course, but an ethic of worldly activism arose in its place; the old clerical hierarchy was dismantled, but political and ecclesiastical government were still formally separate (if informally conjoined); and the church itself was organized along federalistic lines. This, at any rate, was the normative structure that emerged in Switzerland and southwest Germany and spread to the Netherlands, Scotland, New England, and, for a time, to England and France as well. To the degree that this configuration endured, it channelled reform in the direction of partial laicization, considerable decentralization, and a harsher but more activist approach towards the poor. The administration of poor-relief was divided among lay representatives of the church, the state, and various private foundations, who sought, not only to aid the poor, but to reform (or punish) them as well. Post-Tridentine Catholicism exhibited a very different configuration of ideas, actors, and institutions. The soteriology of good works, the independence of the clerical hierarchy and the universal (that is, centralized and transnational) organization of the church were not only retained, but strengthened. The result, at least in the long run, was a system in which church officials (re)claimed direct or indirect (i.e, administrative or supervisory) control over most sources of charity; in which charity in a given locale was often provided by a wide range of different institutions; and in which the religiously normative stance towards the poor was redemptive (rather than reformist or punitive). Insofar as the direction of social reform was influenced by religious factors, then, the key determinants seem to have been: (1) the normative stance of the church towards the poor—passive versus active, reformist versus redemptive; (2) the organization of the clergy and its position vis-à-vis the state—hierarhical versus collegial, dependent or independent; and (3) the structure of church government—territorial, federal or universal.

But, of course, religious factors were not the only factors. Attitudes towards the poor were also informed by nonreligious ideas (for example, humanism and Neostoicism) as well as by political and material considerations (for example, the fear of disease and disorder and the problem of scarce resources). The reforms themselves came in waves that coincided not only with periods of religious reform and renewal (for example, the 1520s), but also with periods of contraction, famine, and disease (for example, the 1590s). And the shape taken by social reform—and confessional settlements—was a product, not only of relations between religious and political institutions and elites, but also between local and national institutions and elites (for example, urban magistrates vs. territorial rulers). If one wished to understand why social reform took the exact shape that it did in a particular case, one would need to look at a range of different factors. But that is not the aim of the foregoing analysis. Its aim is merely show that confession was *one* of the factors that influenced the *general* direction that social reform took.

Political Discipline: The Protestant Ethic and the Spirit of Bureaucracy

For most scholars, the administrative apparatus and the army are the core institutions of the early modern state. One might argue, as I have, for a broader view of the state and the determinants of state power, which would include institutions of local governance and mechanisms of moral regulation. But the administrative apparatus and the army must still figure in that larger view because they were the mechanisms through which states extracted material resources and defended their borders.

Most scholars of state-formation have seen geopolitical competition as the driving force behind administrative rationalization. In my analysis of the Prussian development, however, I stressed a different factor: a disciplinary revolution from above inspired by ascetic Protestantism. It is religion, I argued, and not geopolitics, that set Brandenburg-Prussia apart from most other German states and helps explain its unexpected rise to power. Was the impact of religion unique to Prussia? Or might it also help to explain the degree of administrative rationalization which we observe in other parts of Europe, too? That is, was confession also one of the factors that influenced the general direction of political reform in the early modern period?

Once again, Thomas Ertman's argument provides a useful point of departure. As the reader may remember, Ertman begins his analysis with a distinction between regime structure and state infrastructure. He then uses Weber's theory of legitimate domination to distinguish between two types of state infrastructure: one in which offices are appropriated by officeholders (patrimonialism) and one in which they are not (bureaucracy).[118] He argues that the type of state infrastructure that emerged in the various states of early modern Europe was determined by "the timing of the onset of sustained geo-political competition."[119] Where sustained geopolitical competition began before 1450 (for example, in Spain, France, and Italy), the result was patrimonialism; where it began after 1450 (for example, in Scandinavia and Germany), the result was bureaucracy. The reason, says Ertman, is that the dominant conception of office holding before 1450 was a proprietary one derived from the idea of the ecclesiastical benefice, and the principal source of officeholders were landed nobles and other elite groupings who could drive a hard bargain with territorial rulers. After 1450, by contrast, rulers could draw on a new, nonproprietary notion of office holding, and they could recruit their administrators from the swelling ranks of trained jurists.

This is an extraordinarily complex hypothesis that rests on a whole series of implicit claims regarding, inter alia: the supply of, and demand for, trained jurists and the social composition and educational backgrounds of judicial and administrative elites. If it is correct, we would expect to find temporal and cross-national differences in most or all of these variables. To begin with, we would expect to find significant increases in (a) the number of people studying law and (b) the number of administrators trained in law from 1450 onward. Further, in those countries that later became bureaucratic (that is, the states of Germany and Scandinavia), we would also expect to find that (c) the nobility was underrepresented within the group of lawyer-administrators, that (d) this group made up a large percentage of all administrators, and that (e) it was considerably larger, proportionally speaking, than the group of lawyer-administrators within countries that later became patrimonial (that is, Spain, France, and the Italian states). The more of these claims that prove correct, the more plausible Ertman's argument becomes.

Now, the first claim is unambiguously correct: the number of law students *did* increase substantially after 1450 as did the number of students more generally. Indeed, the size of the student population appears to have grown steadily throughout Europe until the late sixteenth century and even longer in some areas. The main reason for this was the large number of new universities founded during the fourteenth and fifteenth centuries, especially in northern Europe. The second claim is probably correct, too: the overall number of lawyer-administrators does seem to have grown during the period in question, though it should be noted that the evidence is not as complete or as systematic as we might like. Claims three through five, however, are somewhat more problematic. Take the social background of law students and lawyer administrators in Germany. Commoners did indeed dominate for a time. But by the early sixteenth century, German noblemen began entering the universities in large numbers and were soon recapturing lost ground within the royal administrations. And in Sweden, the dominance of bourgeois lawyers was even more short-lived. So while legal studies did serve as an important route into the royal administrations in Germany and Scandinavia, they did not serve as a means for displacing the landed nobility from its traditional prerogatives, at least not for any great length of time. What about the fourth claim, regarding the proportion of lawyer-administrators within the royal services? Let us begin with several examples from the German states. In Bavaria, 55 of the 184 men who served as councillors (*Hof*- or *Hofkammerräte*) between 1550 and 1596 had academic degrees of one sort or another.[120] The proportions in the South Welfish principalities Braunschweig-Wolfenbüttel, Calenberg, and Grubenhagen were a bit lower; there, a little over one-third of the royal counselors who served between 1555 and 1651 had studied, but less than one-sixth had taken degrees.[121] To my knowledge, the Prussian crown employed only a handful of lawyers outside of the courts proper, and Frederick William I, chief architect of the Prussian bureaucracy, had a notoriously low opinion of lawyers.[122] Lawyer-administrators could also be found in the middle and lower tiers of the royal administrations of the German principalities, though almost certainly in lower proportions. These numbers are not inconsiderable. But they are not as high as Ertman's argument might lead us to expect, either. How do these numbers compare with those in patrimonial states? In France, the proportion of lawyers in the high councils was initially quite high, but declined steadily: it was 47 percent between 1286 and 1422, 41 percent between 1422 and 1549, and 27 percent thereafter.[123] We do not have a comparable data series for Spain, but the proportions were almost certainly higher. A number of the royal councils were fully monopolized by trained lawyers, as were around one-third of the *corregimientos*, the regional directors of the royal administration.[124] The Roman Church and the papal state also had many lawyers in leading positions. Thus, there do not seem to have been any large or obvious differences in the proportion of trained lawyers serving in the royal administrations of bureaucratic and patrimonial states. Indeed, if anything, there may have been more lawyers in the patrimonial administrations.

Though far from exhaustive, this evidence is sufficient to cast doubt on Ertman's argument. For while the number of lawyers and lawyer-administrators did increase after 1450, there are no indications that the increase was greater in states that became bureaucratic than in states that became patrimonial, nor does it appear that common-born lawyers displaced landed nobles, at least not for any great length of time. Thus, it is hard to see how the recruitment of lawyers could have played the large and decisive role that Ertman attributes to it. That said, it is clear that late medieval and early modern rulers did hire considerable number of lawyers—as well as a good many commoners and foreigners, some lawyers, some not—partly for their legal and administrative expertise and partly as a means of diluting the power of the indigenous nobility. But this practice seems to have begun quite early and to have been quite general; it began long before 1450 and was used by both patrimonial and proto-bureaucratic rulers alike.[125]

Might there be a simpler, more consistent and more plausible explanation for the variations that Ertman identifies? Recall his coding of the cases: Britain, Scandinavia and the German states are classified as bureaucratic, and Spain, France, Italy, Hungary, and Poland as patrimonial. One might criticize this coding as too crude. Still, when the cases are listed in this order, a striking pattern emerges: the division between bureaucratic and patrimonial states coincides almost perfectly with the Protestant/Catholic divide! Of course, it must be emphasized that the coincidence between confessional allegiance and administrative system is not complete. Some Protestant states were not terribly bureaucratic. Take the Dutch Republic. There, one finds a certain degree of bureaucratization within subaltern posts—in the clerical support staff of the States General or the Amsterdam City Council, for example. But higher level administrative functions were mostly in the hands of the urban regents and their chosen representatives, and the collection of taxes was generally farmed out.[126] Of course, there was no organized system of venality, such as France or Spain had. But then much the same might be said of the Florentine city-state, which was Catholic.[127] Nor were convergences of this sort specific to the more urbanized areas of Europe; they can also be found in agrarian regions. Consider the cases of Saxony and Bavaria, the one Protestant, the other Catholic. In both states, many key administrative posts remained under the control of the territorial diet or *Landtag* and could only be filled with members of the landed nobility—a classic example of the type of patrimonialism that Weber referred to as *ständisch* or estates-based. In the case of Bavaria, however, the *Landtag* ceased to meet during the seventeenth century, and the estates were represented through a standing committee that could more easily be controlled by the king.[128] One might therefore argue that Bavaria was less patrimonial, and more bureaucratic, than was Saxony. It should also be noted that some of the patrimonial states still had bureaucratic features. This is especially true of Spain, France, and the papal state; they combined widespread venality with a hierarchical chain-of-command and a certain degree of supervision and discipline, usually through royal commissaries, such as the French *intendants*. Similarly, it should be noted that the form of patrimonialism that existed in these states was quite different from that found in Hungary or Poland.[129] In the latter countries, offices were appropriated not by private persons but by social groups and, in particular, by the landed nobility. Hungary and Poland were characterized not by venality but by an extreme form of estates-based patrimonialism. Similar observations could be made about the Protestant states of northern Europe. There, too, the spread of bureaucratic administration was often limited by the prerogatives of representative assemblies, albeit not to the degree that it was in Hungary or Poland. And even where such barriers had been removed, as in the "absolute" monarchies of Scandinavia and the Empire, patrimonial elements still remained. Prussian and Swedish officials did not have the sort of contractual and legal protections typical of a modern bureaucracy; they could still be fired without warning and at pleasure—and sometimes were. But while the coincidence between confessional allegiance and administrative system is less than perfect, and the initial contrast between patrimonial and bureaucratic states too sharp and simplistic, it is nonetheless true that the most fully bureaucratic states were Protestant (for example, England, Sweden, and Prussia) while the most deeply patrimonial states were Catholic (Italy, France, Spain, Hungary, and Poland), so that there does, in fact, seem to have been a nontrivial degree of correlation between Protestantism and bureaucracy, on the one hand, and patrimonialism and Catholicism, on the other. The question, of course, is why.

Not surprisingly, the answer I propose focuses, not on geopolitics, but on religion. In particular, it focuses on the impact of two events: the Papal Schism (1378–1417) and the Protestant Reformation (ca. 1500–ca. 1550). For it was during the schism that offices were first sold on a grand scale, and it was from the papacy that secular rulers initially borrowed this device. Venality was thus introduced earliest and spread furthest in precisely those areas where the Roman Church was most influential and most deeply entrenched at this time, namely, France and the Italian and Iberian peninsulas. Of course, venality did not remain confined to these areas; it eventually spread to northern Europe as well. But its roots were never as deep there nor its growth as lush. The Reformers, who first elaborated and instituted a nonproprietary system of office-holding (within the church), targeted the benefice system, and through the influence of their followers venality within the state was nipped in the bud and a proto-bureaucratic form of administration put in its place.

Patrimonialism and Venality: Types and Degrees

Before tracing out the role of the papacy in the invention and diffusion of venal office holding, it is important that we distinguish venality from other types of patrimonialism and identify some of the different forms that it takes. It is a tedious exercise but one that will prove useful in the following analysis.

The appropriation of political offices in early modern Europe took a variety of different forms. If we distinguish between individual and collective forms of appropriation, on the one hand, and permanent and temporary forms on the other, we arrive at the following four-fold typology (see table 4). (1) *Venal office holding* (individual and permanent): in this system, functionally defined offices are treated as the private property of a particular individual and can be legally bought and sold or bequeathed and inherited. (2) *Feudal office holding* (collective and permanent): in this system, geographically defined offices are treated as the private patrimony of a particular lineage; they can be bequeathed and inherited, but not legally bought or

Table 4 Types of Office Holding

Bearer of Offices	Mode of Appropriation	
	Temporary	*Permanent*
Individual	Farming	Venality
Collective	Oligarchy	Feudalism

sold. (3) *Oligarchy* (collective and temporary):[130] in this system, offices of both kinds—functional and territorial—are treated as the corporate patrimony of a particular estate, typically landed nobles or urban patricians, who collectively confer them upon individual members of their estate for some specified time, usually by means of election, rotation, or lottery; such offices cannot be legally bought, sold, bequeathed, or inherited. (4) *Farming* (individual and temporary): in this system, offices are sold to the highest bidder for a specified period of time, but cannot be sold or bequeathed. Obviously, these are ideal types rarely found in pure form. As we will see, mixed types are also possible (for example, venal oligarchies and venal farms).

It is important to note that these four systems differ, not only in the form, but also in the degree of appropriation and, hence, in their susceptibility to rationalization and reform. Under the venal and feudal systems, particular individuals or lineages obtain a *permanent* claim over an office, and merit and performance can play little if any role in the selection of incumbents. Under the oligarchic and farming systems, by contrast, there is greater room for merit- and performance-based recruitment and promotion, for example, via competitive elections in oligarchies or competitive auctions in farms. For this reason, I will assume that oligarchies and farms represent milder forms of patrimonialism, especially when they are competitive.

Because venality is the main focus of this section, it is worthwhile to define it somewhat more precisely and to discuss its various forms and degrees in more detail. In the broadest sense, venality is simply the sale of public offices. Scholars of venality often then distinguish between private and public venality. Private venality involves a transaction between private persons, typically the holder of an office and a would-be purchaser; the sovereign is not a party to the transaction. By contrast, public venality involves a transaction between a public body and a private person, usually the sale of an office to an individual, usually by the sovereign or his representatives or, conversely, the repurchase of an office from an individual.[131] One might also draw a second distinction between de facto and de jure venality. I will speak of de facto venality in two cases: (a) when payment for or exchange of an office is expected or tolerated but not required or institutionalized, as when transfer of an office is preceded by a secret payment (a bribe) or a public gift; or (b) when a payment of some kind is required and institutionalized but does not have the *legal* status of a payment for office, as when the incumbent is required to pay certain fees upon assuming office. These two types may also be seen as stages or degrees of venality, with (b) being the more severe or developed form. To distinguish this latter type in the discussions that follow, I will refer to it as "proto-venality." Finally, I will speak of de jure venality when a payment is not only required and institutionalized but officially and legally regarded *as* a payment for the office. Obviously, the different types of venality distinguished above differ not only in form but also in degree. In its most fully developed form, venality is permanent, public, and de jure. This is the form in which we will be most interested below.

The Development and Diffusion of Venality in Late Medieval and Early Modern Europe: The Role of the Papacy

The case for a papal role in the development and dissemination of venality rests mainly on various forms of circumstantial evidence. The first is *historical timing*. Most scholars of the subject agree that the popes played a pioneering role in the sale of offices. Strong evidence of de facto, public venality, in which gifts to the pope preceded the appointment to benefices, may already be found during the reign of Innocent III (1198–1216).[132] De facto, private venality also appeared around this time in the form of the infamous *resignatio in favorem tertii*, in which the holder of an ecclesiastical benefice resigned his post in favor of a third party who then transferred it to the intended recipient in exchange for a consideration paid to the first party and shared with the third. This device allowed the seller and purchaser to evade the charge of simony. Public, proto-venality was first instituted during the Great Schism by the Roman pope, Boniface IX (1389–1406). The political and administrative chaos of the Schism resulted in a precipitous drop in papal revenues, and Boniface responded by putting many lower level administrative offices up for sale.[133] By the 1440s, these sales had become de jure; they had a legal status recognized by the courts.[134] Under Sixtus IV (1471–1484), clerical offices within the Roman Curia were being created and sold and there is some evidence that higher level offices within the Curia were also for sale.[135] Be that as it may, there can be no doubt that high level offices within the Curia and even the College of Cardinals itself were being openly bought and sold by the first decade of the sixteenth century.[136] In sum, there is evidence of public venality in the Roman Church as early as the twelfth century, and evidence of de jure public venality as early as the mid-fifteenth century.

Amongst the secular rulers of Europe, the kings of France are generally seen as pioneers in the development of venality. In comparison with the popes, however, they were veritable laggards. Of course, the farming out of royal offices was already well established in France by the thirteenth century, and traces of it may even be found three centuries earlier.[137] What is more, private, de jure venality seems to have been quite common by the mid-1300s, and there is indirect evidence of its existence a full century earlier.[138] And it also appears that members of the king's courts and counsels were involved in this traffic, probably from the late fourteenth century onwards.[139] But this traffic was limited to lower level offices, and it was not until the first two decades of the early sixteenth century that we find clear evidence of public venality—of the permanent sale of offices by the French kings themselves. With the establishment of a special "marketing" agency, the *bureau des parties casuelles*, Francis I gave official recognition and legal stature to such sales and began the process of creating new offices as a means of generating revenue. Over the next century and a half, the number and the level of the offices for sale rose fairly steadily. By the time of Richelieu, it is estimated that there were over 40,000 venal offices in France.

It is sometimes claimed that venality was unknown in Spain.[140] And, in fact, it is true that the kings of Spain never instituted de jure, public venality. But recent research has uncovered clear evidence of venality in all its other forms and degrees. De facto, private farming out of municipal offices was practiced in the cities of Castille from the late fourteenth century onwards, and hints of it can be found more than a century earlier.[141] Evidence of de facto, public venality and private proto-venality in the municipal governments may be found in the mid fifteenth century, when the Castillian cortes lodged repeated protests against the creation of new municipal offices by the Spanish Crown and against the use of the *resignatio in favorem* for the transfer of offices to third parties.[142] By the 1480s, a system of public, proto-venality was clearly in place, with offices in the royal judiciary and financial administration being offered for sale, though only on modest scale.[143] And in 1494 private traffic in municipal offices was made legal.[144] The kings of early modern Spain never did legalize the sale of public offices, and they shied away from selling judicial posts. But they did engage in systematic proto-venality and on a grand scale; thousands of posts were sold during the early modern period, not only in Castile and Aragon, but also in Spanish America and the Indies and even in the Spanish Inquisition.[145]

The situation in Italy was inevitably more complex and variegated. In the early modern *mezzogiorno,* venality was both widespread and highly developed. Like their immediate neighbor, the papal state, the governments of early modern Sicily and Naples both practiced systematic, de jure venality, selling a wide-range of offices to the highest bidders from the early sixteenth century onwards.[146] Unfortunately, the development of venality in premodern Sicily and Naples has not been systematically studied, so it is not clear how deep the roots of these practices were.[147] But they cannot have extended back as far as they did in France because thirteenth-century Sicily and Naples both had unusually rational administrative systems, with limited-term appointments, money salaries and other proto-bureaucratic features.[148] In northern Italy, by contrast, venality does not appear to have been as widespread or as fully developed. In Florence, there was no public venality at all and little if any private venality.[149] In Venice, public venality did not appear until the seventeenth century and only on a limited scale; it was used as a financial expedient during a period of fiscal crisis and was never extended to high-level political and judicial posts.[150] The only major exceptions to this rule were Savoy and Milan, where public venality was introduced from outside—by the French in the former case, and the Spanish in the latter.

Of course, venality was not limited to the Catholic polities of Latin Europe. It can also be found in the Protestant countries of the north, albeit in milder and less developed forms. In the Dutch Republic, for example, would-be officeholders sometimes made large gifts to influential magistrates in hopes of gaining an appointment.[151] Gifts of this sort also seem to have played a role in the hunt for offices in Stuart England.[152] Nor was Brandenburg-Prussia immune. During the late seventeenth and early eighteenth centuries, posts in local government and the royal judiciary were sometimes offered for sale, as were titular posts of various ranks.[153] But the private sale of offices was forbidden.

• • •

What the evidence on historical timing shows is that the papacy was the first state to institute a system of full-fledged venal office holding—public, de jure, and permanent. And it strongly suggests that the papacy also led the way in earlier phases of development in both private and public venality. What the evidence on historical timing does *not* show, of course, is that the development of venality in the secular states was stimulated or influenced by developments in the church and the papal state. After all, it could be that the genesis of venality was a case of simultaneous invention, of individual rulers responding to similar circumstances in similar ways, without regard to, or knowledge of, one another's actions. But there are at least two bodies of evidence that speak against such a conclusion.

The first has to do with *geographical proximity and institutional ties*. As it turns out, the areas in which venality was most pervasive and most highly developed—France, Spain, and certain parts of Italy—were also areas that were very close to the papacy, either geographically, institutionally, or both. Consider the case of France. The kings of France housed the popes in Avignon for most of the fourteenth century and parts of the fifteenth, and their subjects dominated the Roman Curia for much of these periods. Their cousins, the Dukes of Anjou, had ruled over Naples during the fourteenth century, and the kings themselves conquered Savoy during the early sixteenth century in the course of a long military campaign on the Italian peninsula. Their chief rivals in this struggle were, of course, the kings of Spain, who gained control over the duchy of Milan in the sixteenth century and whose forbears had ruled over Naples since the fifteenth century and Sicily since the thirteenth. Given their deep involvement in papal politics and their long-standing presences on the Italian peninsula, it is hard to imagine that the kings of France and Spain could have been unaware of the growth of venality in the Roman Curia and the Church more generally. And it is even harder to imagine that the rulers of the Italian states would have been unfamiliar with these practices; the papacy's personnel was overwhelmingly Italian.

When taken together, these circumstances provide strong evidence of papal *influence* in the development and diffusion of venality. But there is additional evidence that the link between the papacy and the spread of venality was stronger still, that it involved not only influence but *imitation*. For the systems of venality instituted in France, Spain, and their dependencies were strikingly similar to those instituted in the Roman Church and the papal states, not only in their broader organization, but even in the minutest of details. Consider the rules governing the resignation of proprietary offices. In the Roman Curia, the resignation had to occur at least twenty days before the incumbent's death; otherwise, the resignation was invalid, and the office reverted to the pope. In France and Spain, the very same rule applied to the *resignatio in favorem*. (In France, however, the period was later extended to forty days.) Indeed, as Otto Hintze first noticed, the language of the documents themselves was borrowed directly from the Church. Or consider the types of offices that could be bought and sold. In Rome, the sale of judicial and ecclesiastical offices was frowned upon by many, and though it was very widespread, especially during the sixteenth century, it was never legalized. Similar restrictions applied in Spain, where judicial offices were never publicly sold, and also in France, where they were not officially put up for sale until the late sixteenth century, long after other categories of offices had been made venal. The reasons for these parallels are not hard to find. They have to do with the influence of canon law, which provided the legal foundations for venal office holding within the Roman Curia and, as it appears, in the secular principalities as well. In this regard, it is striking to note that the countries in which venality took root earliest and most deeply were precisely the countries that had the oldest and most prestigious faculties of canon law—Italy, France, and Spain.

• • •

Of course, venality was not limited to the Latin countries. As we have seen, rulers throughout Europe experimented with it at one time or another. Thus, if we wish to explain variations in the degree of venality, we must understand, not only where the seeds came from, but why they took root and grew in some places but not in others. The answer to this question, I will argue, has a great deal to do with the influence of the Protestant Reformation and, in particular, with the new conception of office it systematized and propagated, a conception that was explicitly antipatrimonial—and extraordinarily bureaucratic.

The Critique of Simony and the Bureaucratization of the Church

The critique of simony—of the use of church offices for personal financial gain—is very old, probably as old as the Western church itself. But it seems to have taken on a new urgency during the fifteenth century, especially in Germany. One of the earliest and best known attacks on the abuses of the Roman Church was the *Reformatio Sigismundi*, which was originally written during the late 1430s, republished five times in manuscript form by 1476 and eight more times in printed form by 1522.[154] Obviously, the *Reformatio* was an influential document. It contained a wide-ranging critique of abuses within the Western church and the Holy Roman Empire, as well as certain suggestions for their reform. The critique of the church focused primarily on the problem of simony, but it catalogued a variety of abuses, including the holding of multiple posts (pluralism), the hiring of substitutes and curés (nonresidence), the collection of common services and annates, and, of course, the sale of indulgences. More interesting, from our perspective, are the proposals for reform, which centered on the elimination of ecclesiastical benefices in favor of a system of fixed salaries and included demands that all clergymen have "a diploma from a university," be subject to regular visitations and participate in diocesan synods, be familiar with the statutes governing their appointments, "have the same income and perform the same tasks," and turn over the tasks of financial administration to a "resident curator." Salaries, technical qualifications, discipline, written rules, functional specialization—the *Reformatio* reads like a blueprint for a Weberian-style bureaucracy! The only thing that distinguished the *Reformatio* was its prescience and cogency. The themes and proposals themselves became virtual commonplaces that were echoed in the writings of well-known humanists and reformers such as Erasmus and Luther, as well as in pamphlets and broadsheets by lesser-known authors.

The systems of clerical office holding that were established in the Protestant polities of Europe during the course of the sixteenth century were remarkably similar to the one proposed in the *Reformatio*.[155] Except in England, benefices were eliminated. And while most clergymen did continue to receive some form of nonmonetary compensation—the use of a field or a house, say—salaries were typically their chief source of income. A certain degree of formal education became a de facto or de jure precondition of office. By the early seventeenth century, the vast majority of Protestant clergymen had spent some time at university, and a sizeable minority boasted university degrees. Nor was this the only hurdle. In many countries, aspiring clergymen also had to pass a formal examination, typically an oral examination by their prospective employer or future colleagues. And once in office most clergymen were also subject to formal oversight of one kind or another—not only by their lay employers and clerical superiors, but often by their peers as well—and those who failed to lead exemplary lives or proved negligent in their duties could be—and often were—subjected to formal admonitions or even expelled from their posts; the expectations were clear and often codified. Conversely, a man who preached well and avoided scandal might reasonably hope to rise through the ranks to become the head minister of a large church or perhaps even a member of the clerical hierarchy. And by the eighteenth century he could also reckon with a certain degree of material security even if he did not achieve any great success—a pension if he lived into retirement or support for his wife and children, if he did not. Separation of person and office, fixed money salaries, technical qualifications, formal examinations, written rules, disciplinary oversight, career ladders, and even pensions—it would be no great exaggeration to say that the Protestant clergyman was the first modern bureaucrat.

What impact did these changes in clerical office holding have on systems of political office holding in Protestant countries? In the short run—meaning the sixteenth century—the answer seems to be: very little. Of course, by openly attacking papal office holding practices and undermining the authority of canon law, the early Reformers probably did help to prevent the spread of venality into northern Europe. But they generally had very little to say about other forms of patrimonialism, such as feudalism or oligarchy, and there is no evidence that they pushed for bureaucratization in the secular sphere. That task fell to the second-generation Reformers of the seventeenth century.

The Protestant Ethic and Bureaucratic Revolution

By the late sixteenth century, the "first" Reformation had run its course; in most of northern Europe, the "lies," "superstitions," and "abuses" of the Roman Church had been removed, and the "true doctrines" and "pure liturgy" of a Reformed church had been put in their place. What was needed now was a second or further reformation, a reformation not just of the church but of life itself, the establishment not only of a godly church but of a godly society. Or such, at least, was the view of a small but vocal minority within the Protestant churches of northern Europe. These groups went by different names in different places and occupied somewhat different positions within their host societies: Puritanism and the Further Reformation were ascetic-reform movements within the Anglican and Reformed churches of England and the Netherlands, respectively; the Second Reformation was a movement for the introduction of Calvinism into the Lutheran territories of Germany; and Pietism was an ascetic-reform movement within the Lutheran churches of Germany and Scandinavia. That said, their agendas were remarkably similar. They railed against laxity within the church, immorality within society, and decadence within the state, and they demanded a stricter application of biblical law and Christian ethics to all classes of society and all spheres of social life.

The impact of these movements varied enormously from one polity to the next. In Brandenburg-Prussia, of course, the Second Reformation and Lutheran Pietism joined forces to carry through a disciplinary revolution from above. In electoral Saxony, by contrast, Lutheran orthodoxy retained its sway in court and country, and Pietism got the cold shoulder. The key difference between these and other cases seems to have been the stance of the monarch and his allies to the precisionist message. Where they were unsympathetic, as in Saxony, precisionist pastors and their followers were driven into quietism—or out of the country, as in Spener's case. Where king and court were receptive, as in Prussia, precisionists were incorporated into an antipatrimonial, reformist alliance. Important examples of the latter dynamic include Sweden and England.

Sweden's disciplinary revolution from above was quite similar to Prussia's. It begins with the reigns of Gustav IX (1590–1611) and Gustav II Adolf.[156] Their predecessor, Sigismund, had converted to Catholicism in hopes of securing election to the Polish Crown. In that enterprise he succeeded, but only at the expense of a religious rebellion at home. The rebellion pitted most of the (Lutheran) clergy and nobility—especially the lower clergy and nobility—against a smaller group of prelates and magnates who had remained loyal to the old faith. The rebels triumphed, and their leader, Gustav Vasa, was eventually proclaimed king. Gustav's reign was a tumultuous one. He alienated the magnates early on through his harsh treatment of the Catholic rebels, many of whom were summarily tried and executed. Subsequently, he alienated many of his orthodox Lutheran supporters through his openly Calvinist sympathies. The marriage of his son, Gustav II Adolf, to a Calvinist princess only served to heighten suspicions that the Vasas were preparing a Second Reformation in Sweden. Such suspicions soon proved false, however, as the new king pledged his loyalty to the Lutheran faith and sought *rapprochement* with the magnates. This *rapprochement* was symbolized by Gustav Adolf's selection of a prominent magnate (Axel Oxenstierna) as his chancellor and closest advisor and institutionalized in the enhanced powers of the magnate-dominated Royal Council (*hovrätt*). But Gustav Adolf's policies towards the magnates were double-edged. The enhanced powers of the magnates were coupled with the recruitment of commoners and foreigners (a good many of them Calvinists) into the lower ranks of the royal administration and the elevation of career civil servants into the hereditary nobility.[157] In this way, Gustav Adolf was able to build a group of loyal supporters within the lower nobility, men who owed their security and status to the state and the monarchy.[158] Following Gustav Adolf's death on the battlefield in 1634, power devolved to a regency government led by Oxenstierna and the Royal Council. Gustav Adolf and Oxenstierna had made great strides in the field of administrative rationalization and centralization, and many of their reforms were codified in a posthumously published document known as the Form of Government.[159] But, as bureaucratic as it may have looked on paper, the royal administration quickly became the private reserve of powerful magnates who asserted control over numerous offices in church and state and paid themselves with plots from the royal domains, while letting the salaries of lesser officials go into arrears for years on end. Not surprisingly, these policies provoked harsh criticism from the lower echelons of the Swedish estates and the royal administration, who insisted that recruitment and promotion to religious and political offices be based on merit, as well as from the peasantry and reform-minded clergy, who decried the devolution of public power into private hands and the use of public monies to finance private decadence.¹⁶⁰ These sentiments were shared by Gustav X, who ascended to the throne in 1650. One of his first acts was a partial reassumption (*reduktion*) of royal lands alienated to the nobility.¹⁶¹ But in 1655 the new king fell on the battlefield, his only heir an infant. A new regency government was put into place, and a new period of magnate dominance began. By this time, precisionist views had begun to penetrate into educated circles, including the circle surrounding Gustav XI, a stern and autocratic man whose rigid personality and ascetic lifestyle strongly resembled those of Frederick William I.¹⁶² Like his Prussian counterpart, Gustav XI wasted little time in tearing down the patrimonial structures of magnate dominance and putting a fully bureaucratic system in its place. By 1686, the leaders of the regency government had been publicly discredited and put on trial, royal lands reclaimed in a massive *reduktion*, and the Swedish bishops stripped of their powers over church liturgy and clerical appointments. The chief beneficiaries of these policies—and the chief supporters of the new regime—were lower-level officials and clergymen and the groups from whom they were recruited—the lesser nobility, the third estate, and the peasantry. The result of these reforms was one of the most thoroughly bureaucratized system of state administration in seventeenth-century Europe.¹⁶³ And while the era of Caroline Absolutism eventually ended when the Swedish estates reasserted their role as corulers of the kingdom in 1718, the legacy of Caroline bureaucracy survived through the Era of Liberty and into the modern era.¹⁶⁴

England is not often compared to Sweden and even more infrequently to Prussia except perhaps as a contrasting case. But whatever the differences in its constitutional development, England's administrative development displays some remarkable similarities with these two absolute monarchies. Like Prussia and Sweden, England entered the seventeenth century with a deeply patrimonial system of administration characterized by a high degree of oligarchy and, unlike them, by a fair amount of private, de jure venality as well.¹⁶⁵ As in Prussia and Sweden, these practices evoked widespread criticism and resentment from precisionist reformers and members of the middle strata who demanded an end to the spoils system, and the establishment of a salaried civil service that would be open to talent. Demands of this sort can already be heard during the early decades of the seventeenth century and eventually wound up on the agenda of the Barebones Parliament and the Cromwellian Protectorate, which largely suppressed the sale of offices, increased the role of salaries in remuneration, and recruited greater numbers of commoners and small gentry into the state administration.¹⁶⁶ Under the Restoration monarchy of Charles II, the three Ps of patrimony, patronage, and payment were restored to their old role in the process of administrative appointments. Following the Glorious Revolution of 1689, however, the throne was once again occupied by an ascetic Protestant monarch (the Dutch stadtholder, William III of Orange) with strong connections to precisionist religion, and the assault on old corruption was renewed, this time to greater and more lasting effect.[167]

• • •

I have argued that differences between Protestant and Catholic states can be explained as the cumulative result of three events: the Papal Schism, the Protestant Reformation, and precisionist revolutions. In closing, it is worth noting that the impact of these events also helps to explain differences *within* the Protestant and Catholic camps. One of the key determinants of intra-Protestant differences was the presence or absence of a precisionist-inspired revolution. Most Protestant states were relatively free of patrimonialism in its severest forms (for example, public venality). But the highest degrees of bureaucratization were attained in states that experienced a precisionist-inspired disciplinary revolution from above. Among Catholic states, involvement in the Italian campaigns of the Renaissance was a key determinant of state infrastructure. Most of the states that were directly involved (Spain, France, Sicily, Naples, and Milan) adopted the papal practice of selling public offices—and on a grand scale; the only major exceptions were Florence and Venice. In these countries, the vested interests of venal officeholders constituted a formidable obstacle to subsequent efforts at proto-bureaucratic reform. Conversely, those states that were not directly involved (for example, Bavaria, Austria, Poland, and Hungary) did not engage in full-blown public venality. Here, antipatrimonial campaigns were more likely to succeed, and higher degrees of bureaucratization could be achieved (as in Bavaria and Austria).

Of course, these events do not explain *all* of the observed variation in levels of bureaucratization. They do not explain why Venice and Florence remained relatively free of public venality, despite their proximity to the papacy, and their involvement in the Italian wars. Nor do they explain why Bavaria and Austria became more bureaucratic than Poland and Hungary. These differences can be more easily accounted for in terms of economic, geopolitical and institutional factors. If Venice and Florence proved more resistant to the lures of venality than their co-combatants, this was probably because they had easier access to capital and less need of financial expedients. France and Spain, on the other hand, would not have been so quick to embrace venality had their treasuries not been so severely taxed by the Italian campaigns. And if Bavaria and Austria became more bureaucratic than their neighbors to the East this probably had much to do with the strength and autonomy of their monarchs vis-à-vis the territorial estates; Poland and Hungary both had strong traditions of representative government, and Poland had an elective (read: weak) monarchy, which made it easier for them to resist efforts at bureaucratization. Thus, there were interaction effects between religious and nonreligious factors. Obviously, the type of state infrastructure that emerged in any given state was the product of numerous factors, of which religion was but one.

What, then, was the contribution of religion? And how might we conceive of its relation to other factors? Clearly, the bellicists are correct in pointing to the enormous fiscal pressures generated by the military revolution of the sixteenth century and by geo-political competition more generally. But the way in which rulers responded to these pressures was mediated by, among other things, the available models of office-holding and their particular religiopolitical ethics. Religion may not have been the driving force behind administrative development in early modern Europe, but it did serve as a switchman that helped to determine the path which those developments took.

Conclusion

There are two main schools of thought about social disciplining in early modern Europe. On the one hand, there are scholars of social welfare who argue that there were no major differences between Catholic and Protestant countries and that early modern social reform was driven by nonreligious forces, such as humanism, capitalism, republicanism, and demography. Their conclusions are based principally upon case-studies of Catholic cities that developed relatively Protestant systems of social welfare during the first half of the sixteenth century. And, on the other, there are scholars of confessionalization. They argue that disciplining was driven by a combination of religious and political forces—specifically, alliances between religious and political elites—but that its effects were relatively uniform across the confessions. Their conclusions are premised mainly on comparisons of Catholic and Protestant systems of religious and moral discipline, which highlight areas of overlap between the confessions.

In my view, the evidentiary basis on which these interpretations are premised is too narrow. To determine whether religion mattered and whether confessional differences existed, we must do three things: (1) we must look at distributions rather than cases, that is, insofar as possible, we must see whether the confessions differed on average, instead of looking for individual cases that appear to defy the rule; (2) we must expand the temporal scope of our analysis beyond the first half of the sixteenth century to include the early modern period as a whole; the differences between the confessions were not clearly delineated until around the middle of the sixteenth century, and the impact of these differences might have taken some time to manifest itself; (3) we must expand the theoretical scope of our analyses, i.e, we should not focus only on religious discipline or social discipline, but examine as many different dimensions of the disciplining process as possible.

This is what I have tried to do in the preceding pages. My conclusion is simple: religion and confession mattered. They mattered in the evolution of ecclesiastical discipline; they mattered in the evolution of social provision; and they mattered in the evolution of state administration. That said, my conclusions are still rather different than the ur-confessionalists'. Unlike them, I see early modern social disciplining as the result of various factors, of which religion was but one—albeit an important one. What is more, I do not see the confessional divide in simple Catholic/Protestant terms; there were also considerable differences between Lutherans and Calvinists and, later, between precisionists and latitudinarians. Nor do I agree with their tendency to equate *Protestantism* with *reform* and *Catholicism* with *reaction*. In the areas of religious discipline and social provision, for example, it could be argued that post-Tridentine Catholicism was actually more intensive and more activist than orthodox Lutheranism.

The most salient difference, at least in the present context, was not between Protestants and Catholics but between Calvinism and other forms of innerworldly asceticism, on the one hand, and nonascetic and/or otherworldly forms of Christianity, such as orthodox Lutheranism and mainstream Catholicism. This difference can be summed up in a single word: discipline. Because of their religiously motivated concerns with self-control, congregational purity, social order, and political duty, innerworldly ascetics pursued individual, ecclesiastical, social, and political discipline with greater vigor than other early modern Christians. And not without success. As we have seen, polities dominated by Calvinists and other ascetic Protestants were more orderly, more regulated, and more fully rationalized than polities dominated by orthodox Lutheranism or reformed Catholicism. While early modern Lutherans and Catholics were no strangers to discipline, they did not experience disciplinary revolutions like those that swept up their Calvinist neighbors. Whether Calvinist-inspired disciplinary revolutions should be seen in a positive or a negative light is beyond the scope of the present study. What is certain is that they have had a lasting impact, not only on the West, but on the world as a whole.

Cover of the Penguin edition of Thomas Hobbes, *Leviathan*.
The foreground and sidebars have been cropped.

CONCLUSION

The image at the left is taken from the cover of a widely used edition of Hobbes's *Leviathan*. It is a cropped and truncated version of the original frontispiece reproduced at the beginning of chapter 1. In this reduced version, the city in the foreground is barely visible and the tableau at the bottom is entirely omitted. And while the sword is still easily recognizable, the crosier now looks more like a scepter, at least to an untrained eye. The Leviathan towers over the landscape, and its stance seems more threatening than inviting. In trimming the frontispiece, I would argue, the editors have not only altered its proportions and reduced its contents; they have simplified its meaning as well.

The early modern state has met with a similar fate in recent work by comparative-historical sociologists. Cities have disappeared from the picture, except perhaps as sources of capital. Churches figure on the margins, if at all, while armies and bureaucrats occupy center stage. The power of the state is equated with the power of the sword. The result is a one-sided and oversimplified picture of the early modern state.

In writing this book, I have had two goals. The first is to undo this work of truncation and reduction by reinserting both the local level and the religious dimension back into the story of the early modern state and by focusing special attention on the crosier—the left, or pastoral, hand of the Leviathan. To put it somewhat more plainly, I have tried to show that both the sources and nature of state power were more complex and multifaceted than the Marxists and the bellicists have allowed. My second goal has been to highlight previously unnoticed connections between seemingly disparate parts of the picture—between Calvinist consistories and Orangist regiments, for example, or between pastoral and political office holding practices. While these connections may be difficult for the modern observer to discern, they were readily apparent to the early moderners themselves, who grouped them together under the master category of discipline. The result, I hope, is a more complete and coherent picture of the early modern state, both of what it was and how it came to be.

In the pages that remain, I will briefly review the main arguments of the book, but my main goal will be to draw out some their broader historiographical and theoretical implications.

The Return of the Repressed: Religion and the Political Unconscious of Historical Sociology

It has been almost two decades now since Peter Evans, Dietrich Rueschemeyer, and Theda Skocpol published *Bringing the State Back In*.[1] The key contention of that volume, as its title suggests, was that sociologists, and social scientists more generally, should pay greater attention to the state, both as a factor in social change and an object in its own right. One of the key implications of *this* volume, I think, is that historical and political sociologists should also pay more attention to religion. In this section, I will try to show how bringing religion back in to the various areas of historical sociology—and social history—could deepen our understanding, not only of state formation, but to other core concerns of historical sociology, including regimes, revolutions, nationalism, and welfare states.

State-Formation

The main focus of this book, of course, has been state-formation, and it may be useful to review its key findings one more time. In summary, I have argued that the intensification of religious discipline in early modern Europe contributed to state strength in at least four distinct but interrelated ways. First, it helped to pacify the popular classes and civilize everyday life, making the task of governing easier and decreasing the need for coercion. Second, it engendered new forms of non–state governance, mechanisms of social control and moral regulation that were consonant with the goals of political elites but not directly and/or formally subject to their authority (for example, ecclesiastical discipline and church-based social provision). Third, it mobilized elite energies for projects of social and political reform by aligning ideal interests in spiritual salvation with projects of social disciplining and self-mastery. Fourth, it generated new models of social regulation and political administration, which could, and did, serve as inspirations or models for secular ones (for example, surveillance of the poor or bureaucratization of state administration). In disciplinary revolutions from below, such as the Dutch Revolt, the first two effects were the most important. In disciplinary revolutions from above, like the one orchestrated by the Hohenzollerns, the third and fourth were primary. And it should perhaps be added that there was at least one disciplinary revolution (that is, the English civil war) in which all of these effects were strongly present, a finding that may well shed some light on the unlikely rise of that island nation to the status of global hegemon in the century that followed.[2]

Regimes

Though I have given less emphasis to this point, it should also be stressed that religion was a factor in early modern regime structure, as well. As we saw in chapter 2, radical Calvinists played a crucial role in the emergence of the Dutch Republic. Their actions touched off the three rebellions that made up the Revolt, and their militancy made compromise impossible. Without them, there might well have been a revolt, but there probably would not have been a republic. Nor was the Dutch case exceptional in this regard. Calvinists played a leading part in many early modern rebellions (for example, in Scotland, France, Bohemia, and Poland).[3] Of course, the adoption of Calvinism did not always lead to the preservation of constitutional rule; the Prussian case is evidence enough of that. There, confessionally charged conflict between crown and estates was a major factor in the genesis of absolutism.[4] Similar patterns and outcomes can be observed in other cases as well. The defeat of the Bohemian uprising led directly to the establishment of royal absolutism. Confessional conflict between a Catholic crown and the Protestant estates also contributed to the weakening of representative government and the expansion of monarchical authority in Bavaria. And many French historians now regard the Wars of Religion as a—or *the*—crucial turning point in the dismantling of the Estates General and the assertion of absolute sovereignty in that country. In each of these cases, the monarch's role as defender of the faith enabled him to rally Catholic members of the privileged classes behind a program of monarchical absolutism as the best defense against heresy. This is not to say that there was a constant conjunction between confession and regime (for example, between Calvinism and republicanism or Catholicism and absolutism); obviously, there was not. Rather, it is to say that confessional conflict was a key *mechanism* that influenced the type of regime—constitutionalist versus absolutist—that emerged in many cases and without which the overall distribution of outcomes cannot be fully understood. In short, to understand why some states developed in a constitutionalist direction, while others took an absolutist shape, we need to look, not only at class constellations and geopolitical competition, but at confessional conflict as well. It is worth noting that countries where constitutionalism was preserved during the early modern era (for example, Switzerland and the Netherlands) also tended to be early democratizers during the modern era, while the countries where absolutism was established (for example, Prussia and Spain) tended towards authoritarianism. Perhaps there should be an addendum to Barrington Moore's classic study, entitled "Religious Origins of Dictatorship and Democracy."

Revolution

Social scientists and social historians have paid relatively little attention to the connection between religion and revolution in early modern Europe.[5] In fact, the book that gave birth to this field and, arguably, to the new historical sociology *tout court*, Theda Skocpol's *States and Social Revolutions*, pays relatively little attention to early modern Europe as such. For in her view, the first social revolution was the French Revolution. In Skocpol's now famous definition: "Social revolutions are rapid, basic transformations of a society's state and class structures; and they are accompanied and in part carried through by class-based revolts from below." They are contrasted with "political revolutions" that "transform state structures but not social structures."[6] According to Skocpol, the English Revolution was a political rather than social revolution because it did not involve a transformation of class structures. Though she does not discuss the Dutch Revolt, it seems likely that she would also place it in the political category. Is she right in doing so? The answer depends upon how one sees the early modern class structure. If one sees it in strict Marxist terms, as a feudal class structure, dominated by the nobility and peopled by the peasantry, then Skocpol's claim is correct. However, if one understands class structure in somewhat broader terms as property relations or social relations of domination, then the Dutch Revolt could certainly be seen as a social revolution and perhaps even as the first modern revolution.[7] For it involved a massive transfer of property and a massive change in relations of power: the expropriation of the (Roman) church and the disenfranchisement of the (Catholic) clergy.

Of course, there are other sociologists, such as Charles Tilly and Jack Goldstone, whose definitions of *revolution* are more encompassing and whose work does include treatments of the Dutch and English cases.[8] However, Tilly's theory of revolution, like his theory of state-formation, focuses mainly on the interaction of geopolitics and class struggle. To the degree that confessional cleavages figure into his accounts, it is usually only as an expression of political or social interests. In his discussion of the Dutch Revolt, for example, Tilly argues that religious preference during the Reformation era was essentially a function of regime structure and that the key issue was, not what the churches preached, but who controlled them.[9] Tilly is right to draw a connection between religious beliefs and political interests, of course, for there were elective affinities between the two.[10] Where he oversteps, I think, is in suggesting, at least implicitly, that the one can be reduced to the other, and at a deeper level, that religion is a realm of beliefs but politics is a realm of interests. It is important to remember that individuals can also have ideal interests (for example, in an afterlife), at least within the context of salvation religions such as Christianity, and that they are sometimes willing to fight and die to defend them, something I suspect they are generally less willing to do for the sake of material interests alone. Of course, this usually holds only for a minority of religious virtuosos. But then again revolutions are most often made by minorities.

The confessionally driven conflicts of the early modern era pose a challenge, not only to Tilly's analysis of revolution but also to a key argument of the contentious politics approach that he and others have championed in recent years, namely, the claim that national-level contention is a relatively recent phenomenon, which first emerges during the nineteenth century, primarily as a response to the centralization of power in territorial states.[11] There are at least two problems with this claim. The first concerns periodization. Why, one wonders, are early modern conflagrations, such as the Dutch Revolt, not classified as national-level contestations? The answer, it appears, is that one of their goals, typically, was the defense of traditional privileges and liberties—that is, local and regional power and autonomy. What this interpretation misses, of course, is that these movements also aimed at national-level institutional transformation—the transformation of the church—a transformation, moreover, that was political by any reasonable definition of that term. The fact that these movements were of national scope—and this is the second problem with the claim—was due, not to the centralization of state power, but rather to the centralization of religious power, and, at a still deeper level, to the fact that religious interests and concerns transcended region.

Confessional conflict also made an important contribution to modern repertoires of contention. For one could argue that Calvinism gave birth to the revolutionary party and the underground movement.[12] The acephalous structure and clandestine character of Calvinist insurgency movements, with their secret networks of churches under the cross and, somewhat later, of the Catholic counterinsurgency movements created to combat them (for example, the various Catholic Leagues), prefigured modern revolutionary parties in terms of tactics and organization and may, indeed, have been their precursors.[13] Nor was this the only tool it contributed to the practice of revolution. For the Confessional Age spawned another, even more basic weapon: the revolutionary ascetic, a personality that cathexes, not with other individuals, but with transcendent causes to which it subordinates its desires.[14] Possessed of utter certainty and lacking emotional ties to those around them, the revolutionary ascetic is capable of attracting dedicated followers and employing any means necessary to achieve his or her ends. From Cromwell through Robespierre to Lenin and Malcolm X, the revolutionary ascetic has been a psychic agent of radical change in the modern West.

Like Skocpol and Tilly, Goldstone regards structural and geopolitical factors as the key *triggers* of revolutionary upheaval, though he does add another mechanism to the mix: demographics. Unlike them, however, he acknowledges, and even emphasizes, the importance of "culture" and "ideology" in determining the *outcomes* of revolutions. "Once the state's fiscal and political woes reduce its authority to nil," he argues, ideologically based groupings rise to prominence by virtue of their "superior organization."[15] And once they are installed at the nucleus of the dominant coalition, their ideas can have real consequences. One reason why the English and French Revolutions brought about more far-reaching changes than contemporaneous uprisings in Turkey and China, Goldstone contends, is that the Puritans and the Jacobins both had linear or progressive understandings of historical time, while their Turkish and Chinese counterparts tended to think in cyclical or restorative terms. While I would agree with much of this analysis, I would like to register one area of dissent. Unlike Goldstone, I would argue that ideology (that is, religion) was important, not only in the outcomes of early modern revolutions, but in their very escalation into revolutions—and for two reasons. First, it introduced a set of intractable issues into early modern politics, issues that significant numbers of people regarded as nonnegotiable, thereby creating the spiraling dynamic of mobilization and countermobilization characteristic of the Dutch Revolt and other early modern conflicts. Second, because the issues it raised were of (putatively) universal scope, the Reformation led to mobilization whose (social) depth and (geographical) scope were far greater than those revolving around particular interests. This is why the early modern era witnessed revolutionary upheavals on a scale and in numbers unlike any previous period—and unlike anything prior to the French Revolution.

Nationalism

Thus far, I have argued that greater attention to religion could enhance our understanding of states, regimes, and revolutions. It is also relevant to a fourth area of historical sociology: the study of nationalism. Confessionalization contributed to the development of Western nationalism in at least two ways: (1) by bringing cultural and political boundaries into closer alignment with one another; and (2) by supplying a discourse through which national distinctiveness could be articulated—and at least partly reconciled with Christian universalism. Like most agrarian societies, medieval Europe possessed an elite, high culture (literate and Latinate) that spanned political boundaries and a crazy quilt of popular cultures (oral and vernacular) that were confined to particular regions. Insofar as confessionalization stimulated the development of mass vernacular cultures that were neither local nor fully European, it helped to create the cultural homogeneities that nationalism would later mythologize and extoll.[16] (It goes without saying that this process was gradual, incomplete, and uneven.) Of course, students of the subject have long argued that nationalism is a secular ideology that first emerges during the French Revolution. But recent work by early modernists has shown this view to be untenable.[17] However one defines it—qua movements, discourse, or category—nationalism can be found in the early modern period. While there were secular forms of nationalist discourse, grounded in narratives of cultural and political distinctiveness, the most common type of nationalist discourse in the early modern period was a religious one, which drew on the Exodus story, and on the notion of chosenness more generally.

Welfare States

Following Esping-Andersen, it has become customary for sociologists to distinguish among three different welfare-regimes: liberal, social-democratic, and corporate-conservative.[18] Esping-Andersen himself concludes that corporate-conservative welfare states were most likely to emerge in predominantly Catholic societies, such as France and Italy. What he does not mention is that liberal welfare states emerged only in areas heavily influenced by Reformed Protestantism (that is, England and its settler colonies) or that social-democratic welfare states emerged only in the homogeneously Lutheran countries of Scandinavia. This is not to deny the importance of class conflict in welfare-state development; rather, it is to suggest that these conflicts may have been mediated or influenced by religious factors (for example, the stance of the church(es) towards the social problem and the relative strength of confessionally based political parties) and that the policies which various countries adopted in response to the social problem may have been influenced by the solutions to pauperism and vagrancy adopted three centuries earlier. For there are remarkable continuities between early modern and modern systems of social provision. Like their Calvinist predecessors, liberal welfare states tend to take a more punitive stance towards the poor and place a higher value on work as a cure for all ills. Similarly, the highly centralized and secular character of social-democratic welfare states was anticipated in their Lutheran forebears, while the more decentralized and less secular character of Christian Democratic welfare states also has premodern roots. It seems unlikely that these continuities are the result of coincidence.

• • •

Given its importance for state formation, revolution, nationalism, welfare states, and other social and historical phenomena, one wonders why religion has figured so little in the work of historical sociologists. This inattention to religion in contemporary historical sociology becomes all the more curious when one considers the centrality of religion in the works of Weber and Durkheim. Indeed, it would be no great exaggeration to say that classical macrosociology was the offspring of comparative religion! Nor should we forget Tocqueville, who took religion quite seriously, so seriously, in fact, that he regarded Puritanism as the handmaiden of liberty—"its companion in struggle and in triumph, its cradle in infancy, the divine source of its laws."[19] And the inattention becomes more curious still when one realizes that religion was also quite important to the work of many postwar American macrosociologists. Bellah, Bendix, Eisenstadt, Lipset, and Rokkan—however diverse they may have been in their interests and outlooks, all incorporated religion into their analyses to one degree or another. The turning point seems to have come during the late 1960s and 1970s when a confluence of developments inside and outside the American academy—the rise of Marxism, the rejection of Parsonsianism, the decline of mainline religion—suddenly made religion seem theoretically and historically irrelevant.[20] Recent developments, such as the rise of cultural sociology, the rediscovery of Durkheim, and the spread of religious fundamentalism suggest that the turn may well have been a wrong one.

Revising State Theory?

The nature of the state and its relation to society, the causes and connections between state autonomy and state capacity, the dynamics and determinants of state-formation—these are the central problems of state theory, broadly conceived. As different as their historical accounts of early modern state formation may be, the positions of the Marxists and bellicists on these more general issues are actually quite similar. Most, I suspect, would happily accept Theda Skocpol's definition of the state as "a set of administrative, policing, and military organizations headed, and more or less well coordinated by, an executive authority," which "first and fundamentally extracts resources from society and deploys these to create and support coercive and administrative organizations."[21] And, like Skocpol, they would probably also agree that state power is "basically organized coercion."[22] And while they might weight them somewhat differently, most Marxists and bellicists would also agree that state power or capacity is essentially a function of (a) the level of economic development, insofar as it determines the overall level of material resources that are available; (b) state structure in the sense of administrative rationalization and/or administrative centralization; and (c) state autonomy in the sense of independence from societal institutions and actors. After all, the more resources a state can extract, the more soldiers, policemen, and administrators it can employ, and the more personnel it has, the more coercion it can exert! This understanding of state power fits well with a top-down view of state-formation in which power-hungry princes and their administrative staffs seize and usurp the power and resources of other actors and institutions (landed nobles, representative assemblies, and so on). The view of the state as a coercive and extractive organization—whose power is a function of its structure, resources, and autonomy and emerges through usurpation and monopolization, all in the pursuit of individual and group domination—this view has dominated comparative-historical work on the early modern state for over a quarter of a century. Borrowing a term from international relations, we might refer to it as the realist consensus.

It should be clear by now that I do not regard this consensus as wrong. On the contrary, I think it contains a great deal of truth. However, I do see it as conceptually incomplete and empirically one-sided. In particular, I would argue that:

1. *States are not only administrative, policing, and military organizations. They are also pedagogical, corrective, and ideological organizations.* Which is to say that their (asserted) functions are broader than the realist perspective allows. Early modern states deployed their resources to support and create schools, orphanages, prisons, workhouses, common chests, diaconates, fraternities, consistories, inquisitions, and many other organizations whose

main purposes were socialization, regulation, and normalization—and not coercion and extraction. In this way, they sought, not simply to bend individuals to their will or strip them of their resources, but to reshape them into obedient and productive subjects. State-formation is not solely a process of institutionalization; it is also, and equally, a process of subjectification. Still, it would be a grave mistake to see the individual subject as a passive agent in this process because:

2. *State power does not operate exclusively, or even primarily, through coercion. It also operates through co-optation.* Overdrawn though it may be in some regards, Hobbes's vision of the social contract is not entirely inaccurate, at least for early modern Europe. Violence and disorder were facts of life, and the war of all against all an ever-looming threat. Under these circumstances, we should not be surprised if the Leviathan's embrace was, for some, an attractive perspective, offering safety and security. Let us not forget that the well-ordered police state was originally a utopian vision! Or that self-discipline was then a sign of freedom and agency rather than subjugation or repression.[23] The disciplinary revolution needed willing cadres and zealous foot soldiers, and it found them in the ranks of the orderly and the godly. The role that such people played in the local institutions and pedagogical projects of early modern states and the close connections that states had to churches suggests that:

3. *State power is not (always just) a function of state structure, material resources, and organizational autonomy. State power is (also sometimes) a function of:*

  A. STATE INFRASTRUCTURE. The realist focus on central institutions misses two other sets of institutions that crucially affect state capacity—and not only regulatory and normalizing capacity but coercive and extractive capacity as well—namely, *local government* and *non-state governance*. One of the most important lessons that we learn from the northern Netherlands and other constitutional republics, is that a combination of strong local government and non-state governance is highly effective not only in maintaining social order but also in extracting material resources—more effective, the numbers suggest, than centralization and despotism alone. Following Michael Mann, I have referred to these two sets of institutions as state infrastructure, a term that evokes images of road networks and power plants. And not incorrectly! For we might think of state infrastructure either as a communications network through which information flows between the central and the local or as a generator that feeds additional power into the state. We should not forget, however, that the fuel for these generators was:

B. HUMAN RESOURCES. *The realist concern with the extraction of material resources overlooks an equally important source of state power: the valorization of human resources.* Ironically, the inadequacy of the realist standpoint is perhaps nowhere more evident than in the military realm, for it is here that disciplinary power is directly transformed into physical coercion through the training of the soldier's body and the coordination of individual action. The putative equivalency of material resources and physical coercion, the assumption that the conversion of money into violence occurs at a fixed rate—an assumption that is implicit within the realist view—therefore proves to be false. Of course, this conversion can also proceed in another direction; disciplinary power can be translated, not only into physical coercion, but into material resources as well. Early modern rulers were aware of this convertibility. That is why they avidly recruited Calvinist artisans and merchants to their own countries. Today, of course, the valorization of human resources occurs, first and foremost, through the various disciplines embodied and inculcated by the educational establishment. However, the regulatory capacity of a state is a function, not only of those institutions that are directly a part of it, but also of the various forms of non–state governance, and it is for this reason that state theory must pay greater attention to:

C. ORGANIZATIONAL ENTWINING. The realist perspective holds that state autonomy enhances state power. And indeed it does—to the degree that we are concerned with state power as "power over" (in the sense of power over social elites and institutions) and insofar as the interpenetration of state and society involves private appropriation of state authority and resources for the sake of personal gain (as in systems of venal office holding). However, to the extent that we are concerned with "power to" (in the sense of power to maintain order, extract resources, defend territory, and so on) and in cases where the state-society relationship involves private support for state authority in the name of the public good, *the power of the state may be enhanced by its connections with social actors and institutions.* The most common form of organizational entwining in the early modern period and the one that has been most central in this book was, of course, the functional dedifferentiation of church and state that typified the confessional age and allowed states to implement long-standing projects of moral regulation and social control. However, one also finds entwining in the economic realm as well: in the close ties between commercial and administrative elites in the Netherlands and Great Britain, for merchants and civil servants in the North Atlantic region, and in the formation of merchant trading companies, which solved collective action problems for the merchants and logistics and supply problems for the administrators. Because the organizations with which the state becomes entwined are often eventually absorbed into it, it is important to bear in mind that:

4. *State-formation* is not (always only) a top-down process driven by material interests. It is (also sometimes) *a bottom-up process channeled by ideal interests*. The realist perspective suggests that state-formation occurs through the creation of new state institutions and their extension through society; it sees state-formation as a process of endogenous growth and institutional expansion. And it assumes that state-builders' actions are strategic responses to external conditions. In my view, both of these assumptions are too simplistic. As we have seen, state-formation can also occur through the emergence of new social practices and institutions and their imitation, co-optation, or absorption by the state. Diaconal poor-relief in the Dutch Republic and the Franckean institutes in Prussia provide two concrete examples of this process. Further, as we have also seen, the state-building strategies of early modern rulers were mediated by their religiopolitical ethics and influenced by religiocultural developments. The clearest example of this is the elective affinity between ascetic Protestantism and bureaucratic office holding discussed in chapter 4. Like all actors, early modern rulers had multiple and potentially conflicting interests—ideal and material, geopolitical and eudaemonistic, personal and dynastic, long-run and short-run, and so on—and their efforts to prioritize and reconcile them were inevitably influenced by individual *habitus* and collective valuations.[24] Merely showing that an actor was pursuing interests explains nothing. The point is to show *which* interests, and why. It is also important to realize that strategy is often more akin to artisanal bricolage than pure engineering. When confronted with a problem—like the creation of administrative machinery—actors piece together solutions using a particular and familiar set of tools. Bureaucracy, for example, was not part of the fifteenth century toolkit. And it became part of the seventeenth century toolkit only because the Protestant Reformation put it there.

• • •

At this point, the reader may wonder whether the question mark behind the section header was not misplaced. But the foregoing revisions to state theory are not really as radical as they may seem; in fact, one could argue that they are not revisions at all! For while they are very much at odds with current theories of early modern state formation, they are remarkably consistent with several bodies of research on the modern state. Consider recent work on social capital.[25] It suggests that the efficacy of government, the development of the economy, the stability of democracy, and various other collective goods are strongly and positively linked to the existence of dense networks of associational life that facilitate cooperation, enforce norms and sustain trust within everyday interaction. To put it in the terms developed here, this work suggests that state strength is partly a function of state infrastructure in the sense of local government and non–state governance. Or take the voluminous literature on corporatism. Theorists of corporatism emphasize the role of organized interests (for example, unions and employers associations) in governing the economy and increasing productivity and argue that organized capitalism yields better outcomes than laissez-faire capitalism or state *dirigisme*. To put it into the terms of the present analysis, they contend that the most effective system of economic governance involves a high degree of organizational entwining. Similar arguments may be found in the growing literature on state embeddedness and state-society synergy, which points to the crucial role of state-society linkages in promoting economic growth in the developing world.[26] There are two other points that bear emphasis in this context. The first is that some of the associations, interests, and linkages in question (for example, social service agencies or labor unions) were the product of reformist movements from below (for example, American progressivism or the European labor movement). The second is the degree to which many of these associations, interests, and linkages have become formally integrated into the central state (for example, through the welfare state or peak bargaining). All of this is well known. What has not been fully appreciated, I believe, is that these, too, could be seen as bottom-up processes of state-formation much like the ones described in this book. As for the role of ideal interests and religiopolitical ethics in state development, it, too, has received a good deal of attention, though mainly in studies of East Asia, and the East Asian miracle. The highly bureaucratized character of most East Asian states is well known, and the role of state bureaucracies in economic development is widely accepted, at least among sociologists and political scientists, as is the role of Confucianism in the genesis of the Chinese bureaucracy and the imitation or imposition of the Chinese model within other parts of the region (for example, Japan and Korea). In Asia, as in Europe, then, the genesis and diffusion of the bureaucratic ethos can be traced back to particular religious reform movements and followed the course of their diffusion. Perhaps one could even speak here of a Confucian disciplinary revolution.

Retrospective: Religion and Social Change in Early Modern Europe—and Beyond

Western Christianity has given rise to numerous movements for internal reform, including medieval monasticism and modern fundamentalism. But few, if any, of these movements have had political and social repercussions as profound and wide-ranging as those sparked by the Reformation. And one of the cardinal failings of recent work on early modern state formation is that it has ignored these repercussions. In closing, I would like to reflect not on the repercussions themselves, which I have detailed above, but on their magnitude. To put it differently, I would like to reflect, not on the effects of the Reformation, but on why those effects were so great.

Part of the answer has to do with the Reformation *message* and, in particular, with the reformers' stress on the *soteriological significance of ethical behavior*, whether as a mark of election (Reformed Pietism), a fruit of conversion (Lutheran Pietism), or an expression of submission and obedience to God (post-Tridentine Catholicism). Though weak or absent in the soteriology of the first generation of Protestant Reformers (for example, Calvin and Luther), this stress on ethical behavior became increasingly prominent in the thinking of second-generation Protestants, such as Calvin and Spener, and also of ascetically minded Catholics, such as the Jesuits and Jansenists. This message stood in sharp contrast with the mainstream soteriology of late medieval Catholicism, which placed far greater weight on *ritual actions* (for example, the rosary) and *clerical interventions* (for example, the Eucharist) than it did on the ethical behavior of individual believers. The importance of this shift, from a sociological point of view, is that it strengthened the connection between an individual's conduct in everyday life and their ideal interest in otherworldly salvation and thereby increased the impact of religious motives on social action.

The Reformation also differed from previous movements in another way as well: its social and geographical *scope*. With the possible exception of the Crusades, earlier movements had generally been confined to small religious or social elites (for example, monasticism, the *devotio moderna*), and those which did have a popular following (for example, Cathars, Wycliffites, Hussites) had been contained within particular regions or kingdoms. The Reformation also began as an elite movement confined to a particular region (namely, the empire). But it soon experienced a rapid and unprecedented expansion facilitated by a variety of factors, including the invention of print, the growth of trading networks, the expansion of the urban populace, the fragmentation of the empire, and the weakness of the papacy, to name only some of the most important.

The third way in which the Reformation differed from previous movements is that it resulted in a lasting split within the Western church and introduced a *new social cleavage* into European political life: confession. Sometimes confession crosscut existing sociopolitical cleavages of estate or nation, creating international religious blocs that transcended political boundaries. At other times, it reinforced existing cleavages, strengthening the solidarity of particular estates or nations and exacerbating preexisting conflicts (for example, between crown and estates or between colonizers and colonized). In both cases, however, it upset existing alliances and equilibria and catalyzed generations of political contestation and realignment.

The fourth and final factor that distinguished the Reformation was *tightened linkages between religious and political elites and institutions*.[27] As we saw in chapter 4, these linkages varied in both strength and form. At one extreme, we find certain Lutheran polities in which the church and the clergy were usually subordinated to the state. At the other, we find various Catholic polities where church and clergy remained formally independent but were subject to informal supervision and control. But some degree of dedifferentiation was a common denominator of the period. Increased cooperation between church and state resulted in intensified control of the population, but also in a transfer of knowledge and practices between the two institutions.

A melding of worldly activity to ideal interests, mobilization of extraordinary depth and breadth, new and lasting sociopolitical divisions and alliances, a tightening of the linkages between state and society—all these factors lent the Reformation its extraordinary transformative power. With its cheery soteriology, its dwindling membership, and its tenuous connections to public life and its institutional divorce from the state, Western Christianity seems unlikely to give rise to another movement of this sort now—or ever. Only three other movements—the Enlightenment, socialism, and fascism—have unfolded a transformative potential of comparative magnitude, and they too seem to have spent their energies. Only outside the West do the chances of religiously inspired disciplinary revolutions still seem significant.

Does this mean that the axle of discipline has stopped turning in the West? By no means! Of course, religious discipline in the name of transcendental ends is practiced only in a small and dwindling number of sectarian communities. But the great discipline of the early modern era has spawned a thousand little disciplines in the pursuit of a thousand mundane ends—physical fitness and beauty, personal happiness and success, sexual pleasure and conquest, intellectual creativity and output, financial success and security. No, the axle of discipline has not stopped turning. But it has been loosed from its moorings and splintered into pieces, which continue to turn, we know not why, beneath our very feet.

NOTES

Introduction
1. There are some important exceptions to this rule, including Philip Corrigan and Derek Sayer, *The Great Arch*, Eiko Ikegami, *The Taming of the Samurai*, and Chandra Mukerji, *Territorial Ambitions*.

Chapter One
1. This is the reading suggested in A. P. Martinich, *The Two Gods of "Leviathan,"* appendix C.

2. On the descending theory of royal authority, see Walter Ullmann, *Principles of Government and Politics in the Middle Ages*.

3. This is the type of reading recommended in Keith Brown, "The Artist of the Leviathan Title-Page."

4. See Martinich, *The Two Gods of "Leviathan."*

5. Thomas Mann, *Werke*, vol. 5/2, p. 1377. Quoted in Heinz Schilling, "Luther, Loyola, Calvin und die europäische Neuzeit"; my trans.

6. The most important Marxist accounts are Perry Anderson, *Lineages of the Absolutist State*, and Immanuel Wallerstein, *The Modern World System*. On the bellicist perspective see especially, Charles Tilly, ed., *The Formation of National-States in Western Europe* and *Coercion, Capital and European States;* G. Poggi, *The Development of the Modern State;* and Brian Downing, *The Military Revolution and Political Change*.

7. See Anderson, *Passages from Antiquity to Feudalism*.

8. Anderson, *Lineages*, p. 18. Anderson thus rejects the traditional Marxist interpretation of absolutism, first set forth by Engels, as a balancing act between the bourgeoisie and the aristocracy.

9. Wallerstein, *Modern World System*, vol. 1, p. 349.

10. Ibid., vol. 1, p. 157.

11. Tilly, *Coercion,* p. 7. Anderson simply ignores the fact that some early modern states, such as Switzerland, the Netherlands, Scotland, England, and Poland, did not develop into absolute monarchies in the first place. In all these countries, monarchical authority was supplanted or strongly limited by the power of representative institutions. Anderson's efforts to explain—or rather explain away—these cases are ad hoc and unsatisfactory. For example, Anderson argues that in England absolutism was stillborn due to an "early bourgeois revolution" "brought on by aristocratic particularism and clannic desperation on its periphery" (*Lineages,* p. 142). He suspends judgement on the Polish case until better scholarship is available and simply excludes the other constitutional regimes from consideration.

12. In fairness to Wallerstein, it should be emphasized that he does not advance an explanation of state-formation per se. He merely offers a general model of capitalist development that purports, among other things, to account for basic variations in state structure. To suggest that his entire theory of the world system is invalidated by its failures on this particular front is therefore logically fallacious. At most, the bellicist critiques of world systems theory merely point up the limitations of Wallerstein's model. See especially Theda Skocpol, "Wallerstein's World Capitalist System."

13. Thomas Ertman, "Rethinking Political Development in Europe."

14. Tilly, *Coercion,* p. 20.

15. Ibid., p. 30.

16. Downing, *Military Revolution,* p. 27.

17. See Ertman, *Birth of the Leviathan.*

18. Ibid., p. 5.

19. The virtue of this schema, as Ertman rightly emphasizes, is that it allows us to grasp important differences between cases that are lumped together in the fiscal-military model, such as Britain and Poland (bureaucratic constitutionalism versus patrimonial constitutionalism) or Prussia and France (bureaucratic absolutism versus patrimonial absolutism). In particular, it highlights the fact that a state's position within the international system—its strength—had more to do with its (administrative) infrastructure than with its (constitutional) structure and helps us to understand why a constitutionalist (but bureaucratic) state such as Britain was ultimately able to best an absolutist (but patrimonial) state such as France. While the former possessed a meritocratic civil service and a market-based system of public finance, the latter was hamstrung by a system of venal and hereditary office holding and was dependent on the whims of private financiers.

20. Ibid., p. 30.

21. Ibid., p. 33.

22. For a critique of falsificationist methodology in social science, see Philip S. Gorski, "The Poverty of Deductivism: A Constructive-Realist Model of Sociological Explanation."

23. For a more extensive statement of the method of "fair causal comparison" employed here, see Richard L. Miller, *Fact and Method,* esp. chap. 5.

24. In his recent book, *The Sinews of Power,* John Brewer has traced out the development of the English civil service in the century after the Glorious Revolution (1689), thereby refuting the received view of the English state as unbureaucratic. See esp. chap. 3.

25. The bellicist tradition originated in the work of Otto Hintze and the historians of the Prussian school; the case of Brandenburg-Prussia continues to be central to bellicist work on state-formation. Tilly, for example, argues that "the later history of Prussia illustrates the process by which national states are formed" (*Coercion,* p. 22). Downing, too, opens the empirical segment of his book with a case study of Prussian absolutism; see *Military Revolution,* chap. 3.

26. The classic statements of this thesis are Francis Carsten, *The Origins of Prussia*, and Hans Rosenberg, *Bureaucracy, Aristocracy, and Autocracy*.

27. Structuralists have tended to exaggerate the historical significance of these events. The army was still quite small (5,000 men) at this time, the bureaucracy tiny (at one point, it had only one member). As Richard Gawthrop has convincingly argued in *Pietism and the Making of Eighteenth-Century Prussia*, there was as yet little difference between Prussia and other German principalities. See also my review of Gawthrop in *German Politics and Society*.

28. A clear and compact overview of the subject may be found in Wolfgang Neugebauer, "Zur neueren Deutung der preußischen Verwaltung im 17. und 18. Jahrhundert in vergleichender Sicht," pp. 541–97. The classic studies of Prussian political development during the eighteenth century are Otto Hintze, *Die Behördenorganisation und die allgemeine Verwaltung in Preußen um 1740, Acta Borussica, Behördenorganisation,* and Conrad Bornhak, *Geschichte des preußischen Verwaltungsrechts*. On administrative reforms under Frederick William I, see especially Kurt Breysig, "Die Organisation der brandenburgischen Kommissariate in der Zeit von 1660–1697," pp. 135–56.

29. The seminal work on the development of the Prussian army is Otto Büsch, *Militärsystem und Sozialleben im Alten Preußen*.

30. Eighteenth-century Prussia might nonetheless seem to offer powerful confirmation for another central tenet of bellicism, namely, that state strength derived, above all, from administrative and political centralization, from the creation of a strong central bureaucracy and the destruction of representative institutions. But if we look further east, this thesis too appears questionable. Petrine Russia exhibited a degree of administrative centralization similar to Prussia; indeed, its administrative system was modelled after Prussia's. Moreover, Russia was even more politically centralized than Prussia, lacking as it did any tradition of representative government above the village level. Yet no one would argue that Peter the Great's Russia was as strong as Frederick the Great's Prussia. On the contrary, Peter's administration was as notorious for its corruption and inefficiency as Frederick's was legendary for its probity and diligence.

31. See Downing, *Military Revolution and Political Change*, chap. 5.

32. This argument is presented with particular force in J. H. M Salmon, *Society in Crisis. France in the Sixteenth Century* and is also advanced in David Parker, *The Making of French Absolutism*, and, more recently, in Mack P. Holt, *The French Wars of Religion, 1562–1629*.

33. As regards the first variable, one could point out that the States General of the Low Countries fought off Spanish absolutism despite the fact that were organized along partly tricurial lines and that the territorial estates of East Prussia succumbed to absolutism, even though they were organized along partly bicameral lines.

As regards the second variable, one might ask, Why 1450? The answer, we are told, is that this was the time at which European universities began producing a steady stream of trained jurists who could be used in high-level administrative posts and that it was the date at which a less feudal and more bureaucratic model of administration first emerged in Germany. And, yet, Ertman presents no evidence about the numbers of university graduates or the rates at which they were employed in public functions. Nor are we given any explanation for why the new model of administration emerged when and where it did. While these are deficits that could at least potentially be remedied, one is left with the lingering suspicion that the date is an ad hoc one that has more to do with the dates of the Hundred Years' War (1338–1453) and the Spanish *reconquista* (ca. 1492) than with the history of legal education and collegial governance.

34. For a more detailed version of this argument, see Gorski, "Calvinism and Revolution: The Walzer Thesis Re-Considered." A very similar argument is advanced in Wayne Te Brake, *Shaping History*, chap. 3.

35. On these events and the political history of the period more generally, see Michael Roberts, *The Early Vasas*. A brief overview may be found in Stewart Oakley, *A Short History of Sweden*, chaps. 5–7.

36. On the role of Petri in these events and on the Swedish Reformation more generally, see Conrad J. I. Bergendoff, *Olavus Petri and the ecclesiastical transformation in Sweden*, and John Wordsworth, *The National Church of Sweden*, chap. 5.

37. The authoritative, English-language study of Swedish politics and society during this period is Roberts, *Gustavus Adolphus*.

38. The old framework was first laid out in Leopold von Ranke, *Deutsche Geschichte im Zeitalter der Reformation* and informed standard accounts of the Reformation such as Roland Bainton, *The Age of the Reformation*.

The term *confessional age* was first coined by Ernst Troeltsch. For an overview of work in the new paradigm, see Harm Klueting, *Das Konfessionelle Zeitalter*, and H. J. Goertz, *Pfaffenhaß und groß Geschrei*. On issues of periodization, see Ernst Walter Zeeden, "Gegenreformation als Modernisierung," and "Zwang zur Konfessionalisierung?" and especially Heinz Schilling, "Die Konfessionalisierung im Reich."

39. The most important figure here is again Schilling. See especially his book *Konfessionskonflikt und Staatsbildung*.

40. See Marc Raeff, *The Well-Ordered Police State*.

41. Schilling, *Aufbruch und Krise*, p. 369; my trans.

42. Of course, they were not always successful. Where reformist currents within the Catholic Church were particularly strong—especially in Spain and Italy—significant poor-relief reforms were sometimes introduced as early as the fifteenth century. On Italy, see the well-known study by Brian Pullan, *Rich and Poor in Renaissance Venice*.

43. For a general overview, see Po-Chia Hsia, *Social Discipline*. On the urban context in particular, see R. Jütte, *Obrigkeitliche Armenfürsorge in deutschen Reichsstädten der frühen Neuzeit*.

44. See Friedrich Paulsen, *Geschichte des gelehrten Unterrichts*, vol. 1, and Lawrence Stone, "The Educational Revolution in England, 1560–1640."

45. See Lewis W. Spitz, "The Importance of the Reformation for Universities."

46. Important recent research in this area includes Martin Ingram, *Church Courts, Sex and Marriage in England, 1570–1640*, and Lyndal Roper, *The Holy Household*.

47. See Max Weber, "Die protestantische Ethik und der Geist des Kapitalismus" *Gesammelte Aufsätze zur Religionssoziologie*, vol. 1.

48. John Calvin, *Selections from His Writings*, p. 386.

49. From the Geneva Confession. Reprinted in Lewis Spitz, *The Protestant Reformation, 1517–1559*, p. 116.

50. David Little, *Religion, Order, and Law*, pp. 41 and 46.

51. See Christopher Hill, *Society and Puritanism in Pre-Revolutionary England*, and Charles L. Cohen, *God's Caress*.

52. Reprinted in Calvin, *Selections from His Writings*, pp. 229–44. On the operation of church discipline, see Robert Kingdon, "The Control of Morals in Calvin's Geneva" and, more generally, "Calvinist Discipline in the Old World and the New."

53. See especially Hajo Höpfl, *The Christian Polity of John Calvin*. Calvin's views on the

relationship between church and state are developed in the concluding sections of *The Institutes of the Christian Religion* and throughout his biblical commentaries, particularly those on the Pentateuch. Also consult William Bouwsma, *John Calvin*.

54. See Kingdon, "Social Welfare in Calvin's Geneva."

55. Paraphrased from Michel Foucault, *Power/Knowledge*, p. 121.

56. I owe the notion of embracing power to John Torpey, *The Invention of the Passport*.

57. Republished as "PrisonTalk" in Foucault, *Power/Knowledge*, p. 39.

58. See the 1977 interview entitled "Truth and Power," in Foucault, *Power/Knowledge*, p. 122.

59. On this point, see the 1976 interview entitled "Questions on Geography" in Foucault, *Power/Knowledge*, esp. pp. 71–72.

60. On this point, see the "Two Lectures" of 1976 republished in Foucault, *Power/Knowledge*, esp. pp. 99–100.

61. Foucault, "1977–78: Sécurité, territoire et population," p. 101.

62. Quoted from Foucault, "Governmentality," p. 87.

63. Whereas the discourse on sovereignty focuses on the interests of the monarch and the means by which he can cement his dominance over his territory and subjects, the discourse on governance focuses primarily on the common good and the types of knowledge and institutions that are necessary to promote it. The art of governance is somewhat stunted by the imperatives of absolutism, argues Foucault, and only reaches full flower with the emergence of political economy during the late eighteenth century. For it is the political economists who first recognize the ways in which state intervention in the market (read: society) may actually be self-defeating, insofar as it stifles the very productive forces that it seeks to nurture. Political economy thus represents a new level of reflexivity in the art of governance.

64. Originally published as *The Tanner Lectures on Human Values* and subsequently republished in Foucault, *Politics, Philosophy, Culture*; references here are to the latter version.

65. See Foucault, *Histore de la sexualité*.

66. Indeed, it was only at the very end of his career that he began to reformulate his theory of power to accommodate the exercise of domination. See the afterword on "The Subject and Power" in Hubert L. Dreyfus and Paul Rabinow, *Michel Foucault*.

67. These methodological precepts are stated most clearly in Foucault, *Language, Counter memory, practice* and especially in the essay entitled "Nietzsche, Genealogy, and History."

68. See Foucault, *Surveiller et punir*.

69. Weber, *Die Protestantische Ethik I*, pp. 12 and 189.

70. See, for example, ibid., p. 116.

71. Ibid., p. 143.

72. This is actually not true for Lutheran Pietism.

73. On the preceding points, see Weber, *Die Protestantische Ethik*, p. 347 and *Wirtschaft und Gesellschaft*, p. 355. Here, too, Weber's interpretation is a bit too simple. As recent scholarship has definitively shown, the rationalization of poor relief cannot be attributed to Calvinism alone. It began in the Renaissance and cut across confessional boundaries. Still, it could be argued—and will be argued here—that Calvinist social reform went further, faster.

74. On the affinity between Calvinism and revolution, see also Michael Walzer, *The Revolution of the Saints*. For a critical discussion of Walzer's argument, see Gorski, "Calvinism and Revolution."

75. Weber, *Wirtschaft und Gesellschaft*, p. 333.

76. Ibid., p. 358.
77. Weber, *Die Protestantische Ethik*, p. 334; *Wirtschaft und Gesellschaft*, p. 683.
78. Weber, *Wirtschaft und Gesellschaft*, p. 290.
79. As we will see, Weber was not the first to make this argument; it was also advanced by various Prussian historians, including Weber's *Doktorvater*, Gustav Schmoller, and Schmoller's protegé, Otto Hintze, and it was from them that Weber probably derived it. In an ironic twist, we will also see that Prussian historians have generally exaggerated the importance of Pietism—and understated the importance of Calvinism. For the moment, however, the key point is that it was in Brandenburg-Prussia the Protestant ethic and the spirit of bureaucracy first formed a lasting union.
80. Weber, *Die Protestantische Ethik I*, p. 286.
81. As anyone familiar with recent developments in early modern historiography will have noted by now, the contrasts that Weber draws between ascetic Protestantism and other denominations are often somewhat overblown. Thanks to the researches of historical specialists, we now know: that the Calvinist system of discipline was more private and the Catholic system more public than he suggests; that the rationalization of poor-relief antedated the Protestant Reformation and cut across confessional boundaries; that the ideological roots of Calvinist revolution are to be found in the writings of Lutheran and Catholic theologians; and that the Catholic Reformation led to an efflorescence of lay organizations which was at least as great as that which was sparked by the Protestant Reformation. But the fact that these differences were smaller than Weber believed does not mean that they were nonexistent—or unimportant. This point will be examined in more detail in chapter 4.
82. In his words: "The development of the modern state is everywhere set in motion by the prince's expropriation of the means of war, administration and finance and of politically useful good of all kinds [from] the autonomous, 'private' bearers of administrative power who assist him" (Weber, *Wirtschaft und Gesellschaft*, p. 824). Weber never elaborated this thesis in any of his writings on the state, which are actually quite meager in scope. But the summary of his views on the subject written by his editor and assistant Johannes Winckelmann suggests that Weber's sociology of the state was quite similar to the analysis of state development elaborated at the turn of the century by Gustav Schmoller, Otto Hintze, and other members of the Borussican school, in that it singled out the absolutist era as the pivotal period in which the distinctive features of the modern state—a specialized bureaucracy and a uniform legal code—first took shape. See Johannes Winckelmann, *Gesellschaft und Staat in der verstehenden Soziologie Max Webers*. See also Andreas Anter, *Max Webers Theorie des modernen Staates. Herkunft, Struktur, Bedeutung*, esp. pp. 163–74.
83. Republished in his *Geist und Gestalt des frühmodernen Staates*, pp. 179–97. This volume, in turn, appeared in English as *Neostoicism and the Early Modern State*. All citations are to the German edition of 1969.
84. Oestreich, "Strukturprobleme," p. 183.
85. Ibid., p. 192.
86. Ibid., pp. 193 ff.
87. An exhaustive though superficial analysis of this legislation may be found in Marc Raeff, *The Well-Ordered Police State*.
88. Oestreich, "Strukturprobleme," p.190. This argument is developed at much greater length in Oestreich, *Antiker Geist und moderner Staat bei Justus Lipsius (1547–1606)*.
89. Oestreich, "Strukturprobleme," pp. 189–90.
90. Ibid., p. 194.

91. See Elias, *Über den Prozess der Zivilisation*, vol. 2. This point is brought out even more clearly in Elias, *Die höfische Gesellschaft*.

92. Elias, *Über den Prozess*, vol. 1, p. 136.

93. Elias makes this point with especial clarity in the opening paragraphs of chapters 2 and 3 of *Die höfische Gesellschaft*.

94. Elias, *Über den Prozess*, vol. 1, p. 106.

95. Ibid., vol. 1, p. 136.

96. This periodization is already implicit in the opening paragraphs of *Über den Prozess*, vol. 1 and is made explicit in the organization of both volumes.

97. John Milton, *The Reason of Church Government*, bk. 1, chap. 1.

98. Tilly, *Coercion, Capital, and European States*, p. 1. The shortcomings of realist definitions of the state will be discussed at length in the conclusion.

99. Some readers may regard this reference to nations as anachronistic; nations and nationalism are often regarded as distinctly modern phenomena that first arose in the late eighteenth century. This assumption has been challenged by a great many historians of late, and I myself do not regard it as tenable. For my views on the subject, and a critical discussion of the literature, see Gorski, "The Mosaic Moment: An Early Modernist Critique of the Modernist Theory of Nationalism."

100. Indeed, as we will see in the discussions of Prussia and France, the level of administrative rationalization is itself partly a function of state ethos.

Chapter Two

1. William Aglionby, *The present state of the United Provinces of the Low-Countries*, vol. 1, pp. A3–5.

2. There are other ways in which it was not so strong. It was not always capable of rapid and unified decision making, nor was it easily able to force its will on recalcitrant elites. State strength has many different dimensions, some of which are not contained in the above specification of the concept.

3. Here I am thinking of Charles Tilly, *Coercion, Capital, and European States*; Brian Downing, *The Military Revolution and Political Change*; and Bruce Carruthers, *City of Capital*, chap. 4.

4. See, especially, Fernand Braudel, *Civilization and Capitalism*, chap. 3; Jonathan Israel, *Dutch Primacy in World Trade*; and Jan de Vries and Ad van der Woude, *The First Modern Economy*.

5. The narrative is based on the following standard accounts of the Dutch Revolt: Pieter Geyl, *The Revolt of the Netherlands*; S. Groenveld et al., *De tachtigjarige oorlog*; Geoffrey Parker, *The Dutch Revolt*; Iwo Schöffer, *De Lage Landen, 1500–1780*, pp. 132–268. Notes in the text refer to more specialized works.

6. See James Tracy, *Holland under Habsburg Rule, 1515–1566*.

7. See Michiel Dierickx, *L'Érection des nouveaux diocèses aux Pays-Bas, 1559–1570*.

8. See Phyllis Mack Crew, *Calvinist Preaching and Iconoclasm in the Netherlands, 1544–1569*.

9. See E. H. Kossman and A. F. Mellink, *Texts Concerning the Revolt of the Netherlands*, document 4, pp. 62–66.

10. See Solange Deyon, *Les "Casseurs" de l'été 1566*.

11. See A. L. E. Verheyden, *Le Conseil des Troubles*.

12. See A. A. van Schelven, *De nederduitsche vluchtelingskerken der XVI eeuw in Engeland en Duitschland*.

13. See H. M. Grapperhaus, *Alva en de tiende pennig.*
14. See J. C. A. De Meij, *De Watergeuzen in de Nederlanden, 1568–1572.*
15. See H. A. E. Enno van Gelder, *Revolutionnaire reformatie.*
16. See J. W. Koopmans, *De Staten van Holland en de Opstand.*
17. See André Despretz, "De Instauratie der Gentse Calvinistische Republiek (1577–79)," and J. Decavele, ed., *Het eind van een rebelse droom.*
18. See H. Q. Janssen, *De kerkhervorming in Vlaanderen.*
19. See Geoffrey Parker, *The Army of Flanders and the Spanish Road, 1567–1659.*
20. See F. G. Oosterhoff, *Leicester and the Netherlands, 1586–1587.*
21. See Jan Den Tex, *Oldenbarnevelt.*
22. See Werner Hahlweg, *Die Heeresreform der Oranier und die Antike,* and J. M. Wijn, *Het Krijgswezen in de tijd van Prins Maurits.*
23. See S. J. Fockema Andreae, *De Nederlandse staat onder de Republiek;* Robert Fruin, *Geschiedenis der staatsinstellingen in Nederland;* and Marjolein C. 't Hart, *Making of a Bourgeois State.*
24. See W. P. C. Knuttel, *De toestand der nederlandsche katholieken ten tijde der republiek,* and A. Th. Van Deursen, *Bavianen en slijkgeuzen.*
25. The classic works on the Dutch state during the ancien régime are Fruin, *Geschiedenis der Staatsinstellingen,* and Fockema Andreae, *De Nederlandse staat onder de Republiek.* For two, more recent overviews, in English, see Hart, *The Making of a Bourgeois State,* and Israel, *The Dutch Republic.*
26. For the details of this process, see E. A. M. E. Jansen, *De opkomst van de vroedschap in enkele hollandsche steden;* Johan E. Elias, *De vroedschap van Amsterdam, 1378–1795;* and P. W. de Lange, "De ontwikkeling van een oligarchische regeringsvorm in een Westfriese stad. Medemblik 1289–1699."
27. There are a number of specialized studies of the provincial states. These include J. W. Koopmans, *De Staten van Holland en de Opstand.;* Caspar van Heel, ed., *Vierhonderd jaar gedeputeerde staten van Overijssel;* F. H. J. Lemmink, *Het ontstaan van de staten van Zeeland en hun geschiedenis tot het jaar 1555;* Wiebe J. Formsma, *De wording van de Staten van Stad en lande tot 1536;* R. Reitsma, *Centrifugal and Centripetal Forces in the Early Dutch republic;* Wybe Jappe Alberts, *De staten van Gelre en Zutphen tot 1459* and *Van standen tot staten;* and C. A. van Kalveen, *Het bestuur van bisschop en Staten in het Nedersticht, Oversticht, en Drenthe, 1483–1520.*
28. On the States General, see also S. J. Fockema Andreae and Herman Hardenberg, eds., *500 jaren Statengeneraal in de Nederlanden,* and John H. Grever, "The Structure of Decision-Making in the States General of the Dutch Republic 1660–68."
29. See Grever, "Committees and Deputations in the Assemblies of the Dutch Republic, 1660–1668."
30. See Van Deursen, "De Raad van State en de Generaliteit (1590–1606)."
31. Here, I am of course referring to the Union of Utrecht (1576). It sealed the alliance of the northern provinces against Spain and came to serve as a constitution of sorts for the republic.
32. The best treatment of this subject is Hart, *The Making of a Bourgeois State.*
33. See H. L. Zwitzer, "Het quotenstelsel onder de Republiek der Verenigde Nederlanden alsmede enkele beschouwingen over de generale petitie, de staat van oorlog en de repartitie."

34. On the administration of the Dutch army, see H. L. Zwitzer, *"De militie van den staat"*; F. J. G. ten Raa and F. de Bas, *Het Staatsche leger, 1568-1795*; C. M. and J. W. M. Schulten, *Het leger in de zeventiende eeuw*; and Wijn, *Het Krijgswezen in de tijd van Prins Maurits*.

35. On the navy and the admiralty colleges, see Gustaaf Asaert et al., *Maritieme geschiedenis der Nederlanden*, vols. 2 and 3; Jaap R. Bruijn, *The Dutch Navy of the Seventeenth and Eighteenth Centuries*; idem, *De admiraliteit van Amsterdam in rustige jaren 1713-51*; and C. T. F. Thurkow, *De Westfriese admiraliteit*.

36. On the States General, see Hart, *Making of a Bourgeois State*, p. 197. On the states of Holland and the city of Amsterdam, see O. Vries, "Geschappen tot een ieders nut," p. 337.

37. For comparisons of naval strength, see G. Modelski and W. R. Thompson, *Seapower in Global Politics, 1494-1993*, pp. 68-70. For comparisons of troop strength, see Parker, "The 'Military Revolution,' 1550-1600—A Myth?" esp. p. 206. More detailed series of figures for each country may be found in Bruijn, *Dutch Navy*; ten Raa and de Bas, *Het staatsche leger*; Anne Blanchard et al., *Histoire militaire de la France* and D. W. Jones, *War and Economy in the Age of William III and Marlborough*.

38. Population figures are from Jan de Vries, *European Urbanization, 1500-1800*, table 3.6.

39. These figures are from Jones, *War and Economy*, table 2.1.

40. See de Vries and Ad van der Woude, *The First Modern Economy*, table 12.3.

41. On this subject, see James D. Tracy, *A Financial Revolution in the Habsburg Netherlands, and* Hart, *Making of a Bourgeois State*, chap. 6.

42. This argument is made quite explicitly in Tilly, *Coercion, Capital, and European States*, and Downing, *The Military Revolution and Political Change*. And it is echoed in Carruthers, *City of Capital*.

43. I derived these figures by converting the total national debts of each country into pounds sterling and dividing by total population. The figures for the national debts are taken from E. H. M. Dormans, *Het tekort*; James C. Riley, *The Seven Years' War and the Old Regime in France*, p. 178; and B. R. Mitchell and Phyllis Deane, *Abstract of British Historical Statistics*, pp. 401-2. The exchange rates are from John J. McCusker, *Money and Exchange in Europe and America, 1600-1775*, table 5.1. Population figures are taken from de Vries, *European Urbanization*, table 3.6.

44. See Sidney Homer, *A History of Interest Rates*, table 16.

45. Ibid., table 15.

46. William Montague, *The Delights of Holland*, p. 138.

47. Ludwig Herzel, ed. *Albrecht Hallers Tagebücher seiner Reisen nach Deutschland, Holland und England 1723-1727*, p. 33.

48. [Charles Lemaitre], *Voyage anonyme et inédit d'un janseniste en Hollande et en Flandre en 1681*, p. 67.

49. See John Lough, *France Observed in the Seventeenth Century by British Travellers*, pp. 167-68.

50. See John Locke, *Travels in France, 1675-1679*, pp. 30-31, 58, 67.

51. See Lough, *France Observed*, p. 105.

52. Ibid, p. 103.

53. Agliongy, *Present State*, p. 61.

54. See Antoni Maczak, *Travel in Early Modern Europe*.

55. The secondary literature on early modern crime is truly vast. For a recent overview of the English literature, see James A. Sharpe, "Quantification and the History of Crime in Early Modern England." On the French literature, see Benoit Garnot, "Pour une histoire nouvelle de la criminalité au XVIIIe siècle." On the German literature, see Joachim Eibach, "Kriminalitätsgeschichte zwischen Sozialgeschichte und Historischer Kulturforschung." On Italy, see Oscar di Simplicio, "La criminalità a Siena (1561–1808)."

56. These numbers are derived from graph 5 in Herman Diederiks, "Quality and Quantity in Historical Research in Criminality and Criminal Justice," pp. 57–76. On criminality in Leiden, see also Els Kloek, "Criminality and Gender in Leiden's *Confessieboeken*, 1678–1794."

57. See Pieter Spierenburg, "Long-Term Trends in Homicide," p. 78.

58. See Anton van den Hoeven, "Ten exempel en afschrik," pp. 40–41; cited in Spierenburg, "Long-Term Trends," p. 79.

59. See Marijke Gijswijt-Hofstra, *Wijkplaatsen voor vervolgden*.

60. These limitations are ably and extensively discussed in Sharpe, "Quantification and the History of Crime," and J. S. Cockburn, "Early Modern Assize Records as Historical Evidence."

61. See Spierenburg, "Long-Term Trends," table 3.1.

62. From 1559 to 1603, 129 people were indicted for homicide. Assuming a population of 52,000, this results in a rate of prosecuted murder of around 5.5 per 100,000 per year. During the period from 1645 to 1679, 185 people were indicted for murder. Because the population was now around 110,000, this yields a rate of prosecuted murder of around 4.8 per 100,000 per year, a rather small decline. The number of people convicted during this period was much smaller: only 48—a conviction rate of 1.25 per 100,000 per year on average. These figures are taken from table 1 in Cockburn, "The Nature and Incidence of Crime in England 1559–1625," and table 14 of Sharpe, *Crime in Seventeenth-Century England*.

63. See table 1 in Cockburn, "Patterns of Violence in English Society."

64. These figures are derived from table 2–1 in Eva Österberg, "Criminality, Social Control, and the Early Modern State." The data are presented and discussed in greater detail in Österberg and Dag Lindström, *Crime and Social Control in Medieval and Early Modern Swedish Towns*. Unfortunately, it is not clear whether these are rates of conviction or of indictment.

65. These figures are derived from Arlette Lebigre, *La Police*, p. 32.

66. While French historians have not been much concerned with the rate of crime, they have spent a good deal of time analyzing the composition of crime. In particular, they have sought to document a shift from violent crimes to property crimes. On the so-called *violence/vol* thesis, see Bernadette Boutelet, "Étude par sondage de la criminalité"; Pierre Deyon, "Délinquance et répression"; and N. W. Mogensen, "Crimes and Punishments in Eighteenth-Century France."

67. For a historical overview, see Philip John Stead, *The Police of France*. Figures are from table 2 in Alan Williams, *The Police of Paris, 1718–1789*.

68. See Lotte C. Van de Pol, *Het Amsterdams hoerdom*, pp. 181, 236.

69. From appendix 1 in Donald Rumbelow, *I Spy Blue*.

70. These impressions are summarized in Julia Bientjes, *Holland und der Holländer im Urteil deutscher Reisender (1400–1800)*, and Charlotte van Strien, *Touring the Low Countries*.

71. From figure 3 in Jan Kok, "The Moral Nation."
72. See Simon Schama, *Embarrassment*, p. 438.
73. See figure 1.2 in Peter Laslett, "Introduction."
74. See Meyer, "Illegitimates," p. 252.
75. See Jacques Depauw, "Amour illégitime et société à Nantes au XVIIIe siècle."
76. See Meyer, "Illegitimates," pp. 252, 254, and *passim*.
77. See figures 2 and 3 in Kok, "Moral Nation."
78. See R. M. Dekker, " 'Wij willen al den duyvel aff hebben!' "
79. See Dekker, *Holland in beroering*. See also C. S. L. Davis, "Peasant revolt in France and England."

80. See Tilly, *European Revolutions*, tables 3.2, 3.3, 3.4, 4.2, and 5.4. It should be noted, however, that these figures tend to overstate the differences between the Netherlands and France. For example, Tilly counts each of the eight wars of religion in France as a separate revolutionary situation. By this logic, it would probably make sense to count the three phases of the Dutch Revolt as distinct revolutionary situations. Even with these adjustments, however, the difference remains quite large.

81. The best overviews of the Dutch consistory are Albertus van Ginkel, *De ouderling*, chap. 4, and Van Deursen, *Bavianen en slijkgeuzen*, chap. 5.

82. On the organization and operation of the classes, see C. A. Tukker, *De classis Dordrecht van 1573 tot 1609*; A. Ph. F. Wouters, *Nieuw en ongezien*; and John Paul Elliott, "Protestantization in the Northern Netherlands." The records of some classes have been transcribed and published. Many of these records are cited below.

83. Substantial portions of their records have been transcribed in J. Reitsma and S. D. van Veen, *Acta der Provinciale en Particuliere Synoden*.

84. Articles 9 and 10 of the Synod of Wezel (1568). The complete text appears in F. L. Rutgers, *Acta van de Nederlandsche Synoden der zestiende eeuw*, pp. 1–55, and in *Kerkelyck Handboekje*, part 8.

85. For an excellent study of everyday life in the Dutch Republic, with many pertinent examples of the thin divide between public and private in Dutch towns, see van Deursen, *Een dorp in de polder*.

86. Synod of Emden (1571), article 32. The full text is reprinted in Rutgers, *Acta*, pp. 55–119.

87. The only instance that I have discovered in which the classis referred such a decision back to the consistory is in *Classicale Acta*, vol. 4, p. 254.

88. See *Classicale Acta*, vol. 1, p. 165, vol. 2, p. 509, and vol. 4, p. 334.

89. As in the case of Aaltje Claeses of Rauwert, who was "reconciled" to the church in 1690 after having been banished for fornication (*hoererij*) six years earlier. See Rijksarchief van Friesland (hereafter RAF), Archief Oude Burgerlijke Stand, inv. nr. 686, Mar. 27, 1684 and Apr. 24, 1690.

90. As in the case of Lysbert Ottes, also of Rauwert, who was repeatedly visited by members of the consistory after being censured for adultery—all to no avail. See RAF, Archief Oude Burgerlijke Stand, inv. Nr. 686, May 27, 1680 to Mar. 27, 1684, *passim*.

91. For example, when Joannes Pibonis, a Reformed pastor in the town of Hommelen, was accused of drunkenness and resisting arrest, the classis of Sneek dispatched two of its members to look into the matter. They commissioned a report on Pibonis's "life and conduct" from several of his colleagues, interviewed a number of eyewitnesses, and eventually discovered that the hapless cleric had also been seen giving a piece of gold to a woman of

ill-repute, at which point he was officially suspended and summoned before the provincial synod (RAF, Archief van de Hervormde Classis van Sneek, inv. nr. 2, Sept. 6, 1625–June 6, 1626, *passim*).

92. See, for example, *Classicale acta, 1573–1620*, Rijks Geschiedkundige Publicatiën, Kleine Serie, vols. 49, 68, 69 and 79 (The Hague: Instituut voor Geschiedenis, 1980–1995), vol. 1: *Particuliere Synode Zuid-Holland, I: Classis Dordrecht, 1573–1600*, ed. J. P. van Dooren, p. 196, and vol. 2: *Particuliere Synode Zuid-Holland, II: Classis Dordrecht, 1601–1620, Classis Breda 1616–1620*, ed. J. Roelevink, pp. 515, 520.

93. See, for example, *Classicale acta*, vol. 2, pp. 150, 652.

94. See, for example, RAF, Archief Oude Burgerlijke Stand, inv. nr. 344a, fos. 40 and 42–43 and inv. nr, 686, Aug. 6, 1688. In the city of Arnemunde, the consistory even ordered that the local bailiff be excluded from communion when the local magistrate dismissed a charge of adultery that he had brought against a fellow church member—in civil court! See *Classicale acta*, vol. 4, *Provinciale Synode Zeeland, Classis Walcheren, 1602–1620, Classis Zuid-Beveland 1579–1591*, ed. J. Boterse, p. 289.

95. They are Hermann Roodenburg, *Onder censuur*; Abels and Wouters, *Kerk en samenleving in de classis Delft*, vol. 2; and Mathieu G. Spiertz, "Die Ausübung der Zucht."

96. On England, see especially Robert von Friedeburg, "Reformation of Manners" and "Sozialdisziplinierung in England?" On Scotland, see especially Michael F. Graham, "Social Discipline in Scotland, 1560–1610."

97. On the French and German congregations, see J. Estèbe and B. Vogler, "La genèse d'une société protestante." For comparative evidence from the Netherlands, see Mathieu Spiertz, "Die Ausübung der Zucht."

98. The key sources on the religious composition of the Dutch population are J. A. de Kok, *Nederland op de breuklijn Rome-Reformatie*, and Hans Knippenberg, *De religieuze kaart van Nederland*.

99. The best discussion of this phenomenon is Van Deursen, *Bavianen*, pp. 128–34.

100. The best discussions of this phenomenon are Joke Spaans, *Haarlem na de Reformatie*, and Benjamin Kaplan, *Calvinists and Libertines*. See also C. C. Hibben, *Gouda in Revolt*.

101. On the church concept of the Dutch Baptists, see Cornelis Krahn, *Dutch Anabaptism*, pp. 112 ff.

102. On religious discipline among the Dutch Baptists, see van Deursen, *Plain Lives in a Golden Age*, pp. 309–10, and W. J. Kühler, *Geschiedenis van de Doopsgezinden in Nederland*, vol. 2:2, *passim*.

103. Van Deursen, *Bavianen*, p. 204.

104. On Dutch Lutheranism, see, in general, Jakob Loosjes, *Geschiedenis der Luthersche Kerk in de Nederlanden*, and J. Happee, J. L. J. Meiners, and M. Mostert, eds., *De Lutheranen in Amsterdam, 1588–1988*.

105. See article 6, "On Christian Discipline and the Church Ban." The church ordinance of 1597 is reprinted in F. J. Domela Nieuwenhuis, *Geschiedenis der Amsterdamsche Luthersche Gemeente*, pp. 32–61.

106. An excellent overview and exhaustive references may be found in Charles H. Parker, *The Reformation of Community*.

107. On this, see especially Spaans, *Armenzorg in Friesland 1500–1800*.

108. The most obvious is the development of confessionally specific systems of indoor relief in many Dutch towns during the late seventeenth and early eighteenth centuries.

109. See, for example, Madeleine van Strien-Chardonneau, *Le Voyage de Hollande*, pp. 69–71, and Montague, *The Delights of Holland*, p. 169.

110. See Charles Parker, *The Reformation of Community*, chap. 2; Charlotte Aleida van Manen, *Armenpflege*.

111. R. B. Evenhuis, *Ook dat was Amsterdam*, vol. 2, p. 75.

112. See Abels and Wouters, *Nieuw en ongezien*, vol. 1, p. 239 and vol. 2, p. 269.

113. See H. ten Boom, "De diaconie der Gereformeerde Kerk te Tiel van 1578 tot 1795."

114. See Van Deursen, *Een dorp in de polder*, p. 213.

115. For example, the civic orphanage of Amsterdam derived about half of its revenues from endowment income. By contrast, the Reformed diacony of Tiel relied mainly on voluntary contributions; they made up about 75 percent of the annual budget.

116. On the following, see Charles Parker, *Reformation of Community*, pp. 83–84.

117. See *Willekeuren, Ende Ordinnantien*, p. 78, and Marco H. D. van Leeuwen and Nicole Lucas, "De diakonie van de Hervormde Kerk," pp. 6–8. A copy is deposited at the library of the Gemeentearchief in Amsterdam (call number: P 0 98).

118. See *Willekeuren, Ende Ordinnantien*, p. 76, and Gemeentearchief Amsterdam (hereafter GAA), P.A. 377, inv. nr. 22, Apr. 8, 1675.

119. See *Willekeuren, Ende Ordonnantien*, p. 82, and Leeuwen and Lucas, "Diakonie," p. 11.

120. GAA, P.A. 377, inv. nr. 22, May 7, 1675.

121. There were at least four such cases in 1675. See GAA, P.A. 377, inv. n. 22, May 3, June 4, Aug. 20, and Oct. 22, 1675.

122. See GAA, P.A. 377, inv. nr. 22, October 22, 1675.

123. On this particular case see GAA, P.A. 377, inv. nr. 1, fos 1–2, and GAA, P.A. 376, inv. nr. 8, fos 271, 273, and 275.

124. See Van Deursen, *Bavianen*, pp. 117–18.

125. The term *Tuchthuis* is often translated as house of correction. Though house of discipline is somewhat less elegant, I prefer it here, for it better conveys the ideological project of which the *Tuchthuis* was a part.

126. The importance of the Dutch houses of correction for the development of the modern prison is discussed in A. Hallema, *Geschiedenis van het gevangeniswezen*; Robert von Hippel, "Beiträge zur Geschichte der Freiheitsstrafe"; and Eberhard Schmidt, *Zuchthäuser und Gefängnisse*.

127. The most detailed description of the Amsterdam *Tuchthuis*, which was razed in the nineteenth century, is contained in Jan Wagenaar, *Amsterdam in zyne opkomst*, vol. 2, pp. 250 ff.

128. This principle was made even more explicit in the ordinances of the Delft *Tuchthuis*, which specified that the inmates should "win their keep (*kost*) with their own hands" (*Beschryving van Delft*, p. 494).

129. The work regimen is described in Thorsten Sellin, *Pioneering in Penology*, chap. 6.

130. This according to the burgermeister of Leiden, Jan van Hout. See Hallema, "Jan van Hout's Rapporten," p. 83.

131. See Sellin, *Pioneering in Penology*, pp. 66–67.

132. Echoing the eighteenth-century chronicler Wagenaar, Spierenburg has recently suggested that the drowning cell was a fiction propagated through the unsubstantiated accounts of foreign travelers. In particular, he argues that the story of the drowning cell can be traced back to the account of several German travelers who could not believe that the Dutch were

able to reform vagrants *without* punitive methods of this sort. This is not implausible. The "observations" of foreign travelers were often borrowed from the accounts of previous travelers, sometimes word for word, and it is quite possible that a story as captivating as that of the drowning cell could have migrated from one account to another without being grounded in reality. But the evidence that could settle this debate—the archives of the *Tuchthuis*—no longer exists and the evidence that Spierenburg presents is hardly conclusive. It could be that the Germans were incredulous at the laxity of the Dutch. Or it could be that Spierenburg and Wagenaar are incredulous at the harshness of their forefathers.

133. *Historie van de Wonderlijcke Mirakelen*. This passage was first quoted in Hippel, "Geschichte der Freiheitsstrafe," p. 492. Here, I cite the English translation in Sellin, *Pioneering in Penology*, p. 70.

134. As Schama astutely points out, the drowning cell was designed not only to teach the value of work but "to be an intensive rehearsal of the primal Dutch experience: the struggle to survive rising waters" (Schama, *Embarrassment*, p. 24).

135. On the types and categories of inmates, see Hallema, "Wie er in de 17e eeuw in het tuchthuis kwamen?" On the incarceration of religious dissenters, see Hallema, "Een pater en twee predikanten in en uit het Amsterdamsche Tuchthuis."

136. This development is explored in detail in Spierenburg, ed., *The Emergence of Carceral Institutions*, and succinctly chronicled in idem, "Voorlopers van de Bijlmerbajes."

137. On the history of the *Werkhuis*, see the brief history written by the regents of the *Spinhuis* during the late eighteenth century contained in GAA, Library, call # J 1.1.28.

138. See *Reglement Voor het WEES-HUYS*, pp. 14–15.

139. Ibid., p. 24.

140. See ibid., p. 21–22.

141. See ibid., p. 12.

142. See GAA, P.A. 446, inv. nr. 1, fo. 19.

143. See GAA, P.A. 446, inv. nr. 1, fo. 17.

144. See GAA, P.A. 446, inv. nr. 1, fos. 195 and 273 and inv. nr. 2, fo. 26.

145. See *Reglement Voor het WEES-HUYS*, p. 5.

146. See GAA, P.A. 446, inv. nr. 1, fo. 17.

147. See GAA, P.A. 446, inv. nr. 1, fo. 100.

148. See GAA, P.A. 446, inv. nr. 1, fo. 292.

149. See Femme S. Gaastra, *De geschiedenis van de VOC*, p. 88.

150. See GAA, P.A. 446, inv. nr. 1, fo. 33.

151. See GAA, P.A. 446, inv. nr. 2, fo. 3.

152. See GAA, P.A. 446, inv. nr. 1, fo. 318.

153. See GAA, P.A. 343, inv. nr. 29, fo. 101 and inv. nr. 30, fo. 9.

154. See GAA, P.A. 343, inv. nr. 30, fos. 20, 22, and 25.

155. See GAA, P.A. inv. nr. 29, fo. 116.

156. The legacies are recorded in the registration books (*inschrijvingsboeken*) of the orphanages.

157. Figures for the three largest orphanages, the *Burgerweeshuis*, *Aalmoezeniersweeshuis*, and *Diakonieweeshuis*, can be found in J. Th. Engels, *Kinderen van Amsterdam*.

158. For Middelburg, see the introduction to C. De Waard, *De Archieven, berustende in het bestuur der godshuizen te Middelburg*. On Leeuwarden, see H. Spanninga, *De blauwe wezen* and M. J. Barnoes van Hemstra, *Old Burger Weeshuis*.

159. The most complete list of places and dates is in Hallema, *In en om de gevangenis van vroeger dagen in Nederland en Nederlandsch-Indië,* pp. 10–17. Hallema is also the author of many detailed local studies too numerous to cite here.

160. The *Tuchthuis* in Leeuwarden, for example, was plagued by serious problems right from the start. In December 1601, two inmates beat and subdued the house warden (*tuchtmeester*), "tearing his clothes to shreds," "threatening him with a knife," and "attempting by these means to get him to relinquish the key" (Gemeentearchief Leeuwarden, Oud-Archief, inv. nr., M1, pp. 164–65).

161. There is also a third question, which has to do with the impetus behind the reforms: Did it come from Calvinism? Humanism? Or somewhere else? In other words, Were its roots religious or secular? These are complex questions that have been hotly debated by Dutch historians and by early modernists more generally. I will discuss them in greater detail in chapter 4. For the moment, suffice it to say that I think the questions themselves are misleading insofar as they rest on a set of false dichotomies between Protestantism and humanism, and religious and secular.

162. This distinction between the central and local state is borrowed from the work of George Steinmetz. See, in particular, George Steinmetz, "The Local Welfare State" and *Regulating the Social.*

163. Brief discussions of marriage laws and religious schools may be found in Chapter 3 of my dissertation, "The Disciplinary Revolution: Calvinism and State-formation in Early Modern Europe, 1550–1750" (Ph.D. diss., University of California, Berkeley, 1996).

164. Moreau to the king of Poland. Cited in Israel, *The Dutch Republic,* p. 850.

165. The so-called Year of Disaster (1672) provides a telling counterexample. Riven by a conflict between the states of Holland and the House of Orange, the Dutch state was caught off guard by Louis XIV's invasion and nearly conquered. On this, see especially D. J. Roorda, *Het rampjaar 1672.*

166. See Hart, *Bourgeois State,* p. 195.

167. See Julian Dent, *Crisis in Finance,* pp. 42, 58.

168. See Hart, *Bourgeois State,* p. 207.

169. See ibid., p. 208.

170. The standard works on the subject are Roland Mousnier, *La Venalité des offices*; Martin Göhring, *Die Ämterkäuflichkeit im Ancien régime*; and William Doyle, *Venality.*

171. See Mousnier, *La Venalité des offices,* pp. 438–39, 449.

172. Several interesting examples may be found in Bruijn, *The Dutch Navy of the Seventeenth and Eighteenth Centuries,* pp. 33–35.

173. See O. Vries, "Geschapen tot een ieders nut," pp. 330, 337.

174. On this subject, see in general Grido de Bruin, *Geheimhouding en verraad.* See also J. G. Smit, "De ambtenaren van de centrale overheidsorganen der Republiek."

175. On the contrary, the available evidence suggests that cases of fiscal impropriety were actually fairly few and far in between, at least in seventeenth-century Holland. Thus, of all the cases recorded by the court of Holland between 1700 and 1811, only three involved charges of official corruption, and two of those concerned law enforcement officers. See Hermann Diederiks, *In een land van justitie.*

176. This paragraph draws mainly on a series of prosopographical studies on the regent class in various cities in Holland: K. W. J. M. Bossaers, *"Van kintsbeen aan ten staatkunde opgewassen"*; Jos. Leenders, *Benauwde verdraagzaamheid, hachelijk fatsoen*; Jacob Johannes

de Jong, *Met goed fatsoen*; Maarten R. Prak, *Gezeten burgers*; and L. Kooimans, *Onder regenten*.

177. Factions and parties have been the subject of three important studies: Roorda, *Partij en factie*; M. van der Bijl, *Idee en interest*; and Groenveld, *Evidente factiën in den staet*. This subject is also treated in considerable detail in Israel, *The Dutch Republic*.

178. For an excellent discussion of the relationship between financial probity and social honor, see Van de Pol, *Het Amsterdams hoerdom*, pp. 68–82.

179. Consequently, errant regents were willing to go to great lengths to conceal their misdeeds. And the local authorities often accommodated them by allowing them to pay fines in lieu of a trial, a process known as composing the offense (*compositie*). But the fines were based on the offender's assets and could be quite substantial. Moreover, there was always the risk that the offense might be made public by one's enemies.

180. See Van de Pol, *Hoerdom*, p. 72.

181. Quoted in Van Deursen, *Plain Lives*, p. 173.

182. A. C. M. Kappelhoff, *De belastingheffing in de Meierij van Den Bosch gedurende de Generaliteitsperiode (1648–1730)*, p. 217.

183. This figure is from Van Deursen, *Plain Lives*, p. 175.

184. This figure is from Kappelhoff, *Belastingheffing*, p. 152. See also Paul Brood, *Belastingheffing in Drenthe, 1600–1822*, p. 115.

185. The term was coined in Michael Roberts, *The Military Revolution, 1560–1660*. For a more extensive (and nuanced) treatment, see especially Geoffrey Parker, *The Military Revolution*.

186. The role of the Dutch was first recognized in Hans Delbrück, *Geschichte der Kriegskunst im Rahmen der politischen Geschichte*. The definitive treatment of the Dutch reforms is Hahlweg, *Die Heeresreform der Oranier und die Antike*. See also Wijn, *Het krijgswezen in de tijd van Prins Maurits*.

187. These drills are described and illustrated in Jacob de Gheyn, *Wapenhandelinghe van roers, musquetten ende spiessen*.

188. On this, see the eyewitness accounts in Lodewijk Mulder, ed., *Journaal van Anthonis Duyck (1591–1602)*, esp. those from 1595.

189. See Max Jähns, *Geschichte der Kriegswissenschaften, vornehmlich in Deutschland*, vol. 2, p. 924.

190. See Geoffrey Parker, *Military Revolution*, p. 20.

191. For details of the reception process, see especially Hahlweg, *Oranische Heeresreform*, chap. 3.

192. See Geoffrey Parker, *The Army of Flanders*, pp. 185–86.

193. According to the Venetian ambassador. See P. J. Blok, ed., *Relazioni veneziane*.

194. On military discipline in the Dutch army, see Wijn, *Krijgswezen*, chap. 3, and Schulten and Schulten, *Het leger*, pp. 57–61.

195. On the Spanish, see Geoffrey Parker, *Army of Flanders*. On the French, see John A. Lynn, "Tactical Evolution in the French Army, 1560–1660."

196. This process of appropriation and adaption is extensively documented in Hahlweg, *Die Heeresform der Oranier*.

197. For Oestreich's views, see especially "Der römische Stoizismus und die oranische Heeresreform," *Geist und Gestalt des frühmodernen Staates*, pp. 11–34. For a general discussion of Neostoicism, see Mark Morford, *Stoics and Neostoics*.

198. See Wolfgang Reinhard, "Humanismus und Militarismus," esp. p. 191 and n. 10.

Chapter Three

1. See Leopold Krug, *Betrachtungen über den Nationalreichtum*, p. 224.

2. For a breakdown of expenditures among Baltic and non-Baltic countries, see http://www.le.ac.uk/hi/bon/ESFDB/images/Korner/swib011.gif and http://www.le.ac.uk/hi/bon/ESFDB/images/Korner/swib012.gif.

3. These figures are taken from Peter Mathias and Patrick O'Brien, "Taxation in Britain and France," pp. 608-9.

4. Based on a figure of 85 million guilders in tax revenues and a national income of 713 million guilders. The first figure is taken from Gustav Otruba, "Staatshaushalt und Staatsschuld unter Maria Theresia und Joseph II," p. 239; and the second, on national income, is taken from J. Marx, Freiherr von Liechtenstern, *Skizze einer statistischen Schilderung des österreichischen Staats*, p. 71.

5. Due to military expenses incurred in the effort to put down the French Revolution.

6. The estimate of national income (261 million Reichstaler) is taken from Krug, *Nationalreichtum des preußischen Staates*, p. 224. The computation of tax revenue is based on Riedel, *Brandenburgisch-preußische Staatshaushault*.

7. The reasons are as follows: (1) 1800 was a peace year in Prussia, so total government expenditures would have been relatively lower; (2) per capita taxes were relatively flat during the second half of the eighteenth century; (3) the Prussian economy was expanding. Taken together, this suggests that the ratio of taxes to national income was probably higher during the middle of the eighteenth century than at the end.

8. See Otruba, "Staatshaushalt und Staatsschuld," table VIIc.

9. See Mathias and O'Brien, "The Social and Economic Burden of Tax Revenue Collected for Central Government," p. 808.

10. See Peter Claus Hartmann, *Das Steuersystem der europäischen Staaten am Ende des Ancien Régime*, pp. 239-41, 260-61, 284-303.

11. See Francis L. Carsten, *The Origins of Prussia*. For a similar interpretation, see also Hans Rosenberg, *Bureaucracy, Aristocracy, and Autocracy*.

12. It inspired another famous work on Prussian political development, Rosenberg, *Bureaucracy, Aristocracy and Autocracy*; underlies the analysis of Prussia in Barrington Moore's *Social Origins of Dictatorship and Democracy*; provided the theoretical basis for Perry Anderson's *Lineages of the Absolutist State* and even influenced more recent works on state-formation such as Charles Tilly's *Coercion, Capital, and European States*.

13. See Gerd Heinrich, "Der Adel in Brandenburg-Preußen," and Peter-Michael Hahn, *Landesstaat und Ständetum im Kurfürstentum Brandenburg während des 16. und 17. Jahrhunderts*.

14. For an excellent discussion of this point, see William W. Hagen, "Seventeenth-Century Crisis in Brandenburg, esp. pp. 318-29.

15. This is particularly evident in Thomas Ertman's *Birth of the Leviathan*, which makes Prussia the exemplar for Germany as a whole. It is also true of Carsten's *Princes and Parliaments in Germany from the Fifteenth to the Eighteenth Centuries*. In this book, Carsten attempts to extend his arguments about Prussia to the rest of Germany.

16. In recent years, several German historians have revived this interpretation—while stripping away its more blatantly hagiograpical and nationalistic elements—by arguing that the Calvinization of the royal service enabled the Prussian electors to bypass and thus short-circuit the authority of the territorial estates. See especially Edgar Melton, "The Prussian Junkers, 1600-1786," pp. 71-109; and Andreas Nachama, *Ersatzbürger und Staatsbildung*.

17. See Carl Hinrichs, *Preußentum und Pietismus*, and Klaus Deppermann, *Der hallesche Pietismus und der preußische Staat unter Friedrich III. (I.)*. Similar arguments may also be found in: Mary Fulbrook, *Piety and Politics*, and Richard L. Gawthrop, *Pietism and the Making of Eighteenth-Century Prussia*.

18. For general overviews, see Hans-Ulrich Delius, "Die Reformation in Berlin," and Felix Escher, "Das Kurfürstentum Brandenburg im Zeitalter des Konfessionalismus."

19. The authoritative account is Bodo Nischan, *Prince, People, and Confession*.

20. On the pamphlet war, see Nischan, *Prince, People and Confession*, pp. 160 ff. For examples of anti-Calvinist persecution, see Fabian zu Dohna, *Die Selbstbiographie des Burggrafen Fabian zu Dohna*, pp. xxiv–xxxi. For an example of popular protest, see the eyewitness report published in Anton Chroust, "Aktenstücke zur brandenburgischen Geschichte unter Kurfürst Johann Sigismund," esp. pp. 18–21.

21. See Nischan, "Johann Peter Bergius."

22. For a particularly lucid discussion of these events, see Otto Hintze, *Die Hohenzollern und Ihr Werk*, pp. 166–77.

23. See Gerhard Oestreich, *Der brandenburg-preußische Geheime*, pp. 10–12.

24. "Eingabe der Deputierten der Stände an Friedrich Wilhelm in Königsberg," Jan. 8, 1641, in *Urkunden und Actenstücke zur Geschichte des Kurfürsten Friedrich Wilhelm von Brandenburg* (henceafter *UA*), vol. 10, p. 88.

25. On the significance of the Dutch example for Friedrich Wilhelm's "estates-friendly domestic policies," see Ernst Opgenoorth, *Friedrich Wilhelm, der Große Kurfürst von Brandenburg*, vol. 1, pp. 50 ff. For a more general discussion of Friedrich Wilhelm's attitudes towards the Estates, see idem, " 'Nervus rerum,' " esp. pp. 108–10, and also Peter Baumgart, "Zur Geschichte der kurmärkischen Stände im 17. und 18. Jahrhundert."

26. See Oestreich, *Geheime Rat*, pp. 15–16. Of the sixteen Privy councillors appointed between 1640 and 1651, nine were native nobles, three were commoners from the Mark, and only four were foreign aristocrats. See Carsten, *Origins*, p. 182.

27. See *UA*, vol. 10, pp. 42 ff.

28. See *UA*, vol. 10, p. 34, n. 1.

29. Chrn. Otto Meylius, *Corpus Constitutionum Marchicarum* (hereafter *CCM*), vol. 6, no. 107, cols. 381–82.

30. Specifically, he rejected the Estates' demand that Lutheran and Reformed professors be appointed to the Royal Gymnasium in Joachimstal and the University of Frankfurt on the Oder as a violation of the "free exercise" of his religion and refused to confirm the nomination of Martin Heinsius, a Lutheran theologian, to the theological faculty at the University of Frankfurt unless he signed a reverse promising to renounce all "bitterness, calumny and blasphemy" in his dealings with the Reformed Church. On the religious grievances of the Estates and Frederick William's reaction, see the Privy Council's "Relation" of July 20, 1642 in *Protokolle und Relationen des Brandenburgischen Geheimen Rathes aus der Zeit des Kurfürsten Friedrich Wilhelm*, ed. Otto Meinardus, vol. I, pp. 323–24; hereafter *PR*.

31. *UA*, vol. 10, pp. 222–25.

32. See Isaacsohn in *UA*, vol. 10, pp. 172 ff.

33. *See UA*, vol. 10, pp. 229–46.

34. *CCM*, vol. 6, no. 115, col. 401.

35. Letter to the Privy Council from May 21, 1652, *UA*, vol. 10, pp. 255–56.

36. The development of the central bureaucracy in Brandenburg-Prussia has been a recurrent focus of historical research since the mid-nineteenth century and is the subject of a voluminous scholarly literature, much of which can be found in the excellent bibliography compiled in Otto Büsch and Wolfgang Neugebauer eds., *Moderne preußische Geschichte 1648–1947*. This older literature tends to play down the role of the native nobility and the territorial estates in the Prussian state; indeed, many of these authors argue that the Hohenzollerns destroyed or abolished the estates altogether. By contrast, the more recent literature tends to play down the power and authority of the central state apparatus; it suggests that the nobility and estates continued to play a significant if diminished role in political administration, particularly at the local level. For this interpretation see especially: Günter Vogler, "Absolutistisches Regiment und ständische Verfassung in Brandenburg-Preußen im 17. und 18. Jahrhundert"; Hahn, *Fürstliche Territorialhoheit und lokale Adelsgewalt;* and, more generally, Jan Peters ed., *Gutsherrschaft als soziales Modell.*

37. *UA,* vol. 10, p. 593.

38. In the words of Paul Gerhard, leader of the orthodox faction. Quoted from Hans-Joachim Beeskow, "Paul Gerhardt," p. 66.

39. Oestreich, *Geheime Rat,* p. 30.

40. See Andreas Nachama, *Ersatzbürger und Staatsbildung,* p. 72. Nachama's figures actually understate the percentage of Calvinists within the Prussian civil service, for they are based solely on an examination of church records from the Berlin Cathedral and thus exclude a number of Reformed officials—such as the Dohnas—who lived outside Berlin.

41. Addendum to the *gravamina* of Oct. 22, 1677, presented to the elector on Dec. 20, 1678. GStAPK HA I, rep. 47, nr. 13.

42. In an ironic footnote to this Lutheran jeremiad, a second chronicle, dated 1735, indicates that von Löben's estate was taken over by one George Abraham Stosch, a descendant, most likely, of the Reformed Court preacher who had played so pivotal a role in promoting the Calvinization of the Prussian elite. Both chronicles are taken from a *Turmknopfeinlage* in the *Kirchenbuch* of Pulzig, which is transcribed in Monika and Paul v. Loeben, "Geschichte der Herren," p. 9.

43. In Georg Küntzel ed., *Die politischen Testamente der Hohenzollern,* p. 44.

44. On the constitutional history of Cleve-Mark before the reign of Frederick William, see A. von Haeften, "Allgemeine Einleitung: Die landständische Verhältnisse in Cleve und Mark bis zum Jahre 1641," in *UA,* vol. 5, pp. 3–82.

45. *UA,* vol. 5, pp. 166–69.

46. See *UA,* vol. 5, pp. 214–16, 236–42.

47. *UA,* vol. 5, pp. 281–87, 297–303.

48. For the negotiations, see *UA,* vol. 5, pp. 309–60. For the agreement, see ibid., pp. 388–95.

49. See *UA,* vol. 5, pp. 416, 432–35.

50. See *UA,* vol. 5, pp. 551–54.

51. See *UA,* vol. 5, pp. 512 ff.

52. See *UA,* vol. 5, pp. 723–25.

53. See *UA,* vol. 5, pp. 688–92.

54. See *UA,* vol. 5, pp. 733–34, and von Haeften, "Einleitung," pp. 607–8.

55. Von Haeften, "Einleitung," in *UA,* vol. 5, p. 793.

56. See *UA,* vol. 5, pp. 962–74.

57. See Otto Hötzsch, *Stände und Verwaltung von Cleve und Mark in der Zeit von 1666 bis 1697*, pp. 155–60.

58. While there were occasional violations of the *ius indigenatus* in lower-level appointments, there is only one known case of a foreigner being appointed to high office. See Hötzsch, *Stände und Verwaltung*, pp. 47–48.

59. See Robert Scholten, *Zur Geschichte der Stadt Cleve*, p. 281.

60. See Martin Gabriel, *Die reformierten Gemeinden in Mitteldeutschland*.

61. See Neugebauer, "Die Stände in Magdeburg."

62. Of course, there were conflicts between the Crown and the estates during the late seventeeth century regarding the spread of Lutheran Pietism. But they are not relevant to the outcome presently under discussion.

63. For a more detailed discussion of these two cases and references to the relevant literature, see Gorski, "The Disciplinary Revolution."

64. I say "one of" because there was at least one other: the Crown had an independent source of revenue in the form of the royal domains. This issue is discussed in more detail below.

65. Frederick was granted the royal title of King in Prussia in 1701. Because he was the third elector named Frederick, but the first king, he is sometimes referred to as Frederick III, other times as Frederick I, and still other times as Frederick III (I). For the sake of simplicity I will simply refer to him as Frederick I.

66. Hintze, *Geist und Epoche der preußischen Geschichte*, p. 347.

67. An entertaining, if unsystematic, overview of these Francophilic tendencies may be found in Adrien Fauchier-Magnan, *The Small German Courts in the Eighteenth Century*. A more theoretically driven account may be found in the introduction to Peter H. Wilson, *War, State and Society in Württemberg, 1677–1793*.

68. On state finance during this period, see especially Kurt Breysig, *Die Centralstellen der Kammerverwaltung und des Heeres*, vol. 1.

69. Brandenburg-Prussia, claimed a well-informed member of the Dutch Council of State in 1704, would be incapable of supporting its army of 30,000 troops without extensive foreign subsidies. Cited from Hans Bleckwenn, *Die Ökonomie-Reglements des altpreußischen Heeres*, p. 8.

70. They sought to gain the king's attention by denouncing one of Wartenberg's cronies, a certain Friedrich Christian von Löben, to the royal prosecutor's office. Von Löben had amassed numerous offices in Halle and Magdeburg and enriched himself by means of various real estate schemes. He was able to deflect most of the charges leveled against him by presenting royal decrees signed by Wartenberg without the knowledge of the king. On the von Löben case, see Brandenburgisches Landeshauptarchiv (hereafter BLHA), Pr. Br. Rep. 4a, 1207.

71. See a detailed account of Wartenberg's fall and the events leading up to it in Hinrichs, *Friedrich Wilhelm I*, pp. 438–90.

72. See J. A. Freylingshausen, *Sieben Tage am Hofe Friedrich Wilhelms I*, Sept. 6, 1727.

73. See Otto Krauske, "Vom Hofe Friedrich Wilhelms I," p. 174.

74. See Friedrich Förster, *Friedrich Wilhelm I*. See especially the discussion of the king's daily regimen in vol. 1, pp. 193 ff.

75. See Freylingshausen, *Sieben Tage*, p. 26.

76. From Frederick William's political testament of 1722, in Küntzel, ed., *Die Politischen Testamente der Hohenzollern,* vol. 1, pp. 70 and 88.

77. On the ethos of the Calvinist clergy, see Rudolf von Thadden, *Die brandenburgisch-preussischen Hofprediger im 17. und 18. Jahrhundert.* The best analysis of the royal officials is Eckhart Hellmuth, *Naturrechtsphilosophie und bürokratischer Werthorizont.* On the position of this group within the royal court during and prior to the early years of Frederick William I's reign, see Hinrichs, *Friedrich Wilhelm I.*

78. See *Krönungs-Ceremonien.*

79. Details in Oskar Schwebel, *Geschichte der Stadt Berlin,* vol. 2, pp. 204–30, and Adolf Steckfuß, *500 Jahre Berlin,* pp. 253–60.

80. The phrase is from Hinrichs, "Der Regierungsantritt Friedrich Wilhelm I," which provides by far the best account of the early days of the new king's reign.

81. See Hinrichs, *Friedrich Wilhelm I,* esp. pp. 209–15 and 491–96.

82. *Acta Borussica* (hereafter *ABB*), no. 149, "Bericht des kaiserlichen Gesandten," Berlin, May 2, 1713.

83. See Ernst Friedländer, ed., *Berliner geschriebene* no. 8 (June 10, 1713).

84. See Riedel, *Brandenburgisch-preußische Staatshaushalt,* "Beilage No. IX."

85. Report of the Dutch representative in Berlin, Baron von Lintelo, Feb. 28, 1713. Cited from Hinrichs, "Regierungsantritt," p. 95.

86. Baron von Lintelo, cited from Oestreich, *Friedrich Wilhelm I,* p. 52.

87. Friedländer, *Zeitungen,* no. 29, Nov. 18, 1713.

88. *ABB,* vol. 2, no. 175.

89. Frédéric le Grand, *Oeuvres,* vol. 1, p. 192.

90. Cited from A. v. Crousaz, *Die Organisation des brandenburgischen und preußischen Heeres seit 1640,* vol. 1, p. 41. These impressions are confirmed by less interested parties such as Albrecht Haller, a Swiss man of letters, who contrasted the poorly trained Württemberger troops he saw in Tübingen with the well-disciplined Prussian units he saw in Halle. See Ludwig Herzel, ed., *Albrecht Hallers Tagebücher seiner Reisen nach Deutschland, Holland und England 1723–1727,* pp. 9 and 77.

91. See the detailed "excurse on the rate of fire" in Hans Delbrück, *Geschichte der Kriegskunst im Rahmen der politischen Geschichte,* vol. 4, pp. 310 ff.

92. See Frederick William's remarks on this subject in Hans Bleckwenn, *Reglement vor die Königl,* p. xxvii.

93. See Siegfried Fiedler, *Grundriß der Militär- und Kriegsgeschichte,* p. 58.

94. See Bleckwenn, *Reglement,* p. xxxiv.

95. Few copies of the earlier *Reglements* have been preserved. One copy of the *Reglement* of 1714 is deposited at the Geheimes Staatsarchiv in Berlin. On the *Reglement* of 1718, see Harald Kleinschmidt, "Zum preußischen Infanteriereglement von 1718."

96. See Kurt Zeisler, *Die "langen Kerls,"* pp. 100–101.

97. Based on the *Reglement* of 1726. Earlier *Reglements* had a slightly larger number of movements.

98. One of the few eyewitness descriptions of routine drilling and the annual review is to be found in the "Curriculum Vitae Militaris Dom. Neubauer," reprinted in Bleckwenn, ed., *Kriegs- und Friedensbilder, 1725–1759,* see esp. p. 249.

99. This is evident, for example, from Friedländer, *Garnisons-Chronik,* which invariably gives long lists of promotions—and demotions—during June and July.

100. See Robert Frhr. von Schrötter, "Die Ergänzung des preußischen Heeres unter dem ersten Könige."

101. Cited from Siegfried Fiedler, "Militärgeschichte im Zeitalter des Absolutismus," p. 121.

102. See *ABB*, vol. 5/2, no. 357.

103. *ABB*, vol. 3, p. 450.

104. See Eugen von Frauenholz, *Das Heerwesen in der Zeit des*, p. 19.

105. The bounty was 12 Reichsthalers, a small fortune for a peasant or artisan. See Wilhelm Stratemann, *Vom Berliner Hofe zur Zeit Friedrich Wilhelms I*, no. 80, May 18, 1730. On the security measures, see Olaf Groehler, *Das Heerwesen in Brandenburg und Preußen von 1640 bis 1806*, p. 23 and Otto Büsch, *Militärsystem und Soziallebem im Alten Preußen*, p. 28.

106. See Max Lehmann, "Werbung, Wehrpflicht und Beurlaubung im Heere Friedrich Wilhelms I."

107. See Curt Jany, "Die Kantonverfassung Friedrich Wilhelms I."

108. See Fiedler, "Militärgeschichte," p. 59.

109. Much has been written about the development of the central state administration in Brandenburg-Prussia. On the subject of administrative organization, the best survey is (still) Conrad Bornhak, *Geschichte des preußischen Verwaltungsrechts*. For a summary of subsequent research and an excellent bibliography, see Neugebauer, "Zur neueren Deutung der preußischen Verwaltung im 17. und 18. Jahrhundert." On the subject of fiscal management, the best survey is Franz Schneider, *Geschichte der formellen Staatswirtschaft von Brandenburg-Preußen*.

110. See *ABB*, vol. 1, no. 123.

111. See *ABB*, vol. 3, no. 295.

112. On the Prussian development and the "cameral sciences" more generally, see Jutta Brückner, *Staatswissenschaften, Kameralismus und Naturrecht*, and Hans Maier, *Die ältere deutsche Staats- und Verwaltungslehre*.

113. Numerous examples may be found in the *Personenregister* in the ABB, which lists all mid- to upper-level administrators and the various offices they held. One particularly famous rags-to-riches story concerns Johan Friedrich Domhardt. It is briefly recounted in the *Allgemeine Deutsche Biographie*, vol. 5, pp. 325–26.

114. The distinguishing features of a bureaucratic administration are listed in Max Weber, *Wirtschaft und Gesellschaft*, pp. 126–27.

115. *ABB*, vol. I, p. 323.

116. From the *Instruction for the General Directory*, *ABB*, vol. 3, p. 558.

117. Based on the *Personenregister* in vols. 1–7 of the *ABB*.

118. Based on the *Personenregister* of the *ABB*, vols. 1–7, and genealogical information culled from the *Heroldbibliothek*, Berlin-Dahlem, and the *Staatsbibliothek I* ("Unter den Linden").

119. See *ABB, Personenregister*, vols. 1–6.

120. See *ABB, Personenregister*, vols. 4.1–5.2.

121. The definitive overview of the Prussian budgetary system is still Riedel, *Brandenburgisch-preußische Staatshaushalt*. More concise (but less complete) overviews may be found in Schneider, *Geschichte der formellen Staatswirtschaft von Brandenburg-Preußen*, and Hintze, *Die Behördenorganisation und allgemeine Verwaltung in Preußen um 1740*, pp. 18–23.

122. Adamant as he was about this rule, the king was not always able to enforce it, particularly in the hinterlands of Prussia, which some officials considered an unacceptable posting.

123. Just how large this network was, however, is unclear. There are several well-known examples, such as those of Katsch and Viebahn within the General Directory and Löllhöffel within the Prussian War and Domains Board (for references, see the following note). Hinrichs also cites fragmentary reports sent to the king by local-level informers. On the whole, however, the documentary record is thin, suggesting that the network may actually have been rather small.

124. See *ABB*, vol. 3, no. 285. See also the instruction for Katsch's successor, Franz Moritz von Viebahn, *ABB*, vol. 4/2, no. 302, and for Löllhöffel, *ABB* vol. 5/1, no. 202.

125. *ABB*, vol. 5.1, p. 806.

126. Wilhelm Stratemann, *Vom Berliner Hofe zur Zeit Friedrich Wilhelms I*, mentions several such inspections. See, for example, nos. 94 and 142.

127. On the Schlubhut case, see "Aktenmäßige Geschichte der Hinrichtung des Geheimen Raths von Schlubhut," *Preußische Monatsschrift* vol. 1 (Dec. 1788). Extracts published in *ABB*, vol. 5.1, no. 132.

128. On the Hesse case, see *ABB* vol. 5/1, no. 271.

129. On the background of the Titius case, see *ABB*, vol. 5/2, no. 163. On his suicide, see Friedländer, *Garnisons-Chronik*, Sept. 27, 1738.

130. On the Drave case, see Wolff, *Berichte*, nos. 58, 98, 100, 123, 124, and 128.

131. Friedländer, *Zeitungen*, no. 9, Mar. 3, 1714.

132. *ABB*, vol. 1, no. 129.

133. See Friedländer, *Zeitungen*, Mar. 24, 1716.

134. Friedländer, *Zeitungen*, Jan. 9. 1717.

135. *ABB*, vol. 2, p. 456.

136. On the Wagner case, see *ABB*, vol 5/1, pp. 517–18, and Friedländer, *Garnisons-Chronik*, Nov. 14, 1732.

137. It is not clear when this practice originated. The first mention of conduct lists I have been able to find is in 1723. (See *ABB*, vol. 4/1, no.122). Frederick William I seems to have dropped the use of conduct lists towards the end of the reign on the grounds that "one cannot get a proper picture of the people from these lists, since those who send them in are influenced too much by their particular passions and personal designs" (*ABB*, vol. 5/2, "Cabinetsordre an den Etatsminister von Happe," Potsdam, Mar. 31, 1738). Frederick the Great subsequently revived it, however, and the Geheimes Staatsarchiv in Berlin and the Brandenburgisches Landeshauptarchiv in Potsdam both have numerous conduct lists from the end of his reign.

138. See Riedel, *Brandenburg-preußische Staatswirtschaft*, pp. 53–54.

139. See ibid., p. 42 and *Beilage* no. IX.

140. Based on the figures in ibid., *Beilage* no. XII, column 10 ("Rest-Ausgabe für Hof- und Civil-Zwecke").

141. The calculation of court expenditure is based on the figures in ibid., *Beilage* no. IX. The other figures are from Schneider, *Geschichte der formellen Staatswirtschaft von Brandenburg-Preußen*, p. 96.

142. See Friedrich von Reden, *Allgemeine vergleichende Finanz-Statistik*, vol. 2, pt. 1, p. 77. Reden's figure includes court expenditures. The figure cited above does not.

143. Compare the salaries given in Hintze, "Einleitende Darstellung," pp. 284–85 with those given in Ernst von Meier, *Hannoversche Verfassungs- und Verwaltungsgeschichte,* vol. 1, pp. 517 ff.; and Hans Schmelze, *Der Staatshaushalt des Herzogtums Bayern im 18. Jahrhundert,* pp. 197–200.

144. This figure is based on the numbers for each branch of the central administration as given in Otto Hintze, "Einleitende Darstellung," *ABB,* vol. 6, pt. 1, pp. 55–197.

145. This figure is an estimate obtained by multiplying the number of provincial governments (nine) times the typical number of officials (roughly 75–100) in each government, as based on Hintze, "Einleitende Darstellung," pp. 289– 492. An exact count is not possible because Hintze does not give complete enumerations for all of the provincial governments.

146. See Eduard Rudolf Uderstädt, *Die ostpreußische Kammerverwaltung.* According to Uderstädt, East Prussia had ten tax collectors (*Steuerräte*), ten justices of the peace (*Landräte*), and fifteen domains managers (*Beamte*). Tax collectors in small villages had four subalterns. Those in Königsberg had considerably more. The justices of the peace were assisted by four engineers (*Kalkulatoren*). No doubt, the domains managers also had subaltern personnel, but Uderstädt does not provide any details. Based on this information, we arrive at a base figure of about one hundred local officials. The other large provinces (that is, East Pomerania, the Old Mark, the New Mark, and Cleve-Mark) had similar numbers of *Landräte,* and there is no obvious reason to assume that the numbers of tax collectors and domains managers were terribly different either, while the smaller provinces (that is, Minden, Halberstadt, Ravensburg and Magdeburg) seem to have had roughly one-third as many officials in each of these categories; see the figures for East Pomerania, Halberstadt, Ravensburg, and the Kurmark in *ABB,* vol. 4, part 1, pp. 181, 766, and 260, and vol. 6, pt. 1, p. 453, respectively.

147. To my knowledge, there is nothing like a comprehensive list of state officials in the Prussian archives. And since the king maintained personal control over all appointments, and since the royal house archives were lost in the Second World War, it is unlikely that such lists are still in existence. Hence, contemporary scholars must depend on the works of prewar scholars, such as Hintze, who had access to a more complete set of archival documents.

148. Despite a fairly intensive search of the published sources and the secondary literature, I was unable to find information on criminality, illegitimacy or social unrest in Brandenburg-Prussia such as I found for the Netherlands and other western European countries. Perhaps the extant sources do not yield this information.

149. On Spener's life and work, see Johannes Wallmann, *Philipp Jakob Spener und die Anfänge des Pietismus,* and Paul Grünberg, *Philipp Jakob Spener.*

150. These included the "prime minister," Eberhard von Danckelmann, the president of the Berlin consistory, Paul von Fuchs, and the Minister for Spiritual Affairs, Marquis Ludwig von Printzen, to name only the most prominent.

151. "It is said that many Reformed Protestants attend my sermons"—thus Spener in a letter to written to Elisabeth Kißweiler in December 1691 (August Nebe, "Aus Speners Berliner Briefen an eine Freundin in Frankfurt").

152. See the register of *Leichenpredigten* contained in the systematic catalogue of the *Staatsbibliothek I* ("Unter den Linden") in Berlin under the call number Ee. The originals, unfortunately, were lost or destroyed during the war.

153. On Prussian poor-law reforms, see Spener, "Letzte theologische Bedencken," in Philipp Jacob Spener, *Schriften,* and Willi Grün, *Speners soziale Leistungen und Gedanken,* chap. 2. In English, see the (rather spotty) account in Reinhold A. Dorwart, *The Prussian Welfare State before 1740,* chap. 8.

154. See Felix Stiller, "Das Berlin Armenwesen vor dem Jahre 1820."

155. See a copy of Spener's *unmaßgebliche Vorschläge* in GStAPK HA I, rep. 47, "Geistliche Angelegenheiten," no. 17a.

156. On the history of private confession within the Lutheran Church and the disputes surrounding it, see Kurt Aland, "Die Privatbeichte im Luthertum von ihren Anfängen bis zur Auflösung" in idem, *Kirchengeschichtlicher Entwürf,* and Laurentius Klein, *Evangelisch-lutherische Beichte.*

157. On Schade and the Berliner Confession Debate, see Dietrich Blaufuß, "Ph. J. Spener, J. Caspar Schade und Sein Freundeskreis," pp. 19 ff.

158. *CCM,* vol. 1, no. 65.

159. On Pomerania, see Hellmuth Heyden, "Briefe Philipp Jacob Speners nach Stargard i.P. Ein Beitrag zur Geschichte des Pietismus in Hinter-Pommern." On Prussia, see Erich Riedesel, *Pietismus und Orthodoxie in Ostpreußen.* On the Mark, see Walter Wendland, "Studien zum kirchlichen Leben in Berlin um 1700," esp. pp. 162–72 and "Märkischer Pietismus," pp. 31–42. On the Rhineland provinces, see Theodor Wotschke, "Zur Geschichte des westfälischen Pietismus," *Jahrbuch des Vereins für westfälische Kirchengeschichte* 32 (1931), pp. 56–100 and 34 (1933), pp. 39–103.

160. See August Hermann Francke, *Segens-volle Fußstapfen,* p. 3.

161. See ibid., p. 12.

162. See ibid., p. 18.

163. See Directorium der Franckeschen Stiftungen, *Die Stiftungen August Herman Francke's in Halle,* p. 74.

164. See ibid., pp. 157–59.

165. The donations are chronicled in great detail in Francke, *Segens-volle Fußstapfen.* On the royal privileges, see Klaus Depperman, *Der hallesche Pietismus und der preußische Staat unter Friedrich I. (III.),* chaps. 8 and 11.

166. For details, see Directorium der Franckeschen Stiftungen, *Die Stiftungen, passim.*

167. See Wolf Oschlies, *Die Arbeits- und Berufspädagogik August Hermann Francke's,* p. 41.

168. Based on the schedules for the *Pädagogium* and the Latin School given, respectively, in Gustav Kramer, *August Hermann Francke,* vol. 1, pp. 225 ff., and Freylingshausen and Gotthilf August Francke, *Ausführlicher Bericht von der Lateinischen Schule des Waysenhauses,* pp. 35–53.

169. Freylingshausen and Francke, *Kurzer Bericht,* p. 43.

170. On the various *Motions- und Recreationsübungen,* see ibid., pp. 18 ff.

171. See Deppermann, *Der hallesche Pietismus,* p. 94.

172. See Francke, *Der von Gott in dem Waysenhause zu Glaucha an Halle ietzo bey nahe für 600 Personen Zubereitete,* p. 12.

173. See Francke, *Segens-volle,* p. 13.

174. As in the case of one young man who drew a picture of the devil and placed it on the footpath in front of his teacher; Francke describes this incident in a letter to Spener dated Dec. 16, 1699. See Kramer, *Beiträge,* p. 425.

175. Freylingshausen and Francke, *Kurzer Bericht,* p. 67.

176. Francke, *Pädagogische Schriften,* p. 98.

177. Ibid., p. 94.

178. On this point, see the memorandum written by a teacher from the *Pädagogium* reprinted in Marianne Doerfel, "Pietistische Erziehung," esp. p. 98.

179. One of Francke's colleagues at the University of Halle, the philosopher and theologian Christian Wolff, charged that graduates of the teacher's college were often unable to understand or summarize theological arguments, and the humanist scholar Christian Thomasius believed that the educational regimen practiced in Francke's schools led to "a subtle form of hypocrisy and self-deception" and compared it, quite rightly, to those of the "strict monastic orders" (cited from Hinrichs, *Preußentum und Pietismus,* pp. 372 ff. and pp. 414 ff.).

180. See Doerfel, "Pietistische Erziehung," p. 94.

181. He obtained the book through Johann Overbeck, a well-wisher who lived close to the Dutch border in the city of Cleve and, by all indications, never returned it despite Overbeck's repeated importunings. See their correspondence in Wotschke, "August Hermann Franckes rheinische Freunde in ihren Briefen," esp. letters no. 68, 69, 74, and 75.

182. See Hinrichs, *Preußentum und Pietismus,* p. 20.

183. Peter Schicketanz ed., *Der Briefwechsel Carl Hildebrand von Canstein mit August Hermann Francke,* no. 485 (Canstein to Francke, Nov. 7, 1711).

184. See Francke, *Segens-volle,* p. 48.

185. See Erich Beyreuther, *August Hermann Francke,* p. 188.

186. According to a letter written to Spener on Jan. 8, 1698, in Gustav Kramer, *Beiträge zur Geschichte August Hermann Franckes,* p. 380.

187. David Sigismund Bohnstedt, a Pietist sympathizer from Cleve, complained in a letter to Francke that "it is costly to hire a candidate from Halle, and we want to have three full-time teachers here" (Wotschke, "Francke's rheinische Freunde," no. 49 [Jan. 8, 1722]).

188. In a letter to Spener, dated Mar. 4, 1701. See Kramer, *Beiträge,* p. 468.

189. See Beyreuther, *Francke,* p. 214.

190. See Oschlies, *Arbeits- und Berufspädagogik,* p. 41.

191. For a good overview and discussion of these developments, see Neugebauer, *Absolutistischer Staat und Schulwirklichkeit in Brandenburg-Preußen,* pp. 545 ff.

192. Ibid., pp. 373–75.

193. On Halle and Magdeburg, see Deppermann, *Der hallesche Pietismus,* chaps. 4 and 9. On Königsberg, see Hinrichs, *Preußentum und Pietismus,* chap. 3, and Reidesel, *Pietismus und Orthodoxie.* On Stettin, see Heyden, "Briefe Philipp Jacob Speners nach Stargard." On Cleve, see Wotschke, "Franckes' rheinische Freunde," esp. letters 24–32 and "Zur Geschichte des westfälischen Pietismus," *Jahrbuch des Vereins für westfälische Kirchengeschichte* 32 (1931), pp. 56–100 and 34 (1933), pp. 39–103.

194. See *CCM,* vol. 1, no. 137.

195. On this point, see esp. Gawthrop, *Pietism,* pp. 215–22.

196. *CCM,* vol. 1, no. 98. It is not clear how efficacious this measure was. Even within the Reformed Church, ecclesiastical discipline appears to have been relatively lax during this period, at least in comparison with the Reformed churches of Switzerland, France, Holland, and Scotland.

197. On this, see especially Fritz Terveen, *Gesamtstaat und Retablissement,* pp. 86–109.

198. See, in general, Erich Wetzel, *Die Geschichte des Königlichen Joachimthalschen Gymnasiums, 1607–1907.*

199. The most recent and most vociferous proponent of this view is Gawthrop, *Pietism and the Making of Eighteenth-Century Prussia.* Similar claims are also advanced in Depperman, *Hallesche Pietismus,* Hinrichs, *Pietismus,* and Fulbrook, *Piety and Politics.*

200. I spent a good deal of time searching for connections between the Pietist movement

and the Prussian bureaucracy but was unable to find any of great note. My procedure was as follows. I first prepared a database containing the names of all royal officials who attained a rank of War councillor (*Kriegsrat*), Domains councillor (*Domänenrat*), War and Domains counsellor (*Kriegs- und Domänenrat*), or higher between 1700 and 1750. Then, I cross-checked these names against the matriculation records of the University of Halle, the letter archives of the Franckean Institutes (*Franckesche Stiftungen*) in Halle, and the church records (*Kirchenbücher*) of the St. Nicolai Church in Berlin. I found only a handful of matches. This suggests that the connections between the Pietist movement and the upper reaches of the Prussian bureaucracy were either very few in number (for example, the well-known examples of Fuchs and Canstein) or of a very informal nature (that is, vague sympathies). Of course, it is still possible that there were strong connections with the lower levels of the Prussian bureaucracy, as suggested in Ernst Opgenoorth, *Ausländer in Brandenburg-Preußen als leitende Beamte und Offiziere, 1604–1871,* and Gerd Heinrich, "Amtsträgerschaft und Geistlichkeit." To my knowledge, however, this hypothesis has never been investigated systematically.

Chapter Four

1. On this point, see Flavio Baroncelli and Giovanni Assereto, "Pauperismo e religione nell'età moderna," esp. pp. 187–89.

2. See Franz Ehrle, "Die Armenordnungen von Nürnberg (1522) und Ypern (1525)," and Georg Ratzinger, *Geschichte der kirchlichen Armenpflege*. See also Ernst Nolfe, *La Réforme de la bienfaisance publique à Ypres au XVIe siècle*.

3. See Otto Winckelmann, "Die Armenordnungen" and "Über die ältesten Armenordnungen"; and G. Uhlhorn, *Die christliche Liebesthätigkeit seit der Reformation*.

4. See, for example, Max Weber, *Wirtschaft und Gesellschaft*, p. 355. It is not clear whether Weber was familiar with Winckelmann's work, though it seems likely that he would have been.

5. It should be noted, however, that many of Pullan's arguments were already prefigured in Brian Tierney, *Medieval Poor Law*.

6. See Brian Pullan, *Rich and Poor in Renaissance Venice*. A brief and lucid survey of the Venetian case may also be found in Bronislaw Geremek, *Poverty*, pp. 131–36.

7. For an overview of the Lyonnais case, see Natalie Z. Davis, "Poor relief, Humanism, and Heresy," and Jean-Pierre Gutton, *La société et les pauvres*.

8. Pullan, "Catholics and the Poor in Early Modern Europe," p. 17.

9. See Robert Jütte, *Obrigkeitliche Armenfürsorge in deutschen Reichsstädten der frühen Neuzeit,* and Linda Martz, *Poverty and Welfare in Habsburg Spain*.

10. As recognized in one recent survey of the subject: Robert Jütte, *Poverty and Deviance in Early Modern Europe*.

11. See Wolfgang Reinhard, "Gelenkter Kulturwandel im siebzehnten Jahrhundert" and esp. "Gegenreformation als Modernisierung?" The relevant essays by Ernst Walter Zeeden may be found in his *Konfessionsbildung*.

12. See esp. Heinz Schilling, "Die Konfessionalisierung im Reich," and Reinhard, "Konfession und Konfessionalisierung." For a fuller discussion and more complete references, see chapter 1, pp. 15–19.

13. The most succinct and complete statement of his position is Geremek, *Poverty*.

14. See Catharina Lis and Hugo Soly, *Poverty and Capitalism in Preindustrial Europe*.

15. Marc Raeff's well-known analyses of German and Russian sumptuary legislation could also be reckoned to the Machiavellian school. See esp. Marc Raeff, *The Well-Ordered Police State*.

16. For example: Sandra Cavallo, *Charity and Power in Early Modern Italy*, and Joel F. Harrington, "Escape from the Great Confinement."

17. On the development of Luther's views and of Lutheran church discipline more generally, see the individual cases, described in detail, in Ruth Götze, *Wie Luther Kirchenzucht übte*, pt. 1, and Martin Brecht, "Lutherische Kirchenzucht bis in die Anfänge des 17. Jahrhunderts im Spannungsfeld von Pfarramt und Gesellschaft."

18. In a letter to the Hessian Synod, dated June 26, 1533, in Martin Luther, *Werke*, vol. 6, nr. 2033. See also Götze, *Kirchenzucht*, p. 107.

19. On the state of current research in the field, see Schilling, "Die Kirchenzucht im frühneuzeitlichen Europa in interkonfessionell vergleichender und interdisziplinärer Perspektive—eine Zwischenbilanz."

20. They parallel the two basic types of ecclesiastical polity (*Kirchenverfassung*) first distinguished in the well-known essay by Karl Müller, "Die Anfänge der Konsistorialverfassung im lutherischen Deutschland." On Lutheran church organization and its regional variations, see also Emil Sehling, *Geschichte der protestantischen Kirchenverfassung*.

21. The Prussian church ordinances of 1568 reproduced the Saxon church ordinances of 1544 with only minor alterations. See Aemilius Ludwig Richter, ed., *Die evangelischen Kirchenordnungen des sechzehnten Jahrhunderts*, no. 127 (hereafter *EKO*).

22. See Gerald Strauss, "Success and Failure in the German Reformation" and *Luther's House of Learning*. Strauss's conclusion that the German Reformation was a pedagogical failure may be too pessimistic, however. Lutheran discipline seems to have been a good deal more effective in Württemberg and other parts of the southwest, as we will see directly.

23. See C. Scott Dixon, *The Reformation and Rural Society*.

24. See Richter, *EKO*, nos. 94 and 131.

25. For an overview, see Brecht, *Kirchenordnung und Kirchenzucht in Baden-Württemberg vom 16. bis zum 18. Jahrhundert*, chap. 1. The two most important church ordinances—the "small" ordinance of 1553 and the "large" ordinance of 1559—are both reprinted in their entirety as nos. 95 and 109 in Richter, *EKO*.

26. On Württemberg, see especially Bruce Tolley, *Pastors and Parishioners in Württemberg*. On Sweden, see Michael Roberts, "The Swedish Church," in Roberts, ed., *Sweden's Age of Greatness, 1532–1718*.

27. Sehling, *EKO*, vol. 8, pp. 107–8, 164, and 208.

28. On this, see Brecht, *Kirchenzucht*.

29. For an overview, see Günther Franz, *Die Kirchenleitung in Hohenlohe in den Jahrzenten nach der Reformation*, esp. chap. 4. For the relevant passages of the church ordinance, see Sehling, *EKO*, vol. 15, p. 127.

30. Richter, *EKO*, no. 97.

31. On Strasbourg, see Thomas A. Brady, Jr., *Ruling Class, Regime, and Reformation at Strasbourg*. On Pomerania, see Richter, *EKO*, vol. 2, no. 117, and esp. p. 239.

32. On Württemberg, see Karl H. Wegert, *Popular Culture, Crime, and Social Control in Eighteenth-Century Württemberg*, and David Warren Sabean, *Power in the Blood*. On Strasbourg, see James M. Kittelson, "Successes and Failures in the German Reformation," and Lorna Jane Abray, *The People's Reformation*.

33. On the history and development of the Spanish Inquisition, see Henry Charles Lea,

A History of the Inquisition in Spain, and, more recently, Henry Kamen, *Inquisition and Society in Spain.*

34. For overviews and syntheses of the contemporary research, see esp. Geoffrey Parker, "Some Recent Work on the Inquisition in Spain and Italy," and, more recently, Francisco Bethencourt, *L'Inquisition à l'époque moderne.*

35. These figures are derived from James Contreras and Gustav Henningsen, "Forty-Four Thousand Cases or the Spanish Inquisition (1540–1700)," p. 118. See also Bartolomé Bennassar, *L'Inquisition espagnole, Xve–XIXe siècle,* esp. chap. 9.

36. On this, see especially E. William Monter, *Frontiers of Heresy;* Stephen Haliczer, *Inquisition and Society in the Kingdom of Valencia, 1478–1834.*

37. See Bennassar, *L'Inquisition espagnole,* pp. 96–98.

38. The figure for Naples cannot be computed because the tribunal there lumped lay and clerical sexual offenses together. These figures and those that follow are derived from Monter and John Tedeschi, "Toward a Statistical Profile of the Italian Inquisitions, Sixteenth to Eighteenth Centuries," pp. 144–46.

39. See Geoffrey Parker, "The Inquisition," p. 530.

40. For a different view, emphasizing the differences between the Spanish and Italian cases, see ibid. Following a closer examination of the statistical evidence, I have concluded that the differences were not as great as Parker assumes.

41. The best treatment of confession in the post-Tridentine church is Jean Delumeau, *L'Aveu et le pardon.* Also useful are Thomas N. Tentler, *Sin and Confession on the Eve of the Reformation,* and Lea, *A History of Auricular Confession.*

42. On this, see esp. Michael W. Maher, "How the Jesuits Used Their Congregations to Promote Frequent Communion."

43. The literature on confraternities is vast. The key studies in English are Ronald Weissman, *Ritual Brotherhood in Renaissance Florence;* Christopher F. Black, *Italian Confraternities in the Sixteenth Century;* Maureen Flynn, *Sacred Charity;* and Nicholas Terpstra, *Lay Confraternities and Civic Religion in Renaissance.* For a brief survey of the recent literature, see Konrad Eisenbichler, "Italian Scholarship on Pre-Modern Confraternities in Italy." And for topical essays by many of the leading scholars, see Johan Donnelly and Maher, *Confraternities and Catholic Reform.*

44. For a masterful analysis of the relationship between the clergy and the confraternities, see Danilo Zardin, "Le confraternite in Italia settentrionale fra XV e XVIII secolo"; Paul V. Murphy, "Politics, Piety, and Reform"; Pierre Lancon, "Les confrèries de rosaire en Rouergue aux XVIe et XVIIe siècles"; and Adriano Prosperi, "Chierici e laici nell'opera di Carlo Borromeo."

45. On the penitential confraternities, see esp. Danilo Zardin, *San Carlo Borromeo ed il rinnovamento della vita religiosa dei laici* and *Confraternite e vita di pietà nelle campagne Lombarde tra 500 e 600;* Andrew Barnes, "The Wars of Religion and the Origins of Reformed Confraternities of Penitents"; and Marc Venard, "Les Formes de la piété des confrèries dévotes de Rouen à l'époque moderne." On the Marian sodalities, the definitive study is Louis Châttelier, *The Europe of the Devout.*

46. The literature on diocesan reform is truly vast. A comprehensive survey of this older historiography may be found in Prosperi, "Missioni popolare e visite pastorali in Italia tra '500 e '600." See also Franco Buzzi and Zardin, eds., *Carlo Borromeo e l'opera della "grande riforma,"* and Keith P. Luria, *Territories of Grace.*

47. Andreas Holzem, "Katholische Konfession und Kirchenzucht."

48. Based on the figures given for the tribunal of Castille, Aragon, Venice, Naples, and the Friuli in Henningsen and Tedeschi, *The Inquisition in Early Modern Europe*.

49. Based on the charts in Holzem, "Katholische Konfession und Kirchenzucht," pp. 312 and 329.

50. See Hermann Roodenburg, *Onder censuur*, table 3.1.

51. On Emden, see Schilling, *Civic Calvinism in Northwestern Germany and the Netherlands*, table. 2.2. On Delft, see A. Wouters, *Nieuw en ongezien*, vol. 2, table 5.3.

52. See Michael F. Graham, "Social Discipline in Scotland, 1560–1610," tables 1 and 2, and also Geoffrey Parker, "The 'Kirk By Law Established' and the Origins of 'The Taming of Scotland.' "

53. Of course, it is possible, even probable, that social sins such as these would often have come out in the confessional. But it seems very unlikely that the discipline of the confessional would have been as effective as the discipline of the consistory, first, because it relied on self-accusation and, second, because it remained private. In other words, it would have been easier to conceal sins and less socially costly to commit them.

54. The most insightful and insistent proponent of this position has been Heinrich Richard Schmidt. See, for example, his *Dorf und Religion;* "Über das Verhältnis von ländlicher Gemeinde und christlicher Ethik"; and esp. "Sozialdisziplinierung?"

55. On Calvinist theories of conversion and justification, see, for example, Charles L. Cohen, *God's Caress*, and W. van 't Spijker, *De verzegeling met de Heilige Geest*.

56. On Luther's views, see Gerhard Krause, "Armut VII. 16–20 Jahrhundert, Luther"; Harold J. Grimm, "Luther's Contributions to Sixteenth-Century Organization of Poor-relief"; and Ingetraut Ludolphy, "Luther und die Diakonie." On the relation of Luther's ideas to earlier movements, see Carter Lindberg, *Beyond Charity*.

57. Erasmus's views on this subject are elaborated in *Enchiridion militis Christiani*. For Kaysersberg's views, see Jakob Wimpheling and Beatus Rhenanus, *Das Leben des Johannes Geiler von Kaysersberg*. For an overview of these and other reformers before the reform and the relation of their ideas to Luther's, see Lindberg, *Beyond*.

58. Cited from the "Address to the Christian Nobility" in Luther, *Works*, vol. 44, p. 190.

59. Cited from Lindberg, " 'There Should Be No Beggars among Christians,' " p. 313.

60. On this point, see especially Karl Holl, "Luther und das landesherrliche Kirchenregiment" in idem, *Gesammelte Aufsätze zur Kirchengeschichte*, vol. 1, pp. 326–80.

61. The first discussion of differences between the Lutheran and Catholic-humanist programs—and, in my view, the best—is to be found in Winckelmann, "Über die ältesten Armenordnungen der Reformationszeit (1522–1525)."

62. This program is most clearly and succinctly articulated in section 21 of Luther's "Address to the German Nobility" *Works*, vol. 44, pp. 189–91. Luther discusses his views on charity, mendicancy, and fraternity at greater length in treatise on "The Blessed Sacrament of the Holy and True Body of Christ and the Brotherhoods" (*Works*, vol. 35, pp. 46–73) and in his long sermon on usury (*Works*, vol. 45, pp. 231–310).

63. The *Beutelordnung* was long attributed to Luther's disciple, Andreas Rudolph Bodenstein (a.k.a., Karlstadt), but now appears to have been written by Luther himself. The case for Luther's authorship was first made in K. Pallas, ed., "Die Wittenberger Beutelordnung vom Jahre 1521 und ihr Verhältnis zu der Einrichtung des Gemeinen Kastens im Januar 1522."

64. For text and discussion see Sehling, *EKO*, vol. 1, no. 160.

65. For text and discussion, see Sehling, *EKO*, vol. 1, no. 109.

66. For examples of imitators, see the numerous local ordinaces in *EKO*, vol. 1.

67. Various versions of the ordinances are reprinted and their origins, influence and significance discussed in Winckelmann, "Die Armenordnungen von Nuremberg (1522), Kitzingen (1523), Regensburg (1523) und Ypern (1525)."

68. On developments in Nuremberg, see Winckelman, "Über die ältesten Armenordnungen," pp. 213 ff.

69. It should be noted that the practice of issuing badges had actually been established much earlier. Before this time, however, the badge was worn by those who were officially permitted to beg rather than by those who were receiving alms, and thus officially prohibited from begging.

70. The religious inspiration—Catholic or Protestant—of this and other reforms of the early 1520s has long been a matter of debate. The literature and arguments are reviewed in Lindberg, " 'There Should Be No Begging among Christians.' "

71. On Strasbourg, see especially Otto Winckelmann, *Das Fürsorgewesen der Stadt Strassburg vor und nach der Reformation bis zum Ausgang des sechzehnten Jahrhunderts*.

72. See Winckelmann, "Über die ältesten Armenordnungen," p. 364.

73. For an overview, see Nolfe, *La Réforme de la bienfaisance publique à Ypres au XVIe siècle*.

74. See Winckelmann, "Über die ältesten Armenordnungen," pp. 377 ff.

75. For the political and social background of the Reformation in Frankfurt, see Sigrid Jahns, "Frankfurt am Main im Zeitalter der Reformation (um 1500–1555)."

76. On the Frankfurt reforms, see Jütte, *Obrigkeitliche Armenfürsorge*, chap. 3.

77. See Franz, *Urkundliche Quellen*, vol. 3, no. 63.

78. Sehling, *EKO*, vol. 8, no. 3.

79. These and other practices were explicitly prohibited in a new "Order of the Common Chest" issued by Philip in 1533. See Franz, *Urkundliche Quellen*, vol. 2, no. 256. For a local example, see ibid, no. 89.

80. See Franz, *Urkundliche Quellen*, vol. 2, nos. 196, 218, 247, and 533.

81. See Sehling, *EKO*, vol. 8, no. 18, p. 211.

82. The best overview of the Reformation in Württemberg is Martin Brecht and Hermann Ehmer, *Südwestdeutsche Reformationsgeschichte*, pts. 3 and 4. See also Julius Rauscher, *Württembergische Reformationsgeschichte*.

83. Reprinted in Rauscher, *Visitationsakten*, vol. 1, no. 8.

84. See Werner-Ulrich Deetjen, *Studien zur württembergischen Kirchenordnung Herzog Ulrichs, 1534–1550*, pp. 124–25.

85. See Rauscher, *Visitationsakten*, vol. 1, no. 25 and *passim*.

86. See Brecht and Ehmer, *Reformationsgeschichte*, p. 323.

87. Viktor Ernst, "Die Entstehung des württembergischen Kirchengutes."

88. Based on the figures cited in Paul Sauer, *Geschichte der Stadt Stuttgart*, vol. 2, p. 167.

89. It is not clear just how systematic this practice was. One example may be found in Rauscher, *Visitationsakten*, vol. 1, no. 73.

90. On this point, see J. Friedrich Battenberg, "Obrigkeitliche Sozialpolitik und Gesetzgebung."

91. The best overview of this subject is Paul Slack, *The English Poor Law, 1531–1782*.

92. On Geneva, see Léon Gautier, *L'Hôpital Général de Genève de 1535 à 1545*, and Robert M. Kingdon, "Social Welfare in Calvin's Geneva." On Emden, see Timothy G. Fehler, *Poor Relief and Protestantism*. On Zurich, see Lee Palmer Wandel, *Always among Us*.

93. On this point, see especially Elsie Anne McKee, *John Calvin on the Diaconate and Liturgical Almsgiving*, pp. 133 ff.

94. For an overview, see Edward O'Donoghue, *Bridewell Hospital*. On the internal workings of Bridewell, see John Howes, *John Howes' ms., 1582*.

95. On the backgrounds of the reformers, see O'Donoghue, *Bridewell Hospital*, chap. 16, and Howes, *John Howes' ms., 1582*. On Ridley, see Jasper Godwin Ridley, *Nicholas Ridley*. On Grafton, see J. A. Kingdon, *Richard Grafton*.

96. These three categories and nine subtypes of poverty are reported by Richard Grafton and were apparently elaborated during discussions among the thirty, that is, the group of men who drafted the reform plan and submitted it to the city council and the king. See Richard Grafton, *Chronicle or History of England*.

97. William Fleetwood, recorder of London from 1571 to 1591, as quoted in O'Donoghue, *Bridewell Hospital*, p. 201.

98. See ibid., chap. 21.

99. On Norwich, see F. M. Leonard, *English Poor Relief*, pp. 101–7.

100. On the creation of a national network of Bridewells, see Joanna Innes, "Prisons for the Poor: English Bridewells," esp. pp. 61–77.

101. On this point, see especially Patrick Collinson, *The Religion of Protestants*, chap. 4. For specific examples, see John F. Pound, *The Norwich Census of the Poor, 1570*, and Slack, "Poverty and Politics in Salisbury 1597–1666." On Ipswich, see John Webb, *Poor Relief in Elizabethan Ipswich*. On Exeter, see Wallace T. MacCaffrey, *Exeter, 1540–1640*. On Terling, see Keith Wrightson and David Levine, *Poverty and Piety*, chap. 7. Other towns are discussed in Leonard, *English Poor Relief*, and Slack, *Poverty and Policy*.

102. So far as I can tell, this interpretation was initially formulated by Protestant historians such as Arwed Emminghaus and Georg Uhlhorn during the second half of the nineteenth century, and then found its way into the writings of Ernst Troeltsch, Max Weber, and R. H. Tawney, rather than the other way around, as Pullan and other historians have argued; see, for example, Brian Pullan, "Catholics and the Poor in Early Modern Europe," p. 15. Tawney, moreover, is the only sociologist of the three who makes this argument in any explicit way, and it is probably to his influence, rather than Weber's or Troeltsch's, that its entrance into the received wisdom of postwar social science is to be traced.

103. The classic statement of the new orthodoxy is Pullan, "Catholics and the Poor." For a more recent defense of this position, see especially Jütte, *Poverty and Deviance in Early Modern Europe*.

104. See Natalie Davis, "Poor Relief, Humanism, and Heresy." An even more detailed discussion of the case of Lyon may be found in Gutton, *La Société et les pauvres*.

105. See Pullan, *Rich and Poor in Renaissance Venice*. A brief and lucid survey of the Venetian case may also be found in Geremek, *Poverty*, pp. 131–36.

106. The most outspoken critics of the socioeconomic explanation of early modern social reform are Ole Peter Grell and Andrew Cunningham, "The Reformation and Changes in Welfare Provision in Early Modern Northern Europe," and Grell, "The Religious Duty of Care and the Social Need for Control in Early Modern Europe." Similar arguments may also be found in Slack, *The English Poor Law*.

107. On Lyon, see Natalie Davis, "Poor Relief," and Gutton, *La Société et les pauvres*. On Paris, see Christian Paultre, *De la répression de la mendicité et du vagabondage en France sous l'ancien régime*. On Rouen, see the introduction to G. Panel, *Documents concernant les pauvres de Rouen extraits des archives de l'Hotel-de-ville*. On Lille, see Robert Saint Cyr and

Duplessis Saint Cyr, "Charité publique et autorité municipale au XVI siècle." On Grenoble, see Norberg, *Rich and Poor.*

108. See Marcel Fosseyeux, "Les Premiers Budgets municipaux d'assistance."

109. See Gutton, *La Société et les pauvres,* pp. 295–326.

110. On this, see especially Jon Arrizabalaga, "Poor Relief in Counter-Reformation Castile."

111. Recent overviews of the literature on poor-relief in Italy include Alessandro Pastore, "Strutture assistenziale fra chiesa e stati nell'Italia della Controriforma," and Pullan, "Support and Redeem." Brief case studies of many of the most important cities, along with citations of the relevant literature, may be found in *Timore e carità.*

112. On Bologna, see Giovannia Calori, *Una iniziativa sociale nella Bologna del '500,* and Terpstra, *Lay Confraternities and Civic Religion in Renaissance,* chap. 5. On Florence, see Daniela Lombardi, "Poveri a Firenze." in *Timore e carità,* pp. 165–84. On Genoa, see Eduardo Grendi, "Pauperismo e albergo dei poveri nella Genova del seicento."

113. On Turin, see Cavallo, *Charity and power.* On Rome, see Delumeau, *Vie économique et sociale de Rome dans la seconde moitié du XVIe siècle,* vol. 1, pp. 403–16.

114. See David Gentilcore, " 'Cradle of Saints and Useful Institutions.' "

115. On Rome, see Michel Fatica, "La reclusione dei poveri a Roma durante il pontificato di Innocenzo XII (1692–1700)." Genoa and Turin are discussed in Black, *Italian Confraternities,* pp. 216 ff.

116. See Saverio Russo, "Potere pubblico e caritá privata," p. 46, and Irene Polverini Fosi, "Pauperismo ed assistenza a Siena durante il principato mediceo," p. 158.

117. See Harrington, "Escape from the Great Confinement," p. 312 n. 8.

118. One could criticize these definitions as too narrow because separation between person and office was only one of the features of bureuacratic administration originally identified by Weber. But there is an underlying logic to Ertman's definition, because many of these features (for example, fixed salaries, separation of the officeholder from the means of administration, and recruitment and promotion based on merit and performance) could not easily have developed in a system where offices were appropriated.

119. Ertman, *Birth of the Leviathan,* p. 25.

120. See Niklas Schrenck-Notzing, "Das bayerische Beamtentum," p. 35.

121. See Notker Hammerstein, "Universitäten," p. 723.

122. So far as I can tell, the only prominent member of the royal cabinet with a legal education was Samuel Cocceji, who was specifically hired for his legal expertise. This conclusion is based on an exhaustive search of the *Personenregister* of the *Acta Borussica, Behördenorganisation* and a complete cataloguing of all royal servants who served in the rank of *Kriegs- und Domänenrat* or higher between 1700 and 1740.

123. See Lucien Karpik, *French Lawyers,* p. 30.

124. See Jean-Marc Pelorson, *Les Letrados,* pp. 68, 133.

125. See Moraw, "Gelehrte Juristen"; György Bónis, "Ungarische Juristen am Ausgang des Mittelalters"; Dieter Stievermann, "Die gelehrten Juristen"; Paul Brand. *The Origins of the English Legal Profession;* Uta-Renate Blumenthal, *Papal Reform and Canon Law;* Lauro Martines, *Lawyers and Statecraft in Renaissance Florence;* and Katarzyna Sójka-Zielinska, "La Rôle des juristes."

126. For further details, see chap. 2.

127. See R. Burr Litchfield, *Emergence of a Bureaucracy.*

128. Overviews and literature in D. Albrecht, "Die Landstände," and Rudolf Kötzschke and Hellmut Kretzschmar, *Sächsische Geschichte,* pp. 254–66.

129. The best short discussion of the Polish case is Hans Roos, "Ständewesen und parlamentarische Verfassung in Polen." In English, see Antoni Maczak, "The Structure of Power in the Commonwealth of the Sixteenth and Seventeenth Centuries." On Hungary, see Boris, "The Hungarian Feudal Diet Thirteenth–Eighteenth Centuries."

130. It is perhaps worth noting that Ertman's definition of patrimonialism omits oligarchy, the very type of patrimonialism Weber regarded as most important in early modern Europe.

131. Some scholars also customarily distinguish between temporary and permanent sales, that is, cases in which the purchaser obtains the office for a specified time, usually of relatively short duration, and cases in which the office becomes the private property of the purchaser and may be resold or bequeathed. The former practice is generally designated as farming. Some scholars view farming as a form of venality; others regard it as a separate type of office holding. Insofar as farming occasionally serves as a transitional stage on the road to permanent appropriation of offices, there is some justice in the former view. But it must also be emphasized that farming represents a much less severe form of appropriation than permanent venality because it affords greater scope for the supervision and control of officials from above. Thus, if farming is to be regarded as a form of venality, it must be considered an especially mild form.

132. See Brigide Schwarz, *Die Organisation kurialer Schreiberkollegien von ihrer Entstehung bis zur Mitte des 15. Jahrhunderts,* pp. 10, 177.

133. See Peter Partner, "Papal Financial Policy in the Renaissance and Counter-Reformation," p. 20.

134. See W. von Hoffmann, *Forschungen zur Geschichte der Kurialen Behörden vom Schisma bis zur Reformation,* p. 171.

135. See Schwarz, *Organisation kurialer Schreiberkollegien,* 177–180), and Hoffmann, *Forschungen zur Geschichte der Kurialen Behörden vom Schisma bis zur Reformation,* vol. 2, p. 41; but see also Bernhard Schimmelpfennig, "Der Ämterhandel an der Römischen Kurie von Pius II bis zum Sacco di Roma (1458–1527)," p. 12.

136. See Barbara Hallman, *Italian Cardinals, Reform, and the Church as Property: 1492–1563* (Berkeley: University of California Press, 1985).

137. See Paul Viollet, *Droit public,* vol. 3, 270–74, and Göhring, *Die Ämterkäuflichkeit im Ancien régime,* p. 13.

138. See Kuno Böse, "Die Ämterkäuflichkeit in Frankreich vom 14. bis zum 16. Jahrhundert," and Roland Mousnier, *La Venalité des offices, sous Henri IV et Louis XIII,* p. 17.

139. See Mousnier, *Venalité,* p. 21.

140. See Willem Frifhoff, "Patterns."

141. Joachim Boër, "Ämterhandel in kastilischen Städten," pp. 148–49.

142. See K. W. Swart, *The Sale of Offices in the Seventeenth Century,* p. 21.

143. See Winfried Küchler, "Ämterkäulichkeit in den Ländern der Krone Aragons," pp. 11–13.

144. See Swart, *Sale of Offices,* p. 21.

145. See Margarita Cuartas Rivera, "La venta de oficios públicos en Castilla-León en el siglo XVI," *Hispania* 1984 44(158): 495–516; Rafael de Lera García, "Venta de oficios en la inquisicion de Granada (1629–1644)," *Hispania* 1988 48(4): 909–62; and Luis Navarro García, "Los oficios vendibles en Nueva España durante la Guerra de Sucesión," *Anuario de Estudios Americanos,* 1975 (32): 133–54.

146. See A. Musi, "La venalità degli uffici in Principato Citra," and Roberto Mantelli, *Il pubblico impiego nell'economia del Regno di Napoli.*

147. See Giuseppe Galasso, *Alla periferia dell'Impero,* p. 16.

148. See Horst Enzensberger, "La struttura del potere nel Regno: Corte, uffici, cancelleria"; Hiroshi Takayama, *The Administration of the Norman kingdom of Sicily;* Pietro Corrao, *Governare un regno.*

149. See Litchfield, *Emergence of a Bureaucracy,* pp. 157–81.

150. See Mousnier, "Le trafic des offices à Venise," and Andrea Zannini, *Burocrazia e burocrati a Venezia in età moderna.*

151. See Michael Erbe, "Aspekte des Ämterhandels in den Niederlanden im späten Mittelalter und in der frühen Neuzeit."

152. See Adolf M. Birke, "Zur Kontinuität des Ämterhandels in England."

153. See Horst Möller, "Ämterkäuflichkeit in Brandenburg-Preussen."

154. See Strauss, *Manifestations of Discontent in Germany,* pp. 3–4.

155. On England, see Rosemary O'Day, *The English Clergy;* Peter Heath, *The English Parish Clergy on the Eve of the Reformation* (London: Routledge & K. Paul; Toronto, University of Toronto Press, 1969); and Viviane Barrie-Curien, "The English Clergy, 1560–1620." On Germany, see Bernard Vogler, *Le Clergé protestant rhénan au siècle de la Réforme, 1555–1619* and "Rekrutierung, Ausbildung und soziale Verflechtung"; Tolley, *Pastors and Parishioners in Württemberg;* and Luise Schorn-Schütte, *Evangelische Geistlichkeit in der Frühneuzeit.* On Switzerland, see Bruce Gordon, *Clerical Discipline and the Rural Reformation.* On the Netherlands, see G. Groenhuis, *De Predikanten.* On Scandinavia, see Grell, *The Scandinavian Reformation.*

156. See Roberts, *Sweden's Age of Greatness, 1532–1718.*

157. See Björn Asker, "Aristocracy and Autocracy in Seventeenth-Century Sweden"; Johan Holm," 'Skyldig plicht och trohet' "; and more generally A. F. Upton, *Charles XI and Swedish Absolutism.*

158. See Göran Rystad, "The King, the Nobility, and the Growth of the Bureaucracy in Seventeenth-Century Sweden," p. 64.

159. See Roberts, *Sweden as a Great Power, 1611–1697,* pp. 18–28.

160. See ibid., pp. 40–48; Rystad, "The Growth of the Bureaucracy," p. 67; and Kaj Janzon "Överdåd på kredit."

161. See Stellan Dahlgren, "Charles X and the Constitution."

162. See Roberts, "The Swedish Church," pp. 148, 152, and Upton, *Charles XI,* pp. 170–71, 216–17.

163. See Michal Kopcynski, "Service or Benefice?"

164. See Werner Buchholz, *Staat und Ständegesellschaft in Schweden zur Zeit des Überganges vom Absolutismus zum Ständeparlamentarismus 1718–1720.*

165. See G. E. Aylmer, *The King's Servants.*

166. See Aylmer, *The State's Servants.*

167. See John Brewer, *The Sinews of Power.*

Conclusion

1. See Peter B. Evans, Dietrich Rueschemeyer, and Theda Skocpol, eds., *Bringing the State Back In.*

2. For a synthetic discussion of English state-formation that has strong resonances with my own analysis, see Michael J. Braddick, *State Formation in Early Modern England, c. 1550–1700.*

3. They were not all (equally) radical or successful, of course. For a discussion of these variations and some of the reasons behind them, see Philip S. Gorski, "Calvinism and Revolution."

4. I discuss this in more detail in chapter 3 of my 1996 dissertation, "The Disciplinary Revolution."

5. The two most important exceptions are probably Michael Walzer, *The Revolution of the Saints,* and Wayne Te Brake, *Shaping History.* Obviously, this charge does not hold for cultural and political historians.

6. Skocpol, *States and Social Revolutions,* p. 4.

7. This argument is inspired by Robert M. Kingdon, "Was the Protestant Reformation a Revolution?"

8. See especially Charles Tilly, *European Revolutions, 1492–1992,* chap. 3, and Jack A. Goldstone, *Revolution and Rebellion in the Early Modern World,* chaps. 2 and 5.

9. See Tilly, *European Revolutions,* esp. pp. 59–61.

10. Tilly's analysis draws on Guy E. Swanson, *Religion and Regime.*

11. The *locus classicus* for this argument is Tilly, *The Contentious.* My critique of it is directly inspired by Michael Young, "Confessional Protest: The Evangelical Origins of Social Movements in the United States, 1800–1840." Ph.D.: New York University, 2001.

12. On this point, see especially Kingdon, "The Political Resistance of the Calvinists in France and the Low Countries," and Helmut G. Koenigsberger, "The Organization of Revolutionary Parties in France and the Netherlands during the Sixteenth Century."

13. On this point, see especially Dale K. Van Kley, *The Religious Origins of the French Revolution.* My thanks to William Sewell, Jr., for drawing this work to my attention.

14. On this concept, see especially Bruce Mazlish, *The Revolutionary Ascetic.*

15. Goldstone, *Revolution and Rebellion,* p. 421.

16. My argument here is, of course, quite similar to Ernst Gellner, *Nations and Nationalism* except that he attributes these sociocultural changes to industrialization rather than confessionalization.

17. For an overview of the debate and the relevant literatures, see Gorski, "The Mosaic Moment."

18. See Gøsta Esping-Andersen, *Three Worlds of Welfare Capitalism.*

19. Alexis de Tocqueville, *De la démocratie en Amérique,* vol. 1, p. 91. Thanks to Chad Goldberg for drawing my attention to this chapter.

20. For a more detailed discussion of these points, see "Religion and the Political Unconscious of Historical Sociology."

21. Skocpol, *States and Social Revolutions,* p. 29.

22. Ibid., p. 26.

23. On this last point, see especially, Michael Schoenfeldt, *Bodies and Selves in Early Modern England.*

24. I am well aware that sophisticated versions of rational-choice theory are capable of addressing more complicated actions and problems of this sort. This is not the place to discuss the various deficiencies I see in this approach. Suffice it to say that I am not persuaded by the tautological invocation of disembedded preference structures as an omnibus solution to the problem of action. As my language suggests, I am more sympathetic to Bourdieuian views of action.

25. The term *social capital* has been used in different ways by different people. I am referring here, of course, to the usage found in Robert Putnam, *Making Democracy Work* and kindred works.

26. The *locus classicus* in this literature is Peter B. Evans, *Embedded Autonomy.*

27. For a more detailed discussion of this point, see Gorski, "Historicizing the Secularization Debate."

BIBLIOGRAPHY

Published Primary Sources

Acta Borussica, Behördenorganisation. Berlin: Paul Parey, 1901.

Aglionby, William. *The present state of the United Provinces of the Low-Countries as to the government, laws, forces, riches, manners, customes, revenue, and territory of the Dutch in three books.* London: Printed for John Starkey, 1669.

"Aktenmäßige Geschichte der Hinrichtung des Geheimen Raths von Schlubhut." *Preußische Monatsschrift* 1, December 1788.

Beschryving van Delft. Delft: Reinier Boitet, 1729.

Blok, P. J., ed. *Relazioni veneziane. Venetiaansche berichten over de Vereenigde Nederlanden van 1600–1795.* The Hague: M. Nijhoff, 1909.

Boterse, J., ed. *Classicale Acta, 1573–1620, vol. 4: Provinciale Synode Zeeland, Classis Walcheren, 1602–1620, Classis Zuid-Beveland 1579–1591.* The Hague: Instituut voor Geschiedenis, 1980–95.

Chroust, Anton. "Aktenstücke zur brandenburgischen Geschichte unter Kurfürst Johann Sigismund." *Forschungen zur brandenburgisch-preußischen Geschichte* 9 (1897): 1–21.

Classicale acta, 1573–1620. The Hague: Instituut voor Geschiedenis, 1980–95.

Dohna, Fabian zu. *Die Selbstbiographie des Burggrafen Fabian zu Dohna (1550–1621) nebst Aktenstücke zur Geschichte der Sukzession.* Leipzig: Duncker & Humblot, 1905.

Dooren, J. P. van, ed. *Classicale Acta, 1573–1620, vol. 1; Particuliere Synode Zuid-Holland, I: Classis Dordrecht, 1573–1600.* The Hague: Instituut voor Geschiedenis, 1980–95.

Erasmus of Rotterdam. *Enchiridion militis Christiani.* Ed. Anne O'Donnel. Oxford and New York: Oxford University Press, 1981.

Francke, August Hermann. *Segens-volle Fußstapfen.* Halle: In Verlegung des Waisenhauses, 1709.

———. *Der von Gott in dem Waysenhause zu Glaucha an Halle ietzo bey nahe für 600 Personen zubereitete Tisch.* Halle: In Verlegung des Waisenhauses, 1729.

———. *Pädagogische Schriften.* Paderborn: Verlag Ferdinand Schöning, 1957.

Freylingshausen, J. A. *Sieben Tage am Hofe Friedrich Wilhelms I. Tagebuch des Professors J. A. Freylinghausen über seinen Aufenthalt in Wusterhausen vom 4. bis 10. September.* Berlin: A. Duncker, 1900.

Freylingshausen, J. A., and Gotthilf August Francke. *Kurzer Bericht von der gegenwärtigen Verfassung des Paedagogii Regii zu Glaucha vor Halle.* Halle: Verlag des Waisenhauses, 1734.

———. *Ausführlicher Bericht von der Lateinischen Schule des Waysenhauses.* Halle: In Verlegung des Waisenhauses, 1736.

Friedländer, Ernst, ed. *Berliner geschriebene Zeitungen aus den Jahren 1713 bis 1717 und 1735.* Berlin: Ernst Siegfried Mittler und Sohn, 1902.

Gheyn, Jacob de. *Wapenhandelinghe van roers, musquetten ende spiessen.* The Hague: n.p., 1607.

Grand, Frédéric le. *Oeuvres.* Berlin: Rodolphe Decker, 1846.

Heyden, Hellmuth. "Briefe Philipp Jacob Speners nach Stargard." *Baltische Studien, Neue Folge* 56 (1970): 47–78.

Historie van de Wonderlijcke Mirakelen, die in menichte ghebeurt zijn, ende noch dagelijk ghebeuren, binnen de vermaerde Coop-stadt Aemstelredam: In een plaats ghenaemt het Tucht-huys, gheleghen op de Heylighewegh. Amsterdam: n.p., 1612.

Howes, John. *John Howes' ms., 1582, being "a brief note of the order and manner of the proceedings in the first erection of" the three royal hospitals of Christ, Bridewell & St. Thomas the Apostle.* London: n.p., 1904.

Kerkelyck Handboekje. Amsterdam: N. Obbes, 1841.

Krönungs-Ceremonien, Welche So wohl bey vorhergehende Proclamation An den 16. Januarii Wie auch auff den Krönungs-Tag selbsten, Den 18. darauff des 1701sten Jahres in Königsberg Höchst feyerlich celebriret worden. Königsberg: n.p., 1701.

Küntzel, Georg, ed. *Die politischen Testamente der Hohenzollern.* Leipzig and Berlin: B. G. Teubner, 1919.

[Lemaitre, Charles]. *Voyage anonyme et inédit d'un janseniste en Hollande et en Flandre en 1681.* Paris: Champion Libraire, 1889.

Luther, Martin. *Werke.* Weimar: Böhlau, 1883–.

Meinardus, Otto, ed. *Protokolle und Relationen des Brandenburgischen Geheimen Rathes aus der Zeit des Kurfürsten Friedrich Wilhelm.* Seven vols. Publikationen aus den Königlichen Preußischen Staats-Archieven, vols. 41, 54, 55, 66, 80, 89, and 91. Leipzig: S. Hirzel, 1889–1919.

Meylius, Chrn. Otto. *Corpus Constitutionum Marchicarum.* Berlin and Halle: Buchladen des Waysenhauses, 1737–51.

Montague, William. *The Delights of Holland: Or, A Three Months Travel about that and the other Provinces with Observations and Reflections on their Trade, Wealth, Strength, Beauty, Policy &c. Together with a Catalogue of the Rarities in the Anatomical School at Leyden.* London: Printed for John Sturton, 1696.

Mulder, Lodewijk, ed. *Journaal van Anthonis Duyck (1591–1602).* The Hague and Arnhem: Martinus Nijhoff and D. A. Thieme, 1862–66.

Panel, G. *Documents concernant les pauvres de Rouen extraits des archives de l'Hotel-de-ville.* Paris: A. Picard, 1917–19.

Rauscher, Julius. *Württembergische Visitationsakten.* Stuttgart: Kohlhammer, 1932.

Reglement Voor het WEES-HUYS Van de ware Gereformeerde Christelijcke Nederduytsche Gemeente, Onder de bedieninge van de Diaconen. Amsterdam: Johannes van Ravesteyn, 1668.

Reitsma, J., and S. D. van Veen. *Acta der provinciale en particuliere synoden.* Groningen: J. B. Wolters, 1892.

Roelevink, J., ed. *Classicale Acta, 1573–1620,* vol. 2; *Particuliere Synode Zuid-Holland, II: Classis Dordrecht, 1601–1620, Classis Breda 1616–1620.* The Hague: Instituut voor Geschiedenis, 1980–95.

Rutgers, F. L. *Acta van de Nederlandsche Synoden der zestiende eeuw.* Utrecht: Kemink & Zoon.

Schicketanz, Peter, ed. *Der Briefwechsel Carl Hildebrand von Canstein mit August Hermann Francke.* Berlin: Walter de Gruyter, 1972.

Spener, Philipp Jacob. *Schriften.* Hildesheim: Olms, 1979–88.

Stratemann, Wilhelm. *Vom berliner Hofe zur Zeit Friedrich Wilhelms I; Berichte des braunschweiger Gesandten in Berlin, 1728–1733,* edited by Richard Wolff. Vols. 48 and 49 of Schriften des Vereins für die Geschichte Berlins. Berlin: Verlag des Vereins für die Geschichte Berlins, 1914.

Urkunden und Actenstücke zur Geschichte des Kurfürsten Friedrich Wilhelm von Brandenburg. Berlin: Georg Reimer Verlag, 1894.

Willekeuren, Ende Ordinnantien, Aengaende het Eleemosyniers-Huys der Stadt Amstelredamme. Amsterdam: Christina Bruynings, 1656.

Winckelmann, Otto. "Die Armenordnungen von Nuremberg (1522), Kitzingen (1523), Regensburg (1523) und Ypern (1525)." *Archiv für Reformationsgeschichte* 10 (1913): 242–88.

Wotschke, Theodor. "August Hermann Franckes rheinische Freunde in ihren Briefen." *Monatshefte für rheinische Kirchengeschichte* 22 (1928–29): 81–373, 23:23–90.

Secondary Literature

Abray, Lorna Jane. *The People's Reformation. Magistrates, Clergy, and Commons in Strasbourg, 1500–1598.* Ithaca: Cornell University Press, 1985.

Aland, Kurt. *Kirchengeschichtlicher Entwürf.* Gütersloh: Gerhard Mohn, 1960.

Alberts, Wybe Jappe. *De staten van Gelre en Zutphen tot 1459.* Groningen: J. B. Wolters, 1950–56.

———. *Van standen tot staten: 600 jaar Staten van Utrecht 1375–1975.* Utrecht: Stichting Stichtse Historische Reeks, 1975.

Albrecht, D. "Die Landstände." In *Handbuch der bayerischen Geschichte, vol. 2: Das alte Bayern,* edited by Max Spindler. Munich: C. H. Beck, 1966.

Allgemeine Deutsche Biographie. Leipzig: Duncker & Humblot, 1900.

Anderson, Perry. *Passages from Antiquity to Feudalism.* London: Verso, 1974.

———. *Lineages of the Absolutist State.* London: Verso, 1979.

Anter, Andreas. *Max Webers Theorie des modernen Staates. Herkunft, Struktur, Bedeutung.* Berlin: Duncker & Humblot, 1995.

Arrizabalaga, Jon. "Poor Relief in Counter-Reformation Castile: An Overview." Pp. 151–76 in *Health Care and Poor Relief in Counter-Reformation Europe,* edited by Ole Peter Grell and Andrew Cunningham. London and New York: Routledge, 1999.

Asaert, Gustaaf, et al. *Maritieme geschiedenis der Nederlanden.* Bussum: De Boer, 1976–78.

Asker, Björn. "Aristocracy and Autocracy in Seventeenth-Century Sweden: The Decline of the Aristocracy within the Civil Administration before 1680." *Scandinavian Journal of History* 15 (1990): 89–95.

Aylmer, G. E. *The State's Servants: The Civil Service of the English Republic, 1649–1660.* London: Routledge & Kegan Paul, 1973.

———. *The King's Servants: The Civil Service of Charles I, 1625–1642.* London: Routledge & Kegan Paul, 1974.

Bainton, Roland. *The Age of the Reformation.* Princeton: Van Nostrand, 1956.

Barnes, Andrew. "The Wars of Religion and the Origins of Reformed Confraternities of Penitents: A Theoretical Approach." *Archives de Sciences Sociales des Religions* 64, no. 1 (1987): 117–36.

Baroncelli, Flavio, and Giovanni Assereto. "Pauperismo e religione nell'età moderna." *Società e storia* 7 (1980): 169–201.

Barrie-Curien, Vivianne. "The English Clergy, 1560–1620: Recruitment and Social Status." *History of European Ideas* 9 (1988): 451–63.

Battenberg, J. Friedrich. "Obrigkeitliche Sozialpolitik und Gesetzgebung." *Zeitschrift für historische Forschung* 18 (1991): 33–70.

Baumgart, Peter. "Zur Geschichte der kurmärkischen Stände im 17. und 18. Jahrhundert." Pp. 131–61 in *Ständische Vertretungen in Europa im 17. und 18. Jahrhundert,* edited by Dietrich Gerhard. Göttingen: Vandenhoek & Ruprecht, 1969.

Beeskow, Hans-Joachim. "Paul Gerhardt." In *Berlinische Lebensbilder,* vol. 5: *Theologen,* edited by Gerd Heinrichs. Berlin: Colloquium, 1990.

Bennassar, Bartolomé. *L'Inquisition espagnole, XVe–XIXe siècle.* Paris: Hachette, 1979.

Bergendoff, Conrad J. I. *Olavus Petri and the Ecclesiastical Transformation in Sweden, 1521–1552: A Study in the Swedish Reformation.* New York: Macmillan, 1928.

Bethencourt, Francisco. *L'Inquisition à l'époque moderne: Espagne, Portugal, Italie XVe–XIXe siècle.* Paris: Fayard, 1995.

Beyreuther, Erich. *August Hermann Francke. Zeuge des lebendigen Gottes.* Marburg an der Lahn: Verlag der Francke-Buchhandlung, 1969.

Bientjes, Julia. *Holland und der Holländer im Urteil deutscher Reisender (1400–1800).* Groningen: J. B. Wolters, 1967.

Bijl, M. van der. *Idee en interest: Voorgeschiedenis, verloop en achtergronden van de politieke twisten in Zeeland en vooral in Middelburg tussen 1702 en 1715.* Groningen: Wolters-Noordhoff, 1981.

Birke, Adolf M. "Zur Kontinuität des Ämterhandels in England." Pp. 205–9 in *Ämterhandel im Spätmittelalter und im 16. Jahrhundert,* edited by Ilja Mieck. Berlin: Colloquium Verlag, 1984.

Black, Christopher F. *Italian Confraternities in the Sixteenth Century.* Cambridge: Cambridge University Press, 1989.

Blanchard, Anne et al. *Histoire militaire de la France.* Paris: Presses Universitaires de la France, 1992–94.

Blaufuß, Dietrich. "Ph. J. Spener, J. Caspar Schade und sein Freundeskreis in der Auseinandersetzung um die Einzelbeichte im Pietismus." *Jahrbuch für berlin-brandenburgische Kirchengeschichte* 48 (1973): 19–53.

Bleckwenn, Hans. *Reglement vor die Königl: Preußische Infanterie von 1726.* Osnabrück: Biblio Verlag, 1968.

———. *Die Ökonomie-Reglements des altpreußischen Heeres.* Osnabrück: Biblio Verlag, 1973.

———, ed. *Kriegs- und Friedensbilder, 1725–1759, Altpreußischer Kommis.* Osnabrück: Biblio Verlag, 1971.

Blumenthal, Uta-Renate. *Papal Reform and Canon Law in the Eleventh and Twelfth Centuries*. Brookfield, VT: Ashgate, 1998.
Boër, Joachim. "Ämterhandel in kastilischen Städten." Pp. 145–57 in *Ämterhandel im Spätmittelalter und im 16. Jahrhundert*, edited by Ilja Mieck. Berlin: Colloquium Verlag, 1984.
Bónis, György. "Ungarische Juristen am Ausgang des Mittelalters." Pp. 65–75 in *Die Rolle der Juristen bei der Entstehung des modernen Staates*, edited by Roman Schnur. Berlin: Duncker & Humblot, 1986.
Boom, H. ten. "De diaconie der Gereformeerde Kerk te Tiel van 1578 tot 1795." *Nederlands archief voor kerkgeschiedenis*, nieuwe serie, 55 (1974–75): 33–69.
Boris, György. "The Hungarian Feudal Diet Thirteenth–Eighteenth Centuries." In vol. 4 of *Gouvernés et gouvernants*. Brussels: Recueils de la société Jean Bodin pour l'histoire comparée, De Boeck University, 1965.
Bornhak, Conrad. *Geschichte des preußischen Verwaltungsrechts*. Berlin: Julius Springer, 1884–86.
Böse, Kuno. "Die Ämterkäuflichkeit in Frankreich vom 14. bis zum 16. Jahrhundert." Pp. 83–110 in *Ämterhandel im Spätmittelalter und im 16. Jahrhundert*, edited by Ilja Mieck. Berlin: Colloquium Verlag, 1984.
Bossaers, K. W. J. M. *"Van kintsbeen aan ten staatkunde opgewassen": Bestuur en beestuurders van het Noorderkwartier in de achttiende eeuw*. The Hague: Stichting Hollandse Historische Reeks, 1996.
Boutelet, Bernadette. "Étude par sondage de la criminalité dans le bailliage de Pont-de-l'Arche (XVII–XVIIIe siècles): De la violence au vol, en marche vers l'escroquerie." *Annales de Normandie* 4 (1962): 235–62.
Bouwsma, William. *John Calvin: A Sixteenth-Century Portrait*. Oxford: Oxford University Press, 1988.
Braddick, Michael J. *State Formation in Early Modern England, c. 1550–1700*. Cambridge: Cambridge University Press, 2001.
Brady, Thomas A. *Ruling Class, Regime, and Reformation at Strasbourg, 1520–1555*. Leiden: E. J. Brill, 1978.
Brand, Paul. *The Origins of the English Legal Profession*. Oxford and Cambridge: Blackwell, 1992.
Braudel, Fernand. *Civilization and Capitalism, Fifteenth–Eighteenth Century, Vol. III: The Perspective of the World*. New York: Harper & Row, 1986.
Brecht, Martin. *Kirchenordnung und Kirchenzucht in Baden-Württemberg vom 16. bis zum 18. Jahrhundert*. Stuttgart: Calwer Verlag, 1967.
———. "Lutherische Kirchenzucht bis in die Anfänge des 17. Jahrhunderts im Spannungsfeld von Pfarramt und Gesellschaft." In *Die lutherische Konfessionalisierung in Deutschland*, edited by Hans-Christoph Rublack. Gütersloh: Gerd Mohn, 1992.
Brecht, Martin, and Hermann Ehmer. *Südwestdeutsche Reformationsgeschichte*. Stuttgart: Calwer, 1984.
Brewer, John. *The Sinews of Power*. Cambridge: Harvard University Press, 1990.
Breysig, Kurt. "Die Organisation der brandenburgischen Kommissariate in der Zeit von 1660–1697." *Forschungen zur brandenburgischen und preußischen Geschichte* 5 (1892): 135–56.
———. *Die Centralstellen der Kammerverwaltung und des Heeres*. Munich: Duncker & Humblot, 1915.

Brood, Paul. *Belastingheffing in Drenthe, 1600–1822.* Amsterdam: Boom Meppel, 1991.
Brown, Keith. "The Artist of the Leviathan Title-Page." *British Library Journal* 4 (1978): 24–36.
Brückner, Jutta. *Staatswissenschaften, Kameralismus und Naturrecht.* Munich: C. H. Beck, 1977.
Bruijn, Jaap R. *De admiraliteit van Amsterdam in rustige jaren 1713–51. Regenten en financiën, schepen en zeevarende.* Amsterdam: Scheltema & Holkema, 1970.
———. *The Dutch Navy of the Seventeenth and Eighteenth Centuries.* Columbia: University of South Carolina Press, 1993.
Bruin, Grido de. *Geheimhouding en verraad: De geheimhouding van staatszaken ten tijde van de Republiek (1600–1750).* The Hague: SDU, 1991.
Buchholz, Werner. *Staat und Ständegesellschaft in Schweden zur Zeit des Überganges vom Absolutismus zum Ständeparlamentarismus, 1718–1720.* Stockholm: Almqvist and Wiksell, 1979.
Büsch, Otto. *Militärsystem und Sozialleben im alten Preußen.* Berlin: De Gruyter, 1962.
Büsch, Otto, and Wolfgang Neugebauer, eds. *Moderne preußische Geschichte 1648–1947. Eine Anthologie.* Berlin, New York: W. De Gruyter, 1981.
Buzzi, Franco, and Danilo Zardin, eds. *Carlo Borromeo e l'opera della "grande riforma": Cultura, religione e arti del governo nella Milano del pieno Cinquecento.* Milan: Silvana, 1997.
Calori, Giovannia. *Una iniziativa sociale nella Bologna del '500. L'Opera Mendicanti.* Bologna: Azzoguidi, 1972.
Calvin, John. *Selections from His Writings.* Missoula, Montana: Scholars Press, 1975.
Carruthers, Bruce. *City of Capital: Politics and Markets in the English Financial Revolution.* Princeton: Princeton University Press, 1996.
Carsten, Francis. *The Origins of Prussia.* Oxford: Clarendon, 1954.
———. *Princes and Parliaments in Germany from the Fifteenth to the Eighteenth Centuries.* Oxford: Clarendon, 1959.
Cavallo, Sandra. *Charity and Power in Early Modern Italy: Benefactors and Their Motives in Turin, 1541–1789.* Cambridge: Cambridge University Press, 1995.
Châttelier, Louis. *The Europe of the Devout: The Catholic Reformation and the Formation of a New Society.* Cambridge: Cambridge University Press, 1989.
Cockburn, J. S. "Early Modern Assize Records as Historical Evidence." *Journal of the Society of Archivists* 5 (1975): 215–32.
———. "The Nature and Incidence of Crime in England 1559–1625: A Preliminary Survey." Pp. 49–71 in *Crime in England 1550–1800,* edited by J. S. Cockburn. Princeton: Princeton University Press, 1977.
———. "Patterns of Violence in English Society: Homicide in Kent, 1560–1985." *Past and Present* 130 (1991): 70–106.
Cohen, Charles L. *God's Caress: The Psychology of Puritan Religious Experience.* New York and Oxford: Oxford University Press, 1986.
Collinson, Patrick. *The Religion of Protestants.* Oxford: Clarendon Press, 1982.
Contreras, James, and Gustav Henningsen. "Forty-Four Thousand Cases of the Spanish Inquisition (1540–1700): Analysis of a Historical Data Bank." In *The Inquisition in Early Modern Europe,* edited by Gustav Henningsen and John Tedeschi. DeKalb: Northern Illinois University Press, 1986.
Corrao, Pietro. *Governare un Regno. Potere, società e istituzioni in Sicilia fra Trecento e Quattrocento.* Naples: Liguori Editore, 1991.

Corrigan, Philip, and Derek Sayer. *The Great Arch: English State Formation as Cultural Revolution*. New York: Blackwell, 1985.

Crew, Phyllis Mack. *Calvinist Preaching and Iconoclasm in the Netherlands, 1544–1569*. Cambridge: Cambridge University Press, 1973.

Crousaz, A. v. *Die Organisation des brandenburgischen und preußischen Heeres seit 1640*. Berlin: F. Niemschneider, 1873.

Dahlgren, Stellan. "Charles X and the Constitution." Pp. 174–202 in *Sweden's Age of Greatness*, edited by Michael Roberts. London: Macmillan, 1973.

Davis, C. S. L. "Peasant Revolt in France and England: A Comparison." *Agricultural History Review* 21 (1973): 122–34.

Davis, Natalie Z. "Poor Relief, Humanism, and Heresy: The Case of Lyon." *Studies in Medieval and Renaissance History* 5 (1968): 217–75.

———. *Society and Culture in Early Modern France*. Stanford: Stanford University Press, 1975.

Decavele, J., ed. *Het eind van een rebelse droom; Brugge in de geuzentijd*. Gent: Stadsbestuur, 1984.

Deetjen, Werner-Ulrich. *Studien zur württembergischen Kirchenordnung Herzog Ulrichs, 1534–1550*. Stuttgart: Calwer, 1981.

Dekker, R. M. *Holland in beroering. Oproeren in de 17e en 18e eeuw*. Baarn: Ambo, 1982.

———. " 'Wij willen al den duyvel aff hebben!' Protesten tegen belastingen in het verleden." Pp. 33–44 in *Fiscaliteit in Nederland*, edited by J. Th. De Smit et al. Zutphen: De Walburg Pers, 1987.

Delbrück, Hans. *Geschichte der Kriegskunst im Rahmen der politischen Geschichte*. Berlin: G. Stilke, 1906–37.

———. *The Dawn of Modern Warfare*. Lincoln: University of Nebraska Press, 1985.

Delius, Hans-Ulrich. "Die Reformation in Berlin." In *Beiträge zur berliner Kirchen-Geschichte*, edited by Günter Wirth. Berlin: Union Verlag, 1987.

Delumeau, Jean. *Vie économique et sociale de Rome dans la seconde moitié du XVIe siècle*. Paris: E. Bocard, 1957–59.

———. *L'Aveu et le pardon: Les Difficultés de la confession: XIII–XVIIIe siècles*. Paris: Fayard, 1990.

Dent, Julian. *Crisis in Finance: Crown, Financiers and Society in Seventeenth-Century France*. London: Newton Abbot, David & Charles, 1973.

Den Tex, Jan. Vo.1 of *Oldenbarnevelt*. Haarlem: H.D. Tjeenk Willink & Zoon, 1960–66.

Depauw, Jacques. "Amour illégitime et société à Nantes au XVIIIe siècle." *Annales ESC* 4 (1972): 115–82.

Deppermann, Klaus. *Der hallesche Pietismus und der preußische Staat unter Friedrich III. (I.)*. Göttingen: Vandenhoeck & Ruprecht, 1961.

Despretz, André. "De Instauratie der Gentse Calvinistische Republiek (1577–79)." *Handelingen der maatschappij voor geschiedenis en oudheidskonde te Gent* 17 (1963): 119–229.

Deursen, A. Th. Van. "De Raad van State en de Generaliteit (1590–1606)." *Bladeren voor vaderlandsche geschiedenis en oudheidkunde* 19 (1964): 1–48.

———. *Bavianen en slijkgeuzen: Kerk en kerkvolk ten tijde van Maurits en Oldenbarnevelt*. Franeker: Van Wijnen, 1991.

———. *Plain Lives in a Golden Age*. Cambridge: Cambridge University Press, 1991.

———. *Een dorp in de polder. Graft in de zeventiende eeuw*. Amsterdam: Uitgeverij Bert Bakker, 1995.

Deyon, Pierre. "Délinquance et répression dans le Nord de la France au XVIIIe siècle." *Bulletin de la Société d'Histoire Moderne*. 14th ser. 20 (1972): 11–15.

Deyon, Solange. *Les "Casseurs" de l'été 1566: L'Iconoclasme dans le nord*. Paris: Hachette, 1981.

Diederiks, Herman. "Quality and Quantity in Historical Research in Criminality and Criminal Justice: The Case of Leiden in the Seventeenth and Eighteenth Centuries." *Historical Social Research* 56 (1990): 57–76.

———. *In een land van justitie. Criminaliteit van vrouwen, soldaten en ambtenaren in de achtiende-eeuwse Republiek*. Hilversum: Verloren, 1992.

Dierickx, Michiel. *L'Erection des nouveaux diocèses aux Pays-Bas, 1559–1570*. Bruxelles: La Renaissance du livre, 1967.

Directorium der Franckeschen Stiftungen. *Die Stiftungen August Herman Francke's in Halle*. Halle: Verlag der Buchhandlung des Waisenhauses, 1863.

Dixon, C. Scott. *The Reformation and Rural Society: The Parishes of Brandenburg-Ansbach-Kulmbach, 1528–1603*. Cambridge: Cambridge University Press, 1996.

Doerfel, Marianne. "Pietistische Erziehung. Johann Christian Lerches Memorandum zu Reformbestrebungen am Pädagogium Regii in Halle (1716/22)." *Pietismus und Neuzeit* 20 (1995): 90–106.

Donnelly, Johan Patrick, and Michael W. Maher, eds. *Confraternities and Catholic Reform in Italy, France, and Spain*. Kirksville: Thomas Jefferson University Press, 1999.

Dormans, E. H. M. *Het tekort. Staatsschuld in de tijd der Republiek*. Amsterdam: NEHA, 1991.

Dorwart, Reinhold A. *The Prussian Welfare State before 1740*. Cambridge: Harvard University Press, 1971.

Downing, Brian. *The Military Revolution and Political Change*. Princeton: Princeton University Press, 1992.

Doyle, William. *Venality: The Sale of Offices in Eighteenth-Century France*. Oxford: Clarendon Press, 1996.

Dreyfus, Hubert L., and Paul Rabinow. *Michel Foucault: Beyond Structuralism and Hermeneutics*. Chicago: University of Chicago Press, 1983.

Ehrle, Franz. "Die Armenordnungen von Nürnberg (1522) und Ypern (1525)." *Archiv für Reformationsgeschichte* 10 (1913): 34–72.

Eibach, Joachim. "Kriminalitätsgeschichte zwischen Sozialgeschichte und historischer Kulturforschung." *Historische Zeitschrift* 263 (1996): 681–715.

Eisenbichler, Konrad. "Italian Scholarship on Pre-Modern Confraternities in Italy." *Renaissance Quarterly* 50, no. 2 (1997): 567–79.

Elias, Johan E. *De vroedschap van Amsterdam, 1378–1795*. Amsterdam: N. Israel, 1963.

Elias, Norbert. *Die höfische Gesellschaft. Untersuchungen zur Soziologie des Königtums und der höfischen Aristokratie*. Neuwied: Luchterhand, 1969.

———. *The Civilizing Process*. Oxford: Blackwell, 1994 [1939].

———. *Über den Prozess der Zivilisation*. Two vols. Frankfurt am Main: Suhrkamp, 1997.

Elliott, John Paul. "Protestantization in the Northern Netherlands: A Case Study—The Classis of Dordrecht, 1572–1640." PhD diss.: Columbia University, 1990.

Engels, J. Th. *Kinderen van Amsterdam*. Zutphen: De Walburg Pers, 1989.

Enzensberger, Horst. "La Struttura del potere nel Regno: Corte, uffici, cancelleria." Pp. 49–70 in *Potere, società e popolo nell'età Sveva (1210–1266)*. Bari: Dedalo, 1985.

Erbe, Michael. "Aspekte des Ämterhandels in den Niederlanden im späten Mittelalter und in der frühen Neuzeit." Pp. 112–30 in *Ämterhandel im Spätmittelalter und im 16. Jahrhundert*, edited by Ilja Mieck. Berlin: Colloquium Verlag, 1984.

Ernst, Viktor. "Die Entstehung des württembergischen Kirchengutes." *Württembergische Jahrbücher für Statistik und Landeskunde* 1911:377–424.

Ertman, Thomas. *Birth of the Leviathan. Building States and Regimes in Medieval and Early Modern Europe*. Cambridge: Cambridge University Press, 1997.

———. "Rethinking Political Development in Europe." In *Annual Meeting of the American Political Science Association*. New York, September 1994.

Escher, Felix. "Das Kurfürstentum Brandenburg im Zeitalter des Konfessionalismus." in *Brandenburgische Geschichte*, edited by Ingo Materna and Wolfgang Ribbe. Berlin: Akademie Verlag, 1991.

Esping-Andersen, Gøsta. *Three Worlds of Welfare Capitalism*. Cambridge: Polity Press, 1990.

Estèbe, J., and B. Vogler. "La Genèse d'une société protestante: Étude comparée de quelques registres consistoriaux langedociens et palatins." *Annales, Economies, Sociétés, Civilisations* 31 (1976): 362–88.

Evans, Peter B. *Embedded Autonomy. States and Industrial Transformation*. Princeton: Princeton University Press, 1995.

Evans, Peter B., Dietrich Rueschemeyer, and Theda Skocpol. *Bringing the State Back In*. Cambridge: Cambridge University Press, 1985.

Fatica, Michel. "La reclusione dei poveri a Roma durante il pontificato di Innocenzo XII (1692–1700)." *Ricerche per la storia religiosa di Roma* 3 (1979): 133–79.

Fauchier-Magnan, Adrien. *The Small German Courts in the Eighteenth Century*. London: Methuen, 1958.

Fehler, Timothy G. *Poor relief and Protestantism: The Evolution of Social Welfare in Sixteenth-Century Emden*. Aldershot, England and Brookfield, VT: Ashgate, 1999.

Fiedler, Siegfried. *Grundriß der Militär- und Kriegsgeschichte*. Munich: Schild Verlag, 1980.

———. "Militärgeschichte im Zeitalter des Absolutismus." In vol. 1 of *Grundzüge der deutschen Militärgeschichte*, edited by Karl-Völker Neugebauer. Freiburg: Rombach Verlag, 1993.

Flynn, Maureen. *Sacred Charity: Confraternities and Social Welfare in Spain, 1400–1700*. Ithaca: Cornell University Press, 1989.

Fockema Andreae, S. J. *De Nederlandse staat onder de Republiek*. Amsterdam: Noord-Hollandsche Uitg. Mij., 1961.

Fockema Andreae, S. J., and Herman Hardenberg, eds. *500 jaren Statengeneraal in de Nederlanden*. Assen: Van Gorcum, 1964.

Formsma, Wiebe J. *De wording van de Staten van Stad en lande tot 1536*. Assen: Van Gorcum, 1930.

Förster, Friedrich. *Friedrich Wilhelm I, König von Preußen*. Potsdam: Verlag von Ferdinand Riegel, 1834–35.

Fosi, Irene Polverini. "Pauperismo ed assistenza a Siena durante il principato mediceo." Pp. 157–84 in *Timore e carità: I poveri nell'Italia moderna*, edited by Giorgio Polti, Mario Rosa, Franco della Peruta. Cremona: Biblioteca statale e libreria civica di Cremona, 1984.

Fosseyeux, Marcel. "Les Premiers Budgets municipaux d'assistance. La Taxe des pauvres au XVIe siècle." *Revue d'histoire de l'église de France* 20 (1934): 407–32.

Foucault, Michel. *Surveiller et punir: Naissance de la prison*. Paris: Gallimard, 1975.

———. *Histore de la sexualité*. Paris: Gallmiard, 1976–82.

———. *Language, Counter-memory, Practice.* Ithaca: Cornell University Press, 1977.
———. *Power/Knowledge.* New York: Pantheon, 1981.
———. *The Tanner Lectures on Human Values.* Cambridge: Cambridge University Press, 1981.
———. "The Subject and Power." Pp. 208–28 in *Michel Foucault: Beyond Structuralism and Hermeneutics,* edited by Hubert L. Dreyfus and Paul Rabinow. Chicago: University of Chicago Press, 1983.
———. *Politics, Philosophy, Culture: Interviews and Other Writings, 1977–1984.* London: Routledge, 1988.
———. "1977–78: Sécurité, territoire, et population." in *Resumé des cours, 1970–1982.* Paris: Julliard, 1989.
———. "Governmentality." In *The Foucault Effect: Studies in Governmentality,* edited by Graham Burchell, Colin Gordon, and Peter Miller. Chicago: University of Chicago Press, 1991.
Franz, Günther, ed. *Urkundliche Quellen zur hessischen Reformationsgeschichte.* Marburg: N. G. Elwert, 1951–57.
———. *Die Kirchenleitung in Hohenlohe in den Jahrzenten nach der Reformation.* Stuttgart: Calwer Verlag, 1971.
Frauenholz, Eugen von. *Das Heerwesen in der Zeit des Absolutismus.* Munich: C. H. Beck, 1940.
Friedeburg, Robert von. "Reformation of Manners and the Social Composition of Offenders in an East Anglian Cloth Village: Earls Colne, Essex, 1531–1642." *Journal of British Studies* 29 (1990): 347–85.
———. "Sozialdisziplinierung in England? Soziale Beziehungen auf dem Lande zwischen Reformation und 'Great Rebellion,' 1550–1642." *Zeitschrift für historische Forschung* 17 (1990): 385–418.
Friedländer, Ernst, ed. *Berliner Garnisons-Chronik.* Schriften des Vereins für die Geschichte Berlins, no. 9. Berlin: R. V. Decker, 1873.
Frifhoff, Willem. "Patterns." Pp. 43–110 in *Universities in Early Modern Europe (1500–1800),* vol. 2 of *A History of the University in Europe,* edited by Hilde de Ridder-Symoens. Cambridge: Cambridge University Press, 1996.
Fruin, Robert. *Geschiedenis der staatsinstellingen in Nederland tot den val der Republiek.* The Hague: Martinus Nijhoff, 1922.
Fulbrook, Mary. *Piety and Politics: Religion and the Rise of Absolutism in England, Württemberg, and Prussia.* Cambridge: Cambridge University Press, 1983.
Gaastra, Femme S. *De geschiedenis van de VOC.* Zutphen: De Walburg Pers, 1991.
Gabriel, Martin. *Die reformierten Gemeinden in Mitteldeutschland: Geschichte und Verfassung einer Bekenntnisminderheit im 18. Jahrhundert und danach.* Witten: Luther Verlag, 1973.
Galasso, Giuseppe. *Alla periferia dell'Impero. Il Regno di Napoli nel periodo spagnolo (secoli XVI–XVII).* Turin: Einaudi, 1994.
Garnot, Benoit. "Pour une histoire nouvelle de la criminalité au XVIIIe siècle." *Revue historique* 288 (1992): 289–303.
Gautier, Léon. *L'Hôpital Général de Genève de 1535 à 1545.* Geneva: Albert Kündig, 1914.
Gawthrop, Richard L. *Pietism and the Making of Eighteenth-Century Prussia.* Cambridge: Cambridge University Press, 1993.
Gellner, Ernst. *Nations and Nationalism.* Ithaca: Cornell University Press, 1981.
Gentilcore, David. "Cradle of Saints and Useful Institutions: Health Care and Poor Relief

in the Kingdom of Naples." Pp. 132–50 in *Health Care and Poor Relief in Counter-Reformation Europe*, edited by Ole Peter Grell and Andrew Cunningham. London and New York: Routledge, 1999.
Geremek, Bronislaw. *Poverty: A History*. Oxford: Blackwell, 1994.
Geyl, Pieter. *The Revolt of the Netherlands, 1555–1609*. London: Cassell, 1988 [1932].
Gijswijt-Hofstra, Marijke. *Wijkplaatsen voor vervolgden: Asielverlening in Culemborg, Vianen, Buren, Leerdam en Ijsselstein van de 16de tot eind 18de eeuw*. Dieren: Bataafsche Leeuw, 1984.
Ginkel, Albertus van. *De ouderling*. Amsterdam: Uitgeverij ton Bolland, 1975.
Goertz, H. J. *Pfaffenhaß und groß Geschrei*. Munich: C. H. Beck, 1987.
Göhring, Martin. *Die Ämterkäuflichkeit im Ancien régime*. Vaduz: Kraus Reprint Ltd., 1965 [1939].
Goldstone, Jack A. *Revolution and Rebellion in the Early Modern World*. Berkeley: University of California Press, 1991.
Gordon, Bruce. *Clerical Discipline and the Rural Reformation: The Synod in Zürich, 1532–1580*. Bern and New York: Peter Lang, 1992.
Gorski, Philip S. "The Poverty of Deductivism: A Constructive-Realist Model of Sociological Explanation." Paper presented to the annual meeting of the American Sociological Association. Los Angeles, 1994.
———. "Review of Gawthrop, *Pietism and the Making of Eighteenth Century Prussia*." *German Politics and Society* 32 (1994): 171–76.
———. "The Protestant Ethic and the Spirit of Bureaucracy." *American Sociological Review* 60, no. 5 (1995): 783–86.
———. "Historicizing the Secularization Debate: Church, State and Society in Late Medieval and Early Modern Europe." *American Sociological Review* 65, no. 1 (2000): 138–68.
———. "The Mosaic Moment: An Early Modernist Critique of the Modernist Theory of Nationalism." *American Journal of Sociology* 105 (2000): 1428–1470.
———. "Calvinism and Revolution: The Walzer Thesis Reconsidered." In *Meaning and Modernity*, edited by Richard Madsen, William M. Sullivan, and Ann Swidler. Berkeley: University of California Press, 2001.
———. "Religion and the Political Unconscious of Historical Sociology." in *The Making and Unmaking of Modernity*, edited by Julia Adams, Elisabeth Clemens, and Ann Shola Orloff. Durham: Duke University Press, forthcoming.
Götze, Ruth. *Wie Luther Kirchenzucht übte*. Göttingen: Vandenhoeck & Ruprecht, 1958.
Grafton, Richard. *Chronicle or History of England*. London: Johnson, 1809 [1558].
Graham, Michael F. "Social Discipline in Scotland, 1560–1610." Pp. 129–57 in *Sin and the Calvinists*, edited by Raymond A. Mentzer. Kirksville: Sixteenth Century Journal Publishers, 1994.
Grapperhaus, H. M. *Alva en de tiende penning*. Deventer: Kluwer, 1982.
Grell, Ole Peter. *The Scandinavian Reformation: From Evangelical Movement to Institutionalisation of Reform*. Cambridge: Cambridge University Press, 1995.
———. "The Religious Duty of Care and the Social Need for Control in Early Modern Europe." *Historical Journal* 39 (1996): 257–63.
Grell, Ole Peter, and Andrew Cunningham. "The Reformation and Changes in Welfare Provision in Early Modern Northern Europe." Pp. 1–42 in *Health Care and Poor Relief in Protestant Europe, 1500–1700*, edited by Ole Peter Grell and Andrew Cunningham. London and New York: Routledge, 1997.

Grendi, Eduardo. "Pauperismo e albergo dei poveri nella Genova del seicento." *Rivista storica italiana* 87 (1975): 621–54.
Grever, John H. "Committees and Deputations in the Assemblies of the Dutch Republic, 1660–1668." *Parliaments, Estates and Representation* 1 (1981): 13–33.
———. "The Structure of Decision-Making in the States General of the Dutch Republic 1660–68." *Parliaments, Estates and Representation* 2 (1982): 125–51.
Grimm, Harold J. "Luther's Contributions to Sixteenth-Century Organization of Poor Relief." *Archiv für Reformationsgeschichte* 60 (1970): 222–34.
Groehler, Olaf. *Das Heerwesen in Brandenburg und Preußen von 1640 bis 1806*. Berlin: Brandenburgisches Verlagshaus, 1903.
Groenhuis, G. *De Predikanten: De sociale positie nan de Gereformeerde predikanten in de Republiek der Verenigde Nederlanden vóór ± 1700*. Groningen: Wolters-Noordhoff, 1977.
Groenveld, S. et al. *De tachtigjarige oorlog*. 3rd ed. Zutphen: De Walburg Pers, 1991.
Groenveld, S. *Evidente factiën in den staet: Sociaal-politieke verhoudingen in de 17e-eeuwse Republiek der Verenigde Nederlanden*. Hilversum: Verloren, 1990.
Grün, Willi. *Speners soziale Leistungen und Gedanken*. Würzburg: Konrad Tritsch, 1934.
Grünberg, Paul. *Philipp Jakob Spener*. Hildesheim and New York: Georg Olms Verlag, 1988.
Gutton, Jean-Pierre. *La Société et les pauvres: L'Exemple de la généralité de Lyon, 1534–1789*. Paris: Société d'Édition "Les belles lettres," 1970.
Hagen, William W. "Seventeenth-Century Crisis in Brandenburg: The Thirty Years' War, the Destabilization of Serfdom, and the Rise of Absolutism." *American Historical Review*. 94, no. 2 (1989): 302–35.
Hahlweg, Werner. *Die Heeresreform der Oranier; das Kriegsbuch des Grafen Johann von Nassau-Siegen*. Wiesbaden: Historische Kommission für Nassau, 1973.
———. *Die Heeresreform der Oranier und die Antike*. Osnabrück: Biblio Verlag, 1987 [1941].
Hahn, Peter-Michael. *Landesstaat und Ständetum im Kurfürstentum Brandenburg während des 16. und 17. Jahrhunderts*. Berlin: De Gruyter, 1983.
———. *Fürstliche Territorialhoheit und lokale Adelsgewalt: Die herrschaftliche Durchdringung des ländlichen Raumes zwischen Elbe und Aller (1300–1700)*. Berlin and New York: Walter de Gruyter, 1989.
Haliczer, Stephen. *Inquisition and Society in the Kingdom of Valencia, 1478–1834*. Berkeley: University of California Press, 1990.
Hallema, A. "Wie er in de 17e eeuw in het tuchthuis kwamen?" *Tijdschrift voor strafrecht* 38 (1926): 222–45.
———. "Jan van Hout's rapporten en adviezen betreffende het Amsterdamsche Tuchthuis uit de Jaren 1597 en '98." *Bijdragen en mededelingen van het Historisch Genootschap* 48 (1927): 69–98.
———. "Een pater en twee predikanten in en uit het Amsterdamsche Tuchthuis." In *Nieuw Rotterdamsche Courant*, March 24, 1929.
———. *In en om de gevangenis van vroeger dagen in Nederland en Nederlandsch-Indië*. The Hague: Gebr. Belinfante, 1936.
———. *Geschiedenis van het gevangeniswezen, hoofdzakelijk in Nederland*. The Hague: Staatsdrukkerij- en Uitgeverijsbedrijf, 1958.
Hallman, Barbara. *Italian Cardinals, Reform, and the Church as Property: 1492–1563*. Berkeley: University of California Press, 1985.
Hammerstein, Notker. "Universitäten—Territorialstaaten—Gelehrte Räte." Pp. 697–735 in

Die Rolle der Juristen bei der Entstehung des modernen Staates, edited by Roman Schnur. Berlin: Duncker & Humblot, 1986.

Happee, J., J. L. J. Meiners, and M. Mostert, eds. *De Lutheranen in Amsterdam 1588-1988.* Hilversum: Verloren, 1988.

Harrington, Joel F. "Escape from the Great Confinement: The Genealogy of a German Workhouse." *Journal of Modern History* 71, no. 2 (1999): 308-45.

Hart, Marjolein 't. *The Making of a Bourgeois State: War, Politics, and Finance during the Dutch Revolt.* Manchester: Manchester University Press, 1993.

Hartmann, Peter Claus. *Das Steuersystem der europäischen Staaten am Ende des Ancien Régime. Eine offizielle französische Enquête (1763-1768) (Beiheft Francia, 7).* Munich: Artemis, 1979.

Heel, Caspar van, ed. *Vierhonderd jaar gedeputeerde staten van Overijssel.* Zwolle: Provincie Overijssel, 1993.

Heinrich, Gerd. "Der Adel in Brandenburg-Preußen." Pp. 259-314 in *Deutscher Adel,* edited by Hellmut Rössler. Darmstadt: Wissenschaftliche Buchgesellschaft, 1965.

———. "Amtsträgerschaft und Geistlichkeit. Zur Problematik sekundärer Führungsschichten in Brandenburg-Preußen 1450-1786." Pp. 179-238 in *Beamtentum und Pfarrerstand 1400-1800. Büdinger Vorträge 1967,* edited by Günther Franz. Limburg an der Lahn: C. A. Starke, 1972.

Hellmuth, Eckhart. *Naturrechtsphilosophie und bürokratischer Werthorizont: Studien zur preussischen Geistes- und Sozialgeschichte des 18. Jahrhunderts.* Göttingen: Vandenhoeck & Ruprecht, 1985.

Hemstra, M. J. Barnoes van. *Old Burger Weeshuis.* Leeuwarden: De Voogdij [van het Old Burger Weeshuis], 1959.

Henningsen, Gustav, and John Tedeschi, eds. *The Inquisition in Early Modern Europe: Studies on Sources and Methods.* Dekalb: Northern Illinois University Press, 1986.

Herzel, Ludwig, ed. *Albrecht Hallers Tagebücher seiner Reisen nach Deutschland, Holland und England 1723-1727.* Leipzig: S. Hirzel, 1883.

Hibben, C. C. *Gouda in Revolt. Particularism and Pacifism in the Revolt of the Netherlands 1572-1588.* Utrecht: HES Publishers, 1983.

Hill, Christopher. *Society and Puritanism in Pre-Revolutionary England.* New York: Schocken, 1967.

Hinrichs, Carl. "Der Regierungsantritt Friedrich Wilhelm I." Pp. 91-137 in *Preußen als historisches Problem,* edited by Carl Hinrichs. Berlin: Walter de Gruyter, 1963.

———. *Friedrich Wilhelm I.* Darmstadt: Wissenschaftliche Buchgesellschaft, 1968.

———. *Preußentum und Pietismus: Der Pietismus in Brandeuburg-Preußen als religiös-soziale Reformbewegung.* Göttingen: Vandenhoeck & Ruprecht, 1971.

Hintze, Otto. *Die Behördenorganisation und die allgemeine Verwaltung in Preußen um 1740, Acta Borussica, Behördenorganisation.* Berlin: Paul Parey, 1901.

———. *Die Hohenzollern und Ihr Werk.* Berlin: Paul Parey, 1915.

———. *Geist und Epoche der preußischen Geschichte.* Leipzig: Koehler & Armelang, n.d.

Hippel, Robert von. "Beiträge zur Geschichte der Freiheitsstrafe." *Zeitschrift für die gesamte Strafrechtswissenschaft* 18 (1898): 419-97 and 608-66.

Hoeven, Anton van den. "Ten exempel en afschrik: Strafrechtspleging en criminaliteit in Haarlem, 1740-1795." PhD Diss: University of Amsterdam, 1982.

Hoffman, W. von. *Forschungen zur Geschichte der Kurialen Behörden vom Schisma bis zur Reformation.* Rom: Preußisches historisches Institut, 1914.

Holl, Karl. *Gesammelte Aufsätze zur Kirchengeschichte*. Tübingen: J. C. B. Mohr, 1948.
Holm, Johan. " 'Skyldig plicht och trohet': Militärstaten och 1634 års regeringsform," *Historisk Tidskrift* 2 (1999): 161–95.
Holt, Mack P. *The French Wars of Religion, 1562–1629*. Cambridge: Cambridge University Press, 1995.
Holzem, Andreas. "Katholische Konfession und Kirchenzucht. Handlungsformen und Deliktfelder archidiakonaler Gerichtsbarkeit im 17. und 18. Jahrhundert." *Westfälische Forschungen* 45 (1995): 295–332.
Homer, Sidney. *A History of Interest Rates*. New Brunswick: Rutgers University Press, 1977.
Höpfl, Hajo. *The Christian Polity of John Calvin*. Cambridge: Cambridge University Press, 1982.
Hötzsch, Otto. *Stände und Verwaltung von Cleve und Mark in der Zeit von 1666 bis 1697*. Leipzig: Duncker & Humblot, 1908.
Hsia, R. Po-chia. *Social Discipline in the Reformation: Central Europe, 1550–1750*. New York: Routledge, 1989.
Ikegami, Eiko. *The Taming of the Samurai: Honorific Individualism and the Making of Modern Japan*. Cambridge: Harvard University Press, 1995.
Ingram, Martin. *Church Courts, Sex, and Marriage in England, 1570–1640*. Cambridge: Cambridge University Press, 1987.
Innes, Joanna. "Prisons for the Poor: English Bridewells, 1555–1800." In *Labour, Law, and Crime*, edited by Francis Snyder and Douglas Hay. London: Travistock, 1987.
Israel, Jonathan I. *Dutch Primacy in World Trade*. Oxford and New York: Clarendon and Oxford University Press, 1989.
———. *The Dutch Republic: Its Rise, Greatness, and Fall, 1477–1806*. Oxford: Clarendon Press, 1995.
J. Marx, Freiherr von Liechtenstern. *Skizze einer statistischen Schilderung des österreichischen Staats:* Im Verlag des Kunst- und Industriekomptoirs, 1800.
Jähns, Max. *Geschichte der Kriegswissenschaften, vornehmlich in Deutschland*. Munich and Leipzig: R. Oldenbourg, 1889.
Jahns, Sigrid. "Frankfurt am Main im Zeitalter der Reformation (um 1500–1555)." Pp. 151–204 in *Frankfurt am Main. Die Geschichte der Stadt in neun Beiträgen*. Sigmaringen: Jan Thorbecke, 1991.
Jansen, E. A. M. E. *De opkomst van de vroedschap in enkele hollandsche steden*. Haarlem: Amicitia, 1927.
Janssen, H. Q. *De kerkhervorming in Vlaanderen*. Arnhem: J. W. & C. F. Swaan, 1866–68.
Jany, Curt. "Die Kantonverfassung Friedrich Wilhelms I." *Forschungen zur brandenburgischen und preußischen Geschichte* 38 (1926): 225–72.
Janzon, Kaj. "Överdåd på kredit: Ett rationellt Val? Några problem kring högadelns economiska verksamhet i Sverige under 1600-talets första hälft." *Historisk tidskrift* 2 (1999): 197–226.
Jones, D. W. *War and Economy in the Age of William III and Marlborough*. Oxford and New York: Blackwell, 1988.
Jong, Jacob Johannes de. *Met goed fatsoen: De elite in een Hollandse stad, Gouda 1700–1780*. The Hague: Stichting Hollandse Historische Reeks, 1985.
Jütte, R. *Obrigkeitliche Armenfürsorge in deutschen Reichsstädten der frühen Neuzeit*. Cologne: W. Kohlhammer, 1984.

———. *Poverty and Deviance in Early Modern Europe*. Cambridge: Cambridge University Press, 1994.
Kalveen, C. A. van. *Het bestuur van bisschop en Staten in het Nedersticht, Oversticht, en Drenthe, 1483–1520*. Groningen: H. D. Tjeenk Willink, 1974.
Kamen, Henry. *Inquisition and Society in Spain*. London: Weidenfeld & Nicolson, 1985.
Kaplan, Benjamin. *Calvinists and Libertines: Confession and Community in Utrecht, 1578–1620*. New York: Oxford University Press, 1995.
Kappelhoff, A. C. M. *De belastingheffing in de Meierij van Den Bosch gedurende de Generaliteitsperiode (1648–1730)*. Tilburg: Stichting Zuidelijk Historisch Contact, 1986.
Karpik, Lucien. *French Lawyers: A Study in Collective Action, 1274 to 1994*. Oxford: Clarendon Press, 1999.
Kingdon, J. A. *Richard Grafton, Citizen and Grocer of London*. London: Privately printed by Rixon & Arnold, 1901.
Kingdon, Robert. "The Political Resistance of the Calvinists in France and the Low Countries." *Church History*, 27, no. 3 (1958): 220–33.
———. "Was the Protestant Reformation a Revolution? The Case of Geneva." Pp. 203–22 in, *Church, Society, and Politics*, edited by Derek Baker. Oxford: Blackwell, 1975.
———. "The Control of Morals in Calvin's Geneva." Pp. 3–16 in *The Social History of the Reformation*, edited by Lawrence P. Buch and Jonathan W. Zophy. Columbus: Ohio State University Press, 1972.
———. "Social Welfare in Calvin's Geneva." *American Historical Review* 76 (1972): 50–69.
———. "Calvinist Discipline in the Old World and the New." Pp. 521–32 in *The Reformation in Germany and Europe*, edited by Hans R. Guggisberg and Gottfried G. Krodel. Gütersloh: Gütersloher Verlagsanstalt, 1993.
Kittelson, James M. "Successes and Failures in the German Reformation: The Report from Strasbourg." *Archiv für Reformationsgeschichte* 73 (1982): 153–75.
Klein, Laurentius. *Evangelisch-lutherische Beichte. Lehre und Praxis*. Paderborn: Verlag Bonifacius, 1961.
Kleinschmidt, Harald. "Zum preußischen Infanteriereglement von 1718." *Zeitschrift für Heereskunde* 47 (1983): 117–20.
Kloek, Els. "Criminality and Gender in Leiden's *Confessieboeken*, 1678–1794." *Criminal Justice History* 11 (1990): 1–29.
Klueting, Harm. *Das konfessionelle Zeitalter*. Stuttgart: Ulmer, 1989.
Knippenberg, Hans. *De religieuze kaart van Nederland: Omvang en geografische spreiding van de godsdienstige gezindten vanaf de Reformatie tot heden*. Assen: Van Gorcum, 1992.
Knuttel, Willem Pieter Cornelis. *De toestand der nederlandsche katholieken ten tijde der republiek*. The Hague: M. Nijhoff, 1892–1894.
Koenigsberger, Helmut G. "The Organization of Revolutionary Parties in France and the Netherlands during the Sixteenth Century." Pp. 224–52 in Koenigsberger, *Estates and Revolutions*. Ithaca: Cornell University Press, 1971.
Kok, Jan. "The Moral Nation: Illegitimacy and Bridal Pregnancy in the Netherlands from 1600 to the Present." *Economy and Social History in the Netherlands* 2 (1990): 7–35.
Kok, J. A. de. *Nederland op de breuklijn Rome-Reformatie: Numerieke aspecten van protestantisering en katholieke herleving in de noordelijke Nederlanden, 1580–1880*. Assen: Van Gorcum, 1964.

Kooimans, L. *Onder regenten: De elite in een Hollandse stad: Hoorn 1700–1780.* The Hague: Stichting Hollandse Historische Reeks, 1985.

Koopmans, J. W. *De Staten van Holland en de Opstand. De ontwikkeling van hun functies en organisatie in de periode 1544–1588.* The Hague: Stichting Hollandse Historische Reeks, 1990.

Kopcynski, Michal. "Service or Benefice? Officeholders in Poland and Sweden of the Seventeenth Century." *European Review of History* 1, no. 1 (1994): 19–28.

Kossmann, E. H., and A. F. Mellink, eds. *Texts Concerning the Revolt of the Netherlands.* London: Cambridge University Press, 1974.

Kötzschke, Rudolf, and Hellmut Kretzschmar. *Sächsische Geschichte.* Frankfurt am Main: Wolfgang Weidlich, 1965.

Krahn, Cornelis. *Dutch Anabaptism.* The Hague: M. Nijhoff, 1968.

Kramer, Gustav. *Beiträge zur Geschichte August Hermann Franckes.* Halle: Verlag der Buchhandlung des Waisenhauses, 1861.

———. *August Hermann Francke. Ein Lebensbild.* Halle: Verlag der Buchhandlung des Waisenhauses, 1880–82.

Krause, Gerhard. "Armut VII. 16–20 Jahrhundert, Luther." Pp. 98–105 in *Theologische Realenzyklopädie,* edited by Gerhard Krause and Gerhard Müller. Berlin: Walter De Gruyter. 1977–.

Krauske, Otto. 1901. "Vom Hofe Friedrich Wilhelms I." *Hohenzollern Jahrbuch* 5 (1977): 174.

Krug, Leopold. *Betrachtungen über den Nationalreichtum des preußischen Staates und über den Wohlstand seiner Bewohner.* Aalen: Scientia Verlag, 1970 [1805].

Küchler, Winfried. "Ämterkäulichkeit in den Ländern der Krone Aragons." Pp. 1–26 in *Spanische Forschungen der Görresgesellschaft,* vol. 27: *Gesammelte Aufsätze zur Kulturgeschichte Spaniens.* Münster: Aschendorffsche Verlagsbuchhandlung, 1973.

Kühler, W. J. *Geschiedenis van de Doopsgezinden in Nederland.* Haarlem: H. D. Tjeenk Willink & Zoon, 1932–50.

Lancon, Pierre. "Les Confrèries de rosaire en Rouergue aux XVIe et XVIIe siècles." *Annales du Midi* 96 (1984): 121–33.

Lange, P. W. de. "De ontwikkeling van een oligarchische regeringsvorm in een Westfriese stad. Medemblik 1289–1699." *Hollandse Studiën* 3 (1972): 119–46.

Laslett, Peter. "Introduction: Comparing Illegitimacy over Time and between Cultures." Pp. 1–70 in *Bastardy and Its Comparative History,* edited by Peter Laslett, Karla Oosterveen, and Richard M. Smith. London: Edward Arnold, 1980.

Lea, Charles Henry. *A History of Auricular Confession.* Philadelphia: Lea Brothers & Co., 1896.

———. *A History of the Inquisition in Spain.* New York: AMS Press, 1966 [1906–7].

Lebigre, Arlette. *La Police: Une Histoire sous influence.* Paris: Gallimard, 1993.

Leenders, Jos. *Benauwde verdraagzaamheid, hachelijk fatsoen: Families, standen en kerken te Hoorn in het midden van de negentiende eeuw.* The Hague: Stichting Hollandse Historische Reeks, 1992.

Leeuwen, Marco H. D. van, and Nicole Lucas. "De diakonie van de Hervormde Kerk." Amsterdam: unpublished manuscript, 1981. A copy is deposited at the library of the Amsterdam Gemeentearchief.

Lehmann, Max. "Werbung, Wehrpflicht und Beurlaubung im Heere Friedrich Wilhelms I." *Historische Zeitschrift* 67 (1891): 254–89.

Lemmink, F. H. J. *Het ontstaan van de staten van Zeeland en hun geschiedenis tot het jaar 1555.* Roosendaal: n.p., 1951.

Leonard, E. M. *The Early History of English Poor Relief.* London: Frank Cass & Co., 1965.

Liehr, Reinhard. "Ämterkäuflichkeit und Ämterhandel im kolonialen Hispanoamerika." Pp. 159–81 in *Ämterhandel im Spätmittelalter und im 16. Jahrhundert,* edited by Ilja Mieck. Berlin: Colloquium Verlag, 1984.

Lindberg, Carter. "There Should Be No Beggars among Christians': Karlstadt, Luther, and the Origins of Protestant Poor Relief." *Church History* 46 (1977): 313–34.

———. *Beyond Charity: Reformation Initiatives for the Poor.* Minneapolis: Fortress, 1993.

Lis, Catharina, and Hugo Soly. *Poverty and Capitalism in Preindustrial Europe.* Sussex: Harvester Press, 1979.

Litchfield, R. Burr. *Emergence of a Bureaucracy: The Florentine patricians, 1530–1790.* Princeton: Princeton University Press, 1986.

Little, David. *Religion, Order, and Law.* Chicago: University of Chicago Press, 1984.

Locke, John. *Travels in France, 1675–1679, as related in his Journals, correspondence and other papers.* Cambridge: Cambridge University Press, 1953.

Loeben, Monika v., and Paul v. Loeben. "Geschichte der Herren, Freiherren und Gräfen von Löben." Berlin-Dahlem; an unpublished manuscript deposited in the Heroldbibliothek, Geheimes Staatsarchiv–Preußischer Kulturbesitz, 1975.

Lombardi, Daniela. "Poveri a Firenze. Programmi e realizzazioni della politica assistenziale dei Medici tra Cinque e Seicento." Pp. 165–84 in *Timore e carità: I poveri nell'Italia moderna,* edited by Giorgio Polti, Mario Rosa, Franco della Peruta. Cremona: Biblioteca statale e libreria civica di Cremona, 1982.

Loosjes, Jakob. *Geschiedenis der Luthersche Kerk in de Nederlanden.* The Hague: M. Nijhoff, 1921.

Lough, John. *France Observed in the Seventeenth Century by British Travellers.* Stocksfield: Oriel Press, 1985.

Ludolphy, Ingetraut. "Luther und die Diakonie." *Luther* 38 (1967): 58–68.

Luria, Keith P. *Territories of Grace: Cultural Change in the Seventeenth-Century Diocese of Grenoble.* Berkeley: University of California Press, 1991.

Luther, Martin. *Works.* Philadelphia: Fortress, 1966.

Lynn, John A. "Tactical Evolution in the French Army, 1560–1660." *French Historical Studies* 14 (1985): 176–91.

MacCaffrey, Wallace T. *Exeter, 1540–1640.* Cambridge: Harvard University Press, 1958.

Maczak, Antoni. "The Structure of Power in the Commonwealth of the Sixteenth and Seventeenth Centuries." Pp. 109–34 in *A Republic of Nobles,* edited by J. Federowicz, Maria Bogucka, and Henryk Samsonowicz. Cambridge: Cambridge University Press, 1982.

———. *Travel in Early Modern Europe.* Cambridge and Oxford: Blackwell, 1995.

Maher, Michael W. "How the Jesuits Used Their Congregations to Promote Frequent Communion." Pp. 75–95 in *Confraternities and Catholic Reform in Italy, France, and Spain,* edited by Johan Patrick Donnelly and Michael W. Maher. Kirksville: Thomas Jefferson University Press, 1999.

Maier, Hans. *Die ältere deutsche Staats- und Verwaltungslehre.* Munich: C. H. Beck, 1980.

Manen, Charlotte Aleida van. *Armenpflege in Amsterdam in ihrer historischen Entwicklung.* Leiden: A. W. Sijthoff, 1913.

Mann, Thomas. *Gesammelte Werke.* Frankfurt am M.: Fischer, 1960–75.

Mantelli, Roberto. *Il pubblico impiego nell'economia del Regno di Napoli: Retribuzioni, reclutamento e ricambio sociale nell'epoca spagnuola (sec. XVI–XVII)*. Naples: Istituto italiano per gli studi filosofici, 1986.

Martin, Jean-Marie. "L'Organisation administrative et militaire du territoire." Pp. 71–122 in *Potere, società e popolo nell'età sveva*, edited by Cosimo D. Fonseco et al. Bari: Dedalo, 1985.

Martines, Lauro. *Lawyers and Statecraft in Renaissance Florence*. Princeton: Princeton University Press, 1968.

Martinich, A. P. *The Two Gods of Leviathan: Thomas Hobbes on Religion and Politics*. Cambridge: Cambridge University Press, 1992.

Martz, Linda. *Poverty and Welfare in Habsburg Spain: The Example of Toledo*. Cambridge and New York: Cambridge University Press, 1983.

Mathias, Peter, and Patrick O'Brien. "Taxation in Britain and France, 1715–1810: A Comparison of the Social and Economic Incidence of Taxes Collected for the Central Governments." *Journal of European Economic History* 5 (1976): 601–50.

———. "The Social and Economic Burden of Tax Revenue Collected for Central Government." Pp. 805–42 in *Prodotto lordo e finanza pubblica secoli XIII–XIX*, edited by Annalisa Guarducci. Florence: Le Monnier, 1988.

Mazlish, Bruce. *The Revolutionary Ascetic: Evolution of a Political Type*. New York: Basic Books, 1976.

McCusker, John J. *Money and exchange in Europe and America, 1600–1775: A Handbook*. Chapel Hill: University of North Carolina Press, 1977.

McKee, Elsie Anne. *John Calvin on the Diaconate and Liturgical Almsgiving*. Geneva: Librairie Droz, 1984.

Meier, Ernst von. *Hannoversche Verfassungs- und Verwaltungsgeschichte*. Leipzig: Duncker & Humblot, 1898–99.

Meij, J. C. A., de. *De Watergeuzen in de Nederlanden, 1568–1572*. Amsterdam: Noord-Hollandsche Uitgevers Maatschappij, 1972.

Melton, Edgar. "The Prussian Junkers, 1600–1786." Pp. 71–109 in *The European Nobilities in the Seventeenth and Eighteenth Centuries, vol. II: Northern, Central, and Eastern Europe*, edited by H. M. Scott. London and New York: Longman, 1995.

Miller, Richard L. *Fact and Method*. Princeton: Princeton University Press, 1997.

Mitchell, B. R., and Phyllis Deane. *Abstract of British Historical Statistics*. Cambridge: Cambridge University Press, 1962.

Modéer, Kjell A. "Die Rolle der Juristen in Schweden Im 17. Jahrhunderet. Eine rechtshistorische Skizze." Pp. 123–37 in *Europe and Scandinavia: Aspects of the Process of Integration in the Seventeenth Century*, edited by Göran Rystad. Lund: Wallin & Dalholm Boktr, 1983.

Modelski, G., and W. R. Thompson. *Seapower in Global Politics, 1494–1993*. Seattle: University of Washington Press, 1988.

Mogensen, N. W. "Crimes and Punishments in Eighteenth-Century France: The Example of the Pays d'Auge." *Histoire sociale* 20 (1977): 337–52.

Möller, Horst. "Ämterkäuflichkeit in Brandenburg-Preussen im 17. und 18. Jahrhundert." Pp. 156–77 in *Ämterkäuflichkeit: Aspekte sozialer Mobilität im europäischen Vergleich*, edited by Klaus Malettke. Berlin: Colloquium Verlag, 1980.

Monter, E. William. *Frontiers of Heresy: The Spanish Inquisition from the Basque lands to Sicily*. New York: Cambridge University Press, 1990.

Monter, E. William, and John Tedeschi. "Toward a Statistical Profile of the Italian Inquisitions, Sixteenth to Eighteenth Centuries." In *The Inquisition in Early Modern Europe*, edited by Gustav Henningsen and John Tedeschi. DeKalb: Northern Illinois University Press, 1986.

Moore, Barrington. *Social Origins of Dictatorship and Democracy: Lord and Peasant in the Making of the Modern World*. Boston: Beacon, 1966.

Moraw, Peter. "Gelehrte Juristen im Dienst der deutschen Könige des späten Mittelalters (1273–1493)." Pp. 77–147 in *Die Rolle der Juristen bei der Entstehung des modernen Staates*, edited by Roman Schnur. Berlin: Duncker & Humblot, 1986.

Morford, Mark. *Stoics and Neostoics: Rubens and the Circle of Lipsius*. Princeton: Princeton University Press, 1991.

Mousnier, Roland. "Le Trafic des offices à Venise." *Revue historique du droit français et etranger* 30 (1952): 552–65.

———. *La Venalité des offices, sous Henri IV et Louis XIII*. Paris: Presses Universitaires de France, 1971.

Mukerji, Chandra. *Territorial Ambitions and the Gardens of Versailles*. Cambridge: Cambridge University Press, 1997.

Müller, Karl. "Die Anfänge der Konsistorialverfassung im lutherischen Deutschland." Pp. 175–90 in *Aus der akademischen Arbeit*, edited by Karl Müller. Tübingen: J. C. B. Mohr, 1930.

Murphy, Paul V. "Politics, Piety, and Reform: Lay Religiosity in Sixteenth-Century Mantua." In *Confraternities and Catholic Reform in Italy, France, and Spain*, edited by Johan Patrick Donnelly and Michael W. Maher. Kirksville: Thomas Jefferson University Press, 1999.

Musi, A. "La venalità degli uffici in principato citra." *Rassegna storica salernitana* 5 (1986): 71–91.

Nachama, Andreas. *Ersatzbürger und Staatsbildung: Zur Zerstörung des Bürgertums in Brandenburg-Preußen*. Frankfurt am Main: Peter Lang, 1984.

Nebe, August. "Aus Speners Berliner Briefen an eine Freundin in Frankfurt." *Jahrbuch für brandenburgische Kirchengeschichte* 30 (1935): 115–55.

Neugebauer, Wolfgang. "Zur neueren Deutung der preußischen Verwaltung im 17. und 18. Jahrhundert. Eine Studie in vergleichender Sicht." *Jahrbuch für die Geschichte Mittel- und Ostdeutschlands* 26 (1977): 86–128.

———. "Die Stände in Magdeburg, Halberstadt und Minden im 17. und 18. Jahrhundert." Pp. 170–207 in *Ständetum und Staatsbildung in Brandenburg-Preußen*, edited by Peter Baumgart. Berlin and New York: Walter de Gruyter, 1983.

———. *Absolutistischer Staat und Schulwirklichkeit in Brandenburg-Preußen*. Berlin and New York: Walter de Gruyter, 1985.

Nieuwenhuis, F. J. Domela. *Geschiedenis der Amsterdamsche Luthersche Gemeente*. Amsterdam: J.H. Gebhard & Co., 1856.

Nischan, Bodo. "Johann Peter Bergius." Pp. 35–59 in *Berlinische Lebensbilder*, edited by G. Heinrich. Berlin: Colloquium, 1990.

———. *Prince, People, and Confession: The Second Reformation in Brandenburg*. Philadelphia: University of Pennsylvania Press, 1994.

Nolfe, Ernst. *La Réforme de la bienfaisance publique à Ypres au XVIe siècle*. Gent: E. Van Goethem & Cie, 1915.

Norberg, Kathryn. *Rich and Poor in Grenoble, 1600–1814*. Berkeley: University of California Press, 1985.

Oakley, Stewart. *A Short History of Sweden*. New York and Washington: Praeger, 1966.

O'Day, Rosemary. *The English Clergy: The Emergence and Consolidation of a Profession, 1558–1642*. Leicester: Leicester University Press, 1979.

O'Donoghue, Edward Geoffrey. *Bridewell Hospital: Palace, Prison, Schools, from the Earliest Times to the End of the Reign of Elizabeth*. London: Lane, 1923.

Oestreich, Gerhard. *Der brandenburg-preußische Geheime Rat*. Würzburg: Konrad Troltsch, 1936.

———. *Geist und Gestalt des frühmodernen Staates*. Berlin: Duncker & Humblot, 1969.

———. *Friedrich Wilhelm I*. Göttingen: Musterschmidt, 1977.

———. *Neostoicism and the Early Modern State*. Cambridge: Cambridge University Press, 1982.

———. *Antiker Geist und moderner Staat bei Justus Lipsius (1547–1606): Der Neustoizismus als politische Bewegung*. Göttingen: Vandenhoeck & Ruprecht, 1989.

Opgenoorth, Ernst. *Ausländer in Brandenburg-Preußen als leitende Beamte und Offiziere, 1604–1871*. Würzburg: Holzner Verlag, 1967.

———. *Friedrich Wilhelm, der Große Kurfürst von Brandenburg*. Göttingen: Musterschmidt, 1971.

———. " 'Nervus rerum.' Die Auseinandersetzungen mit den Ständen um die Staatsfinanzierung." In *Ein sonderbares Licht in Teutschland. Beiträge zur Geschichte des Großen Kurfürsten von Brandenburg, 1640–1688*, edited by Gerd Heinrich. Berlin: Duncker & Humblot, 1989.

Oschlies, Wolf. *Die Arbeits- und Berufspädagogik August Hermann Francke's*. Witten: Luther Verlag, 1969.

Österberg, Eva. "Criminality, Social Control, and the Early Modern State: Evidence and Interpretations in Scandinavian Historiography." In *The Civilization of Crime*, edited by Eric A. Johnson and Eric H. Monkkonen. Urbana: University of Illinois Press, 1996.

Österberg, Eva, and Dag Lindström. *Crime and Social Control in Medieval and Early Modern Swedish Towns*. Stockholm: Almqvist & Wiksell, 1988.

Oosterhoff, F. G. *Leicester and the Netherlands, 1586–1587*. Utrecht: Hes Publishers, 1988.

Otruba, Gustav. "Staatshaushalt und Staatsschuld unter Maria Theresia und Joseph II." Pp. 197–249 in *Österreich im Zeitalter der Aufklärung*. Vienna: Verlag der österreichischen Akademie der Wissenschaften, 1985.

Pallas, K., ed. "Die Wittenberger Beutelordnung vom Jahre 1521 und ihr Verhältnis zu der Einrichtung des Gemeinen Kastens im Januar 1522. Aus dem Nachlasse des Professors Dr. Nic. Müller—Berlin." *Zeitschrift des Vereins für Kirchengeschichte in der Provinz Sachsen* 12 (1915): 1–45 and 100–137.

Parker, Charles H. *The Reformation of Community: Social Welfare and Calvinist Charity in Holland, 1572–1620*. Cambridge: Cambridge University Press, 1998.

Parker, David. *The Making of French Absolutism*. London: Edward Arnold, 1983.

Parker, Geoffrey. *The Army of Flanders and the Spanish Road, 1567–1659*. Cambridge: Cambridge University Press, 1972.

———. "The 'Military Revolution,' 1550–1600—A Myth?" *Journal of Modern History* 48 (1976): 195–214.

———. "Some Recent Work on the Inquisition in Spain and Italy." *Journal of Modern History* 54, 3 (1982): 519–32.

———. *The Dutch Revolt*. London: Peregrine, 1988.

———. *The Military Revolution: Military Innovation and the Rise of the West, 1500–1800.* Cambridge: Cambridge University Press, 1988.

———. "The 'Kirk By Law Established' and the Origins of 'The Taming of Scotland': Saint Andrews, 1559–1600." In *Sin and the Calvinists,* edited by Raymond A. Mentzer. Kirksville: Sixteenth Century Journal Press, 1994.

Partner, Peter. "Papal Financial Policy in the Renaissance and Counter-Reformation, *Past and Present* 88 (1980): 17–62.

Pastore, Alessandro. "Strutture assistenziale fra chiesa e stati nell'Italia della controriforma." Pp. 435–65 in *Storia d'Italia. Annali vol. 9: La chiesa e il potere politico,* edited by Georgio Chittolini and Giovanni Miccoli. Turin: Einaudi, 1986.

Paulsen, Friedrich. *Geschichte des gelehrten Unterrichts.* Berlin: Walter de Gruyter, 1919–20.

Paultre, Christian. *De la répression de la mendicité et du vagabondage en France sous l'ancien régime.* Geneva: Slatkine-Megariotis Reprints, 1975.

Pelorson, Jean-Marc. *Les Letrados. Juristes Castillans sous Philippe III.* Le Puy-en-velay: L'Éveil de la haute Loire, 1980.

Peters, Jan, ed. *Gutsherrschaft als soziales Modell: Vergleichende Betrachtungen zur Funktionsweise frühneuzeitlicher Agrargesellschaften.* Munich: R. Oldenbourg, 1995.

Poggi, G. *The Development of the Modern State.* Stanford: Stanford University Press, 1979.

Pol, Lotte C. Van de. *Het Amsterdams hoerdom. Prostitutie in de zeventiende en achttiende eeuw.* Amsterdam: Wereldbibliotheek, 1996.

Pound, John F. *The Norwich Census of the Poor, 1570.* London: Cox and Wyman, 1971.

Prak, Maarten R. *Gezeten burgers: De elite in een Hollandse stad: Leiden, 1700–1780.* The Hague: Stichting Hollandse Historische Reeks, 1985.

Prosperi, Adriano. "Chierici e laici nell'opera di Carlo Borromeo." *Annali dell'Istituto Storico Italo-Germanico in Trento* 14 (1988): 241–72.

———. "Missioni popolare e visite pastorali in Italia tra '500 e '600." *Mélanges de l'Ecole Française de Rome. Italie et Méditerranée* 109 (1997): 767–783.

Pullan, Brian. *Rich and Poor in Renaissance Venice: The Social Institutions of a Catholic State.* Oxford: Blackwell, 1971.

———. "Catholics and the Poor in Early Modern Europe." *Transactions of the Royal Historical Society* 26 (1976): 15–34.

———. "Support and Redeem: Charity and Poor Relief in Italian cities from the Fourteenth to the Seventeenth Century." *Continuity and Change* 3 (1988): 177–208.

Putnam, Robert. *Making Democracy Work: Civic Traditions in Modern Italy.* Princeton: Princeton University Press, 1993.

Raeff, Marc. *The Well-Ordered Police State: Social and Institutional Change through Law in the Germanies and Russia, 1600–1800.* New Haven: Yale University Press, 1983.

Ranke, Leopold von. *Deutsche Geschichte im Zeitalter der Reformation.* Berlin: Duncker & Humblot, 1852.

Ratzinger, Georg. *Geschichte der kirchlichen Armenpflege.* Freiburg im Br.: Herder, 1884.

Rauscher, Julius. *Württembergische Reformationsgeschichte.* Stuttgart: Calwer Vereinsbuchhandlung, 1934.

Reden, Friedrich von. *Allgemeine vergleichende Finanz-Statistik.* Darstadt: Verlag der Hofbuchhandlung von G. Jonghaus, 1856.

Reinhard, Wolfgang. "Gelenkter Kulturwandel im siebzehnten Jahrhundert: Akkulturation in den Jesuitenmissionen als universalhistorisches Problem." *Historische Zeitschrift* 223 (1976): 529–90.

———. "Gegenreformation als Modernisierung? Prologomena zu einer Theorie des Konfessionellen Zeitalters." *Archiv fur Reformationsgeschichte* 68 (1977): 226–52.

———. "Humanismus und Militarismus. Antike-Rezeption und Kriegshandwerk in der oranischen Heeresreform." Pp. 185–204 in *Krieg und Frieden im Horizont des Renaissancehumanismus*, edited by Franz Josef Worstbrock. Weinheim: Acta humaniora, 1986.

———. "Konfession und Konfessionalisierung: 'Die Zeit der Konfessionnen (1530–1620/30)' in einer neuen Gesamtdarstellung." *Historisches Jahrbuch* 114 (1994): 107–24.

Reitsma, R. *Centrifugal and Centripetal Forces in the Early Dutch Republic: The States of Overijssel, 1566–1600*. Amsterdam: Rodopi, 1982.

Richter, Aemilius Ludwig, ed. *Die evangelischen Kirchenordnungen des sechszehnten Jahrhunderts*. Nieuwkoop: B. De Graaf, 1967.

Ridley, Jasper Godwin. *Nicholas Ridley, a Biography*. London and New York: Longmans, Green, 1957.

Riedel, Adolph F. *Der brandenburgisch-preußische Staatshaushalt in den beiden letzten Jahrhunderten*. Berlin: Ernst & Korn, 1866.

Riedesel, Erich. *Pietismus und Orthodoxie in Ostpreußen*. Königsberg: Ost-Europa Verlag, 1937.

Riley, James C. *The Seven Years' War and the Old Regime in France: The Economic and Financial Toll*. Princeton: Princeton University Press, 1986.

Roberts, Michael. *Gustavus Adolphus: A History of Sweden, 1611–1632*. London: Longmans, Green and Co., 1953.

———. *The Early Vasas: A History of Sweden, 1523–1611*. Cambridge: Cambridge University Press, 1968.

———. *Sweden as a Great Power, 1611–1697*. London: Edward Arnold, 1968.

———. "The Swedish Church." Pp. 132–73 in *Sweden's Age of Greatness*, edited by Michael Roberts. London: Macmillan, 1973.

———. *The Military Revolution, 1560–1660: An Inaugural Lecture Delivered before the Queen's University of Belfast*. Belfast: M. Boyd, 1988 [1956].

———, ed. *Sweden's Age of Greatness, 1532–1718*. London: Macmillan, 1973.

Roodenburg, Hermann. *Onder censuur: De kerkelijke tucht in de gereformeerde gemeente van Amsterdam, 1578–1700*. Hilversum: Verloren, 1990.

Roorda, D. J. *Partij en factie. De oproeren van 1672 in de steden van Holland en Zeeland, een krachtmeting tussen partijen en facties*. Groningen: J. B. Wolters, 1961.

———. *Het rampjaar 1672*. Bussum: Fibula–Van Dishoeck, 1972.

Roos, Hans. "Ständewesen und parlamentarische Verfassung in Polen." Pp. 310–67 in *Ständische Vertretungen in Europa im 17. und 18. Jahrhundert*, edited by Dietrich Gerhard. Göttingen: Vandenhoeck & Ruprecht, 1969.

Roper, Lyndal. *The Holy Household: Women and Morals in Reformation Augsburg*. Oxford: Clarendon, 1989.

Rosenberg, Hans. *Bureaucracy, Aristocracy, and Autocracy: The Prussian Experience 1660–1815*. Cambridge: Harvard University Press, 1958.

Rumbelow, Donald. *I Spy Blue: The Police and Crime in the City of London from Elizabeth I to Victoria*. London and New York: Macmillan and St. Martin's, 1971.

Russo, Saverio. "Potere pubblico e carità privata. L'assistenza ai poveri a Lucca tra XVI e XVII secolo." *Società e storia* 23 (1984): 45–80.

Rystad, Göran. "The King, the Nobility, and the Growth of the Bureaucracy in Seventeenth-Century Sweden." Pp. 59–70 in *Europe and Scandinavia: Aspects of the Process of Integra-*

tion in the Seventeenth Century, edited by Göran Rystad. Lund: Wallin & Dalholm Boktr, 1983.

Sabean, David Warren. *Power in the Blood: Popular Culture and Village Discourse in Early Modern Germany*. Cambridge and New York: Cambridge University Press, 1984.

Saint Cyr, Robert, and Duplessis Saint Cyr. "Charité publique et autorité municipale au XVI siècle: L'Exemple de Lille." *Revue du nord* 59 (1977): 193–219.

Salmon, J. H. M. *Society in Crisis. France in the Sixteenth Century*. London: Methuen, 1975.

Sauer, Paul. *Geschichte der Stadt Stuttgart*. Stuttgart: Kohlhammer, 1993.

Schama, Simon. *The Embarrassment of Riches*. Berkeley: University of California Press, 1988.

Schelven, A. A. van. *De nederduitsche vluchtelingskerken der XVI eeuw in Engeland en Duitschland*. The Hague: Martinus Nijhoff, 1909.

Schilling, Heinz. *Konfessionskonflikt und Staatsbildung*. Gütersloh: Gütersloher Verlagsanstalt, 1981.

———. "Die Konfessionalisierung im Reich: Religiöser und gesellschaftlicher Wandel in Deutschland zwischen 1555 und 1620." *Historische Zeitschrift* 246 (1988): 1–45.

———. *Aufbruch und Krise: Deutschland, 1517–1648*. Berlin: Siedler, 1988.

———. "Luther, Loyola, Calvin und die europäische Neuzeit." In *Inaugural Lecture*. Humboldt University, 1991.

———. *Civic Calvinism in Northwestern Germany and the Netherlands: Sixteenth to Nineteenth Centuries*. Kirksville: Sixteenth Century Journal Publishers, 1991.

———. "Die Kirchenzucht im frühneuzeitlichen Europa in interkonfessionell vergleichender und interdisziplinärer Perspektive—eine Zwischenbilanz." Pp. 11–40 in *Kirchenzucht und Sozialdisziplinierung im frühneuzeitlichen Europa*, edited by Heinz Schilling. Berlin: Duncker & Humblot, 1994.

Schimmelpfennig, Bernhard. "Der Ämterhandel an der Römischen Kurie von Pius II bis zum Sacco di Roma (1458–1527)." Pp. 3–40 in *Ämterhandel im Spätmittelalter und im 16. Jahrhundert*, edited by Ilja Mieck. Berlin: Colloquium Verlag, 1984.

Schmelze, Hans. *Der Staatshaushalt des Herzogtums Bayern im 18. Jahrhundert*. Stuttgart: J. G. Cotta'sche Buchhandlung Nachfolger, 1900.

Schmidt, Eberhard. *Zuchthäuser und Gefängnisse*. Göttingen: Vandenhoek & Ruprecht, 1960.

Schmidt, Heinrich Richard. "Über das Verhältnis von ländlicher Gemeinde und christlicher Ethik: Graubünden und die Innerschweiz." *Historische Zeitschrift* Beiheft 19 (1991): 455–87.

———. *Dorf und Religion: Reformierte Sittenzucht in berner Landgemeinden der frühen Neuzeit*. Stuttgart and New York: G. Fischer, 1995.

———. "Sozialdisziplinierung? Ein Plädoyer für das Ende des Etatismus in der Konfessionalisierungsforschung." *Historische Zeitschrift* 265 (1997): 639–82.

Schneider, Franz. *Geschichte der formellen Staatswirtschaft von Brandenburg-Preußen*. Berlin: Duncker & Humblot, 1952.

Schnith, Karl. "Zum Problem des Ämterkaufs in England vom 12. bis zum 14. Jahrhundert." Pp. 196–203 in *Ämterhandel im Spätmittelalter und im 16. Jahrhundert*, edited by Ilja Mieck. Berlin: Colloquium Verlag, 1984.

Schoenfeldt, Michael. *Bodies and Selves in Early Modern England: Physiology and Inwardness in Spenser, Shakespeare, Herbert, and Milton*. Cambridge: Cambridge University Press, 2000.

Schöffer, Iwo. *De Lage Landen, 1500–1780*. Amsterdam: Elsevier, 1983.

Scholten, Robert. *Zur Geschichte der Stadt Cleve.* Cleve: Fr. Boss, 1905.
Schorn-Schütte, Luise. *Evangelische Geistlichkeit in der Frühneuzeit: Deren Anteil an der Entfaltung frühmoderner Staatlichkeit und Gesellschaft.* Gütersloh: Gütersloher Verlagshaus, 1995.
Schrenk-Notzing, Niklas. "Das bayerische Beamtentum, 1430-1740." Pp. 27-49 in *Beamtentum und Pfarrerstand, 1400-1800*, edited by Günther Franz. Limburg an der Lahn: C. A. Starke Verlag, 1972.
Schrötter, Robert Frhr. von. "Die Ergänzung des preußischen Heeres unter dem ersten Könige." *Forschungen zur brandenburgschen und preußischen Geschichte* 23 (1910): 403-67.
Schulten, C. M., and J. W. M. Schulten. *Het leger in de zeventiende eeuw.* Bussum: Fibula van Dishoeck, 1969.
Schwarz, Brigide. *Die Organisation kurialer Schreiberkollegien von ihrer Entstehung bis zur Mitte des 15. Jahrhunderts.* Tübingen, M. Niemeyer, 1972.
——. "Die Entstehung der Ämterkäuflichkeit an der Römischen Kurie." Pp. 61-67 in *Ämterhandel im Spätmittelalter und im 16. Jahrhundert*, edited by Ilja Mieck. Berlin: Colloquium Verlag, 1984.
Schwebel, Oskar. *Geschichte der Stadt Berlin.* Berlin: Brachvogel & Rankft, 1888.
Sehling, Emil. *Geschichte der protestantischen Kirchenverfassung.* Leipzig: Teubner, 1907.
Sellin, Thorsten. *Pioneering in Penology.* Philadelphia: University of Philadelphia Press, 1944.
Sharpe, J. A. *Crime in Seventeenth-Century England: A County Study.* Cambridge: Cambridge University Press, 1983.
——. "Quantification and the History of Crime in Early Modern England: Problems and Results." *Historical Social Research* 56 (1990): 17-32.
Simplicio, Oscar di. "La criminalità a Siena (1561-1808). Problemi di ricerca." *Quaderni storici* 17 (1982): 242-64.
Skocpol, Theda. "Wallerstein's World Capitalist System: A Theoretical and Historical Critique." *American Journal of Sociology* 82 (1976): 1075-90.
——. *States and Social Revolutions.* Cambridge: Cambridge University Press, 1979.
Slack, Paul. "Poverty and Politics in Salisbury 1597-1666." Pp. 164-203 in *Crisis and Order in English towns, 1500-1700*, edited by Peter Clark and Paul Slack. London: Routledge & Kegan Paul, 1972.
——. *Poverty and Policy in Tudor and Stuart England.* New York: Longman, 1988.
——. *The English Poor Law, 1531-1782.* Cambridge: Cambridge University Press, 1995.
Smit, J. G. "De ambtenaren van de centrale overheidsorganen der Republiek in het begin van de zeventiende eeuw." *Tijdschrift voor Geschiedenis* 90 (1977): 382-83.
Sójka-Zielinska, Katarzyna. "Le Rôle des juristes dans le mouvement de la codification du droit en Pologne à l'époque de la Renaissance." Pp. 191-203 in *Die Rolle der Juristen bei der Entstehung des modernen Staates*, edited by Roman Schnur. Berlin: Duncker & Humblot, 1986.
Spaans, Joke. *Haarlem na de Reformatie.* The Hague: De Bataatsche Leeuw, 1989.
——. *Armenzorg in Friesland 1500-1800.* Hilversum: Verloren, 1997.
Spanninga, Hotso. *De blauwe wezen van Leeuwarden: Geschiednis van het Nieuwe Stadsweeshuis.* Leeuwarden: Stichting het Nieuwe stads Weeshuis, 1988.
Spierenburg, Pieter. "Voorlopers van de Bijlmerbajes. Amsterdam als bakermat van de gevangenisstraf." *Ons Amsterdam* 34 (1982): 260-63.
——. "Long-Term Trends in Homicide: Theoretical Reflections and Dutch Evidence, Fif-

teenth to Twentieth Centuries." Pp. 63-105 in *The Civilization of Crime*, edited by Eric A. Johnson and Eric H. Monkkonen. Urbana: University of Illinois Press, 1996.

———, ed. *The Emergence of Carceral Institutions: Prisons, Galleys, and Lunatic Asylums, 1550-1900*. Rotterdam: Erasmus Universiteit, 1984.

Spiertz, Mathieu G. "Die Ausübung der Zucht in der Ijsselstadt Deventer in den Jahren 1592-1619 im Vergleich zu den Untersuchungen im Languedoc und in der Kurpfalz." *Rheinische Vierteljahresblätter* 49 (1985): 139-72.

Spijker, W. van't. *De verzegeling met de Heilige Geest: Over verzegeling en zekerheid van het geloof.* Kampen: De Groot Goudriaan, 1991.

Spitz, Lewis. *The Protestant Reformation, 1517-1559*. New York: Harper & Row, 1985.

———. "The Importance of the Reformation for Universities: Culture and Confession in the Critical Years." Pp. 42-67 in *Rebirth, Reform, and Resilience: Universities in Transition 1300-1700*, edited by James E. Kittelson and Pamela Transue. Columbus: Ohio State University Press, 1984.

Stead, Philip John. *The Police of France*. New York: Macmillan, 1983.

Steckfuß, Adolf. *500 Jahre Berlin*. Berlin: B. Bigl, 1880.

Steinmetz, George. "The Local Welfare State: Two Strategies for Social Domination in Urban Imperial Germany, 1871-1914." *American Sociological Review* 55 (1990): 891-911.

———. *Regulating the Social: The Welfare State and Local Politics in Imperial Germany*. Princeton: Princeton University Press, 1993.

Stievermann, Dieter. "Die gelehrten Juristen der Herrschaft Württemberg im 15. Jahrhundert." Pp. 229-72 in *Die Rolle der Juristen bei der Entstehung des modernen Staates*, edited by Roman Schnur. Berlin: Duncker & Humblot, 1986.

Stiller, Felix. "Das berliner Armenwesen vor dem Jahre 1820." *Forschungen zur brandenburgischen und preußischen Geschichte* 21 (1908): 175-97.

Stone, Lawrence. "The Educational Revolution in England, 1560-1640." *Past and Present* 28 (1964): 41-81.

Storey, Robin L. "England: Ämterhandel im 15. und 16. Jahrhundert." Pp. 196-203 in *Ämterhandel im Spätmittelalter und im 16. Jahrhundert*, edited by Ilja Mieck. Berlin: Colloquium Verlag, 1984.

Strauss, Gerald. *Manifestations of Discontent in Germany on the Eve of the Reformation*. Bloomington: Indiana University Press, 1971.

———. "Success and Failure in the German Reformation." *Past and Present* 67 (1975): 30-63.

———. *Luther's House of Learning*. Baltimore: The Johns Hopkins University Press, 1978.

Strien, Kees van. *Touring the Low Countries: Accounts of British travellers, 1660-1720*. Amsterdam: Amsterdam University Press, 1998.

Strien-Chardonneau, Madeleine van. *Le Voyage de Hollande: Récits de voyageurs français dans les Provinces-Unies, 1748-1795*. Oxford: Voltaire Foundation at the Taylor Institution, 1994.

Sur, Bernard. *Histoire des avocats en France des origines à nos jours*. Paris: Dalloz, 1998.

Swanson, Guy E. *Religion and Regime: A Sociological Account of the Reformation*. Ann Arbor: University of Michigan Press, 1967.

Swart, K. W. *The Sale of Offices in the Seventeenth Century*. The Hague: M. Nijhoff, 1949.

Takayama, Hiroshi. *The Administration of the Norman Kingdom of Sicily*. Leiden: E. J. Brill, 1993.

Te Brake, Wayne. *Shaping History: Ordinary People in European Politics, 1500-1700*. Berkeley and Los Angeles: University of California Press, 1998.

Ten Raa, F. J. G., and F. de Bas. *Het Staatsche leger, 1568–1795*. Breda: De Koninklijke Militaire Academie, 1911.

Tentler, Thomas N. *Sin and Confession on the Eve of the Reformation*. Princeton: Princeton University Press, 1977.

Terpstra, Nicholas. *Lay Confraternities and Civic Religion in Renaissance Bologna*. Cambridge: Cambridge University Press, 1995.

Terveen, Fritz. *Gesamtstaat und Retablissement: Der Wiederaufbau des nordlichen Ostpreußen unter Friedrich Wilhelm I*. Göttingen: Musterschmidt, 1954.

Tex, Jan den. *Oldenbarnevelt*. Cambridge: Cambridge University Press, 1973.

Thurkow, C. T. F. *De Westfriese admiraliteit*. Enkhuizen: Fas Frisiae, 1946.

Tierney, Brian. *Medieval Poor Law: A Sketch of Canonical Theory and Its Application in England*. Berkeley: University of California Press, 1959.

Tilly, Charles, ed. *The Formation of National-States in Western Europe*. Princeton: Princeton University Press, 1974.

———. *The Contentious French*. Cambridge: Belknap, 1986.

———. *Coercion, Capital, and European States 1000–1990 A.D.* Oxford: Blackwell, 1990.

———. *European Revolutions, 1492–1992*. Oxford: Blackwell, 1993.

Timore e carità. Cremona: Biblioteca statale e librerera civica, 1982.

Tocqueville, Alexis de. *De la démocratie en Amérique*. Paris: Gallimard, 1961.

Tolley, Bruce. *Pastors and Parishioners in Württemberg during the Late Reformation, 1581–1621*. Stanford: Stanford University Press, 1995.

Tomás y Valiente, Francisco. "Les Ventes des offices publics en Castille aux XVIIe et XVIIIe siècles." Pp. 89–113 in *Ämterkäuflichkeit: Aspekte sozialer Mobilität im europäischen Vergleich*, edited by Klaus Malettke. Berlin: Colloquium Verlag, 1980.

Torpey, John. *The Invention of the Passport: Surveillance, Citizenship, and the State*. Cambridge: Cambridge University Press, 1999.

Tracy, James D. *A Financial Revolution in the Habsburg Netherlands: Renten and Renteniers in the County of Holland, 1515–1565*. Berkeley: University of California Press, 1985.

———. *Holland under Habsburg Rule, 1506–1566: The Formation of a Body Politic*. Berkeley: University of California Press, 1990.

Tukker, C. A. *De classis Dordrecht van 1573 tot 1609. Bijdrage tot de kennis van in en extern leven van de gereformeerde kerk in de periode van haar organisering*. Leiden: Universitaire Pers, 1965.

Uderstädt, Eduard Rudolf. *Die ostpreußische Kammerverwaltung, ihre Unterbehörden und Lokalorgane unter Friedrich Wilhelm I. und Friedrich II. bis zur Russenokkupation (1713–1756)*. Königsberg in Pr: Buch- und Steindruckerei von Otto Kümmel, 1911.

Uhlhorn, G. *Die christliche Liebesthätigkeit seit der Reformation*. Stuttgart: Gundert, 1890.

Ullmann, Walter. *Principles of Government and Politics in the Middle Ages*. London: Methuen, 1966.

Upton, A. F. *Charles XI and Swedish Absolutism*. Cambridge: Cambridge University Press, 1998.

Van Gelder, H. A. Enno. *Revolutionnaire reformatie*. Amsterdam: P. N. van Kampen & Zoon, 1943.

Van Kley, Dale K. *The Religious Origins of the French Revolution: From Calvin to the Civil Constitution, 1560–1791*. New Haven: Yale University Press, 1996.

Van Strien, Charlotte. *Touring the Low Countries: Accounts of British Travellers, 1660–1720*. Amsterdam: Amsterdam University Press, 1998.

Venard, Marc. "Les Formes de la piété des confrèries dévotes de Rouen à l'époque moderne." *Histoire, Économie et Société* 10, 3 (1991): 283–97.
Verheyden, A. L. E. *Le Conseil des troubles*. Flavion-Florennes: Editions le Phare, 1981.
Viollet, Paul. *Droit public. Histoire des institutions politiques et administratives de la France*. Paris: L. Larose et Forcel, 1890–1903.
Vogler, Bernard. *Le Clergé protestant rhénan au siècle de la Réforme, 1555–1619*. Paris: Ophrys, 1976.
———. "Rekrutierung, Ausbildung und soziale Verflechtung. Karrieremuster evangelischer Geistlichkeit." *Archiv für Reformationsgeschichte* 85 (1994): 225–33.
Vogler, Günter. "Absolutistisches Regiment und ständische Verfassung in Brandenburg-Preußen im 17. und 18. Jahrhundert." Pp. 209–32 in *Die Bildung des frühmodernen Staates—Stände und Konfession*, edited by Heiner Timmerman. Saarbrücken: Dader, 1989.
Von Thadden, Rudolf. *Die brandenburgisch-preussischen Hofprediger im 17. und 18. Jahrhundert; ein Beitrag zur Geschichte der absolutistischen Staatsgesellschaft in Brandenburg-Preussen*. Berlin: De Gruyter, 1959.
Vries, Jan de. *European Urbanization, 1500–1800*. Cambridge: Harvard University Press, 1984.
Vries, Jan de, and Ad van der Woude. *The First Modern Economy: Success, Failure, and Perserverance of the Dutch Economy, 1500–1815*. Cambridge: Cambridge University Press, 1997.
Vries, O. "Geschappen tot een ieders nut. Een verkennend onderzoek naar de Noordnederlandse ambtenaar in de tijd van het Ancien Regime." *Tijdschrift voor geschiedenis* 90 (1977): 328–49.
Waard, C. De. *De Archieven, berustende in het bestuur der godshuizen te Middelburg*. Middelburg: J.C. & W. Altorffer, 1907.
Wagenaar, Jan. *Amsterdam in zyne opkomst, aanwas, geschiedenissen, voorregten, koophandel, gebouwen, kerkenstaat, schoolen, schutterye, gilden en regeeringe*. Amsterdam: Isaak Tirion, 1760–88.
Wallerstein, Immanuel. *The Modern World System*. New York: Academic Press, 1976–87.
Wallmann, Johannes. *Philipp Jakob Spener und die Anfänge des Pietismus*. Tübingen: J. C. B. Mohr, 1970.
Walzer, Michael. *The Revolution of the Saints*. New York: Athenaeum, 1970.
Wandel, Lee Palmer. *Always among Us: Images of the Poor in Zwingli's Zurich*. Cambridge: Cambridge University Press, 1990.
Webb, John. *Poor Relief in Elizabethan Ipswich*. Ipswich: Cowell Limited, 1966.
Weber, Max. *Die Protestantische Ethik I*. Gütersloh: Gerd Mohn, 1984 [1920].
———. *Wirtschaft und Gesellschaft*. Tübingen: Mohr, 1985 [1922].
———. "Die protestantische Ethik und der Geist des Kapitalismus." In *Gesammelte Aufsätze zur Religionssoziologie*. Tübingen: J. C. B. Mohr, 1988 [1920].
Wegert, Karl H. *Popular Culture, Crime, and Social Control in Eighteenth-Century Württemberg*. Stuttgart: F. Steiner, 1994.
Weissman, Ronald. *Ritual Brotherhood in Renaissance Florence*. New York: Academic Press, 1982.
Wendland, Walter. "Studien zum kirchlichen Leben in Berlin um 1700." *Jahrbuch für brandenburgische Kirchengeschichte* 21 (1926): 129–97.
———. "Märkischer Pietismus." In *Festgabe zum deutschen Pfarrertag, Berlin 1927*. Eberswalde: Volkskirchlicher und pädagogischer Verlag, 1927.

Wetzel, Erich. *Die Geschichte des Königlichen Joachimthalschen Gymnasiums, 1607–1907.* Halle: Buchhandlung des Waisenhauses, 1907.

Wijn, J. M. *Het Krijgswezen in de tijd van Prins Maurits.* Utrecht: n.p., 1934.

Williams, Alan. *The Police of Paris, 1718–1789.* Baton Rouge and London: Louisiana State University Press, 1979.

Wilson, Peter H. *War, State, and Society in Württemberg, 1677–1793.* Cambridge: Cambridge University Press, 1995.

Wimpheling, Jakob, and Beatus Rhenanus. *Das Leben des Johannes Geiler von Kaysersberg.* Munich: Fink, 1970.

Winckelmann, Johannes. *Gesellschaft und Staat in der verstehenden Soziologie Max Webers.* Berlin: Duncker & Humblot, 1957.

Winckelmann, Otto. "Über die ältesten Armenordnungen der Reformationszeit (1522–1525)." *Historische Vierteljahrschrift* 17 (1914–15): 187–228 and 361–400.

———. *Das Fürsorgewesen der Stadt Strassburg vor und nach der Reformation bis zum Ausgang des sechzehnten Jahrhunderts, Quellen und Forschungen zur Reformationsgeschichte.* Leipzig: M. Heinsius Nachfolger, 1922.

Wordsworth, John. *The National Church of Sweden.* London: A. R. Mowbray, 1911.

Wotschke, Theodor. "Zur Geschichte des westfälischen Pietismus." *Jahrbuch des Vereins für westfälische Kirchengeschichte* 32 (1931): 56–100.

———. "Zur Geschichte des westfälischen Pietismus." *Jahrbuch des Vereins für westfälische Kirchengeschichte* 34 (1933): 39–103.

Wouters, A. and Abels Ph. F. *Nieuw en ongezien: Kerk en samenleving in de classis Delft en Delfland 1572–1621.* Delft: Eburen, 1994.

Wrightson, Keith, and David Levine. *Poverty and Piety in an English Village: Terling, 1525–1700.* New York: Academic Press, 1979.

Zannini, Andrea. *Burocrazia e burocrati a Venezia in età moderna: I cittadini originari (sec. XVI–XVIII).* Venezia: Istituto veneto di scienze, lettere ed arti, 1993.

Zardin, Danilo. *Confraternite e vita di pietà nelle campagne Lombarde tra 500 e 600: La pieve di Parabiago-Legnano.* Milan: NED, 1981.

———. *San Carlo Borromeo ed il rinnovamento della vita religiosa dei laici: Due contributi per la storia delle confraternite nella diocesi di Milano.* Legnano: Società arte storia Legnano, 1982.

———. "Le confraternite in Italia settentrionale fra XV e XVIII secolo." *Società e storia* 35 (1987): 81–137.

Zeeden, Ernst Walter. "Gegenreformation als Modernisierung." *Archiv für Reformationsgeschichte* 68 (1977): 226–52.

———. "Zwang zur Konfessionalisierung? Prologomena zu einer Theorie des konfessionellen Zeitalters." *Zeitschrift für historische Forschung* 10 (1983): 257–77.

———. *Konfessionsbildung: Studien zur Reformation, Gegenreformation und Katholischen Reform.* Stuttgart: KlettCotta, 1985.

Zeisler, Kurt. *Die "langen kerls": Geschichte des Leib- und Garderegiments Friedrich Wilhelms I.* Frankfurt am Main: Ullstein, 1993.

Zwitzer, H. L. "Het quotenstelsel onder de Republiek der Verenigde Nederlanden alsmede enkele beschouwingen over de generale petitie, de staat van oorlog en de repartitie." *Mededelingen van de Sectie Militaire Geschiedenis—Landmachtstaf* 5 (1982): 5–47.

———. *"De militie van den staat": Het leger van de Republiek der Verenigde Nederlanden.* Amsterdam: Van Soeren, 1991.

INDEX

absolutism: bureaucratic, 7, 8, 9, 174n. 19; Marxist interpretation of, 173n. 8; military-bureaucratic, 6, 11–12; monarchical, 79, 85, 159; origins of, 3–4, 31; patrimonial, 7, 8, 174n. 19; Prussian genesis of, 79, 159; and social discipline, 29, 31; struggle against, and religious reform, 13
ad hoc commissions, 8
administrative efficiency: defined, 103; in Dutch Republic, 67–71; in Prussia, 99, 103–5
administrative power, 35
administrative rationalization, 138, 151, 179n. 100
Aerschot, Duke of, 43
Aglionby, William, 39, 51
Almoners, 129
alms, 19
almshouses, 60
Almsmen's Orphanage, Amsterdam, 65
Alva, Duke of, 42
Amsterdam: crime rate, 51; ecclesiastical discipline, 123; homicide rate, 52; poor-relief, 60, 134; social reform process, 62–66
Amsterdam *Tuchthuis*, 63–64, 66, 67, 75, 130, 132

Anderson, Perry, *Lineages of the Absolutist State*, 3–4, 5, 10, 174n. 11
Anglican church, 150
annates, 148
Antiblasphemy Commission, Venice, 122
anticlericalism, 16
anticonfessionalism, 117, 135–36
Aragon, 121, 145
Archdiaconal Court, Munster, 123
asceticism: of Frederick William I, 94; inner-worldly, 26, 27, 155; revolutionary, 162
ascetic Protestantism, 26–28, 168, 178n. 81
ascetic-reform movements, 150
Aschersleben, George Wilhelm von, 100
Augsburg Confession, 14, 87
Aumône générale, Lyon, 131
auricular confession, 108
Austria, 82, 153, 154

bailiwicks, 45
Baltic provinces, 79
ban, 120
bankruptcy, 70
baptisms, 19
Baptist sects, discipline in, 58
Barebones Parliament, 152
Battle of Nieuwpoort, 73

Bavaria, 80, 141, 153, 154, 159
Becquer, Bernhard Friedrich, 101
begging: legislation on, 62, 66, 135; Luther's views on, 125; by mendicant clergy, 126; prohibition of, 127, 128
Beichtpfennig, 108
Belgium, 41
Bellah, Robert, 164
bellicism: critique of world systems theory, 174n. 12; model of Prussian state-formation, 11, 80, 83–84; models of state formation, 5–10, 28, 39, 40, 154, 165, 174n. 25, 175n. 30
Bendix, Reinhard, 164
benefices, 138, 148, 149
Bentham, Jeremy, 23, 67
Berg, 90
Bergius, Johannes, 86
Berlin, 96
bicameral legislatures, 7–8, 9
biconfessional congregations *(Simultankirchen),* 88
blasphemy, 123
Bodenstein, Andreas (a.k.a. Karlstadt), 126
body politic, 1
Bohemian estates, revolt of, 17, 159
Bologna, 133
Boniface IX, 144
bookkeeping, 69
Borussican school, 178n. 82
Brandenburg, 79; Calvinist Reformation, 86–92; Lutheran Reformation, 85–86
Brandenburg-Prussia. *See* Prussia
Braunschweig-Wolfenbüttel, 139
Brederode, Duke of, 42
Brewer, John, *The Sinews of Power,* 174n. 24
bribe, 144
Bridewell Hospital, 130–31
Brill, 42
Bringing the State Back In (Evans, Rueschemeyer, and Skocpol), 158
Britain. *See* England
brotherly love, imperative of, 127
Bruges, 43
Bucer, Martin, 17
bureaucratic absolutism, 7, 8, 9, 174n. 19
bureaucratic constitutionalism, 7, 8, 9, 174n. 19

bureaucratic vs. patrimonial state structure, 7, 138–42
bureaucratization: of clerical office holding, 149–50, 168; defined, 138, 205n. 118; and disciplinary revolution from above, 153–54, 159; and Protestant ethic, 28, 138–42, 150–53, 168; and state strength, 175n. 30
burgomasters, 45, 70

Calenberg, 139
Calvin, John, 17, 116, 170; beliefs about poor-relief, 130; *Ordonnances ecclésiastiques,* 20–21
Calvinism: consistories, 123–24; and constitutionalism, 13; conversion, 124; ecclesiastical discipline, 119, 123–25; impact on Dutch military practices, 72–75; impact on Dutch military uprisings, 41, 44–45, 159; impact on Dutch political institutions, 67–72, 89; impact on strength of Dutch Republic, 75–79; and modern revolutionary parties, 161–62; and political revolution, 27–28, 159–60; rise of in Low Countries, 41–42; role of in disciplinary revolution, xv, xvii, 19–22, 27; theology, 20
Calvinist Reformation, 14, 86–92, 150, 178n. 81
canon law, 148
canton system *(Kantonsverfassung),* 98
capital-intensive state formation, 5
capitalism, 154; laissez-faire, 169; spirit of, 26; world system, 4
capitalized-coercion state formation, 5
captain-general, Dutch Republic, 46
Caroline Absolutism, 152
Carsten, Francis L., 83
case studies, 118
Castille, 121, 133, 145
Cathars, 170
Catholic Church: counterinsurgency, 17, 162; and patrimonialism, 138–42; poor-relief, 115–16, 132–37; Post-Tridentine, 122, 137, 155, 170; Reformation, xvii, 121, 178n. 81
Catholic Leagues, 162
Catholics, Dutch, 59

238 : Index

centralization: and absolutism, 29; administrative, 5, 8, 31, 151, 165, 175n. 30; of poor-relief, 129, 130, 132, 133, 136
Charlemagne, 10
Charles I, 13
Charles II, 152
Charles V, 16, 41
Charles IX, 14
China, 28
Christian activism *(tätiges Christentum)*, 107
Christian Democratic welfare states, 164
Christian polity *(res publica christiana)*, 21
Christoph, Duke, 128
church and state: dedifferentiation, 171; differentiation, 167
church-building, and state power, 18
church councils. *See* consistories
church discipline. *See* ecclesiastical discipline
city council, 45
city-states, 6
civility. *See* social discipline
Claeses, Aaltje, 183n. 89
classis, 56, 57, 124, 183n. 91
class structure, 160
clerical interventions, 170
clerical office holding, bureaucratization of, 149–50
Cleve, 79, 86, 90–91, 99, 111
Cleve-Mark, 86, 90–91, 99
clientelism, 69
Cocceji, Samuel, 205n. 122
Cockburn, J. S., 53
coercion-intensive state formation, 5, 6
coercive discipline, 32–33
coercive state power, 35
colonial state power, 35
commerce, 3–4
common chests, 128
communal discipline, 27, 32, 124–25
comparative politics, xv
comparative state power, 36
composing the offense *(compositie)*, 188n. 179
compulsory state power, 35
conduct lists, 195n. 137
confederal states, 6
confession, sacrament of, 122, 202n. 53

confessional age, 176n. 38
confessionalization paradigm, 2–3, 116; church-building and state-building under, 17–19; and disciplining, 36, 154; as new interpretation of early modern period, 15–17
confessional politics, 171; and division between bureaucratic and patrimonial states, 138–42; in Prussia, 15; in Sweden, 13–14
confraternities, 122, 123, 124
Confucianism, 169, 170
consistories, 18; vs. confessional, 202n. 53; functions of, 21, 22, 58, 59; Lutheran, 119–20; members of, 55–56; powers of, 57; Reformed vs. Catholic, 123–24
constitutionalism: bureaucratic, 7, 8, 9, 174n. 19; and Calvinism, 13; vs. military-bureaucratic structure, 6; patrimonial, 7, 8, 9, 174n. 19
contracts of correspondence, 70
conventicles *(ecclesiola in ecclesia)*, 106
conversion, Calvinist, 124
conversos, 121
corporate-conservative welfare states, 163
corporatism, 169
corrective discipline, 32
Council of State, Dutch Republic, 43, 46, 47
Council of Trent, 14, 17, 134
countermarch, 73, 74
court preachers *(Hofprediger)*, 88
Court Treasury *(Hofkammer)*, 99
Covenanter's revolt, 17
Creutz, Ehrenreich Bogislav von, 102–3
crime rates, 51–52
criminal justice systems, 53
Cromwellian Protectorate, 152
Crusades, 170
cuius regio, eius religio, 16–17
cultural sociology, 164

Danckelmann, Eberhard von, 93
Dark Age empires, 7
Davis, Natalie Zemon, 115, 131
decentralization, of poor-relief, 137
"dedoctrinization" *(Enttheologisierung)* of politics, 29

de facto venality, 143–44, 145
de jure venality, 144, 145, 146
Delft, 60, 123
democracy: rise of, 6; in United States, 28
democratization, 6
demography, 154, 162
Denmark, 8, 9, 12, 120
Depperman, Klaus, 84
Deputized States, Dutch Republic, 46
desertion rate, Prussian army, 98
deserving poor, 61, 66, 115, 131, 135
diaconates, 59, 61, 62–63, 122, 130, 134
Diet *(Landtag)*, 45–46, 47, 83, 87, 141
disciplina, 20
disciplinary revolution, 155, 171; from above, 34, 95–96, 112, 138, 150–54, 159; from below, 34, 159; defined, xvi, 33–34; role of Calvinism in, xv, xvii, 19–22, 27. *See also* social discipline
disciplined church *(église dressée)*, 20–21
discrimination, 129, 132, 133
domain revenues, 82
Domains Directory, Prussia, 99
Don Juan of Austria, 43
Dort, 129
double predestination, 26
Downing, Brian, *The Military Revolution and Political Change*, 5–6, 7, 8, 10, 11–12, 174n. 25
Drave, Hans, 102
Drenthe, 44, 46, 47
drilling, military, 72, 74, 97
drowning cell, 185n. 132, 186n. 134
Dudley, Robert, Earl of Leicester, 43–44
Durkheim, Emile, 164
Dutch Calvinism: impact on Dutch Republic, 41, 44–45, 67–72, 75–79, 89, 159; rise of, 41–42; system of church discipline, 55–58
Dutch Catholics, 59
Dutch Lutherans, 58–59
Dutch Republic, 6; administrative efficiency, 68–71; birth of, 44; bureaucracy, 48, 141; diaconal poor-relief, 168; economic strength, 40; impact of Calvinism on infrastructure of, 75–79; impact of Calvinism on military practices, 72–75; impact of Calvinism on military uprisings, 41, 44–45, 159; impact of Calvinism on political institutions, 67–72, 89; interest rates, 50; local control over religious affairs, 40, 47; local political system, 69–71; nonmilitary expenditures, 68; political efficiency, 67–68; poor-relief reform, 59 67, 129–30, rebellion levels in, 55; stability of, 39–40, 51–55; state-formation, 9–10; strength of, 48–55; strength of local state, 67; structure, 45–48; taxes, 46–50; threat of Spanish reconquest, 72–75; venality in, 146; Year of Disaster, 187n. 165
Dutch Revolt, 13, 17, 28, 39, 40–45, 162; role of Calvinism in, 41, 44–45, 159; as social revolution, 160–61

early modern Europe: core states, 10; intertwining of religion and politics, 3; state formation, xv
East Asian miracle, 169–70
eastern Europe, military threat posed by west European absolutism, 4
East India Company, 65
East Pomerania, 79, 91
East Prussia, 15, 79, 91, 93, 112, 175n. 33
ecclesiastical courts *(Episkopalgerichtsbarkeit)*, 18
ecclesiastical discipline, 32, 36, 117, 158; Calvinist vs. Catholic, 123–25; Catholic, 121–25; Dutch system, 40, 47, 55–58; effect on Dutch society, 58–59; Lutheran, 119–20
ecclesiastical polity *(Kirchenverfassung)*, 27
economic development, and military mobilization, 5
educational institutions, Prussian, 109–10
Ehrle, Franz, 115
Eighty Years' War, 40
Eisenstadt, Shmuel, 164
elect, 21
election, 170
elementary schools, 19
Elias, Norbert, 23, 30–31, 117
Emden, 123
Emminghaus, Arwed, 204n. 102
Engels, Friedrich, 173n. 8
England: administrative development, 152–

240 : Index

53; bureaucratic constitutionalism, 8, 9, 174n. 19; civil service, 174n. 24; civil war, 159; illegitimacy rate, 54, 124; murder rate, 53; navy, 48; parliaments, 12–13; poor-relief reform, 130; public debt, 50; theories of state formation, xvii, 10, 12
English Revolution, 160
Enlightenment, 113, 171
Era of Liberty, 152
Erasmus of Rotterdam, 16, 22, 125, 149
Ertman, Thomas, *Birth of the Leviathan*, 5, 7–10, 12, 15, 138–40, 174n. 19, 175n. 33, 205n. 118, 206n. 130
Esping-Anderson, Gosta, 163
estates-based *(ständisch)*, 141
Estates General, 159
ethical behavior, soteriological significance of, 170
Eucharist, 170
evangelical movement, 15, 16
Evans, Peter, 158
exchange relations, 4
excise taxes, 47, 49
excommunication, 21, 56, 57, 119
exogenous sources, of power, 35
external power, 35

familiares, 121
famine, 116
Farnese, Alexander, Duke of Parma, 43, 72, 73
fascism, 171
feudal class structure, 160
feudalism, 3, 150
feudal office holding, 142–43
Finland, 120
First Nordic War, 88
fiscal-military model, of state formation, 5–10, 11, 174n. 19
fiscal reforms, Prussian, 101–3
Flanders, 44
Florence, 76, 133, 141, 146, 153
Fontane, Theodor, 79
food coupons, 62
Form of Government, 151
Foucault, Michel, xvi, xvii, 3, 22; on discipline, 25, 31–32, 67; *Discipline and Punish,* 23; on governance, 177n. 63; history of sexuality, 25; "Politics and Reason," 24–25; state theory, 23–26
France, 8, 38; bureaucratic features, 141; crime levels, 51; domain revenues, 82; illegitimacy rates, 54, 124; interest rates, 50; lawyer-administrators in royal services, 140; military-bureaucratic absolutism, 11–12, 174n. 19; monarchical absolutism, 159; navy, 48; public debt, 50; state-building, 11–12; ties to papacy, 147; venality, 68–69, 145, 153; Wars of Religion, 13, 17
Franciscans, 122
Francis Hercules, Duke of Anjou, 43
Francis I, 145
Francke, August Hermann, 108–11, 198n. 179
Francke's method, 109–11
Frankfurt am Main, 106, 127
fraternal admonishment, 56
Frederick Henry, 86
Frederick I, 85, 97, 99, 192n. 65; nonmilitary expenditure under, 103–5; poor-law reforms, 107; reign of, 92–93; social discipline, 111–12
Frederick II, 96
Frederick's Hospital, 107, 108
Frederick the Great, 83, 96, 113, 175n. 30
Frederick William I, 85, 93; administrative efficiency under, 99, 104–5; asceticism, 94, 152; austerity program, 95–96; belief in the efficacy of discipline, 94; and conduct lists, 195n. 137; disciplinary revolution from above, 80, 112; fiscal and administrative reforms, 11, 98–103; low opinion of lawyers, 140; military reforms, 11, 96–98; promotion of Pietist movement, 111–12; religiopolitical ethos of, 93–95
Frederick William of Hohenzollern, Prince, 73
Frederick William (the Great Elector): and Cleve-Mark, 90–91; establishment of standing army, 11; "Political Testament" of 1667, 89–90; relations with territorial estates, 80, 83, 85, 86–92; religious policies, 88–90
French Revolution, 160
Friesland, 44, 45, 46, 60

Friuli, 121
fundamentalism, 170
furlough system *(Beurlaubungssystem)*, 98
Further Reformation, 105, 150

garrisons, 74
Gawthrop, Richard, *Pietism and the Making of Eighteenth-Century Prussia*, 175n. 27
Gelderland, 46
General Finance Directory, Prussia, 99, 100
General Hospital, Geneva, 130
Generality Lands, 46
General Superior Finance, War and Domains Directory, Prussia, 99
General Superior Finance War and Domains Commissary, Prussia, 11
General War Commissary, Prussia, 11, 86, 88, 99
Geneva, 38, 120, 130
Genevan consistory, xvii
Genevan mission, 17
Genoa, 133, 135
Gent, 43
geopolitical competition, 8, 12, 84, 138
George William, 86
Geremek, Bronislaw, 116
German Peasants War, 16
German states: bureaucratic absolutism, 8; crime, 51; houses of correction, 131; poor-relief reform, 130; proportion of lawyer-administrators in the royal services, 139–40
Gijswijt-Hofstra, Marijke, 52
Glorious Revolution of 1689, 153
Goldstone, Jack, 160, 162
good works, 115, 136, 137
governance: Foucault on, 24, 177n. 63; new infrastructure of in early modern Europe, xvi; non-state, 166, 169
grace, Luther's views on, 125–26
Graft, 61
Great confinement *(grand renfermement)*, 132–33, 135
Great Schism, 144
Grenoble, 132
Groningen, 46
Grubenhagen, 139
Gustav II Adolf, 151

Gustav IX (Gustav Vasa), 9, 13–14, 151
Gustavus Adolphus, 14
Gustav X, 152
Gustav XI, 152
Gutton, Jean-Pierre, 115

Haarlem, 52
Habsburgs, 13, 41–43, 128
Halberstadt, 79, 86, 91, 92, 99
Halle, 111
Hanover, 82
Hansa, 6
hedge sermons, 42
Hegel, G. W. F., 79
Henry III, 43
Henry IV, 11–12, 13
heresy, 122, 123
Hesse, Adam Friedrich, 102
Hessia, 38, 120, 128, 129
Hessia-Cassel, 120
heterodoxy, 57
hierocratic discipline, 27
Hinrichs, Carl, 84
Hintze, Otto, 84, 92, 147, 174n. 25, 178nn. 79, 82
historical comparison, 118
historical contingency, 12, 13
historical institutionalism, 40
historical sociology, xv, 158, 164
Hobbes, Thomas: *De Cive*, 1; *Leviathan*, xviii, 1–2, 37, 156, 157, 166
Hohenlohe, 120
Hohenzollern, House of, 79, 80, 86, 159; attempt to impose Second Reformation, 15; impact of Calvinism on, 84–85; invasion of Julich and Berg, 90; political rationality, 82–85. *See also* Prussia; *specific Prussian rulers*
Holland, xvii, 42; Calvinism-dominated republican regime, 44; nonmilitary expenditures, 68; Pacification of Gent, 43; political organization, 45; in States General, 46; tax burden, 47
Hôpital général, Paris, 133
hospitals, 59
house of discipline *(Tuchthuis)*, 63–64, 66, 67, 75, 110, 130, 132, 185n. 125
House of Orange, 86

House of Orange-Nassau, 46
houses of correction, 59, 131
houses of the Lord, 59
humanism, 29, 116, 117, 131, 132, 137, 154
human resources, 167
Hundred Years' War, 9
Hungary, 8, 12; estates-based patrimonialism, 141; lack of bureaucratization, 153, 154; parliaments, 13; rebellion, 17
Hussites, 170
Hutten, Ulrich von, 16

idealist theory, of Prussian state-building, 80, 84–85
ideal-typical bureaucracy, 12, 99–100
Ignatius Loyola, 116
illegitimate births, 54, 124
image breaking, 42
Imperial domination, 7
Imperial Electorates *(Kurfürstentümer)*, 81
indigenous sources, of power, 35
individual discipline, 32–33
indoor relief, 59, 60, 61, 66, 115, 135, 184n. 108
indulgences, sale of, 148
industrial revolution, xv–xvi
innerworldly asceticism, 26, 27, 155
Innocent III, 144
Inquisition. *See* Italian Inquisition; Spanish Inquisition
institutional discipline, 32
institutionalization, 29, 40
intendants, 141
interest rates, 50
internal power, 35
intraconfessional uniformity, 36. *See also* ecclesiastical discipline
Italian Inquisition, 121–22, 123
Italy: geopolitical competition, 8; illegitimacy rates, 124; northern city-states, 76; poor-relief, 133; venality, 145–46; workhouses, 135
ius reformandi, 16

Jacobins, 162
Jansenists, 170
Japan, 169
Jesuits, 19, 122, 170

Joachimsthalsches Gymnasium, 112
Julich, 90
Junkers, 83
jurists, trained, 138–39
justification, 20

Kastenordnung, 128, 129
Katsch, Christoph von, 101
Kaysersberg, Geiler von, 125
Kleve. *See* Cleve
Knyphausen, Dodo von, 93
Königsberg, 86, 95, 111
Korea, 169
Krafft, Adam, 128

labor movement, 169
laicization, of poor-relief, 129, 130, 132, 133, 136, 137
laissez-faire capitalism, 169
Landräte, 196n. 146
Landtag. See Diet *(Landtag)*
Landtags-Rezesse, 83
Lasco, Johannes à, 14
Latin Europe, 8
latitudinarians, 155
lawyer-administrators, in bureaucratic and patrimonial states, 139–40
legitimate domination, theory of, 138
Leiden, 51, 52, 129
Lemaitre, Charles, 51
Lesnig church ordinances, 126
liberal welfare states, 163, 164
Lille, 132
Limburg, 44
Lipset, Seymour Martin, 164
Lipsius, Justus, 74, 75
Lis, Catharina, 116
Löben, Friedrich Christian von, 192n. 70
local government: in Dutch Republic, 40, 47–48, 67, 69–71; role in state formation, 6, 7, 12, 166, 169
Locke, John, 51
Lodewijk, Willem, 74
Lombardy, 133
Louis XIII, 11, 13
Louis XIV, 13, 82, 85, 92
Low Countries: division of, 41; rise of Calvinism in, 41–42

Lucca, 135
Lütern, Heinrich von, 128
Luther, Martin, 116, 149; on church discipline, 119; evangelicalism, 16; lack of stress on ethical behavior, 170; Ninety-five Theses, 15; views on poor-relief, 125–27
Lutheran consistories, 119–20
Lutheranism: Dutch, 58–59; ecclesiastical discipline, 119–20; emphasis on pure doctrine, 105; marriage courts, 119, 124; orthodox, 155; and poor-relief reform, 125–29; in Prussia, 84; and reform, 136; in Sweden, 14
Lutheran Pietism, 170
Lyon, 115, 118, 132, 134, 135

Maasluis, 54
Machiavelli, Niccolò, *The Prince*, 24
macrosociology, 164
Magdeburg, 79, 91, 92, 120
magic, 121
magistrates, 45
Mann, Michael, 37, 166
Mann, Thomas, *Joseph und seine Brüder*, 3
Margaret of Parma, 42
Marian sodalities, 122
Mark, 79, 86
marriage ordinances, 19
Marschall, Samuell von, 100
Marxism: and bellicism, 165; and early modern class system, 160; interpretation of absolutism, 173n. 8; models of state formation, 10; stage theories, 5; theory of Prussian state-building, 83
Masters of the Holy Spirit, 129
materialism, 80
Maurice of Nassau, 44
Maurice of Orange, 72, 73, 74, 75
Mazarin, Cardinal Jules, 11
"medieval charity," 133
Melancthonian Formula, 14
mendicant orders, 37, 127, 135
merchant trading companies, 168
Micron, Martin, 14
Milan, 146, 147, 153
military, of Dutch Republic, 47–49
military-bureaucratic absolutism, 6, 11–12

military-bureaucratic vs. constitutionalist state structure, 6
military competition, as the driving force behind state-formation, 5, 6
military power, 35
military practices, 72–75
Milton, John, 31
Minden, 86
monasticism, 170
monopolies, 31
Moore, Barrington, 160
Moore, Benjamin, 6
municipal court *(schepenenbank)*, 69
Munster, 123
murder rates, 52, 53
mutinies, 73

Nantes, 54
Naples, 121, 133, 146, 147, 153
national debt, of Dutch state, 50
nationalism, and confessionalization, 163
national-states, 5
neoconfessionalism, 117
neo-Machiavellianism, 117
neo-Malthusianism, 117
neo-Marxism, 3–10, 117
Neostoicism, 29, 74, 76, 119, 137
nepotism, 69, 100
Netherlands, xvii, 6, 10, 12, 38, 41, 124, 160. *See also* Dutch Republic
Neubauer, Georg Heinrich, 108, 110
Nieuwpoort, Battle of, 73
Ninety-five Theses, 15
nonabsolutist state, 7
nonresidence, 148
non–state governance, 166, 169
normative discipline, 32–33
Northern Netherlands, 6, 42
Nuremberg, 115, 126–27

observation, technology of, xvi
Oestreich, Gerhard, 23; "Structural Problem of European Absolutism, 29–30, 31, 32, 74, 116–17
office holding, 168; clerical, 149–50; conception of, 138; new models of, 8; types of, 142–43. *See also* venality
oligarchy, 143, 150, 152, 206n. 130

On Constancy (Lipsius), 74
On the Roman Army (Lipsius), 74
Order for a Common Chest *(Kastenordnung)*, 126
Order for a Common Purse *(Beutelordnung)*, 126
organizational entwining, 167–68, 169
organized capitalism, 169
orphanages, 59, 61, 64–66, 67
Österberg, Eva, 53
Ottes, Lysbert, 183n. 90
outdoor relief, 59, 60, 62, 66
Overijssel, 44, 46
overseers, 56
Oxenstierna, Axel, 151

Pacification of Gent, 43
Pädagogium, 109, 111
Palatinate, 79, 82
panopticon, 23, 67
papacy, role of in development of venality, 144–48
Papal Schism, 153
Paris: illegitimacy rate, 54; murder rate, 53; poor-relief, 132
parish poor rates, 130
parliaments, effects of, 7, 9–10, 12–13
Parma, 75
patrimonial absolutism, 7, 8, 174n. 19
patrimonial constitutionalism, 7, 8, 9, 174n. 19
patrimonialism, 150; vs. bureaucratic state structure, 12, 138–42; estates-based, 141; and oligarchy, 152, 206n. 130; under the Restoration, 152; and venality, 142–44, 153
patronage, 152
payment, 153
Peace of Augsburg, 14, 15
peak bargaining, 169
pedagogy, 109
pensionaries, 46
Pérez de Herrera, Cristobal, 133
Perpetual Edict, 43
Peter the Great, 175n. 30
Petri, Olavus, 13
Pfalz-Neuburg, Duke of, 90
Philip II, 10, 41, 42, 44

Philip of Hessia, 128
Pia Desideria (Spener), 106, 107
Pibonis, Joannes, 183n. 91
Pietism: and Prussia, 28, 84, 85, 178n. 79, 198n. 200; reformed, 170; and social reform, 105–12, 134, 150
pillarized social provision, 60
Plotho, Ludwig Otto Edler von, 102
pluralism, 148
Poland, 6, 8, 12, 174n. 19; bureaucratization, 153, 154; estates-based patrimonialism, 141; gentry movement, 17; parliaments, 13; patrimonial constitutionalism, 9; "Republic of Nobles," 6
police legislation, 29
police state *(Polizei- und Ordnungsstaat)*, 29, 117
political economy, 177n. 63
political efficiency, 67–68
political revolution, 27–28, 159–60
Pomerania, 79, 92
poor-relief, 154; Calvinism and, 27; centralization of, 129, 130, 132, 133, 136; church-based, 158; confessional differences in, 155; continuities between early modern and modern systems, 163–64; decentralization of, 137; differences between Protestant and Catholic systems of, 115–16, 133–37; Dutch system of, 59–67; laicization of, 129, 130, 132, 133, 136, 137; Luther's views on, 125–27; ordinances, 19; pillarized system, 60; rationalization of, 132, 177n. 73, 178n. 81; reform, 107, 125–37; Reformation and, 18–19
poverty, 204n. 96
power. *See* state power
precisionism, 150, 152, 153, 155
predestination, 20, 26, 94
premarital sexual activity: in Calvinist-dominated societies, 124; in Dutch Republic, 54; in England, 54
presbyterian disciplinary system, 120
print, invention of, 171
prison, 23
private sins, 56
private venality, 143, 144, 145; de jure, 152; proto-, 145

Privy Council *(Geheimer Rat)*, 86, 88
progressivism, 169
Protestant ethic, 20; and bureaucratic revolution, 28, 138–42, 150–53, 168; and early modern state, 26–28
Protestantism: ascetic, 26–28, 168, 178n. 81; poor-relief systems, 115–16, 129–31, 133–37
Protestant Reformation, 3, 153; disciplinary revolution unleashed by, xv, xvi; interaction with other historical processes, 17; linkages between religion and politics, 3, 171; message of, 170; social and geographical scope of, 170–71; and social change, 170–72; and social reform, 18–19, 37, 136; and struggle against absolutism, 13; three overlapping segments, 15–16; traditional accounts of, 15, 116
proto-Erastian systems of discipline, 120
proto-venality, 144, 145
provincial diets (provincial states), 45–46, 47
Prussia, 2, 15, 92, 160, 174n. 19; absolutism, 79, 159; administrative efficiency, 99, 103–5; army, 80–81, 96–98; bellicist model of state-formation, 11, 80, 83–84; bureaucraticization, 99–100, 178n. 79, 191n. 36; Calvinist elite, 92; Calvinists in Royal Service, 89, 189n. 16; confessional politics, 15; Diet *(Landtag)*, 87; disciplinary revolution from above, 95–96, 112, 138, 150; disciplinary revolution from below, 105–12; Domains Directory, 99; educational institutions, 109–10; fiscal reforms, 101–3; Franckean institutes in, 168; under Frederick I, 92–93; General Finance Directory, 99, 100; idealist theory of state-building, 80, 84–85; lawyer-administrators in royal services, 140; Lutheran consistories in, 119; Lutheranism, 84; Marxism theory of state-building, 83; meritocratic administration, 100–101; patrimonial elements, 141; peculiar character of, 80–82; Pietism, 28, 84, 85, 178n. 79, 198n. 200; possible explanations for rise of, xvii, 38, 83–85; public finance, 81–82; puritanism, 93–95; ratio of taxes to national income, 189n. 7; royal domains, 82; in seventeenth-century, 79–80; state autonomy, 85–95, 112; taxes, 81–82; territorial expansion under Frederick William, 78; venality, 146
public finance: in Dutch Republic, 50; in Prussia, 81–82
public sins, 56
public venality, 143, 144, 145, 146, 153
Pullan, Brian, 115, 116, 131–32, 133
Puritanism, 105, 134, 150, 162, 164
Puritan revolution, 13, 54

Raeff, Marc, 117
Ranke, Leopold von, 15
Rasp House, 63
rational-choice theory, 208n. 24
rationalization, 26, 113, 165; administrative, 99–105, 138, 151, 179n. 100; of poor-relief, 132, 177n. 73, 178n. 81
Ratzinger, Georg, 115
Ravensburg, 79
real estate taxes, 47
realist consensus, 165, 166, 167, 168
Rebellion of the Imperial Knights, 16
Rebeur, Philippe, 94
recession, 116
Reden, Friedrich von, 104
reduktion, 152
reform. *See* social discipline
reformation from above *(obrigkeitliche Reformation)*, 15–16
Reformatio Sigismundi, 148–49
Reformed Pietism, 170
Reformed Protestantism. *See* Calvinism
regents, 69, 70, 71
regime structure, 7, 12; and confessional conflict, 13, 159–60; vs. state infrastructure, 138
regional visitation committees, 120
Reglement, 97
regulatory power, 35
Reinhard, Wolfgang, 116
relative power, 36
relief agencies, 129
religion. *See* Protestant Reformation; *specific religions*

religious authority, and temporal authority, 2
religious dialogues *(Religionsgespräche)*, 88
religious discipline. *See* ecclesiastical discipline
religious uniformity, 17–18
Renaissance: humanists, 22; Italian campaigns, 153
republicanism, 44, 154
Requesens, Don Louis, 43
resignatio in favorem tertii, 145, 147
res publica christiana (Christian polity), 21
Restoration, 9, 152
retirement homes, 59, 61
revolution, and religion, 160–62
revolutionary ascetic, 162
Rhineland provinces, 79
Rich and Poor in Renaissance Venice (Pullan), 115, 132
Richelieu, Cardinal, 145
Riksdag, 9, 13, 14
ritual actions, 170
Rokkan, Stein, 164
Rome, 133, 135
rosary, 170
Rotterdam, 54
Rouen, 132
royal authority, descending theory of, 173n. 2
Royal Council *(hovrätt)* (Sweden), 151
royal courts, and civilizing process, 30
Rueschemeyer, Dietrich, 158
Russia, 175n. 30

St. Nicolai Church, Berlin, 107
Salamanca, 134
salvation by faith, 136
Savoy, 146, 147
Saxony, 38, 80; church discipline, 119, 120; domain revenues and nonmilitary expenditures, 82; Lutheran orthodoxy, 150; patrimonialism, 141; poor-relief reform, 129
Sayn-Wittgenstein, Duke August of, 93
Scandinavia, 8
Schilling, Heinz, 15, 18, 19, 116
Schlubhut, Albrecht von, 102
Schmalkaldian League, 16

Schmoller, Gustav, 84, 178nn. 79, 82
Schwarzenburg, Count Adam von, 86
Scotland, 8, 76, 123, 124
scriptural law, 20
Sea Beggars, 42
Second Reformation, 15, 120, 150
second serfdom, 4, 83
self-discipline, 20, 32, 33, 36, 124, 166
seminarium praeceptorum, 109, 111
sexuality, regulation of, 19
sheriff *(schout)*, 45, 70
Sicily, 146, 147, 153
Siena, 135
Sigismund, Johann, 86, 89, 151
simony, 144, 148–50
sin, 56, 202n. 53
sin taxes, 61, 107
Sixtus IV, 144
Skocpol, Theda, 158, 165; *States and Social Revolutions*, 160
social capital, 169, 208n. 25
social contract, 166
social-democratic welfare states, 163, 164
social discipline, 154, 158; from above, 32–33; and absolutism, 13, 29, 30–32; basic models of, 117–19; from below, 32–33, 169; and Calvinism, 19–22; Catholic vs. Reformed, 27; as civilizing process, 30–31, 32, 117; communal, 27, 32, 124–25; confessional differences, 154–55; debate about, 115–19, 154; levels and modes of, 32–33; local control over in Dutch Republic, 47–48; proto-Erastian systems of, 120; and state power, 36
social history, xv
social infrastructure, and state power, 37–38
socialism, 171
social provision. *See* poor-relief
social revolution, 160
social sins, 202n. 53
Society of Jesus, 122
sociology: cultural, 164; historical, xv, 158, 164; of the state, 178n. 82
sociopolitical ethics, and state power, 38
Soly, Hugo, 116
Sorbonne, 127
South Welfish, 139

Index : 247

Spain, 8; absolutism, 160; bureaucratic features, 141; illegitimacy rates, 124; lawyer-administrators in royal services, 140; ties to papacy, 147; venality, 145, 153
Spanish Armada, sinking of, 44
Spanish Habsburgs, 13, 41–43, 128
Spanish Inquisition, xvii, 42, 121, 123, 145
Spener, Philipp Jacob, 106, 107, 111, 150, 170
Spierenburg, Pieter, 52, 185n. 132
Spinhuis, 64
stadtholders, 46
Ständestaat, 6
ständisch (estates-based), 141
state: as a coercive and extractive organization, 165; defined, 35; as a pastoral organization, xvi
state autonomy: origins of in Prussia, 85–92, 112; and state power, 165, 167
state *dirigisme*, 169
state efficiency. *See* administrative efficiency
state formation: ascending analysis of, 23–24; as bottom-up process, xvi–xvii; capital-intensive, 5; coercive-intensive, 5, 6; descending analyses of, 23; and disciplinary revolution, 158–59; fiscal-military model, 5–10, 11, 174n. 19; and geopolitical competition, 8, 12, 84, 138; social-scientific literature on, xv, 2; sociological theories of, 3–15; standard theory of, 40; as top-down process, xvi, 31
state infrastructure, 75–79, 138, 166–67, 169, 174n. 19
state of war *(Staat van Oorlog)*, 47
state power: and church-building, 18; complexity, 157; connection with social actors and institutions, 167–68, 169; defined, 35; and human resources, 167; and social discipline, 36; and social infrastructure, 37–38; and sociopolitical ethics, 38; and state infrastructure, 166–67; and state organization, 37; types of, 35; and wealth, 40
States General, of Dutch Republic, 43, 46–47, 48, 68, 141, 175n. 33
state strength, 179n. 2
state structure, 7, 12, 75

state theory, 22–23, 37, 76, 164–68, 169
Sten Sture, 13
Stettin, 111
Stevin, Simon, 44, 72, 74
Stockholm: Bloodbath of 1520, 13; murder rate, 53
Stoicism, 113
Strasbourg: disciplinary system, 120; ordinances of 1523, 127
"sturdy beggars," 107, 108
Stuttgart, 128, 129
subjectification, 166
Sully, duc de, 11
surveillance, xvi
Sweden, 6, 8, 12; bureaucratic absolutism, 9; confessional politics, 13–14; disciplinary revolution from above, 150–52; patrimonial elements in, 141; regional visitation committees, 120; social background of lawyer administrators, 139
Swedish estages, 151–52
Switzerland, 76, 130, 160
synods, 56, 124

Tawney, R. H., 204n. 102
taxes: in Dutch Republic, 46–50; in Prussia, 81–82; sin, 61, 107
tax farmers, 71
tax farming, 143, 145, 206n. 131
temporal authority, 2
tercio, 73
territorial churches, 17, 18
territorial church fund *(Kirchengut)*, 128
territorially fragmented states, 5
Thirty Years' War, 11, 17, 86, 91
Thomasius, Christian, 198n. 179
Tiel, 60–61
Tilly, Charles, 7; *Coercion, Capital and European States*, 5–6, 8, 35; *European Revolutions*, 55; on state-formation, 174n. 25; theory of revolution, 160–61
Titius, Andreas, 102
Tocqueville, Alexis de, 164
town council, 69
trading networks, 171
travelers' hostels, 59, 61
tribute-taking empires, 5
Tridentine Decrees, 121

Troeltsch, Ernst, 115, 176n. 38
Trolle, Gustav, 13
Troltsch, Ernst, 204n. 102
Tuchthuis. *See* house of discipline *(Tuchthuis)*
Turin, 133, 135

Uhlhorn, Georg, 115, 204n. 102
Ulrich, Duke, 128, 129
undeserving poor, 61, 63, 66, 115, 131, 135
Union of Utrecht, 43, 180n. 31
United Provinces, 43, 44. *See also* Dutch Republic
universities, 8, 19, 139
University of Halle, 108, 111, 198n. 179
urban expansion, 171
urban leagues, 6
ur-confessionalists, 117, 126, 136, 155
Utrecht, 44, 46

vagabonds, 66
vagrancy laws, 62
vagrants, 107, 108
van Oldenbarnevelt, Johan, 44
venality, 12, 167; defined, 143; in Dutch Republic, 9, 141, 146; farming, 143, 145, 206n. 131; in France, 68–69, 145, 153; and imitation, 147; in Italy, 145–46; papal role in development of, 144–48; and patrimonialism, 142–44, 153; in Spain, 145; types of, 143–46
Venice, 6, 38, 76, 118; Inquisition, 121; poor-relief, 132, 134, 135; public venality, 146; venality, 153
verponding, 47
Vives, Juan Luis, 22

Wagenaar, Jan, 185n. 132
Wagener, Johann Tobias, 103
Wallerstein, Immanuel, *The Modern World System*, 3, 4, 5, 10, 174n. 12
war. *See* military competition
War and Domains chambers, 101
War of the Spanish Succession, 50

Wars of Religion, 11–12, 13, 17, 159
Wartenberg, York von, 192n. 70
wealth, and state power, 40
Weber, Max, xvii, 22, 37, 94, 115, 204n. 102; on ascetic Protestantism, 178n. 81; centrality of religion in works, 164; *Economy and Society*, 27, 32; estates-based patrimonialism, 141; ideal-typical bureaucracy, 12, 99–100, 205n. 118; on oligarchy, 206n. 130; overlooking of relations between discipline and state, 23; on predestination, 20; *The Protestant Ethic*, 26–27; "The Protestant Sects," 27, 28, 178n. 79; on relationship between religion and discipline, 3; sociology of the state, 178n. 82; state theory, 26–28; theory of discipline, 31, 32; theory of legitimate domination, 138
welfare state, 163–64, 169
Willem Lodewijk, Prince, 72
William III of Orange, 153
William Louis, 75
William of Orange (William the Silent), 42, 43, 44, 45
Winckelmann, Johannes, 178n. 82
Winckelmann, Otto, 115
witchcraft, 121, 122, 123
Wittenberg: church ordinances of 1522, 126; poor-relief, 134; regional visitation committees, 120
Wolff, Christian, 198n. 179
workhouses, 59, 61, 63, 135
worldly activism, ethic of, 136
worldly calling, 115
world systems theory, 40
Württemberg, poor-relief reform, 120, 128–29
Wycliffites, 170

Year of Disaster, 187n. 165
Ypres, 127

Zeeden, Ernst Walter, 15, 116
Zeeland, 42, 43, 44, 46
Zwingli, Ulrich, 17

www.ingramcontent.com/pod-product-compliance
Lightning Source LLC
Chambersburg PA
CBHW050901300426
44111CB00010B/1334